W9-CAN-838

THE CONTESTED METROPOLIS

WITHDRAWN
FROM
UNIVERSITY OF PENNSYLVANIA
LIBRARIES

This is an INURA book

Editor: Raffaele Paloscia

Editing Supervisor: Lorenzo Tripodi

Editorial Board: Constance Carr (Berlin), Stefan De Corte (Brussels), Giancarlo Paba (Florence), Michael Edwards, Louanne Tranchell (London), Roger Keil (Toronto), Christian Schmid (Zurich)

Graphic Design: Manuela Conti/Ogino Knauss

Linguistic Revision: Donald Bathgate, Brenda Porster

Contact: http://www.inura.org

This book has been supported by:
Regione Toscana - Assessorato alla Cultura
Comune di Firenze - Assessorato alla Cultura
Università di Firenze - Dipartimento di Urbanistica e Pianificazione del Territorio
INURA Berlin, INURA Brussels, INURA Florence, INURA London, INURA Toronto, INURA Zurich

A CIP catalogue record for this book is available from the Library of Congress, Washington D.C., USA.

Bibliographic information published by Die Deutsche Bibliothek
Die Deutsche Bibliothek lists this publication in the Deutsche Nationalbibliografie; detailed bibliographic data is available in the internet at http://dnb.ddb.de.

This work is subject to copyright. All rights are reserved, whether the whole or part of the material is concerned, specifically the rights of translation, reprinting, re-use of illustrations, recitation, broadcasting, reproduction on microfilms or in other ways, and storage in data banks.
For any kind of use, permission of the copyright owner must be obtained.

© 2004 Birkhäuser – Publishers for Architecture, P.O. Box 133, CH-4010 Basel, Switzerland
Part of Springer Science+Business Media Publishing Group.
© 2004 INURA Firenze, Via Micheli 2, 50121 Firenze, Italy

Printed on acid-free paper produced from chlorine-free pulp. TCF

Printed in Italy by Tipografia Editrice Polistampa, Florence
ISBN 3-7643-0086-8

9 8 7 6 5 4 3 2 1   http://www.birkhauser.ch

INURA

THE CONTESTED METROPOLIS

SIX CITIES AT THE BEGINNING OF THE 21st CENTURY

Birkhäuser – Publishers for Architecture
Basel • Boston • Berlin

HAPF 7/2/04
Fine Arts / HT / 151 / C6344 / 2004

Contents

UNIVERSITY OF PENNSYLVANIA LIBRARIES

Introduction

TEXT..Raffaele Paloscia
PHOTOS ....Raffaele Paloscia
TRANSLATION...Donald Bathgate

1.

The clammy, overpowering heat of this unbelievable August is blanketing Florence, a city I have lived in and enjoyed a love-hate relationship with for more than 30 years. I'm trying to concentrate on the opening words that would immediately make the spirit of this book clear, something that would exemplify this collective enterprise presenting the "contested metropolis" at the beginning of the new millennium, a work which many friends have contributed to, friends who despite working in very differing *milieux*, identify with INURA and who, in their work, attempt to put its principles into practice.
The Italian press agencies are running a minor piece of news which is as unbelievable as it is emblematic. "Sitting Prohibited" states the notice posted in the square in front of Florence Cathedral below Brunelleschi's dome and Giotto's bell-tower, next to the steps perennially crowded with passers-by, students, vendors of all colours, street-artists, kids with guitars round their necks and tourists from the campsites, youth hostels, and small hotels, with their sandwiches and drinks – and certainly not the patrons of the nearby hotels, restaurants and open-air cafés and their stratospheric prices. People enjoying a rare, free-of-charge pause, enjoying being one of a crowd, getting to know their neighbour, trying to understand each other in different languages all the while taking in, subconsciously or not, the rigorous, clean geometrical lines of the green and white marble of the medieval Baptistery and the soft, gilded shapes of the Door to Paradise, which marked the beginning of the Renaissance, people sitting on steps put there to welcome the religious, the faithful, pilgrims, travellers, peddlars, jugglers and beggars all of whom have used them for centuries.
Not any longer.
Thus has the firmly left-wing municipal authority of this town ruled, opting for a misplaced sense of "decorum" linked to an equally misplaced concept of urban "security"; this authority which, only a few months ago and in the face of ferocious opposition, hosted and supported the extraordinary event that was the European Social Forum. After a myriad of meetings held to develop new ideas and new projects for a fairer, more sustainable world, over a million people paraded through the streets of Florence on the Social Forum's last day calling for peace in an up-beat but never violent demonstration, a compact, festive crowd whose numbers and like this city had never witnessed before.
This is one of the many contradictory swings we have come to expect, alternating between upholding and legitimising the intrinsic value of urban society's multi-faceted expressiveness, while falling in line with the push of the most retrograde factions of Roman Catholicism in combination with the powerful, intolerant lobbies, both local and otherwise, of the monolithic tourism-based economy, towards repressive rules, excluding those for whom such an economy has no use.
Or perhaps it is not too late.
Indeed people have been trickling back to sit on the Cathedral square steps during these recent, late-summer days in a procession of small improvised groups, but also in more organized acts of civil disobedience. Action groups which have deep roots in the area, the Florence Social Forum and the *Laboratorio per la Democrazia* first and foremost, have been strenuous in upholding everyone's right to the city and the use of its spaces, especially those considered most characteristic. This, by contrast, is the legitimate premise and guarantee of a "decorum", the expression of a city with no desire to see itself relegated to a marketplace, shop-window or museum but wants to stay alive, throbbing and deeply, unconditionally free.
It is again possible.
Just as this book was going to print, and pressured by an imminent large-scale demonstration to protest against a misplaced use of public space, the more open-minded, aware sector of the municipal administration won the day and, after only three week from its promulgation, the prohibition has been abolished!

Florence, 2003, Cathedral Square

2.

This is what our book is about:: the series of happenings, alluded by an episode like this to, that occur in the transformation of the metropolitan contexts the book describes and analyzes with an eye to a new urban way of life that we must decide on and draw up together. The general theme is the "contested metropolis" meaning an objective, non-eliminable condition, structurally innate to the very idea of metropolis, a complex, structured, multi-faceted city thronged with ways of life, cultures, languages, hopes in a natural consolidation of every kind of relationship and social confrontation. Contested metropolis in the two, complementary meanings of the adjective:

- the metropolis *fought over* by the various actors and driving forces that populate and claim it, often in an inevitably conflictual manner, the right to live in it, work in it and enjoy oneself in it using its resources in a way suitable to one's own needs. The contenders who come out on top now are the bearers of the mercantile-oriented ideology in its strongly competitive, globalizing version, the champions of the transformation of urban fabric, of its network of metropolitan values (and thus supranational) in particular aiming towards profit and the pursuit of it at all costs. A situation which we attempt in many ways to overturn in order to give the big city back its multi-faceted, continually evolving identity and its special role as a place for recomposing urban living based on co-existence, and welcoming, receptive solidarity.
- the metropolis *not accepted* as such in its present economical, physical, social and cultural configuration, rejected for what it offers its inhabitants (and its non-affluent visitors), which seems very little compared with what the metropolis takes and demands from a great number of them. A metropolis which, from the viewpoint of those who query it most, should become the emblem of another possible world, the promoter and guarantor of infinite alternatives, both tried and able to be tried, for social survival, as well as reciprocal acceptance and a pluralist, shared sense of belonging.

London, 2003, inside Modern Tate

3.

There is something undoubtedly utopian in this approach to the metropolis and its process of transformation. This we do not deny; on the contrary we affirm it with such vehemence that, before going more deeply into the issues related to each single metropolis, we make it the proper starting point of the book.
Two authors (both speakers at the 2001 Florence INURA Conference) who have set themselves the task of delving deeply into the issue of urban society and its concretisation into the physical elements that contain it, present us with their view of "utopia". There are a number of essential factors common to both. Both explicitly reject the centrality of economics and point to the urgent need to broaden the democratic foundation through direct participation by all participants, the marginal and antagonistic no less than others, for the process of transformation of society and of the physical spaces where it condenses and unfolds. Both authors are aware of the need for institutional mediation and hence a reformulation of the mechanisms of representation, for innovation in municipal administrations to make them more effective and directly expressive of the inhabitants of their community. Both, to all intents and purposes, refer not to a low-yield ideal-type organization of urban living, but to a practicable utopia achievable within a continual process.
However, the approaches they suggest are very different.
The scenario outlined by the first, Sandercock, emerges as the result of an almost instinctive behaviour pattern, emotive, blurred and at once very dense. It hinges on an innate capacity for collective mobilization which seems to be appearing in increasingly broader sections of society which are stimulated to bring it out in a process of radical renewal. Weight is given to the "thousand[s] of tiny empowerments" towards the freeing of a world made oppressive by being structured solely towards achieving economic objectives and controlling them. She places great attention on telling, narrating and disseminating a multitude of minor but highly evocative and stimulatory experiences.
The second author, Magnaghi, suggests a structured vision, clear and defined in detail, almost a continuation of the great utopias of past centuries. The "local project" is expressed through a point-by-point critique of the no-longer acceptable anti-sociality of present-day living and of the times and ways it has been constructed. This is no decontextualized, sterile model but almost a creative overview of what recent decades have expressed in terms of criticism of a model of development and of globalizing society, here revised, enriched in concept and translated into the constituent parts of a possible, revitalizing process of refoundation to be modelled in accordance with single realities.
The common intent is the abandonment of a society, a city, a metropolis which is ill, unjust and bad for both humans and nature, in the attempt to move towards a utopian vision, a horizon that promises another, possible world. A horizon and an aim which can never be fully achieved, but which will keep us moving in the right direction with passionate intensity.

Brussels, 2000, *Façadisme*

4.

Berlin Brussels Florence London Toronto Zurich. Six cities (all of them seats of an annual INURA Conference) in an affluent West, all with a well-characterized, strong image, the sign, apparent at least, of success in one or more areas within the new geography of finance, services, media, commerce, tourism and entertainment, and the new economy in general.
Each of these cities, with their differences in terms of activity and size from compact Florence to sprawling London, are well-defined component parts of the system of the global economy and the global market. They manage to grab a large slice of what is produced elsewhere; in other words they keep a firm hold on the functions of command, finance and organizational strategy of broad sectors of production and services which lead to the concentration of wealth in monetary terms. This takes place through a process of compression, in some cases to the limit for survival, of quotas distributed to poorer areas whether they be in those same cities regions or countries, or on the planet as a whole. All these urban areas produce wealth but they also produce a proportional quantity of poverty (London/Edwards), which creates a sort of social and economic as well as environmental footprint.
There is an increasing proportion of the population who are becoming aware of this and who are no longer willing to be subjected to the ideals underpinning the process. In this book, therefore, attention is focused on what is happening within metropolitan territories, what is within the immediate grasp of the inhabitants, the settled communities and what scope is there for their reaction, their direct participation without forgetting, obviously, the significance that local actions, increasingly networked, can have in the transformation of the globalized world.
The issues dealt with are familiar, interconnected among themselves, and linked directly to the widespread, intensifying shift towards the supremacy of the global economy and the polarization, destructuring and fragmentation of urban and social fabrics: the never-ending changes in the uses to which public spaces are put and their encroaching privatisation and the reactions this provokes; the rise in social, economic and cultural exclusion; the manner in which foreigners, different and marginalized people are accepted or rejected; the competitive commercialisation of the city and the spectacularization of its symbolic places; the new, emerging growth of the urban subculture, a kind of delayed-action victory which in some cases can backfire into exploiting the issue of safety to introduce controls and, not infrequently, into episodes of full-scale ethnic cleansing; the upholding of a not always clear, well-defined idea of sustainable city; the various declensions of the issue of new citizenship; inhabitants' participation in the process of transformation of the actual physical space vis-à-vis also the urgency of re-establishing planning concepts as well as the tools they use; the need to redefine the concept of urban identity and give it a fluid, open, more cosmopolitan meaning, and many more issues still.

Berlin, 2003, Potsdamer Platz

5.

The good city, the global city, the sustaining city, the insurgent city, the gated city, the erased city, the barred city, the forbidden city, the contested city, the un-contested city, the fragmented city, the sustainable city, the frigid city, the hybrid city, the substitute city, the creole city, the diaspora city, the soft city, the playful city, the invisible city, the safe city, the competitive city, the solidarity city, the multicultural city, the deregulated city, the post-industrial city, the mediterranean city.
The list is long and far from complete, compiled to provide a synthetic, informative list of the issues touched on and many others, and with them the many often conflictual aspects of a multishaped multifaceted metropolis which in this book are dealt with in lesser or greater depth and outline. The most varied adjectives are combined with each other in the headings of chapters and paragraphs or in the actual text alongside the noun "city" (or "metropolis" or "capital") in some cases with opposing meanings. Some will be easily recognizable by their having been introduced as concise, summarizing metaphors by major scholars on urban phenomena: philosophers, sociologists, economists, planners, literati, historians, including exponents of the principal doctrine of reference mentioned in the texts, Bourdieu, Lefevbre, Friedmann, Harvey, Sassen (some of whom, it must be said, have been highly participatory guests over the years at INURA conferences). Others are paradoxes coined for the occasion by the authors in an attempt to lend an immediate description to a phase in the development of one of the metropolises, or to a function or recognizable, shared urban condition, or even a little-known network of relationships within a city, a process of transformation of an apparently marginal niche of urban society for better or for worse not immediately perceivable, of a new, ever more widespread code of conduct vis-à-vis urban spaces and their uses.
Many of the issues tackled are the same and are found across the board emphasized to a lesser or greater extent in all chapters. Each case, however, does have its own prevailing viewpoint, a specific metropolitan focus on which the article as a whole hinges. What is highlighted for **Berlin,** the symbol of the fall of communism and the victory of the western, capitalist "one best way", is how it is shown as having become commercial, the rendering of its most representative spaces as a spectacle, functional to global competition which, up to now at least, does not seem to have produced the desired results. Instead, the reunified city seems to have been destructured and be in the throes of an identity crisis which only the strength of what its deep-seated sub/counterculture produces seems able to combat. **Brussels** shows up the set of conditions which stem from its bi-partition tradition and from its dependence on the state. A multi-ethnic, fragmented city par excellence, its more progressive sectors seek innovative cultural exchanges through the improvement of local areas as a positive link to bridge differences, and the organization of symbolic events capable of lending a unitary but pluralist voice to all players in urban life. **Florence** is represented through the experiences of its insurgent components who reject marginalisation, and uphold their life-styles through a process of continual physical adaptation of the public space enacted by the most diverse of the city's components (children, non–EU citizens, sex workers, squatters, social centres, gays etc.), who from antagonists become protagonists of urban life. **London** is viewed through the achievements of the new, highly innovative metropolitan government, palindromic in its attention to the most diverse minorities and its involvement in a process of real democratization of metropolitan life, while also being committed to the growth of the global city in accordance with a set of rules of the most unprincipled competitiveness. The contradictions which emerge are assessed from highly different viewpoints. **Toronto** underlines its multicultural essence now jeopardised by a sinister process of "creolisation" which deconstructs every ethnic identity only to recompose their various single parts into a myriad of new eclectic fusions. Urban policies are exploiting this so as to define the specific identity of a global city while relaxing planning regulations in order to attract new exponents of the dot com economy. Reactions to this strategy, however are becoming louder and more widespread. In conclusion, **Zürich** turns its attention to ways, times, spaces, effects and contradictions in the process of the formation of the global city. Emphasis is placed on the strength of the part played by alternative culture, born in the unrests of the 80s which has led to the conflicting developments of today, a commercially-oriented response to the requirements of the global market on the one hand, an essential component for successful experimentation in new ways of living coherent with the environment and, on the other, human solidarity.

Zürich, 1997, The Rote Fabrik

6.

Those seeking a coherent, closely-woven comparative analysis with a politico-sociological-urbanistic slant of large, western cities which attempts to reduce the processes presently unfolding to a single interpretative model will be disappointed by this book. Similarly, those who read it hoping to embark on a simulated journey through the various expressions that urban sub/counterculture provides in different contexts linked by global-wide networks will not find what they are looking for. These are indeed present in the book but not systematic or catalogue-like.
Indeed the ambition and the stuff of the book is different. It sets out to be the story and a direct, immediate representation of these six cities, told with differing slants and from different standpoints – in some cases indeed unprecedented and surprising, sometimes with internal contradictions – prepared by a group of highly varied individuals from very different geographical backgrounds but who are united by belonging, either from its outset or from more recent times, to INURA (International Network for Urban Research and Action) which in its collective name takes the responsibility for the whole book. The authors are a cross section of this association: urbanists, squatters, artists, old- and new-generation activists, geographers, students, architects, local authority officials, representatives of urban movements, sociologists and social centre association members. They share the ideal of actively working and participating in the various phases of the process of transformation of the cities they live in, in a dimension out of the ordinary, declined in the widest possible manner, and of conducting research and implementing urban action networking among themselves, inspired by the principles summarised in the Declaration: An Alternative Urban World is Possible", which is repeated in full at the end of the book. The different cultural backgrounds and the ways of relating to the places where one intervenes lead to different forms of writing, representing reality and narrating experiences. What Fred Robinson defined in the closing text of the book is held true by all: The Spirit of Inura: an attitude towards the world of a "network of people opposed to global capitalism, exploitation, sexism, racism, consumerism, and keen to bring about change".

Toronto, 1998, From the CN Tower

berlin bruxelles/brussel firenze london toronto zürich

Achievable Utopias

TEXT...Leonie Sandercock

Practicing Utopia: Sustaining Cities

The ancients sang their way all over the world. They sang the rivers and ranges, salt pans and sand dunes. They hunted, ate, made love, danced, killed; wherever their tracks led, they left a trail of music. They wrapped the whole world in a web of song.
(Bruce Chatwin *The Songlines*)

Introduction

In the wake of the manifold planning disasters of the 20th century, many of which were brought about by the best of intentions for social improvement, dare we continue to support the idea of planning as a utopian social project? If the answer is Yes, then what kind of planning imagination/s might avoid a repetition of past disasters and actively promote the kind of urban diversity and adaptability that would counterpoint the hubris of high modernist interventions? At the beginning of the 21st century, what are the possibilities for *an art of urban engagement* which takes a position on issues such as democracy, power, social justice and sustainability? And what does this have to do with planning, as we know it? These are the questions that frame this paper.

Cities are neither organisms nor machines. They are flesh and stone intertwined. They are 'built thought'. They are the containers of dreams and desires, hopes and fears. They are an assemblage of active historical agents making daily choices of how to live well. They are an assemblage of communities: communities of interest as well as communities of place; invisible communities of the dead as well as of the unborn. Cities are the repositories of memories, as well as memory's texts: their layered surfaces, their coats of painted stucco, their wraps of concrete register the force of these currents both as wear and tear and as narrative. That is, city surfaces tell time and stories. Cities are full of *stories in time.*

Urban narratives of loss, yearning, hope, desire, fear and memory are what I want to talk about today. Through these stories I imagine an end to planning as we know it - bureaucratic planning. I see planning as an always unfinished *social* project whose task is managing our co-existence in the shared spaces of cities and neighborhoods in such a way as to sustain and enrich human life, to work for social, cultural, and environmental justice. This social project, to be sure, has an imperfect past, and an uncertain future, but as an enduring social project it needs to come to terms with these enduring narratives. Is there an/other planning imagination which can be harnessed to this task?
I suggest that there is such an emerging imagination, and that, among other things, it requires an expanded, more communicative conception of planning, and a more emotionally rich language available to practitioners. It also requires a different social representation of planning. What follows is an outline of a *dialectical* planning imagination *and* its actually existing practices.

This text, presented at the INURA - Florence conference 2001, was already published with the same title in *Documentation - Information on Swiss Planning (DISP) n. 148 / 2002*

I want to suggest a different sensibility from the bureaucratic (or regulatory) planning that has dominated the 20th century — a more dialectical planning imagination. Not dialectical in the Hegelian or Marxist sense but in the postmodern spirit of 'both/and', or in the concept of yin and yang, suggesting the quest for a balance and complementarity, but a balance which is dynamic rather than static. A pessimism of the intellect and an optimism of the will; explanatory/critical moments and anticipatory/utopian moments; the politics of social theory and the poetics of social action; a Nietzschean metaphysics of the body and its drives and affects, and a Cartesian metaphysics of cognitive being and idealising. Jonathan Rabin's 'soft city'. Henri Lefebvre's ludic city, and also his analysis of the production of space. Calvino's 'invisible cities' alongside Guy Debord's 'society of the spectacle'. Relph's 'spirit of place' juxtaposed with Harvey's 'speculative production of place'. Communicative action as well as institutional reform. And an acknowledgement of the repressive *and* transformative powers of both state *and* community.

For as long as the operations of capital are set on processing the earth into dust, a critique of globalizing capitalism must continue to be a major focus of critical urban inquiry. But that doesn't tell us all we need to know about the practices of power in the modern world. There's more than one enemy/antagonist in our drama - a theme I'll need to return to. Managing global city regions in this new century when the whole world will become urban requires a complex imagination of cities: their emotional affect as well as their material effects. It takes a capacity for learning about self and society, a capacity for strategic thinking in a range of spatial and substantive contexts, and a capacity for empathy as well as for intellectual inquiry, an imagination which can move back and forth between those critical/analytical modes and more narrative/receptive sensibilities.

I listen to Calvino (1974), whispering that we must seek and learn to recognize who and what, in the midst of the inferno, are not inferno, then make them endure, give them space. Within the dominant society there are always cracks in which other realities begin to take shape. With apprehension then, but armed with actual examples rather than urban science fiction, I *want to suggest that more and more of our work, if we want to work towards sustaining cities, will be bound up with organizing hope, negotiating fears, and mediating memories.* What follows is a discussion of such planning practices - which require a different kind of planning imagination from the one that has characterized the modernist era and its search for order, clarity and certainty.

The Organization of Hope

Ken Reardon's work in East St. Louis is one of the most successful and inspiring models for *the organization of hope.* Reardon (2002) tells the story of a ten-year university/community partnership, which has transformed one of the worst black ghettoes in the USA into an area which has attracted US$45 million of public and private investment in urban regeneration. This transformation process began ten years ago with one small action, namely the 'sweat', the labor of students and residents over one weekend to clean up two vacant, but trash-filled plots of land, and then to convert that space into a safe playground for children. Reardon gives us an old-fashioned story of heroism against impossible odds, with faith and quiet determination as the weapons, an inspirational story. The overall lesson is that none of this would have happened without the faith, hope, and sweat of the quietly determined leaders and residents of East St. Louis.

The result, a decade later, is not only the US$45 million in new public and private investment which has come to this once-devastated neighborhood, but also that, in the process, more than 350 University of Illinois students have had a powerful, and for some, life-transforming, learning experience. This was a step-by-step approach to regeneration - what I have, elsewhere, called '*a thousand tiny empowerments*' (Sandercock 1998). Some of the tools involved are technical: bubble charts, excel files, GIS, wall maps, interview schedules. But nothing would have happened if a trusting relationship had not been developed between the residents and the students, which required openness and communicative skills on both sides. And the deeper meaning of the story is its inspirational quality, its description of a *process of organizing hope, in spite of, or in a context in which the institutional perspective had literally written off, abandoned this community.*

Negotiating Fear

There are multiple and competing discourses of fear in any city, and these discourses seek to define who and what is to be feared in the process of change, and in so doing, to influence the management and direction of change in ways that privilege the rights of some at the expense of others, the sense of place of some at the expense of others. Discourses of fear function ideologically to shape our attention, to convey a comprehensible and compelling story of the fate of the city, and to provide reasons for how we should act in response to perceived problems. Discourses of fear are maps of a social reality perceived as problematic in moments when we are unsure what direction to take:- where and how to live, where to invest, what schools to send our children to. The reality of city fear is always mediated by these discourses or representations of it.

Portraying parts of cities as sites of physical and/or moral decay, of economic and/or social disorganization, as places to avoid, has intended or implicit policy consequences — clearance, clean-up, redevelopment. Portraying certain groups in the city as people to be feared, junkies, gays, the homeless, immigrant/youths, Aborigines, and so on, also has intended policy consequences, from police sweeps, to increasing the hardware of surveillance, to defensive architectural and design practices. I could use Capetown, or Sao Paulo, or Los Angeles as spectacular illustrations, or more mundane but no less vicious examples like the attempt of the JAG Team (Juvenile Aid Group) in the Australian city of Perth, who for the past 6 years have mounted operations to cleanse the city of young people, 'youth', who might constitute a threat to families (Iveson 2000).

Planning and urban management discourses are, and always have been, *saturated with fear*. If we accept that fear will always be with us, then we do need to think about how to manage fear in the city, but we need to think about this in a very different way than we have in the past. The consequences of the 'enclaving and hardware' approach to managing fear include changes in the character of public space and of citizens' participation in public life. One of the most tangible threats to public culture, as Zukin (1996) has argued, comes from the politics (and discourses) of everyday fear. When public space is perceived as too dangerous to venture into, then the principle of open access, of a civic culture, is utterly destroyed.

This enclaving of the city builds on particular discourses of fear which seek to cleanse and purify the city as a moral order, as well as to make the city safe for consumption, and so to protect the economic order. Rather than being swept under the carpet as undiscussable, or tackled as an issue of increasing urban fortification, urban fears need to be communicated and negotiated if we are to keep alive the idea of the city as a vital public sphere in which common goals and solutions can be achieved.

I've written a lot this past year about how the future of planning in cities of difference requires a coming to terms with the existence of fear in the city, fear of the stranger/foreigner/outsider (Sandercock 2000; 2001). The recent emphasis in the planning literature on more 'communicative approaches' for handling planning disputes acknowledges the need for more process-based methods of conflict resolution, but their emphasis on rational discourse avoids the emotions at the heart of conflict, and thus often avoids the real issues at stake. A possible way forward is through a more narrative and dialogical approach, which begins with an analysis and understanding of this *fear of the other* and develops processes for working through these fears.

In the new journal *Planning Theory and Practice* I discuss just such a case, where an apparently insoluble conflict between indigenous people and Anglo-Australian residents in an inner Sydney neighborhood was eventually solved by an innovative practitioner who spent nine months creating the space in which these antagonistic residents could begin a conversation with each other, which ultimately led to greater understanding and the possibility of peaceful co-existence (Sandercock 2000). This resonates with the innovative work of people like John Forester and Howell Baum. Forester insists that emotions cannot be left at the door as one enters a negotiation: that anger, suspicion, fear, grief, and other equally powerful emotions are an unavoidable part of public policy issues. Through participation, he argues, we not only reproduce, but can reconstitute social relationships. 'When we learn about the significant historical experiences of others and articulate our own in public settings, he argues, we may change ourselves as well as our strategies and sense of priorities' (Forester 1999).

Baum suggests that it is important for planners working in emotionally charged situations not to try to suppress conflict, for to do so is to sabotage the work of grieving and healing which needs to be done as part of a process of change. Helping people to discuss their fears, he argues, is a way of seeing past them toward the future. What is emerging is a notion that the planning process must be able to create a transitional space between past and future, where people can imagine stepping away from past memories without feeling that they have lost their identity or betrayed the objects of memory. They must be able to imagine alternative futures (Baum 1997).

This kind of planning work, involving confrontation, dialogue and negotiation across the gulf of cultural (or other) differences, requires its practitioners to have a highly developed planning imagination which includes, but goes well beyond, socio-spatial and political economic analysis: it requires fluency in a range of ways of knowing and of communicating - from storytelling to listening to interpreting visual and body language. In such cases, in carefully designed public deliberative processes, the use of narrative, of people telling their own stories about how they perceive the situation, becomes a potential consensus-building tool for unearthing issues unapproachable in a solely rational manner. When the parties involved in a dispute have been at odds for generations, or come from disparate cultural traditions, or where there is a history of marginalization, something more than the usual tool-kit of negotiation and mediation is needed, some 'method' which complements but also transcends the highly rational processes typical of the communicative action model.

What particularly interests me about this approach is the possibility of social transformation, of a process of public learning, which results in permanent shifts in values and institutions. If we want to 'practice utopia', then we have to be able to imagine how such instances can produce, or lead to, these permanent shifts. That, inevitably, requires some thinking about institutions.

Mediating Memories

In 1993, on the outskirts of Budapest, the Statue Park Museum opened. Since 1989 heated public debate had raged over what to do with the statuary, memorials and monuments from the former socialist period. In the case of Budapest, its elected Assembly resolved this by proposing a process in which the choice of statues to be removed or kept would be decided by each district of the city, individually, by referendum. Citizens would have one of three choices for each monument: a) keep it in place; b) have it destroyed; c) contribute it to the Statue Park Museum (Trowell 2000).

The choice to attempt a democratic process in such a situation was more complex, and potentially more volcanic and divisive than if the new-born state had simply erased all cultural traces of former Soviet and socialist connections, as has been the case in some of the former socialist countries of Eastern Europe. The process brought to the surface a lot of pain, hatred and anger, with unexpected allegiances and unforeseen senses of ownership, often for non-ideological reasons. It's probably too soon to know whether this cultural process, which was so deeply uncomfortable in the short term, has enabled the country to come to terms with its history more fully and profoundly than it might have done through overnight erasure. Hungary is the only country in the former socialist east that dared to investigate the popular significance of such symbols, and to do this through a street-by-street democratic process. This makes the new Statue Park Museum an extraordinarily potent realization of the previously unimaginable.

The idea for the Museum had first come from a literary historian who had proposed that all the various Lenin statues from all over Hungary be gathered in a 'Lenin Garden'. This proposal could have been perceived as an ironic joke, but instead, it led to a profound civic process - what John Forester (1999) would call a 'deep public deliberation'. The elected Assembly in Budapest took a risk. They dared to believe that people could decide for themselves, directly, *and* that the process could be as important as the outcome.

This story illustrates another important dimension of the work of building sustaining cities and communities, that of *mediating memories*. All neighborhoods have histories, and that accumulation of history is constitutive of local identity. Part of the work of community building involves invoking this history, these memories. But it should never be assumed that there is only one 'collective memory' of place. More likely, there are conflicting memories, and layers of history, some of which have been rendered invisible by whoever is the culturally dominant group.

There are many interesting examples of recognition of the need to deal with memory in order for reconciliation, healing, and social transformation to occur. Best known perhaps are the Vietnam War Memorial in Washington DC, and the holocaust museum in Berlin, both of which have been controversial. South Africa's Truth and Reconciliation Commission was a process rather than a memorial. Lesser known is the case of Liverpool, England, a city which by the 1980's, after two decades of economic decline, was on the brink of 'city death', with disastrous levels of unemployment, out-migration of young people, appalling race relations, and a deteriorated and neglected built environment. How can a city regenerate from such despair and demoralization?

There were, according to Newman and Kenworthy's account (1999), three catalysts. The first was a community mobilization around housing rehabilitation. The second was a major effort to combat racism — starting an arts anti-racist program, and tackling racism in the police force. But perhaps of greatest spiritual and symbolic impact was the opening the Museum of Slavery in the new Albert Dock tourism complex. This award-winning museum shows how Liverpool was central to the slave trade. It graphically depicts the whole process of slavery, and names the many established Liverpool families who made their fortunes from slavery. Here is a case where the telling of a buried story or stories provides some ground for healing a divided city, and in so doing, acts as a catalyst for regeneration and growth.

What's common to all the stories I've told in this paper, from Budapest to East St. Louis to Liverpool, is their demonstration of a social process in which diverse publics and interests are able to negotiate possibilities, partaking of dreams of a world which is better, but is not a dream. The real debate, of course, lies in how much significance to give to such stories - how to interpret them. So now I want to think about that question, by examining five propositions that have been implicit in my arguments thus far.

Let me remind you of my opening questions. Can there be an art of urban engagement which takes a position on issues such as democracy, power, social and environmental justice? And what does this have to do with planning as we know it? My outline of a dialectical planning imagination has proceeded by narrative examples which have concentrated on the utopian/anticipatory rather than the critical moments. I now want to reiterate some of these apparently utopian propositions that I've advanced, and critically examine them.

Proposition 1: that democratizing planning decisions is the solution, as in the Budapest story.

This all-too-easy conclusion is one I'm prepared to stand by, but we only have to look at the infantile public consultation processes employed by many public agencies to cast doubt on the argument. It takes a book length case study like that of Rebecca Abers (2000) on the success of participatory municipal budgeting in Porto Alegre to explain why there are grounds for confidence. Cryptically, all I can say here is that the secret is in the recipe, the 'how' of the participatory process, and that there are critical decisions about scale which always have to be made - what territorial and temporal scale for what kinds of decisions.

Proposition 2: that self-help rather than bureaucratic help gets the results, so community-based planning should be privileged over planning by the state.

This might seem a logical conclusion based on much of the community activist literature (Heskin 1991; Leavitt and Saegert 1990), but there's a need for a tougher analysis. Communities aren't always progressive, and states aren't always repressive (Holston 1998). There has to be some broader societal recourse when communities act in exclusionary ways, just as there has to be some grassroots recourse when states act in repressive ways. Community-based planning still needs the state, both for resources and for institutionalizing changes in values, processes and distributions. The power balance between the two will always be contested.

Proposition 3: that planning is all about talk. Communicative action rules, ok!

I have emphasized the importance of talk and of narrative, and elsewhere I've elaborated this as a 'therapeutic model of planning' (Sandercock 2000). But I won't defend this, as some have, as THE new planning paradigm. Talk is an important form of intervention and action, but planning cannot be reduced to talk, and certainly not to talk as neutral mediation. There are at least three qualifications to be made. What has to accompany talk, and here's where the skill resides, is judgement, valuing, interpretation. And, complementing talk, we have to be able to draw on design skills, legislative drafting skills, and all sorts of substantive and technical knowledges. Finally, we have to consider the weight of institutions, a topic too little discussed in the emerging literature on community-based planning.

My comments today belong to a way of conceptualizing planning as a social activity carried out by individuals. There is an equally powerful and equally important way of conceptualizing planning as a quality of institutions. Imagining utopian possibilities, we must be able to imagine the institutions that we desire, as well as imagining the citizens and planners who will maintain and transform them. But we also have to analyze the institutions that currently frame and constrain our work. The long march through the institutions cannot, alas, be avoided.

Proposition 4: that we can make planning more meaningful by reconceptualizing it as organizing hope, negotiating fear, mediating memory.

The search for meaning, for re-enchantment, is palpable in the world, especially among the young, but a sceptic might ask:- so what's changed simply by reconceptualizing planning's tasks as you've done here? What power relationships have changed, for example? My argument - and I'm certainly not the first to make it - is that social representation matters. If we only write books documenting the hegemonic power of capital, we are not simply reflecting reality but helping to constitute it. What if we were to take seriously the performativity of social representations, the ways in which they are implicated in the worlds they represent. What if we emphasized, rather than swept under the carpet, alternative forms of planning, alternative imaginations and practices. That discursive struggle has been one of my projects in this paper.

Proposition 5: the very idea of planning as a social project, an art of urban engagement, is a dangerous Enlightenment delusion which misunderstands and/or underestimates the imperatives of both capital and the state.

My paper has both faintly suggested and firmly denied this proposition. Let's examine it more closely.
The Enlightenment dream of the perfectibility of man became, by degrees, a belief in the perfectibility of the social order and a new conception of the state was born - the idea that a central purpose of the state was the improvement of all members of society, their health, housing, skills, education, longevity, productivity, not to mention their morals and family life. The *will to plan* comes out of this *improving impulse*, which was best expressed in 20th century self-confidence about scientific and technological progress, a mentality which was unscientifically optimistic about the possibilities for the comprehensive planning of human settlements.

It was not only capital which got in the way of these dreams. The administrative ordering of society and nature proved an equally formidable enemy. The seemingly unremarkable tools of modern statecraft, tools of measurement, accounting, mapping, record-keeping, are tools vital to our welfare and freedom. They undergird the concept of citizenship and the provision of social welfare. But they are also constitutive of a new social order. They privilege the center, and the synoptic view, and marginalize local knowledges. We have gradually come to understand, thanks to Foucault and others, that modern statecraft is largely a project of internal colonization. Or, as James C. Scott puts it, 'the builders of the modern nation-state do not merely describe, observe, and map: they strive to shape a people and landscape that will fit their techniques of observation' (Scott 1998). Thus categories that begin as artificial inventions of cartographers, census takers, police officers, and urban planners, can end by becoming categories that organize people's daily existence, precisely because they are embedded in state-created institutions that structure that experience. The state is thus the vexed institution that is the ground of both our freedoms and unfreedoms.

The dilemma then, is (as always), *what can we do?* Noir intellectuals like Nietzsche delight in showing us our inconsistencies, contradictions, weaknesses. 'Human, all too human'. The enemy, in other words, is also ourselves. Knowing that, and knowing that the nature of the city is flux and change - *my personal* answer is to reverse the dictum of Daniel Burnham of Chicago a hundred years ago: 'Make no little plans'. My 21st century response is threefold:
- to think big, in the sense of seeing the big planetary picture, but to proceed by a thousand tiny empowerments;
- to critique the system world, but also to under stand that we cannot do without it;
- and to think, metaphorically, about the Songlines...

Conclusion: The Work of the Songlines

I've argued that in working towards more sustaining cities, we need some new models of planning practice which expand the language of planning beyond the realm of instrumental rationality and the system world, and speak about (and develop the skills for) organizing hope, negotiating fear, and mediating memory, as well as developing the habits of a critical/analytical mind. This transformed language would reflect the emotional breadth and depth of the lived experience of cities: cities of desire, cities of memory, cities of play and celebration, cities of fear, cities of struggle.

The sensibility underpinning this transformation includes the ability to tell, to listen to, and above all, to make space for stories to be heard. We use stories in various ways: to keep memory alive, to celebrate our history/identity; to derive lessons about how to act effectively; to inspire action; and as a tool of persuasion in policy debates. We uncover buried stories. We create new stories. We invent metaphors around which policy stories pivot. Stories, carefully told and carefully heard, have the potential to act as a bridge between ingrained habits and new futures. Stories can (usefully) disrupt habits of thought and action that control everyday life. The will to change has to come from an ability - a planner's ability and also a city user's ability - to imagine oneself in a different skin, a different story, a different place, and then desire this new self and place that one sees. An effective storytelling practice is perhaps that which is able to conscript readers or residents to suspend their habits of being and come out in the open and engage in dialogue with strangers.

I've provided some examples of this kind of planning work, from the US, Australia, and the UK, which I think of as the work of the Songlines. So let me finally explain this allusion. Pre-colonial Australia was the last landmass on earth peopled neither by farmers nor by city dwellers but by hunter gatherers. Along a labyrinth of invisible pathways, known to us as Songlines, the Aboriginals traveled in order to perform all those activities which are distinctly human - song, dance, marriage, exchange of ideas, and arrangements of territorial boundaries by agreement rather than by force. The Songlines, in Aboriginal culture, are what sustain life. The task of a new planning imagination is to search for the city's songlines, for all that is life sustaining, in the face of the inferno.

References

Abers, R. (2000), *Inventing Local Democracy. Grassroots Politics in Brazil* Boulder, Colorado: Lynne Riener Publishers

Baum, H. (1998), *The Organization of Hope* Albany, NY: SUNY Press

Calvino, I. (1974), *Invisible Cities* NY: Harcourt, Brace, Jovanovich

Forester, J. (1999), *The Deliberative Practitioner* . Cambridge, Mass.: MIT Press

Holston, J. (1998), "Spaces of Insurgent Citizenship", in: Leonie Sandercock (ed), *Making the Invisible Visible.* Berkeley, CA: University of California Press

Iveson, K. (2000), "Beyond Designer Diversity", in: *Urban Policy and Research*, 18, 2, 219-238.

Newman, P. and J. Kenworthy (1999), *Sustainability and Cities* Washington, DC: Island Press

Reardon, K. (2002), "Ceola's Vision, Our Blessing: The Story of an Evolving Community/University Partnership in East St. Louis, Illinois", in: B. Eckstein and J. Throgmorton (eds.), *Making Space for Stories that Sustain: Planning, Storytelling, and the Sustainability of American Cities.* Cambridge, Mass.: MIT Press

Sandercock, L. (1998), *Towards Cosmopolis. Planning for Multicultural Cities.* London: John Wiley and Sons

Sandercock, L. (2000), "When Strangers Become Neighbours: Managing Cities of Difference", *Planning Theory and Practice,* 1,1: 13-30.

Sandercock, L. (2001), "Difference, Fear and Habitus", in: J. Hillier ed. Habitus: *A Sense of Place.* Aldershot: Ashgate.

Scott, J. (1998), *Seeing Like a State.* New Haven, Conn.: Yale University Press

Trowell, J. (2000), "The Snowflake in Hell and The Baked Alaska: Improbability, Intimacy and Change in the Public Realm", in: S. Bennett and J. Butler (eds) *Advances in Art and Urban Futures. vol.1, Locality, Regeneration and Divers[c]ities.* Bristol: Intellect Books

Zukin, S. (1996), *The Cultures of Cities.* NY: Blackwell

TEXT..Alberto Magnaghi

The Local Project: Summing up a Political Vision

The Territorialist Approach: Towards Self-Sustainable Local Development

The starting point of the Italian "territorialist" school's contribution to the current planning debate lies in the integration of the standard approaches to sustainable development (basic needs, self-reliance, eco-development) and in the emphasis on balance in its three objectives, reformulated as follows: aiming development towards fundamental human requirements (over and above those of a material nature); developing self-reliance in the form of local self-government; and enhancing the quality of the environment.

From this premise, the territorialist approach (Magnaghi, 1992) has focused on the increasing relevance of local roles, developing the concept of "self-sustainable local development", and has carried out analytical applications and experiments in various territorial contexts, both in Italy and abroad (Magnaghi 1998a, 1998b, 2000a; Paloscia 1998). This approach is based on the assumption that only an innovative relationship of co-evolution between local inhabitants/producers and the territory can, by "caring", lead to a lasting equilibrium between human settlements and the environment. "Self-sustainable local development" is therefore produced by investing heavily in local environmental, territorial and cultural heritages, broad social participation in creating developmental agreements; and non-hierarchical exchanges within and among urban regions.

In this context, liberation from territory is seen as a short-term and barely sustainable historic event, which produces new developmental poverty (Sachs 1992). Against this, the "territorialist" school perceives the place as a heritage; it gives weight to caring for the human environment, interpreting long-term identities, unifying inhabitant and producer, and creating new networks of local societies and social practices. A constellation of towns, villages and regions linked by solidarity, each governing its own territory with local styles of self-sustainable development which is the requirement for sustainability in third world megalopolises too.

The local society into which the locally-based project is grafted is not "handed down" or inherited, but can only be the outcome of a political project which reconsiders a number of issues:

- 'urban' practices and policies must shift to a 'regional' context proper to manage the ecological footprint, aiming for sustainable management of cycles of primary resources (food, water, waste etc.);
- actors potentially initiating change must shift from a predominantly urban dweller concept to countryside people as producers of new consumer products (*terroir* products, organic and quality food, landscapes, hydro-geological safeguards, environmental maintenance and restoration, local economic districts);
- from the dwellers/producers distinction, typical of Fordist industrial society, a shift towards a merging (in the post-fordist self-employment society) of these two roles into a commonly held, shared responsibility for local production and quality of life;
- from closed local societies, stable in time and place, to multiethnic and shifting local societies whose identity is built by planning a common future together.

The concept of self-sustainability requires a far-reaching re-dimensioning of the economic sub-system which, since it is predominant has caused a de-stabilization in the processes of self organization of the social and natural sub-systems. Social conflict has shifted, in post-Fordism, from capital versus labour to a new conflict pitting the upholding and the destruction of local cultures against each other; social polarization and fragmentation on the one hand and assertion of diversities, life styles, cultures, and the insurgence of new communities on the other. 'Territory' (the urban region) has become the new 'factory' within the molecular organization of post-fordist self-employment with the result that the conquest of 'territorial *plus valorem*' by new dwellers/producers can already be perceived as humus for future social conflict. Globalization has already produced local-identity-oriented revolts, and the search for new rooting and place-care processes. Pointing this new place consciousness towards outcomes far from violence and war is the main issue for urban and regional politics and policies.
The concept of self-sustainability also involves the need for the role of local governments to develop in parallel. In order to bridge the existing gap between conflicts of interests and desirable fair dealing in local development, representative democratic institutions need to be supplemented with tools and agencies of direct democracy, so that the decision-making process becomes open to a growing number of contributing voices.
The new municipality (Magnaghi *et al.* 2002) is therefore conceived as the institution where local agents can create a convergence between institutional policies and social practices, fostering the building of local constitutional pacts, defining its "statute of places" and producing collective scenarios for action.
In a word, these principles of the "territorialist approach" represent the roots for creating a local project.

Making Local Society

Developed within the territorial approach to self-sustainable local development, local projects imply a political vision of new forms of democracy shaped by actions aimed at developing or "making" local societies. Expressing this in politics, and in local government policies, language and actions, is a slow contradictory process. In the most advanced realities, however, it leads to increased acknowledgement of the need to facilitate the growth of local societies intent on constructing virtuous relations with their own constructed environment by re-interpreting local territorial values.
From this point of view the local project is the political manifestation of a need, a requirement, or an idea in response to the challenge of globalization, and aims at getting beyond the current twofold reaction to it, both alternatives of which involve non-sustainability: on the one hand, the isolationist resistance of local communities defending their own identity through closure, refusal to innovate or entertain outside relations; and, on the other, the competition among local systems that exploit and despoil their environmental, territorial and human patrimony in the eager race to gain advantages by slavishly following exogenous rules created for the world market.
Caught in this contradiction, a local society which attempts to go beyond this impasse by reinterpreting and enhancing its own identity - its own unique nature and heritage - within the context of a system open to relations and exchanges is not at all a certainty. It exists potentially only in the presence of a series of factors: identity-seeking fragments holding out against the trend towards uniformity; the planetary scale struggle against the processes of economic globalization; local drives towards re-identification; practices that produce values to be used as guidelines by the self-employed, especially in the tertiary sector; practices of caring for the environment and places; tendencies towards molecular re-appropriation of innovation. But so that this local society can act as a vehicle of change, it must be helped to grow as a nodal point with a dense network of a plurality of voices that create a bottom-up "globalization". In this densely-woven network, the construction of a local society is a project or idea that can gain political force; it is no longer simply a static heritage to be collected and preserved.
In the local project the density of social and economic interactions taking place is what is required to create a sufficiently closed system in opposition to the potential destructuring deriving from pressure from globalization. At the same time, the project needs to be sufficiently open

that it does not fall into the isolation of “sad localisms” which are unable to react to the larger context. The risk is that the local, in turn, may be destructured (like the excessively open system) through marginalisation and impoverishment. The nodes in the network, the “places” of local society, must have a strong identity and internal cohesion; otherwise they become mere junctions in the wide-flung networks of the global. These networks transform local nodes for their own purposes and consumption, assigning them a place in a hierarchy that follows the laws of production technology and the market in the global economic system, thus stripping them of all identity and autonomy. Colonization (local behaviour dictated from elsewhere) or marginalisation are the two dangerous extremes affecting local societies in the age of globalization. A balanced relation between closure and openness gives the local project a cosmopolitan vision, both internally and in its relations with the world. The pact of solidarity among local actors for the purposes of enhancing places is not based on the preservation of given historical identities, but on the emergence of an identity shared by all the agents involved in building the project through a constructive re-interpretative dialogue with the long-term socio-cultural models present in a given place. The new inhabitants (new farmers, new producers and new consumers who choose the path of local self-sustainable development) interpret the identity of a place (its values and contextual wealth), and are careful to produce transformation that will increase its value. The new inhabitants of the “Creole” city, made up of a multi-ethnic, immigrant society, do not necessarily identify with local residents (who are at times the representatives of vandalistic localism or distorted uses of the local context that drain and exploit its energy for global competition). The agents interpreting the “spirit of place” (Casey 1997, Paba 1998) and designing self-sustainability must come from everywhere to cooperate in constructing the local project and its relations with the world.

From Class Consciousness to Place Consciousness

If the reaction to globalization is an identity-seeking ethic of isolationism – an easy prey to authoritarian nationalism – we must not merely on these grounds dismiss the need for identity together with the many violent and culpable forms of its political governance. The Left has often done this in the name of universalistic western modernization, failing to grasp the strategic importance of the question of identity following the end of geopolitical blocs and Fordism. In the post-Fordist period, the contrast between capital and labour is being shifted to one pitting uniformity, destruction of cultures, polarization and social fragmentation on one hand against the affirmation of differences, diversities, cultural uniqueness and social re-composition on the other. In other words, this contrast is found in the clash between regulations handed down from without and self-government. It can be seen in the search for various models of development based on the appropriation and use of resources by producer-inhabitants in different relations of social production that necessitate new statutes of self-employed labour in different forms of direct democracy pacts, and in different strategic sectors of the economy.
“From class consciousness to place consciousness”: this formula coined by Becattini (1999) nicely sums up the radical change in the conflict. The territory of complex, molecular post-Fordist society has become the place of the production of value. “Place consciousness” alludes to the recognition by the community of the value of their territorial patrimony in producing lasting wealth and new processes of self-government. The form of appropriating added territorial value (exogenous or endogenous) becomes the object of conflict. The local project is the scenario in which to recompose the various stakes involved in the development and social appropriation of the common good represented by the territorial patrimony. In this perspective the need for identity should be politically reinterpreted as constructive energy fostering the growth of place consciousness and development styles based on recognition of specific socio-cultural features, on care for and enhancement of local resources (environmental, territorial, productive) and on networks of non-hierarchical fair trading among local societies. But this positive evolution of the enormous energies deriving from the contradictions of globalization requires a radical transformation of the centralist political culture towards neo-municipal forms of federalism, in which the development of the territory and its specific features as the producer of real wealth takes place in the name of enhancement and cooperation among diversities, instead of exploitation - exogenous or endogenous - of human and material resources.

The first cultural and political breakthrough required would seem to be to channel the identity-seeking revolt and the processes of neo-racination towards the building of local societies, without denying the *a priori* needs and aspirations produced by new forms of poverty, or resorting to an abstract, universalistic proclamation of values.

The Statute of Places: a Constitutional Pact to Develop the Territorial Patrimony

The construction of the local project is based on the pact involving various agents, who, starting from descriptions of conflicts of interest, redefine their own projects and action frameworks in relation to the development of the common patrimony through the coordination of local development objectives. This process must go beyond the traditional forms of representation and delegation and lead to the construction of new institutions of direct democracy. These, in turn, must attempt to reposition guidelines and settle conflicts by orienting the process of transformation towards scenarios of self-sustainable development. The transformation can take place if the system of agents (both public and private) experimenting the new institutions is sufficiently broad and complex as to guarantee visibility and presence for those who usually have no say – the weaker members of society with their problems (social sustainability) – as well as to pinpoint and strengthen innovative energies which can be potentially active in developing the patrimony.
The territorial patrimony (Choay 1992) is made up of a complex system of values (cultural, social, productive, environmental, artistic and urban) which the local project reinterprets by exploiting energies that are born from contradiction and innovation. A pact among the agents, based on the development of the patrimony as the material basis for the production of wealth, generates the rules of conduct and reciprocal guarantees to safeguard and enhance the environment (environmental sustainability) as well as the quality of life (territorial sustainability). These rules and guarantees spring from the very construction of the project, in which caring and trusting relations are established through the collective recognition of the shared common good. There is also a check on conditions for individual action (by producers and inhabitants) which is not harmful to the patrimony, and as such is recognized as a collective good. Conscious recognition leads to social self-control and virtuous guiding actions. This process in turn helps planning to evolve into forms of social production of the territory through the collective construction of its statutes, as regards both the preservation and transformation of the patrimony. The statute of places is thus a constitutional act, the self-aware expression of "place consciousness", worked out by the inhabitant-producers in the process of the collective construction of decisions, to create an original style of development (Magnaghi 2000b).
The construction of the statute of places thus becomes the founding act of the local project. It goes beyond the exogenous laws and restraints on the social individual, and collective action towards regulations and pacts for transformation aided by shared common meaning, built up through forms of self government and new institutes of direct democracy (political sustainability). As the social production of the territory, the local project uses indicators of wealth and well-being which are not only those of economic growth (GDP) which is given less importance compared to other criteria; these include the widespread ownership of the means of production, self-government, environmental quality, living quality, solidarity and the development of non-business caring relations (Daly and Cobb 1994). Through these assessment criteria, the local project reduces the dominance of the economic system in favour of the socio-cultural system. And it is by following these criteria that local project creates the conditions of its realisation - the transformation of lifestyles, of modes of consumption and production - by building up local economic systems able to produce added territorial value (economic sustainability).

Innovative Statutes of Citizenship

In the age of the crisis of citizenship and the social statutes of waged labor, the local project highlights the importance of forms of self-employment, crafts, and micro-firms. This complex molecular production fabric is now the widely accepted terminal for networking multinational enterprise and financial capital. However, if the local project has its own statutes, knowledge

and internal trust among locally self-managed firms, it can form the productive base of local development by building integrated local economic systems - from agriculture to the advanced tertiary sector. The local project can implement new space-time statutes and new rights of citizenship, bringing the figures of the inhabitant and self-employed producer closer together by "domesticating" labour (also with the aim of raising the quality of life) and removing significant portions of productive activity from the market.
In this context, it is vital not to look back nostalgically on the corporate statutes of waged labour and Fordism. The construction of self-managed, self-sustainable local companies will only be possible by releasing the energy of widespread molecular labour in post-Fordist society, thus encouraging the creation of complex networks of inhabitant-producers - the owners of the means of production who make their own production companies by adhering to a pact for the development of their *own* territorial patrimony. The components of local society acquire citizenship rights not according to previous appurtenances but rather according to their active participation in the construction of new societal statutes.
Local society cannot be invented from scratch. It develops by making the most of virtuous energies and new forms of labour already present in the territory. A fundamental aspect of building local society consists, therefore, in working on the new societal statutes of self-government of "the second generation of self-managed labour" (Bologna 1997), within which the tertiary sector can be the cultural and ethical guide that helps enterprises to go beyond a monolithic, "economic-based" identity.
To go beyond the political forms associated with the statute of waged labour, it is necessary "not to work in a homogeneous group, but connect, contaminate... gather together heterogeneous elements, translate social languages and join them up in a horizontal grid" (Revelli 1999). This form of politics is just being born. It has to do with the promotion of new community aggregates, new forms of democracy founded on communicative action, where a host of stakes, values, and differences are expressed in continuously evolving concerted pacts accompanied by conflict but also by the acknowledgment of otherness. Making local society is thus an ongoing process of weaving the web of civic networks, involving a widely varying group of insurgent agents: women, children, the elderly, ethnic groups, associations, social centres, and voluntary groups, who recreate the public space of the city; new farmers who produce public goods (environmental quality, landscape, and local economies); producers who develop the environment and local cultures; and fair trading and ecobanks. At present all these groups still represent a great outburst of fragmented energies hostile to globalization scattered over the territory. Thus, another important aspect of building local society lies in joining up these fragments of innovative energy so that they come together in the same territory by initiating an open, cooperative process of transformation carried out by the network of diverse agents who are working to create shared scenarios.

The New Municipality Governs the Local Project

A radical change in the role of local government, and especially municipalities, takes place within this process. The local project presupposes the growth of powers and competencies in communal administrations and higher territorial entities, which are also expressions of the municipalities insofar as they represent a higher order of the local. In a sustainability project based on the development of territorial patrimony, public authorities are asked to transform their roles in two convergent directions: on the one hand to change from governing services to governing development, i.e. orienteering decisions involving the economy and production activities towards developing the local patrimony; on the other, to change from being institutes of delegation to become new institutes of direct democracy, able to implement fostered statutes of governed development. In this complex system of governance by implementing new planning rules and new institutes of democracy the municipality is in a position to denote and promote agents and energies that will develop the patrimony. At the same time, it can discourage and contrast the strong exogenous and endogenous powers which simplify the complexity of the decision-making system and tend to take over resources to exploit use them for their own profit, thereby damaging and consuming the common good.

In promoting and consolidating intermediate institutes of democracy (local development agencies, pacts, committees, workshops, etc.), the municipality can create a fertile meeting ground for top-down policies and bottom-up social networks. This is the key issue. We are witnessing a powerful drive (the European Union, regions, municipal administrations) towards processes of participation and local development projects in which the construction of the institutes of coordination among local agents is a prerequisite for funding. This thus provides the conditions for an encounter between the workplaces of local societies and the institutions. But this must be a two-way encounter, able to produce new events, new structures, and networks. The implementation of top-down policies will not necessarily make local society grow, if the projects are prefabricated, or the agents at the negotiation table are few and powerful, or the regulations of development are dictated by economic globalization and market competition. Therefore, networks of self-organized agents must be able to gain access to these tools. The negotiation tables must be as broad as possible and represent the interests of the weakest, and the projects proposed by different agents should be assessed for their contribution in terms of the enduring development of the territorial and environmental patrimony so as to satisfy the needs and aspirations of the inhabitants, and not simply to comply with exogenous market laws.
In this halfway meeting-point the new municipality can take on functions which are crucial to building the local society, provided it correctly uses its new powers to manage the various aspects involved. Those, above all, are the qualification and widening of new institutions of coordination, and democratic communication networks; finding and encouraging agents who can pursue sustainable initiatives to develop the environment; selecting and giving incentives to virtuous production activities; and creating a style of development of its own territory through a broad constitutional and statutory path in constructing local society (Sullo 2002).

Towards Bottom-up Globalization

In the "glocalist" theory, local development is created insofar as the local community is contaminated by the global, thus bringing into the local the innovations that derive from opening relations with long and short worldwide networks. Local development occurs where local society manages to build horizontal networks in the global system. But here we are faced with a problem nor unlike squaring the circle (establishing mutual relations between the local and the global), since global intervention in the local tends to drain energies and resources and to restore dominance. The issue at stake, then, is how to combine these long networks with the depth of the territory without the local losing out as a consequence.
The alternatives are either coexistence with the global through its long networks or active resistance to the global and the construction of equitable networks (bottom-up globalization?). In favour of the second approach, it must be said that at present the global does not permit an equitably-balanced dialectic relationship, because its rules exclude the sustainability of the local by placing greater emphasis on competition than cooperation, the exploitation of resources rather than the development of patrimony, social polarization rather than greater complexity, and so on. In the global the long networks are joined up (by the market, powerful technologies, finance, etc.) and deal with each individual local reality separately through hierarchical "tree" relations in which the position of each individual region in the hierarchy is pre-established. Each individual region is therefore forced to take part in the competition according to rules imposed from outside.
This ideal a global network of local societies is still weak and must be strengthened in order to build a relationship with the current centralist forms of economic globalization that does not place it at a disadvantage. It must do so primarily by constructing:
- inter-local informative relations, fair-trading networks that interface with the global networks;
- a proliferation of cities able to build non-hierarchical global relations through the spread of rare services in peripheral regional networks as a response to the processes that tend to concentrate power and command in the global cities;
- eco-friendly, fair commercial and financial relationships that develop local and translocal networks in the world economy market;

- local self-sustainable production systems based on the development of the patrimony, that join the world market as agents actively producing a new quality of wealth and as agents spreading original new models of production and consumption;
- networks of local development agencies that create an interface between top-down projects and bottom-up projects
- South-South cultural relations; South-North relations intensifying interconnections laid over the North-South networks – self-representation as opposed to representation by the centre.
Albeit to different degrees, in the possible relations between the local and global, and in the presence of an overdetermined global, overflowing, which deals separately with each individual local that has been sucked in by global competition, the problem lies in implementing all policies, actions and projects aimed at achieving the following:
- strengthening internal cohesion in each local system, constructing self-perpetuating social bonds, and the capacity to express particular features of a self-sustainable developmental style (by which we mean the capacity for self-reproduction of the physical and man-made territory); this requires the development of a culture and "consciousness" of place, of a different kind of rationality, since only the local, or short networks, generate sociality (a scarce resource), which generates value added and positive sum games.
- building medium and long local-to-local networks to modify the highly hierarchical system of global cities in the direction of more complex multiple regional subsystems; encouraging relations (between cities, regions, and local economic systems) to intensify non-hierarchical networks of fair trading, subsidiarity, complimentarity, and reciprocal consolidation within macro-regions (the Alpine region, the Mediterranean region, the European Union, etc.), instead of global economic networks.

By strengthening the internal cohesion in local society and its complex integrated production structure, the local project lays the basis for the independence necessary to implement a system of relations with other non-hierarchical, federative, caring local societies, thus setting in motion a process of bottom-up globalization that responds to the objective of raising the quality of life in non-selective and non-exclusive forms. This objective contrasts with top-down economic globalization, which produces processes that increase poverty, because of the rules of competition in which each local agent, business or city, is forced to adopt imposed laws of globalization: i.e. lower labour costs and less consideration of environmental factors.

In conclusion, the local project is seen as a political proposal of bottom-up globalization to spread and connect the energy that is emerging as a response to economic globalization, a utopian allusion to a plural, de-hierarchized, fair world (Brecher and Costello 1995). As such, the local project recognizes the deep disparity in the current relationship between the local and the global. The local project thus makes no claims to solve problems through hastily resorting to competition among poor regions, a competition destined to produce short circuits, with disastrous effects for the development of local societies. What the local project proposes as a strategic priority is to work on the growth of local networks and their social density as the indispensable condition for confronting relations and pressures from the long networks of the global.

References

Becattini, G. (1999), *Lo sviluppo locale*, Prato: Iris

Bologna, S. (1997), "Dieci tesi per la definizione di uno statuto per il lavoro autonomo", in: Bologna, S. and Fumagalli, A. (eds.), *Il lavoro autonomo di seconda generazione*: Milano: Feltrinelli

Brecher, J. and Costello, T. (1995), *Global Village or Global Pillage* (it., *Contro il capitale globale*, Milano: Feltrinelli 1996)

Casey, E.S. (1997), *The Fate of Place*. Berkeley: University of California Press

Choay, F. (1992), *L'allegorie du patrimoine.* (it., *L'allegoria del patrimonio*, Roma: Officina, 1995)

Daly, H.E. and Cobb J. (1994), *For the Common Good*. Boston: Beacon

Magnaghi, A. (ed.) (1992), *Il territorio dell'abitare. Lo sviluppo locale come alternativa strategica*. Milano: Angeli

Magnaghi, A. (ed.) (1998a), *Il territorio degli abitanti. Società locali e autosostenibilità*. Milano: Dunod

Magnaghi, A. (1998b), "Territorial Heritage: A genetic code for sustainable development", in: INURA (eds.), *Possible Urban Worlds*. Basel: Birkhauser

Magnaghi, A. (2000a), *Il progetto locale*. Torino: Bollati Boringhieri

Magnaghi, A. (2000b), "Identità dei territori e identità dei luoghi", in: Cinà, G. (ed.), *Descrizione fondativa e statuto dei luoghi.* Firenze: Alinea

Magnaghi, A. et al. (2002), *Charter for a New Municipium*. Firenze: Centro A-Zeta

Paba, G. (1998), *Luoghi comuni*. Milano: Angeli

Paloscia R. (1998), "The La Habana/Ecopolis Project. Urban Regeneration and Community Development ", in: INURA (eds.), *Possible Urban Worlds*. Basel: Birkhauser

Revelli, M. (1999), "Fare società", in: *Carta dei cantieri sociali* (supplement to *Il Manifesto)* 2, 6

Sachs, W. (ed.) (1992), *Dizionario dello sviluppo*. Torino: Gruppo Abele

Sullo, P.L. (ed.) (2002), *La democrazia possibile*. Napoli: IntraMoenia berlin bruxelles/brussel firenze london toronto zürich

Berlin: from MetropoLUST to MetropoLOST

Photo sequence in front pages of this chapter by Manuela Conti / ogi:no knauss

TEXT..........Constance Carr, Ute Lehrer

Introduction

Berlin, quite irrevocably, has changed and metamorphosed at a scale and magnitude that leaves most of its urban spaces unrecognizable compared with its appearance of years ago. The fall of the Wall on November 9, 1989 was not only a symbolic manifestation of a world in flux but it was the starting point of a period of new expectations for Berlin. City boosters quickly announced Berlin's future as that of a metropolis, a global city, a bridge-head to the East. The drive to become global was complemented with speculative activies in the real estate business, financed mainly from outside. The arrival of new investments and new players collided with local conventions, while at the same time the two distinct local practices of city-building had to be renegotiated. Through the erection of impressive speculative buildings, it was hoped to find the spatial manifestation of a new hegemony, where alternative ways of thinking became marginalized. Everyday life experiences as well as work relations have in a way that created new disparities and contradications. The articles in this chapter are aimed at giving the reader a glimpse into what has become of Berlin's transformation and the associated ramifications thereof.

If to understand a city one must first understand its socio-political and geographical history, then one must understand the depth and scope of what has transpired in Berlin's last ten years. Summing up the decade of reconstruction following the fall of the Wall, Constance Carr gives an overview of the planning obstacles that were faced by Berlin planners as they connected two radically different cities to create Germany's capital. One is reminded, however, that the story does not end in the happily-ever-after, fairytale-like optimism that one might have liked to predict back at the time of reunification. Instead, the story simply isn't over: like urban transformation in metropoles around the world, it is an ongoing process. Berlin now has new problems that create new divisions and new disparities, some that still stem from the original two Berlins, some that have simply evolved as a result of the transformation process.

The construction cranes that stretched across the districts of Mitte and Tiergarten over the nostalgic Potsdamer Platz have become a world famous symbol - so overused that it is now sometimes regarded as cliché. The production and marketing of Berlin as a city reborn is where Ute Lehrer´s piece takes us. By telling the story of the bright red Info-Box that stood at the centre of one of the world's largest construction sites, she shows that this deceivingly modest addition to the construction process was an integral part of a particular marketing strategy to promote Potsdamer Platz. This symbolizes a city planning strategy that mimics new trends also followed by large firms, whereby the production of an image seems to become more important than the product itself. Furthermore, Lehrer underscores the conflicting realities and non-realities that reflect through and out of this policy of the image.

Volker Eick shows that the reproduction of Berlin's urban space did not and does not occur within a static political economic context. Instead, Berlin like many other cities, is restructuring politically and economically in the name of flexibilization. Specifically, as Berlin's financial budget tightens, public services are devolved to private and third sector organizations. He focuses on the governmental downsizing of public safety services and the instrumental use of the third sector and workfare participants as their replacement - a process that further justifies itself through "communitarian and inclusionist/integrationist discourses". Further, as suggested in his title, Eick reveals some of the new social polarities that have arisen as a consequence of this situation.

Connecting theory with real life examples, Ahmed Allahwala and Constance Carr show that counter publics take on a secondary role in Berlin's urban space, and how public spaces not only retain a standardized normative character, but remain systematically exclusive to non-hegemonic discourses. Historically, strong counter-public and social movements such as feminist movements, anti-racist action movements, environmental movements, have all been pushed to the fringe.

With the fall of the Wall, subcultures and counter-cultures were revived and reached new heights in Berlin, when new energies and new territories became the site of a lively Techno as well as of a more experimental electronic music scene. In his contribution, Ingo Bader identifies off-culture as a pioneer for redevelopment in obsolete industrial areas. He addresses the problem of the commercialization of counter-cultures whereby cultural products are not only material goods but also contributors to lifestyle choices for the middle classes.

While heterogenous in their individual approaches, all the authors share a critical perspective on Berlin's recent spatial, political, social, cultural and economic transformation, and their contributions question Berlin's Lust, and the strategies selected for becoming a metropolis again.

TEXT..Constance Carr
PHOTOS..Constance Carr

Berlin: Re-Unified, but Not in One Piece

Berlin has become famous for its extraordinary situation. It is a city that has undergone unprecedented change in the last 15 years - a change that was sparked by the fall of the Wall, and a change that has met extraordinary challenges as Berliners and Berlin city planners faced the overwhelming challenge of reconnecting, reconstructing and reunifying the two Berlins.

In addition to the physical and social barriers that needed to be overcome, Berlin's situation could be singled out because of its location, because of how and why it was divided, and because of concurrent trends in political-economic regulation. For the first time as a whole since the War, Berlin could integrate with the surrounding region. For decades, Berlin was also one of the world's few locations where socialism came in direct contact with capitalism. Reunification meant that the two governments that were formed after the War would have to work together, harmonize under one government, and co-ordinate under one form of regulation. Berlin would also have stakeholders at local, national and international levels, as local interests battled with the interests of a nation's new capital city, which was emerging as privatization and neoliberalization swept other metropoles around the world.

Now, almost 15 years later, the divided Berlin is again whole, but it continues to change in ways that create new faults and fissures. The goal of a united Berlin was something that many sought to achieve after the fall of the Wall. However, the new fragments that have been created only show that this vision is yet to be seen.

City and Region: Initial Physical Barriers

Immediate problems of a physical nature were (Frick, 1991): 1) how to deal with development inside the inner city (the territory encircled by the S-Bahn Ring or S4 subway line); and 2) how to develop the different city centres. Until 1990, the area inside the S-Bahn Ring consisted of two main city centres, *Kurfürstendamm/Zoologischer Garten*, and *Mitte* - two city centres that date back to the initial foundation of Charlottenburg in 1705. After reunification, the initial dialogues that circulated around the question of what to do with this land varied (ibid.). Many looked forward to the growth of a lively inner city, while others worried that this land would be devoured by investors interested only in services and market-oriented redevelopment. These hopes and fears were augmented by the more pragmatic but equally daunting task of structural amendments needed in order to recombine the eastern part with the western. Old blocked off streets, for example, had to be reconnected - a process that during the 1990s involved an average yearly expenditure of 5.3 million German Marks (DM), peaking in 1995 at 6.5 Million DM (*Senatsverwaltung für Stadtentwicklung*, 2000). Similarly, old railways and subway lines had to be rejoined.

Another planning problem was how Berlin, a city of 3.4 million inhabitants living at a density of 3,820 persons per km2 (ibid.), was going to expand into the surrounding State (*Land)* of Brandenburg, an area with 2.57 million individuals occupying nearly 30,000 km2 (*ibid.*). Unlike other post-war cities, urban sprawl did not occur in Berlin. West Berlin was surrounded by a wall, and therefore could not be structurally, economically, or culturally integrated with the surrounding German Democratic Republic (GDR). East Berlin did not expand either, as was typical geographical of socialist cities. Suddenly, with the breakdown of the iron curtain, not only was development at the periphery possible, but so was full integration with the "New States of the Federal Republic of Germany"(*Neue Bundesländer*).

Berlin is now (but perhaps not for long) one of three cities in Germany that enjoy City-State [1] status (the other two being Hamburg and Bremen). The primary advantage of this status is that a city can administer by itself many of the responsibilities usually allocated to state levels of government. Disadvantages do exist, however, such as obligatory negotiations between the City-State and the surrounding State (*Land*)). City-States do not have jurisdiction beyond their boundaries and therefore, and not surprisingly, cannot force neighbouring municipalities to act. This dynamic may be particularly awkward because different levels of government may become involved in the negotiation processes.

Postdamer Platz 2000

Frick (1991) discussed the concept of a "star-shaped" development pattern that would extend Berlin into the surrounding Brandenburg - a pattern that would follow the old railway lines that were built in the 1920s and 1930s. Each axis of the star would reach out to neighbouring townships (Oranienburg, Bernau, Königswusterhausen, Strausberg, Zossen, Wünsdorf, Michendorf, and Neuen), and the territory along each axis would be reserved for housing and built-up areas, while the areas in between the axes would be reserved for "open space." The main problem with this plan was its realization. Existing complex bureaucratic planning structures in both Berlin and Brandenburg inhibited the process (*ibid.*). If the City-Sate of Berlin wanted to expand into the surrounding region with either strategically placed housing or industry - or anything else concerning policing, elections, environmental protection, public health, waste disposal, education, housing construction, traffic administration, public service facilities, culture, or recreation (Council of Europe, 1992) - then it was required to negotiate with Brandenburg, whose aims and goals could possibly be very different.

Currently there are discussions aimed at amalgamating Berlin with Brandenburg under one state government, a plan that was defeated in a referendum in 1996. Brandenburgers voted 62% against an amalgamation, while Berliners voted 53.6% in favour - with the majority of "yes" votes coming from western districts (Statistisches Landesamt Berlin, 1996). A move to begin amalgamation could only have been initiated if both regions produced more than 50% in favour; thus, the idea was vanquished. Today, the governments of both States want to re-ignite the amalgamation debate, arguing that the fusion of census, regional planning, secondary education, radio and broadcasting, transportation and other sectors will have great benefits. The hope is now to achieve amalgamation by 2009 (Senatskanzlei, 2003).

Whether amalgamation is achieved or not, however, development in this region will have ripple effects on surrounding states, and perhaps even Poland. A look at municipal city plans [2] (*Flächennutzungsplan*, or *F-Plan*) will show this. Cities in the coastal State of Mecklenburg-Vorpommern, for example, are encouraging further tourism and trade, and this is neatly integrated and harmonized with development in Berlin. The growth of maritime activity involved with regional trade is being encouraged. To attract more tourism, the beaches and nature reserves are being promoted as attractive sports and recreation destinations. Smaller cities are also being turned into places for well-being [3] (*Badeorte*). This area will also be well-connected to Berlin by transportation systems (especially the B11 highway and railroad southward towards Berlin) that are currently under construction. The North-East of Poland is also undergoing redevelopment, increasing trade and tourism in the area. This development may, however, not only be linked to its proximity to Metropole Berlin, but also to its position as a future European Union State.

From Socialism to Capitalism

Piecing together the two radically different cultural systems also presented a major problem (Guskind, 1991). It didn't follow that the breakdown of the physical wall in 1989 would lead to a simple process of architectural and bureaucratic change, because another barrier existed: the so-called, "Wall in the Mind" (*die Mauer in den Köpfen*). Both Easterners and Westerners had to re-accustom themselves to the idea of possibly living in communities that could physically as well as socially cross the now non-existent boundary. Although there has been quite a bit of migration (for example, the westerners who jumped at the opportunity of cheaper rents in the eastern tenements, and easterners who searched for employment in the west), many communities have not moved and have remained relatively insular. Non-German residents, for example, have remained in western districts (thus raising the question of what their reservations about the east are). Likewise, neo-Nazi groups have remained in their communities in the east (e.g. the neighbourhood of Hellersdorf). This phenomenon was perhaps in part reinforced by the fact that all facets of everyday life are fulfilled in respective neighbourhoods. Migration, at least on a daily basis, is not necessary. Many public transportation routes have also stayed in their respective part of town. Although remarkable changes have been made to the city street layout and underground subway systems, streetcars still run only in the eastern districts, while double-decker buses still run only in the western districts, thus limiting cross-city travel to a certain extent.

Upon re-unification, a central question, or rather, assumed question, was what was to be done with the former socialist structures produced through socialist thought. The characteristics that defined East Berlin between 1945 and 1989 reflected just that [4]: 1) the "artistic" design of urban centres to reflect the success and prosperity of the socialist regime (and likewise the worthlessness of market-oriented development); 2) a distinction between rural and urban living, resulting in no suburbanization; 3) a neglect for pre-socialist physical structures, such as tenement housing (said to have been left as showcases of the pitfalls of capitalism); 4) an absence of segregation based on economic status (resulting in next to no homelessness or unemployment, and the full inclusion of women into the workplace), although political status and capability played a differentiating role; and 5) an extreme centralization of power and decision-making, resulting in token (if any) municipal participation and relatively high corporate power at the local level, which was dominated primarily by vertically integrated industry.

After the Wall came down, it was generally assumed that the socialist structures would be dismantled. The continuous flight of East Germans during the 1950s, the hundreds of escape attempts after 1961 (the year the wall was built), and the countless narratives of state repression as a result of living under a central government policed by the Stasi, remain a testament to the unpopularity of the socialist regime implemented by the Soviet Union. However, after the "protective wall against (western) fascism" (*Antifaschistischer Schutzwall*) was demolished and the process of rebuilding the united Germany and Berlin began, it would soon be revealed that some aspects of the socialist creation would not only be torn down, but also missed - especially by former residents of the GDR.

Postdamer Platz 2001

With the fall of communism in the GDR, Berlin was seen as a geographically strategic gateway to eastern markets, and many authors and planners studied and discussed Berlin's redevelopment with only glancing reference to East Berlin as a former socialist city.
The argument was that the structure of the now non-existent GDR regime was generally not relevant to new planning processes. What followed, however, is what could be described as the invasion of a capitalist, corporatist democratic regime [5] into the communist-socialist territory that was formerly the GDR. Following Article 23 of the West German Constitution, the apparatus of the GDR was formally nullified (Schulz, 1995), and the GDR's administration, bureaucracy, and workforces were dismantled and replaced with those of the existing Federal Republic of Germany. The official East German party, the SED (*Sozialistische Einheitspartei Deutschland*), changed its name to the PDS, *(Partei des Demokratischen Sozialismus)*, and was swallowed into the West German governmental system as an independent party - a party that, today, is supported not only by old defenders of the socialist regime, but also by a new, young and committed generation of radical anarcho-communists. The GDR currency became obsolete and the West German Mark was introduced. Soon, East German exports to former member states of the Comecon block fell by more than 75% (from almost 30 billion DM to 7 billion), leaving almost 40% of the East German workforce unemployed, while West German exports increased by 23% (Schulz, 1995). Moreover, socialist monuments were purged and socialist spaces removed - processes that did not occur without a struggle. Although, for example, places like Alexander Platz were a reminder of the strongly criticized socialist state, they were still places of community events and everyday life and therefore places of value to be remembered.

Intense competition between the east and west has, however, a tradition in Berlin. Before the Wall came down, they were embattled in a fierce competition with one another to prove who had it better - citizens of socialism or citizens of capitalism. Each side eagerly flaunted its accomplishments and successes, its prosperity, wealth and riches. West Berlin, an outpost of western capitalism in the "Red Sea," became a "showplace of western consumerism," (Guskind, 1991). The cult film, "*Sonnenallee*" told, in part, the tale of teenage boys in the East who eagerly bought forbidden underground music from the West, and of East Germans who would smuggle for their family members coffee or stockings over the border back into the East (a phenomenon still confirmed by many German citizens still today). On the flip side, the East flaunted other attributes, such as its architectural accomplishments, the most famous of which is the television tower (*Fernsehturm*), which towered 365 metres over Mitte and was visible from any point inside the two Berlins.

The new Berlin was also, as Guskind (1991) put it, "a city with two or more of everything," and this proved to be a new problem in the reorganization of the city. Such questions, for example, as to whether it should be the symphony of the former East or the symphony of the former West to continue to receive government funding would cause sensitive political negotiations - yet another bone of contention in the climate of competition. This, in combination with the drastic deindustrialization that led to particularly high levels of unemployment, and the fight to retain socialist space, furthered even more the psychological divide and fostered prejudices that each side held for the other [6]. The ramifications of such a radical transition as that from socialism to capitalism - and some economists, at least, have predicted that the economic gap will take 50 years to close (Schulz 1995) - remains of particular relevance to urban planners and theorists today, if equality between "Westerners" and "Easterners" is ever to be reached.

Local versus National versus International

Berlin is a City-State within the federal structure of Germany, divided into 12 administrative subdivisions or districts (*Bezirke*). It is also in the midst of building a nation's capital, and becoming increasingly tied to international economic, social and cultural interaction. This means that spaces in Berlin are subject, albeit not evenly, to interests from community, municipal, national and international levels.

The national debate over the decision whether to move the capital city of Germany to Berlin or to stay in Bonn focused on three general issues (Häußermann and Strom, 1994): 1) the capital city as a symbolic place; 2) the capital city as a "political milieu"; and 3) the capital city as a "catalyst of regional development". After the Second World War, the idea of Berlin as the Capital City (*Berlin als Hauptstadt*), once again the site of country's governmental headquarters, remained a mere burning ember. It was a small flame that both Bonn and Berlin fanned as a memorial to the divided Germany, and in hopes of a future reunification. Immediately after the fall of the Wall, the realization of this dream attracted international attention and investors. Several years after reunification, it also turned away or disappointed investors, as internal national debates over the process of relocation were prolonged (Häußermann and Strom, 1994). Not everyone agreed that Bonn would benefit from the relocation, for example. Now, one decade (and a bit) later, the German Parliament and 17 federal ministries have moved from Bonn to Berlin. This has involved the reconstruction of 500,000 square meters of office space, moving 11,400 jobs, and the relocation of 7,500 workers (Senatsverwaltung für Stadtentwicklung, 2000). This does not include the hundreds of private firms and non-profit organizations that also relocated, and the thousands of commuters with expensive and time consuming transportation obligations.

Postdamer Platz 2002

According to the reconstruction of Berlin as a united capital city, Berlin was divided into two conceptual planning zones (Häußermann and Strom, 1994): 1) the areas that would house the capital city functions and government buildings, which were primarily along the site of the Wall, called "Development Areas"; and 2) the neighbourhoods tangential to the development area, called "Adjustment Areas." Special adjustments were made to the decision-making structure for this specific planning process. Under normal circumstances, district governments participated in urban planning activities. For decisions concerning the building of government buildings, however, these steps were eliminated. It would be inaccurate to say that citizens had absolutely no opportunity to participate, since many political boards worked with local organizations for feedback and consultation - a normal dynamic of urban politics in many urban centres. However, since the right to veto or appeal decisions had been taken away, opportunities for citizen input had consequently been substantially diminished.

The building of the nation's capital was taking place under a particular set of special circumstances: namely, as one of Europe's largest metropolises redeveloping at an accelerated speed fuelled by the potential of enormous international capital investment (Krätke, 1992). Many authors have already shown how that the power of potential capital investment underscored and influenced redevelopment in Berlin. Strom (1996a) showed how the production of space was a consequence, at least in part, of the dynamics between public policy and real-estate-market pressure. Krätke (1992) argued that that the interests of internationally active real-estate companies and large industrial service-sector firms with an interest in property investments were the driving forces behind Berlin's reconstruction. Berry and McGreal (1995) showed how the Investment Priority Act (a follow-up to the Restitution Act that offered to return properties to their original Jewish owners) gave priority of land ownership to "economically productive" investors. However, "potential" was the operative word in the opening sentence of this paragraph. By the mid-1990s, it was becoming clear that international financial interests were not so great as was originally expected.
Instead, the economic landscape of Berlin was dominated by large German enterprises, such as the German Rail System (*Deutsche Bahn AG*), Siemens, and IBM Deutschland Holding, who all moved their headquarters to Berlin, while international investors stayed away, leaving Berlin, in this sense, a very "national space".

This lack of international financial attention, however, did not curb the wave of neoliberalization and flexibilization that other metropolises around the world also experienced. Furthermore, if the Internet is a porthole to the building of international relations, and if one sees that privitization, at least, opens the door for international firms to deliver services, then Berlin is, indeed, intimately tied to the international community. As deindustrialization in Berlin set in, leaving unemployment as high as 26% in some neighbourhoods, the service sector grew (Senatsverwaltung für Stadtentwicklung, 2000). Around the turn of the millennium, popular use of the cell phone and high-speed Internet exploded: the second-most-common web address ending, after .com, is now .de. The Senate Administration for Economy, Labour and Women (*Senatsverwaltung für Wirtschaft, Arbeit und Frauen*) now even boasts of Berlin as an "Information Society" (*Informationsgesellschaft*), and Berlin-Brandenburg as the European model for information and technological (IT) development.
With the motto, "We Make IT," clusters of firms specializing in media or information technology have emerged throughout Brandenburg, and the whole region of Berlin-Brandenburg is now the location with the highest number of DSL internet connections in Europe, the testing ground for "Universal Television" (DVB-T), and home to more than 10,000 firms driving the IT industry, with an 11-billion Euro turnover (*ibid.*). It is further vaunted, too, that the jobs lost by de-industrialization have been replaced by jobs created in the IT industry. However, unemployment continues to rise (Senatsverwaltung für Stadtentwicklung, 2000) and social disparities continue to polarize (Krätke, 2003), as Berlin faces a dismal financial crisis.

After the War, Berlin was never a well-to-do city. During post-war years, West Berlin received substantial subsidies from the West German government. As East Germany's capital city, it also received financial support from the East German government. Today, however, Berlin carries an enormous financial debt that is around the billions of Euro dollars (Krätke, 2003) - a situation that has arisen partly as a result of the not wholly successful replacement of the manufacturing industry with the information technology industry, and partly from an unexpected downturn in the value of financial investments made by the city at the turn of the millennium.

This financial situation has now set the stage for a sharpened neoliberal agenda that the city budget quite clearly reveals. Financial projections up to 2006 call for the reduction of work places in civil services. Among the targeted administrations are those of the fire department, police [7], school system and city planning (Senatsverwaltung für Finanzen, 2002). Besides the outright slashing of jobs, other measures include "widening the options for part-time work" for those who might be interested in early retirement, and requiring teachers to take on heavier teaching loads. At the same time, in a handbook entitled "What Costs How Much?", published by the Senate in 2001, the (high) costs of services such as child immunization, health and hygiene controls, foster parenting, playgrounds, kindergartens and welfare administration are also analyzed. These measures show the typical pattern of neoliberal agendas, which always begin with the "need" to cutback "unnecessary" governmental services. Once decided, the government outsources their management and delivery (which turned out to be, in fact, somehow necessary) to either the private or non-profit sector, forfeiting citizen's democratic control along with it - and this is the case in Berlin. Local needs such as housing, secondary education, recreational services, employment training services and policing have all been devolved or are being devolved to either the non-profit or profit sector.

Conclusion

Rebuilding Berlin certainly represented a demanding task for city planners, and today (2003), much of the building frenzy and fervour has already subsided. The “Info Box” (the information centre and viewing platform for visitors) has been dismantled. The sea of construction cranes that once dominated the scenery at Potsdamer Platz is rapidly receding. Daimler-Benz, which somehow acquired property there at an astounding 100DM/m2 (Pepchinski, 1993), has completed its project which now marks the skyline at Potsdamer Platz neighbouring the Sony Centre. Many of the old buildings on Unter den Linden have reopened. The government meets daily in the now open and functioning Reichstag. The old tenement buildings of the district of Mitte are newly renovated, sanitized and shiny, and are now thriving with day and night-life. Ostbahnhof (the east train station) boasts new architecture, and nearby one can view one of the remaining sections of the Wall, newly and neatly painted and preserved (and named a modish East Side Gallery).

In the spring of 2000, the Senate Administration for City Development (*Senatsverwaltung für Stadtentwicklung*) showcased an uncritical exhibit that celebrated the diversity and dynamics of the reunified Berlin. This entertaining interactive exhibition displayed Berlin as state of the art, clean, fun. There was nothing negative about Berlin. The “many-sided economic and socio-spatial divides characteristic of the metropolitan process,” that Krätke (1992) had predicted for Berlin evidently did not develop during that previous decade.

Although Berlin has gone through enormous physical and structural alterations, further organizational changes lie on the horizon with the pending amalgamation with Brandenburg. Berlin’s socialist history has been integrated into capitalism. Yet inequalities and prejudices between East and West still linger, and xenophobia and fear of xenophobia are still detectable. There has been an attempt to replace the industries lost during the 1990s with a prosperous information technology industry, but it was not particularly successful. Further, flexibilization and increased privatization continues to threaten citizen participation in the development and delivery of public services, and unemployment remains high. Berlin has reunited. However, new divides have been created. The possibility of a “one piece” appears (at least as yet) nowhere in sight.

References

Berry, J. and McGreal, S. (1995), "Berlin", in: J. Berry and S. McGreal. (eds), *European Cities, Planning Systems and Property Markets*, London: E & FN Spoon.

Council of Europe (1992), *Structure and Operation of Local and Regional Democracy: Federal Republic of Germany*, Council of Europe.

Frick, D. (1991), "City development and planning in the Berlin conurbation", in: *Town Planning Review.* 62, 1, 37-49.

Guskind, R. (1991), "Making Berlin whole", in: *Planning.* American Planning Association. May 1991.

Häußermann, H. "From the socialist to the capitalist city: experiences from Germany", in: Andrusz, G., Harloe, M., and Szeleny, I. (eds) (1996), *Cities After Socialism.* Oxford: Blackwell.

Häußermann, H. and Strom, E. (1994), "Berlin: the once and future capital", in: *International Journal for Urban Regional Research.* 18, 2, 335-346.

Häußermann, H. and Kapphan, A. (2000), *Berlin: von der Geteilten zur Gespaltenen Stadt.* Opladen: Leske & Budrich.

Krätke, S. (1992), "Berlin: the rise of a new metropolis in a post-Fordist landscape", in: Dunford, M. and Kafkalas, G. (eds) (1992), *Cities and Regions in the new Europe.* London: Belhaven.

Krätke, S. (2003), "Berlin's socio-economic situation",in: *Bulletin of the International Network for Urban Research and Action*, No. 24.

Musterd, S. (1994), "A rising European underclass? Social polarization and spatial segregation in European cities", in: *Built Environment*, 20, 2, 185-191.

Pepchinski, M. "Report from Berlin", in: *Progressive Architecture*, November 1993.

Schulz, B. (1995), "Germany, the United States and future core conflict", in: *Journal of World-Systems Research*, 1, 13.

Senatskanzlei (2003), "Zusammen Arbeit Berlin-Brandenburg", published online at: http://www.berlin.de/rbmskzl/berlinbrandenburg/index.html

Senatsverwaltung für Finanzen (2001), *Was Kostet Wo Wie Viel.* Berlin: Druckerei JVA Tegel.

Senatsverwaltung für Finanzen (2002), *Finanzplanung von Berlin 2002 bis 2006*, Berlin: Daab Druck & Werbe GbmH.

Senatsverwaltung für Stadtentwicklung (eds) (2000), *z.B. Berlin: Zehn Jahre Transformation und Modernisierung.* Berlin: Runz & Casper Publishers.

Stadt Wolgast (1997), *Erläuterungsbericht zum Flächennutzungsplan*, Wolgast: Stadt Wolgast.

Statistisches Landesamt Berlin (2003), "Amtliches Ergebnisse über den Zusammenschluß der Bundesländer Berlin und Brandenburg am 5. Mai 1996." Published online at: http://www.statistik-berlin.de/wahlen/

Strom, E. (1996), "The political context of real estate development: central city rebuilding in Berlin", in: *European Urban and Regional Studies*, 3, 1: 3-17.

Endnotes

[1] A City-State is a city that is given the same jurisdiction as a state. For an explanation of the constitutional and legal basis of the district, municipal, and state structures as articulated in the German Constitution (Grundgesetz), as well as corresponding jurisdictions of each level of government, tasks and responsibilities of the electorate, and the organization of terms and conditions of public participation, see Council of Europe (1992). "Structure and Operation of Local and Regional Democracy: Federal Republic of German." *Council of Europe.*

[2] See for example the official plans of Stadt Wolgast, 1997.

[3] In Germany, certain townships are designated as wellness centres. Often linked to a city´s location or history, such as nearness to nature or the presence of springs, the economy of these towns is based on the provision of health care services (e.g. physiotherapy, massage, nutritional consultation) as a preventative health-care measure for citizens of Germany.

[4] See also Häußermann, 1996.

[5] Musterd (1994) defined the "conservative corporatist state," as a regime that seeks to preserve status differentials by granting social rights according to status and class (in contrast to the models of the UK, or Sweden - that have been called respectively, the "liberal welfare state" and the "social democratic state").

[6] This aggression can been seen, in part, in the German language itself, as 'Easterners' have acquired the derogatory name, '*Ossies*', and 'Westerners', likewise have acquired the equally derogatory name, "*Wessis.*" Each carries its own set of stereotyping.

[7] See also Eick in this book.

TEXT..........Ute Lehrer
PHOTOS..........Ute Lehrer

Reality or Image? Place Selling at Potsdamer Platz

This article is based on my dissertation on "Image Production and Globalization: City-Building Processes at Potsdamer Platz, Berlin", University of California, Los Angeles (UCLA), 2002.

The Spectacularization of the Building Process

In recent years, one can see a trend in multinational corporations expanding their public relations and marketing budget to focus on image production for their products. The more these corporations become diversified the more, it seems, they are interested in creating images for specific aspects of their products. This new emphasis on developing marketing strategies can be read as part of the new economy in which firms that used to be based in manufacturing increasingly shift toward administration and service functions (King, 1990, p.17; Gutmann, 1988). The same can be said about cities. As the planning historian Steven Ward notes there has been a growing emphasis on cities adopting a professional approach to marketing strategies: "Unlike the 'innocent crassness' (...) of most earlier boosterist efforts, place selling campaigns were now more likely than ever to be the work of marketing experts." (1998, p. 199). City marketing strategies have become a collaboration between the private and public sector, involving the press offices of city departments and the public relations agencies of the investors, along with public-private agencies hired to promote the image of the city. While the motivation and the goals may be very different, all these departments and offices share one thing - they produce images in order to focus attention on a particular place. This already established form of boosterism (Hall and Hubbard, 1998; Jonas and Wilson, 1999) has now evolved into a coordinated effort to turn cities into spectacles and the urban experience into image consumption. This is particularly true for large-scale projects where it is difficult (for both the specialist and the non-specialist) to imagine the future shape of new built environments and their impact on the urban fabric.

The events of the Fall of 1989 and the merging of two parts into one big city required a symbolic and spatial manifestation. The vast open land around Potsdamer Platz, located in the geographic middle of the city, seemed to present a unique chance of knitting together the two cities into one. Perceived as a no-man's land, the area became one of the prime objects of large-scale international investment in the reunified Berlin and simultaneously the symbol of Berlin's search for a reinvented central-urban identity. The redevelopment at Potsdamer Platz was one of the first and the biggest single building projects in the reunited Berlin, and was soon referred to as "Europe's largest construction site."

I argue that the spectacularization of the building process was central in the appropriation of Potsdamer Platz as the new center of Berlin and as a symbol of Berlin's anticipated new role as capital city. This investigation of image production and the spectacularization of the building process of Potsdamer Platz is presented from two distinct perspectives. The first one addresses the increased importance that built environments play in major cities in attracting both name recognition and investment of capital. Issues of form, size and temporality all define the relevance of built environments to image production. Although these characteristics are not necessarily mutually exclusive, size is the most important in regard to image production. Large-scale projects, partly by virtue of their sheer volume and the role they play in urban infrastructure and politics, have become places of spectacles. The second perspective addresses the processes, means and strategies for transforming the construction site at Potsdamer Platz into an extraordinary urban spectacle.

Potsdamer Platz in Berlin is a good example of such spectacularization of the building process, where a number of different strategies were used to draw attention to the construction site and its future. All three approaches of image production in the built environment - signature architecture, mega-event, and large-scale project - share the objective of making a particular city more competitive on the global stage. They are seen as having the added benefit of temporarily attracting tourists to a specific location which otherwise would "merely" enjoy more long-term impacts such as the relocation of established firms, the opening of branches or subsidiaries or the creation of start-up businesses.

Promoters and investors at Potsdamer Platz had a number of obstacles to deal with. Some of the hurdles had to do with the site itself, others had to do with the investors and the nature of their project. The first difficulty was that the site used had been dissected by the Wall and, over several decades, had become a wasteland in the imagination of the general public. Secondly, because of the sheer size of Potsdamer Platz and its specific boundaries, it was difficult, even for the trained eye, to imagine the completed project and its relation to the rest of the city. Thirdly, the historical significance of the location, including its proximity to a number of significant offices of the Nazi period, had to be redefined. Fourthly, multinational corporations were not always greeted more or less sympathetically, and, particularly in the case of Daimler Benz, had to undergo some major polishing of their public images. And finally, investors needed to attract other businesses to lease office or retail space in the newly-erected complex. In sum, it became clear that the public relations teams were not only dealing with the urban impact of redevelopment, but also with the acceptance of the project by the general public. Hence, it was important for the public relations departments to establish and maintain good relations with the local media.

The spectacularization of the building process at Potsdamer Platz has reduced public debate over new projects to a discussion of architectural form. Previously the debate included considerations of property ownership, land use, ecology, social justice, and so forth. Of course, the focus on architecture has not meant that these issues disappeared; rather they were transposed into different discourses employing the lexicon of urban form. In this sense, different actors in the city-building process, in their collective attempts to create something that was significant beyond the specific location of Potsdamer Platz, had to relate their discursive interventions to the new architectural master discourse. As a result, the predominance of architectural discourse created a new hegemony for a specific group of powerful actors. While the team responsible for the spectacularization of Potsdamer Platz might have had internal differences in their specific agendas, their combined interest was in using the building process to pursue city development goals and corporate strategies that went beyond the immediate architectural achievement of the Potsdamer Platz project.

Production of Real and Imagined Images: Info Box

The most successful image production creator for Potsdamer Platz was Info Box. The bright red Info Box located right in the center of the construction site played a crucial role in the Potsdamer Platz redevelopment project as a microcosm of image production at Potsdamer Platz. As a marketing strategy, the Info Box exhibition/building had two main objectives. On the one hand, Info Box created a concrete "place" in the middle of a wide-open space in Berlin's geographic center, a real-physical place that became a point of attraction for tourists and Berliners alike. On the other hand, Info Box produced not only a certain interest by itself, but also alleviated the negative disturbances associated with such a large-scale project (beyond the imagination of most people.)
Moreover, it turned the site and its building process into the happening place for the New Berlin. Info Box therefore played a crucial role in the spectacularization process at Potsdamer Platz as both an exhibition building and a clever advertisement strategy for the team of investors.

Borrowing the concept developed by Venturi, Izenour and Scott Brown (1977) in analyzing the urban signage system in American cities, Info Box can be described both as a billboard and as a duck. It was a billboard because of its shape, its color and its elevated position right in the middle of the construction site. As the first new building on this vast, relatively empty site, it was a sign, readable from all four directions. And it was a duck because it indicated from the outside what the inside held; it was an exhibition place of the construction processes surrounding the oversized red container.

The exhibition/building Info Box, named the "first house" at Potsdamer Platz by its sponsors, opened on October 16, 1995. In a speech, Walter Nagel, then Senator for Construction, made a clear link between building activities and image production when he said:

Our Info Box is the most important contribution to Berlin's location and city marketing so far. While others are discussing things, we are taking action. If we want to take the people with us on this voyage of radical change in Berlin, we have to let them get on. So, come and join us on the info star-ship, climb aboard the box with the answers (Nagel in Info Box, 1995).

The "box with the answers", as Nagel called it, was home to an impressive exhibition (with architectural drawings, models, multimedia virtual walk, and historical photographs), explaining the scale and scope of the construction project as well as the site's historical significance. Images of the past and the future challenged the imagination of the residents and visitors. The past, however, was a higly selective view, focusing on a special time when Potsdamer Platz was supposedly one of the main centers of Berlin. The link to the past was dominated by images presenting the nightlife of the roaring twenties with neon light, café culture, and cabaret entertainment. These images contrasted with the activities of the future rising outside the walls of the exhibition/building. Hence, the Info Box building was also a "window" and a "lookout" platform overseeing the construction activities at Potsdamer Platz.

It is important to recall that there was a tradition of exhibition places in European cities—in comparison to North America, where a single panel presenting the construction team is simply posted at the entry of the site. Berlin, in particular, can look back on a well-established practice of explaining major construction activities to the general public. In East Berlin, all large-scale projects (e.g. Mahrzahn or Hellersdorf) were accompanied by temporary exhibition places in portables of substantial size (300 to 400 sq. meters), explaining the upcoming construction activities not only to the interested audience but also to construction workers. Most of these exhibition pavilions were planned as temporary buildings but sometimes they became regular features of a site. An example is the Berlin Pavillion designed by local architects as a temporary exhibition place for the international building exhibition Interbau from 1957, showing maps, architectural drawings, pictures and models of the building activities. It was supposed to be demolished after the building exhibition was over but is still in use today as a restaurant and exhibition venue.

The design of the Info Box was an outcome of an invited architectural competition. The objective of this competition was to create an image "which would stand up to the surrounding busy optical area of a large-scale construction site. It should set an accent for the establishment of a new center" (Info Box, 1997, p. 10). The first prize went to Till Schneider and Michael Schumacher, a firm from Frankfurt am Main, which modeled their competition entry after the construction office containers that one finds in large numbers not only on Potsdamer Platz but also on all construction sites throughout the city. However, their design of an "oversized container" emphasized and distorted some of the original features: by increasing its size, Info Box appears like a pop art object in the middle of the construction site. With its raised elevation on columns it works as a sign system, while the bright red metal panels on Info Box' façades made an unmistakable visual statement in contrast with the messiness of the construction site. Glass panels interrupted the geometry of the metal panels and opened up views of the building activities going on right outside of the box. As a result, the Info Box not only marked the center of the building activities but also served as an advertisement for the Potsdamer Platz project in the form of a tridimensional billboard.

BARESEL
3.6

In contrast to the competition inviting ideas for Potsdamer Platz, there was no quarrel about the result of the Info Box competition. To the contrary, the winning design actually drew a lot of support even from those who were generally opposed to the redevelopment of Potsdamer Platz. The acclaimed modern style design succeeded because it created something relatively unique and innovative while producing an image that found immediate acceptance among the general public. The bright red prefabricated metal panel building benefited from its temporary status, premised on the fact that it would disappear by the time the redevelopment project was completed. As one of the critics said in an "obituary" for Info Box: The architects "from Frankfurt brought some southern German lightness to Berlin and into the heavy discussion about building heights and granite façades. They hold up a mirror for the local architects: this is how one could build" (Bernau, 2000).

The prefabricated system of I-beams allowed for a relatively easy assembling and dismantling of the Info Box building - and therefore the building stood in the great tradition of temporary exhibition architecture, including Paxton's Crystal Palace for the World Exhibition in London of 1851.

With a total floor area of 2,200 square meters over three stories, the Info Box stood 8 meters above ground, forming a rectangle 23 meters high, 62.5 meters long, and 15 meters wide. The total floor space was divided into 1,200 square meters of exhibition space, 210 square meters of cafeteria space, 100 square meters for a sales area, while the remaining 610 square meters facilitated inner circulation. The construction cost was roughly 10 million German Marks and was paid by the investors in Potsdamer Platz (Info Box, 1997, p. 10-11). A special flight of metal stairs led to a roof terrace as a lookout point on the construction site; this terrace could also be rented for parties after the closing hours of the Info Box.

The architectural competition for the Info Box took place in 1994, and its construction started in June 1995. Because of its prefabricated metal panels construction technique, the building was completed in three months, with the inside finished in six additional weeks. Info Box opened its doors to the general public on October 15, 1995 and stayed open until December 31, 2000. In spite of being one of the main attractions in Berlin, it was subsequently dismantled in January 2001.

While at the beginning there was some concern about the acceptance of the unusually shaped, positioned and colored structure, Info Box soon became one of Berlin's favorite tourist attractions. The numbers exceeded the projected estimate of visitors by about ten times. In the first year, 1.7 million people visited Info Box and the Potsdamer Platz construction site, and this number remained relatively constant over the five years of its existence, with a total of 8.25 million visitors (naturally there were more visitors during the summer months than during winter time).[1]

In the early years of the redevelopment project, Info Box appeared as the only solid, permanent building structure on the whole site, and functioned as an anchor within all the messiness and constant changes arising on the Potsdamer Platz construction site. While at the beginning visitors came to Info Box to get some information about the imminent transformations of the desolate site in the heart of Berlin, Info Box later became a place where visitors wanted to see how Potsdamer Platz was being transformed. The constant pilgrimage of visitors was also supplemented by a good number of teenagers who took advantage of free access to the Internet on some of its computers.

Daily activities at Info Box ranged from services to visitors, to upholding the permanent exhibition, and maintaining good relations with the press - D&D Kommunikation Verlag Dirk Nishen GmbH and Co KG teamed up with Rhenus Baulogistik GmbH. The concept of Info Box was more sophisticated than just an exhibition center for building activities in the city. It was also a money-making machine with a busy cafeteria and a bookstore that sold publications on the history of Potsdamer Platz and on Info Box itself (both published by D&D Nishen), as well as selling an array of souvenirs. Info Box had a high capacity utilization rate (76 percent) for renting space for conferences, meetings and other social gatherings. It even advertised itself as an extraordinary alternative to churches and city halls for marriage ceremonies.

The promoters of Info Box used every occasion to celebrate its success. When after only nine months of operation the first one million people had visited the Info Box, a press announcement commemorated the fact that the Info Box had many more visitors than Berlin's main indoor attraction, the Pergamon Museum, which received "only" 720,000 visitors per year). Celebrating this special occasion, investors at Potsdamer Platz sponsored a huge cake in the form of the Info Box.

After 500 days of existence, the 2,222,222nd visitor received a free helicopter ride, flying over the construction site; the voucher was presented to her by the person who had been identified as the 500,000th visitor on March 22, 1996. While celebrations for lucky individuals were standard, the marking of the 5 millionth visitor was a bit more unusual. Everyone who came to visit the Info Box on the morning of August 26, 1998 was invited to search the exhibition space for a mock-up of the Info Box. The grand prize was a 4-day trip for two people to Lisbon (flight, accommodation, and pocket money included), which at that time was the site of extensive building activities in preparation for Expo 1998 and therefore was very similar to Potsdamer Platz in terms of image production through the built environment.

The popularity of Info Box made officials reconsider its demolition. When on May 22, 1998, at its projected mid-life point, then Senator Jürgen Klemann of the Senate for Construction, Housing and Transportation announced his commitment to the success of Info Box and suggested that "when [Info Box] finally has to make way for further buildings we shall find a new central site in Berlin for the red box." But when the time was up for Info Box at Potsdamer Platz, it was dismantled and, in contrast to earlier announcements, never reassembled at a new site. Ideas for relocating Info Box within Berlin vanished as did rumors of selling it to interested parties in Japan. At that point, Info Box had exhausted all its novelty to Berlin city boosters and politicians. The bright red building has certainly been a marker in the urban landscape of Berlin.

Figure 1: Visitors at Info Box (October 1995 to December 2000)

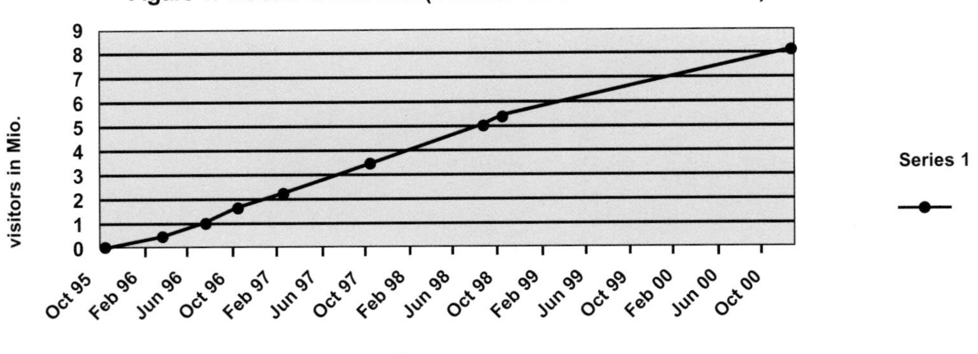

The end of Info Box remained within the tradition of producing images around the construction process. On December 30, 2000, just a few days before dismantling started, Info Box was host to over 1,000 celebrity guests that were wined and dined. The last remaining pieces of the prefabricated metal panels were auctioned off (the majority of the panels had been sold earlier through an electronic auction that had started in October). The fundraising party and the auction went for an anti-racist initiative (Gesicht zeigen! Aktion für ein weltoffenes Deutschland e. V.), and raised 133,794 German Marks. During this event, Peter Strieder, in his function as the Senator for Urban Development, celebrated Info Box as “worldwide, the most successful model for contemporary marketing of construction sites” (Küppers, 2001).

Conclusion

The successful transformation of Potsdamer Platz was in the interest not only of multinational investors but also of local politicians, planners, architects, and other groups that stood to profit from enhancing the role of Berlin. The aim of these groups, which together sometimes acted as an alliance similar to those described in the literature on regimes (Stone and Sanders, 1987) and growth machines (Molotch, 1980, 1993), was to catapult Berlin back into the orbit of significant places in the global economy, while at the same time marking its new beginning.

Images of the built environment are frequently used to promote the image of a city, from multi-media presentations for international events or competitions to promotional trade brochures, to the omnipresent postcards depicting the local skyline or architecture. Yet, in the past, the medium had not entirely become the message. This changed drastically in the case of the Potsdamer Platz, where the object of construction - the actual buildings to be erected - became merely secondary in significance - at least temporarily - to the building process itself. Consequently, the production of images seemed to take priority over the production of buildings. The erection and promotion of Info Box encapsulated this image production through spectacles. Not surprisingly, the image production campaign for the redevelopment of Potsdamer Platz was the result of collaboration among the public relations departments of the investors, various City departments and a newly-founded agency for the promotion of post-Wall Berlin. In this unprecedented campaign, public relation played a central role in fostering good relations between investors and city boosters on the one hand and the local print media on the other.

While not unprecedented as such, the example of Potsdamer Platz presents a new high point in place marketing. What is special about this case is the intensity with which image production took place on a multitude of levels. In this sense Potsdamer Platz potentially pointed in a new direction for city-building and place-marketing which is now applied and practiced around the world, from Las Vegas, to Toronto, to Singapore.

References

Bernau, N. (2000 December 29), *Das Provisorium war eine Chance.* Berliner Zeitung.

Gutmann, R. (1988), *Architectural Practice: A Critical View.* Princeton, NJ: Princeton Architectural Press.

Hall, T. and P. Hubbard.(eds) (1998), *The Entrepreneurial City: Geographies of Politics, Regime and Representation.* Chichester: John Wiley & Sons.

Info-Box (1997), *Der Katalog.* Berlin: Nishen.

Info-Box. (1995), *Press Release.* October 16.

Jonas A.E.G. and D. Wilson. (eds) (1999), *The Urban Growth Machine.* Albany, N.Y.: State University of New York Press.

King, A. D. (1990), *Global Cities: Post-Imperialism and the Internationalisation of London.* London, New York: Routledge.

Küppers, K. (2001), “Die Info-Box ist abgegessen” in: *Taz*, January 2, 16.

Molotch, H. (1980), “The City as a Growth Machine: Toward a Political Economy of Place”, in: *American Journal of Sociology*. 82, 309-32.

Molotch, H. L. (1993), “The Political Economy of Growth Machines”, in: *Journal of Urban Affairs*. 15 (1).

Stone, C. N., and H. T. Sanders. (1987), *The Politics of Urban Development.* Lawrence: University Press of Kansas.

Venturi R., S. Izenour and D. Scott Brown (1977), *Learning from Las Vegas: The Forgotten Symbolism of Architectural Form.*

Ward, S. V. (1998), *Selling Places: The Marketing and Promotion of Towns and Cities 1850-2000.* New York: Routledge.

Endnotes

[1] The dates in this section are taken from a variety of press releases from Info Box.

TEXT......Volker Elck
PHOTOS......Volker Elck, Christian Ditsch

From SOLIDARI*City* to *Segregatio*TOWN

The Death of the Social in Berlin's Nonprofit Organizations?

"Indeed, local action does not make sense if it leads to reinforcing boundaries and barriers. [...] In a time of growing social inequalities, it is important to observe how citizens fight these inequalities," thus starts the invitation for the early summer meeting of INURA 2002 in France. This paper deals with a (futile) search for "the opposite possibilities" within the nonprofit sector in Berlin: Nonprofits are said to fight against social inequalities in the field of local labor market integration and the social welfare sector. But mobilizing unemployed people and welfare recipients within an "activating social state" leads to new forms of social exclusion - now including communitarian and inclusionist/integrationist discourses within a neo-liberal workfare system.

"How citizens fight inequalities" is specifically important for cities like Berlin, the city with the highest number of welfare recipients in Germany - and the highest number of nonprofit organizations as well. Berlin has faced tremendous economic and political changes since the early 1990s. These can be interpreted as indicating the city's shift from a highly subsidized western outpost against Communism to one acting as an entrepreneur in a globalized world economy under neo-liberal conditions. It now finds itself in a financial crisis no other (German) metropolis has ever seen before.

In the first five years following unification, East and West Berlin experienced a loss of 280,000 manufacturing jobs. As of March 2003 the number of unemployed was around 318,000, the unemployment rate 18.7%. About 38,000 of these are under 25. The number of welfare recipients was 262,000 (7.8%) in December 2001. The number of welfare recipients under the age of 18 stood at 88,000 in the same year.
This development path is a result of the locally specific articulation of globalization processes: Berlin still faces many obstacles in its projected transition to a post-Fordist service industry metropolis (Krätke/Borst 2000, Strukturpolitische Expertenkommission 1992, Mayer 1997). Recent research claims that Berlin's failure in the global inter-urban/interregional competition can be explained by both the relative de-industrialization of West Berlin during the Cold War [1] and by the de-industrialization of East Berlin's industrial core since unification.[2] Lacking almost any industrial base, and without the conditions for post-industrial services in place, severe increases in unemployment rates (especially in the East) and of welfare dependency rates (particularly in the West) have become structural [3] and have occurred as part of Berlin's financial crisis.[4]

The Devolution of the Welfare System and the Nonprofit Sector

The devolution of the welfare system is intriguing for German policy makers, a process associated with a new form of governance. In order to effectively deal with the complexity of contemporary social problems at local level, stakeholders from all spheres of society are being brought together to cooperate with the municipality and with each other. With the devolution of welfare production, the blurring of borders between traditional policy fields (such as labor-market, economic development, and social policies) and security policies (Veblen 2000; Eick 2000) can be observed. In all sectors involved with welfare production (public, private, voluntary and nonprofit) shifts in values, habits, and organizational structures (e.g. an increasing market orientation among the non-profits) can be identified. All this is happening in an environment increasingly defined by devolution.

Nonprofit or third-sector organizations [5] are said to be the likely repositories of the devolutionary process, given their capacity for quickly taking up the new opportunities and challenges this devolution process might produce. This is especially true for those nonprofit organizations that are working in the fields of local labor and social welfare 'markets'. However, the typically idealistic mind-set (and practice) of both traditional and alternative nonprofits in Germany (the latter having developed out of the new social movements in the 1960s and 1970s, see Mayer 1987) are being replaced by a new pragmatism attempting to accommodate post-Fordist socioeconomic imperatives which lead to a Schumpeterian workfare regime (Jessop 1997, 2000).

Nonprofits Joining the Security Market

Many authors have discussed the interdependence of poverty and crime (Garland 2001; Body-Gendrot 2000; Eick 1998a). Despite fiscal restraints and parallel restructuring of the active labour market and the social welfare system during the early 1990s, requests for intervention and public commitment in the field of poverty and crime continue to be common, and in recognition of this interdependency, Germany has established new agencies to deal with '(in)security' and '(dis)order'.

During the last decade, community crime prevention councils, security and order partnerships, security guards and voluntary police services have been established, mainly on the grounds that disorder problems have been growing. Discussions about the specific local differences among such organizations (along with the observed trends and growth of commercial security services) have found their way into social scientific literature. Particular attention has been given to emerging private security businesses and community crime prevention methods.[6] In recent years, these initiatives have become standard and integral components of the (re)organized interior security system of the Federal Republic of Germany. Two trends are highlighted in the literature. First, such initiatives are characterized as oriented towards specific small-scale localities and particular 'problems'. In addition, these trends are substantiated by the emergence of so-called 'operational forces' (*Operative Gruppen*) and 'special task forces' of the state police (*Landespolizei*) and federal police (*Bundesgrenzschutz*). Both the state and federal police focus their activities on specific 'marginalized' groups or particular urban spaces. Public-private partnerships are common and have become institutionalized between police authorities and profit-oriented security services.[7] In contrast, little attention has been given in social scientific literature to non-state actors like the nonprofit organizations that have become an active part of this market during the last decade. In an effort to tackle growing unemployment rates as well as alleged disorder problems and so-called incivilities, police and commercial security agencies are increasingly accompanied by new 'colleagues' working in informal control agencies. Nonprofits today are part of the security market.

There are reasons, however, for this absence of discussion of nonprofits in criminology, in crime policy and corresponding sociopolitical and economic discussions. Lindenberg speculates that these organizations and their respective programs have been ignored because they do not have, "at least at first glance, a crime policy function" (2000b: 8). Rather, they were designed as instruments of the active labor market, and, thus were not part of political debates concerning crime and security. At the same time, the precise function of nonprofit organizations until now has seldom been an explicit research topic in social scientific research on labour market policy.

Moreover, these organizations have been seen as progressive and therefore have received little criticism. In Berlin, both in the Western and Eastern parts of the city, the reason might be that they came into being out of local settings and therefore had strong anchors in their neighbourhoods. In the Western part they emerged from new social movements, while in the East they developed from the industrial enterprises that created strong ties with the surrounding districts and neighbourhoods.[8]

The resulting organizations attempted to redefine and redevelop different approaches to replace the former state-repressive models of security. Many nonprofits tried to respond with programs that were not only sensitive to articulated demands for crime reduction and social stabilization of neighbourhoods, but also to risks of stigmatization and social exclusion of the "usual suspects" - mostly ethnic youth. With regard to assessing the success of welfare reform, these programs have aimed to go beyond the comparatively easy task of transferring "employable" welfare recipients into the workforce. These initiatives have taken up the challenge of addressing the complexity of social, economic, spatial and racial discrimination that has kept so-called "problem groups" from entering the labour market.

Meanwhile, with an "activating social state" in place, the local and federal government administrations have increased pressure on nonprofits (and their 'clients'). This activating social state focuses on workfare schemes, on keeping the unemployed busy at any price, and concentrates on work obligations for the unemployed instead of delivering adequate training programs or just paying unemployment benefits and welfare. It is based on the concept of duties for the unemployed and the acceptance of a low wage sector.

At the same time, Berlin's state administration and nonprofit organizations both execute exclusion processes through integration measures. Activating the unemployed and welfare recipients through subsidized workfare schemes into the (subsidized) labour market is described as 'integration' by the public administrations. At the same time, nobody talks about the fields of activity that the unemployed and welfare recipients are pushed to. Currently more than 700 persons [9] are allocated to the field of (in)security, (dis)order and control services (Eick 2003). This happens in a "huge and murky industry of 'training'", where, as Rose (1996: 347) suggests, "unemployment is re-problematized as a matter of the lack of individual and marketable skills among the unemployed themselves, to be countered by a multitude of training organizations that are private and compete in a market for public contracts and public funds" (Rose 1996: 347). The strong dependence of German third-sector organizations on public funding (Anheier *et. al.* 1997) puts stronger pressure on the nonprofit organizations to follow the demands of public authorities.[10] However, for nonprofits this 'workfare industry' is not without its benefits. The CEOs and high ranking administrative staff of nonprofits hold well paid, secure, attractive jobs. Therefore, Rose (1996: 347) correctly observes that now, as before, "the management of misery and misfortune can become, once more, a potentially profitable activity."
Compared to the public and private sector, nonprofits are said to be more innovative, more creative, more flexible and closer to the local needs of the so-called problem groups. Moreover, it remains highly important that these organizations be defined in this way, and this underpins the (self-)understanding of the nonprofit stakeholders. In addition to Lindenberg's comments above, these attributes might be responsible for the fact that nonprofit organizations have rarely been objects of critical discussion. The specific mélange "of neo-liberalism, remainders of social-democratic state interventionism and libertarian trends, which won intellectual influence as disintegration products of the post-68 protest movement" (Hirsch 2002: 172, author's translation), has been responsible for widespread immunization against criticism of these organizations.

Post-Fordist Innovations in Local Labour, Welfare and Security Markets

Today, strong market orientation and the simultaneous reduction of public funding describe both active labour market policies and the "mixed economy of policing" (Nogala 2001). Increased forced labour for the long-term unemployed as well as welfare recipients characterizes the broadening of the "activating social state". With the lifting of the monopoly that employment offices (*Arbeitsämter*) maintained on work placement in 1994, nonprofits have been expected to place the long-term unemployed into the first (or unsubsidized) labour market. Filling work placement quotas became the principal criterion in determining if nonprofit organizations would continue to receive grants. This structure forced the nonprofits to compromise their objectives, which had previously aimed to help unemployed persons with a long-term and viable perspective. In combination with the observed (im)moralization of unemployment that defines work as an obligation to the *Gemeinschaft*, this results in a work placement ethic with the motto: "work at any price" ("Arbeit um jeden Preis").

For Michael Ehrke, "revisionism", which he denotes as the neo-social-democratic model of the Third Way, is basically a matter of:

the age-old message to the worst-off that they should accept their material disadvantages and seek a form of secondary gratification in doing their duty. The most important duty is gainful employment, the incentive for which is neither attractive material reward nor job satisfaction - but duty. [...] *Here the moral imperative is directed first and foremost at the prospective victims of modernization, the recipients of welfare benefits* [...]. *The less likely the prospect of 'good jobs' (i.e. tolerably secure and acceptably paid employment), the more strongly this duty is emphasized. The rhetoric of duty is likewise applied to the socializing function of regular work, the converse of which is also countenanced - 'tough on crime and tough on the causes of crime' - i.e. for cases where socialization through gainful employment is unsuccessful.*
(Ehrke 1999: 18, 14, author's translation).

As nonprofits were obliged to and thus decided to operate according to these changes, they opened up to the conventional low wage employment sectors, forcing their 'clients' into these kinds of occupational circumstances - most commonly the hotel and restaurant sectors, building sanitation and branches of private security services (Pohl/Schäfer 1996; see Ehrenreich 2001).

The *Industrie - und Handelsschutz GmbH* (Industry and Trade Protection Company, IHS) stands for an aggressive orientation towards the low-wage market. As early as 1991, the company established a nonprofit organization as a subsidiary (IHS BQ GmbH).

By order of the Berlin Senate the *IHS BQ GmbH* called for the procurement of 500 long-term unemployed and trained them in *Arbeitsbeschaffungsmaßnahmen* or ABMs (federally funded programs for job creation) as passenger assistants in public transport. The stated aim was to transfer them into the first or regular labour market, but this goal was not achieved. Nevertheless, today 300 persons a year are employed in ABMs.[11]

In carrying out its tasks, the IHS BQ GmbH:

also perceives a function for the employment offices while reporting those welfare recipients unwilling to work within the measures. There is no wage-scale commitment, the scales are close to the industrial low wage sector. [...] To concentrate on the low wage sector remains reasonable also in the future. At the same time, this implies calculating very low staff expenditures within the working measures. The expenses per job in ABMs at the IHS BQ gGmbH are one third less than at other nonprofits
(IHS gGmbH 2000: 3, 7, author's translation).

Upon analyzing base-line wages required for basic necessities, this system can be described as a downward spiral. In addition, various evaluations indicate that a growing percentage of workfare participants are dependent on supplementary social assistance; meanwhile, the number of participants receiving this additional welfare has risen to nine percent (Senatsverwaltung für Arbeit 2001; Arbeitsamt Berlin Ost 1999).

After the early 1990s, socio-political questions concerning city development and zoning policies were addressed primarily within the context of internal security (*Innere Sicherheit*). 'Security' advanced as a central focal point in urban restructuring, and in this context (re)activated existing instruments, players and concepts at varying levels of command. Thus, the production and reproduction of this security discourse took place on a (local) state, commercial(ized), and private (or more popular: civil society) level; all these developments were not without influence on the development of active labour market policies (see Eick 2003). These changes might be interpreted in the context of post-Fordism (Hirsch 2002; Jessop 2000), in which metropolises convert from integrative into exclusive growth machines under neo-liberal globalization. As a result of regional competitiveness, welfare rights lose their importance and are instead transformed into workfare duties. Moreover, they become subordinated to, and more strictly controlled by market forces (Jessop 1997). At the same time, socio-economic problems are transferred to the sphere of the individual's responsibility.

The neo-liberal strategy accordingly consists of:

the delegation of responsibility for social risks such as illness, unemployment, poverty etc., and the delegation of the organization of (surviving) life within society in the scope of collective and individual subjects (individuals, families, associations) and transforms it into a problem of self-care. The specific attribute of the neo-liberal rationality is founded in the intended congruence between a responsible-moral and a rational-calculating subject. [...] *Since the choice of options to act within neo-liberal rationality appears to be an expression of one's own free will, the consequences of acting are ascribed to the subject alone, and actors are held responsible for themselves*
(Lemke 2000: 38, author's translation).

These processes, which accompany an emerging (inter)national hierarchy of cities and polarization within cities, also work themselves out socio-spatially. Intensified competition between localities and entrepreneurial city policies lead to 'prosperity enclaves' on the one hand and 'islands of poverty' on the other. This fragmentation and polarization of urban spaces and society should not to be separated from the restructuring of state-run, private and commercial security.
This is especially clear in the private or, more precisely, commercial security business. Profits not only stem from the outsourcing of a whole range of services by public authorities, industrial and service sectors (see table I), but also from the further outsourcing by the private security services themselves.

Some of the nonprofit organizations described here were founded out of private security companies as their own non-profit branches (GmbH) in order to give the commercial sector access to the subsidized or second labour market (*Zweiter Arbeitsmarkt*), which, as stated above, can use public funds to subsidize its own profitability.

The (joint) activities of different players in social and labour market politics are referred to in the social sciences as "welfare mix" (Evers/Olk 1996). If commercial actors like private security agencies push themselves onto the active labour market, while at the same time the political field of internal security is opened up to nonprofit organizations and local state players, we can then speak of a corresponding "Security Mix". The intensified cooperation of private security agencies with the state and federal police can be described as a 'police-private-partnership'. This partnership is completed by nonprofits in the context of workfare programs.

To the (local) administration, nonprofit organizations offer intermediary opportunities of intervention that, in the frame of new governance structures, might lead to broadened options for the (local) state (Jessop/Peck 1998; Eisenschitz/Gough 1996).

Table I: Private security agencies and their current fields of activity

Older Fields of Activity			**New Fields of Activity**
airport services	emergency services	security counseling	city patrols
alarm *persecution*	escort services	security post during track building	criminal investigation
building site guards	event/show services	security transports	management of:
controlled key management	facility management	special custody	deportation prisons
cordoning off services	factory fire brigades	special services (military)	homes for asylum seekers
data security	factory security officers (spying/anti-sabotage)	technical reports	parking spaces
district control patrols	fair/ museum services	telephone service	prisons
doormen service	fire protection	training	psychiatric clinics
door opening/ key finding services	guarding of real estate	vehicle protection	radar traffic control
education	holiday services	vessel protection	security points
electronic room protection	money management	workplace security	pollution control ("Ranger")
elevator control	money/asset transport		private security agencies in public transport
emergency call centers	profit and loss control		second labor market
	property protection		
	reception services		
	security analysis		

These structures do not require direct intervention, since through:

the development of [such] partnerships the state tries to profit from both the logic and the institutions of non-state government and tries to obviate those partnerships with the intention to 'govern at a distance'. The state tries to 'control' and to encourage others to take the responsibility for 'rowing'. It is a development that leads to a system of labour division: on the one hand the state remains the most important source for security, since it has access to the resource of violence; on the other hand non-state resources are mobilized to create security networks that function on the basis of risk management
(Shearing 1997: 273, author's translation).

Such programs initially secure the position of nonprofits in an increasingly narrow second labour market. In this highly subsidized sector of the German economy, nonprofit-organizations in Berlin are heavily dependent on administrative authorities (employment offices, Senate and local district authorities) that follow a totally different way of thinking, different procedures and methods. In the end, nonprofits (prepared to cooperate) could be assigned to specific functions that the (local) state would like to off-load (mainly on the grounds of fiscal restrictions).

In direct contrast, nonprofit organizations are challenged twice, due to market-oriented labour policies, by the simple fact that they need money, and by the fact that their fields of activity are situated between compensation and exclusion of interests. Therefore, these fields of activity are contradictory to the (self-) description of nonprofits as 'holistic' and 'integrative' actors.
As a result, nonprofit-organizations compete with commercial security services. Due to the 'marketization' of active labour market policies, both sets of players are now able to develop new fields of activity for profit realization. More and more tasks that up to now remained under the jurisdiction of the "*Monopol legitimen physischen Zwangs*" ("the state monopoly on violence", Max Weber) are withdrawn from the state. Such tasks are now 'secreted' from the state's responsibility.

Nonprofits as Intermediary Conflict Solvers

From the point of view of the political and economic elites' feces are a crucial location - and security-factor (Rouhani 2000; Hearne 1987; Eick 1998a). The *Jahreszeiten gGmbH* has been put into action to manage the 40 tons of droppings produced by the 100,000 dogs owned by Berlin's 'civil society'. *Jahreszeiten* is a nonprofit organization founded by the commercial security service *Securitas GmbH*. This nonprofit was founded in 1993 in response to vandalism problems that are said to cost 15 million Euros annually in Berlin. By placing long-term unemployed people together with regular employees, "Green Cops" were put in control of parks in the eastern sections of Berlin. These quasi-uniformed workers were responsible for ensuring that dogs were kept on leashes, enforcing the no-cycling by-laws within the park, and reporting suspected vandals to the police. The essential goal of this program was to convey a (fantasy) uniformed presence in the public sphere to help raise perceptions of security.

For corporations like *Securitas GmbH*, programs like "Green Cops" and nonprofit subsidiaries like *Jahreszeiten* became an effective means of recruiting subsidized personnel at low cost. Moreover, through the reinforced market orientation of the active labour market, the subsidized labour market became an attractive market segment. On the one hand this is because the employment offices pay for training and employment of the long-term unemployed. So, should the occasion arise, integration of such people into the commercial company can occur with ease. At the same time, despite particular restrictions (Eick/Grell 2002), increased profits are easily achievable, since all recruitment preparation is financed by the employment offices.

Because of Berlin's difficult fiscal situation, neither the department responsible for public gardens nor the city-run cleaning company *Berliner Stadtreinigung* (BSR) are able to hire enough personnel to deal with the droppings in public streets, parks, and squares. At the same time, the state police refuse to take action against this kind of defilement. Thus, police services have reduced, or removed altogether, their presence in the parks in which *Jahreszeiten GmbH* was active. From the point of view of the state police, such local needs as controlling dog-owners or cyclists are district tasks and have become relegated to the realm of community responsibility.

Through the institutionalization of this strategy, poorly trained long-term unemployed people at *Jahreszeiten* are employed to enter into direct confrontation with local residents, sometimes resulting in aggressive and highly emotional conflicts and/or even demonstrations (dog-diaper demonstrations, 'nappy' noise).[12]

Since neither neighbourhood or state politicians, nor the police display any readiness to deal with these struggles, *Jahreszeiten* has been put into action. Thus, this nonprofit was instructed to convene a so-called citizens' round table (*Runder Tisch*) to find solutions to these local problems. The goal of the round table was to resolve the conflict on a local level, but assault and battery resulted. Dog-owners attacked *Jahreszeiten* employees, while the latter proceeded to take action against particular dog-keepers (young migrants, punks). This, in turn, necessitated intervention by the state police.

By activating non-governmental organizations and the round table, the government instituted a prototype strategy of devolution that corresponds to the neo-social democratic political model of the "*Neue Mitte*" ("New Center", Bundesregierung 1999). This enables (with all the appropriate ideology) the governing of security and social cohesion. A new mode of governance known in social science as "governing at a distance" emerged, following the logic of "contractual communities" (Shearing 1997).

Nonprofits as Space and Sweep Squads

In *Berlin-Pankow* the deployment of nonprofit security services was conveniently planned after the governmental administration had concentrated numerous homeless people and welfare recipients in a sub-district of *Pankow* called *Französisch-Buchholz*. As problems with these 'clients' were expected in the public realm, the goal of the nonprofit's employment was to instruct welfare recipients already living in this area to observe behavior in this residential quarter. The mayor of Stuttgart has to date been the most outspoken proponent of this strategy. At the Baden-Württemberg conference on "Community Crime Prevention" in July 1998, he said that the employment of nonprofit security workers against marginal groups in the inner city of Stuttgart:

> *has been successful, because some of them were sitting on park benches before and can say to the others now: 'Come on, you can take your bottle of beer with you.' For me that is a social-political sign, too. That's much better than to continue to pay welfare and to have a discussion about whether begging should be allowed or not* (Schuster 1998: 24).

Politicians like Schuster try to employ the poor against the poor. Through workfare programs, former welfare recipients and the long-term unemployed are activated to police the behavior of currently unemployed people and welfare recipients.

Helmholtzplatz, a square situated in the district *Prenzlauer Berg*, is considered a "problem area" and is one of the present 17 *Quartiersmanagementgebietes* (neighbourhood management districts). These are so-called "disadvantaged areas", assigned to management programs that are aimed at stabilizing locally specific situations seen as 'problematic' (Häußermann/Kapphan 2000). *Helmholtzplatz* is also one of the present 24 so-called "dangerous places" (Eick 2001b) which, according to the General Security and Order Law of Berlin (*Allgemeines Sicherheits- und Ordnungsgesetz*, ASOG), give police officers the power to suspend citizens' rights (ID checks without cause for suspicion, bodily searches, eviction).

While *Helmholtzplatz* is a meeting place for homeless people, punks (with dogs) and alcoholics, it is under gentrification pressure. Thus, homeless people, punks and alcoholics are a thorn in the side of district politicians, middle-class neighbourhood organizations, and inhabitants who have moved in recently. The presence of a poor population on *Helmholtzplatz* is seen as inhibiting their efforts to redevelop and increase the value of properties in the area.
Upon the suggestion of the *Quartiersmanagement* and district administration (*Bezirksamt*), four former welfare recipients were stationed in the neighbourhood under the supervision of the nonprofit organization *Berlin macht mit e.V.* They are dressed in berets and black jackets, equipped with walkie-talkies and trained in general citizens' rights and public garden laws. According to the non-profit's chair they are appointed

"not to chase people away, but to make sure that everything takes place in a reasonable way. That is to say, to take care that dogs keep off the lawn, and that the playground isn't full of dog dirt, and that they don't drink that much. And that's what they are doing, and somehow it works" (see Eick 2003, author's translation).

In recent years, the police and nonprofit organizations' methods have changed. From 1998, the time the square was under reconstruction, until its re-opening in July 2001, there were regular expulsions and a permanent threatening police presence. These expulsions were accompanied by a so-called "Social Work Concept" ("*Konzept Soziale Arbeit*"), whereby social-pedagogic nonprofit organizations and social workers were obliged to provide their services to the homeless, punks, and alcoholics - but outside the vicinity of *Helmholtzplatz*. For the coordinator responsible for the "Social Work Concept"

ridding the square of the [homeless] *group is the prerequisite for integrative social work. Only when positive use is possible without disturbance can attempts be made to integrate these persons and their deviant behavior*
(cited in: Holm 2001a: 9, author's translation).

Meanwhile, permanent patrolling has been replaced by a police tactic of systematic detainment in the side-streets. The nonprofit organization functions as an information service for the police; in particular the pleasantness of *Helmholtzplatz* as a place to spend time has decreased, especially for young men of Arab appearance.

As a further initiative of the *Quartiersmanagement* a parallel program has been developed to target marginal groups and divide them into groups that include: users of non-illegal drugs who live in the area; users of non-illegal drugs who do not live in the area, but come as 'booze-tourists' (they are said to keep the big dogs); and buyers and sellers of illegal drugs (Holm 2001a: 10). Different tactics are applied to the respective groups. Surveillance, control and arrest of the third group clearly falls under the jurisdiction of the police who rely on information from the other actors.
Information-gathering about and treatment of the two other groups is more complicated. Lacking practical information they cannot be distinguished clearly. In everyday life those who accept the new (dis)order rules and take part in events organized by the *Quartiersmanagement* (e.g. garbage removal, construction of a meeting point, festivities) and thus accept and identify with the changes in the square-are thought to be part of the neighbourhood and the *Gemeinschaft*.
The treatment of the groups described above shows that "government through community, even when it works on pre-existing bonds of allegiance, transforms them, invests them with new values [...] and re-configures relations of exclusion" (Rose 1996: 336). In this case the "pre-existing bonds of allegiance" are represented by the coalition of district politicians, middle class oriented neighbourhood organizations, and the inhabitants that moved in recently; together they build a gentrification-coalition. *Gemeinschaft* in this sense states that their coalition acts in the interest of all.[13]

Meanwhile the group of 'integrated' alcoholics and the employees of *Berlin macht mit* watch every new group of 'booze-tourists' distrustfully and keep them under observation. Thus, the alcoholics are converted into quasi-square-watchers, now being part of the supervision and exclusion strategy. The combination of special police legislation (ASOG), the permanent police presence, the employment of the nonprofit *Berlin macht mit*, the flexible exclusion and partial integration strategy, "Social Work Concept", translated into action by social-pedagogic nonprofit organizations, social workers, and the *Quartiersmanagement* together, has proved to be (almost) successful. Currently a debate is going on as to whether to enclose the whole of *Helmholtzplatz*. Starting with a repressive strategy to enforce the restructuring of the square, the management of *Helmholtzplatz* has been replaced by a partial integration strategy (see Holm 2001b) based on the hope (more than the expectation) that the neighbourhood will be capable of self-regulation.[14] All new exclusionary practices, including the planned enclosure, are presented as integration measures.

Broken Neighbors as Targets of an Integrative Exclusion Strategy

This contribution focuses on the political engagement of nonprofits in the field of security and order within the approaching new 'global area', in which diverse state and non-state actors determine the field of the security economy and divide up the whole market into different cooperation and competition arrangements. Concrete, multiple security markets are emerging that, with regard to specific geographical or social entities, require, one could say, 'customer specific' forms of insecurity and disorder management.

With regard to the labour market it is obvious that the low wage sector is extended by nonprofits, too. Issues like labour conditions, minimum wage or livelihood are pushed into the background and become overshadowed by moralized work obligations.[15] The unemployed and welfare recipients are meant to emphasize duties to and responsibilities for the *Gemeinschaft* - this is also true for the security market. The above described order and control measures are called 'integrative projects' by all actors involved. However, the specific connection of both policy fields (labour market policy and internal security) that leads to new exclusion is disregarded. Three spheres of functions can be distinguished: First, control and order services run by nonprofits are used as conflict-adjusting instances and are directed towards resolving user conflicts. Second, in so-called disadvantaged areas nonprofit organizations are seen as a tool to move problematic neighbourhoods towards self-regulation. The poor are employed against the poor, and nonprofit security agencies are brought into action for disciplining and supervision. Third, inclusion and exclusion processes are connected. Low-wage security workers, employed by nonprofits, have to expel low income individuals from inner city territories.
Also worthy of note is expulsion-training for unemployed people and welfare recipients by federal and state police, by (multi-national) security companies, and nonprofits - all financed with public money. All participants celebrate these exclusionary strategies as integration of the unemployed into the labour market, and further as a contribution towards the cohesiveness and strength of the neighbourhood and 'civil society' as a whole. As a result, particular norms instead of common rights are enforced: What is at stake is the identification, control, reprimanding, and, if need be, expulsion of undesirables.

In the end, these security and order services are highly compatible with small-scale and problem-oriented strategies within current urban development and labour market policies. Both focus explicitly on strategies and tactics *in each case* differing *from place to place*. The recent emergence of non-state actors is frequently misunderstood as a retreat of the (nation) state.

The enforcement of a "civil society from above" (Lanz 2000), coupled with a "mixed economy of policing" (Nogala 2001), aspires to the stronger participation of local stakeholders, to allow state administrations to govern at a distance.

Among a growing number of nonprofits,[16] the planning, implementation, translation into action, and evaluation of such projects are seen as anything but exclusionary - indeed, quite the opposite.[17] Informalization and fragmentation of (access) rights and small-scale control policies against marginalized sections of the population are seen as inclusive strategies. It may be attractive to organize any kind of job that might connect with the first or regular labour market. This may be especially attractive in the presence of mass unemployment. Fighting unemployment and social exclusion is honorable. However, if (in)security and (dis)order come into play, there is a need to look twice. It seems, that in attempts to achieve *SolidariCity*, nonprofits today are (no longer) reliable agents.

References

Anheier, H., Priller, E., Seibel, W., Zimmer, A. (Eds.) (1999), *Der Dritte Sektor in Deutschland. Organisationen zwischen Staat und Markt im gesellschaftlichen Wandel*. Berlin.

Arbeitsamt Berlin Ost (1999), "Vermittlungsteam/ABM-Service: Ortübliche Vergütung in ABM/SAM", Ms. (unpublished) Berlin.

Beste, H. (2001), "Zonale Raumkontrolle in Frankfurt am Main im ausgehenden 20. Jahrhundert", in: Dinges, M., Sack, F. (Eds.), *Unsichere Großstädte? Vom Mittelalter zur Postmoderne*, p. 333-353, Konstanz.

Body-Gendrot, S. (2000), *The Social Control of Cities? A Comparative Perspective*. Oxford.

Bundesregierung (1999), *Moderner Staat - Moderne Verwaltung. Leitbild und Programm der Bundesregierung (Kabinettsbeschluss)*. Berlin.

Ehrke, M. (1999), *Revidierter Revisionismus. Der Dritte Weg und die europäische Sozialdemokratie*. Bonn.

Eick, V. (1998a), "Neue Sicherheitsstrukturen im "neuen" Berlin. "Warehousing" öffentlichen Raums und staatlicher Gewalt", in: *ProKla*, 28 Jg. n. 110, 95-118, Münster.

Eick, V. (1998b), "Der deutsche Bahnhof - Zentrale oder Filiale der panoptischen Stadt des 21. Jahrhunderts? Aktuelle Sicherheitsdiskussionen, -strategien und -praxen bei und im 'Umfeld' der Deutschen Bahn AG" (www.bigbrotherawards.de/2000/.gov/add.html).

Eick, V. (2000), "Integrative Strategien der Ausgrenzung: Der exklusive Charme des kommerziellen Sicherheitsgewerbes", in: Hamburger Institut für Sozialforschung (Ed.), *Ausgegrenzte, Entbehrliche, Überflüssige*. Hamburg, 63-76.

Eick, V. (2001), "Land unter in Neukölln? Die Wohnungsbaugesellschaft 'Stadt und Land' spielt soziale Stadt", in: *Berliner MieterEcho*, No. 285, 20-21.

Eick, V. (2002a), "From Welfare to Work - Ending Police Force as we know it..." (Paper presented at the Annual Conference of the Association of American Geographers, 19.-23. March, unpublished), Los Angeles.

Eick, V. (2003), ""Wenn Ihr einen schönen Tag haben wollt, müsst Ihr lächeln..." Zur Rolle von ABM-Ordnungsdiensten in der Sicherheitsproduktion", in: Elsbergen, G. v. (Ed.), *Kustodialisierung der Inneren Sicherheit. Wachen, Kontrollieren, Patrouillieren,* Opladen: in print.

Eick, V., Grell, B. (2002), "Mit der Sozialen Stadt von Welfare zu Work? Zur Rolle von freien Trägern in der neuen Sozial- und Beschäftigungspolitik", in: Walther, U.-J. (Ed.), *Soziale Stadt - Zwischenbilanzen,* Opladen, 181-192.

Eisenschitz, A., Gough, J. (1996), "The Contradictions of Neo-Keynesian Local Economic Strategy", in: *Review of International Political Economy*, 3. Jg., Vol. 3, 434-458.

Garland, D. (2001), *The Culture of Control. Crime and Social Order in Contemporary Society*. Oxford.

Hearne, V. (1987), *Adam's Task. Calling Animals by Name*. New York.

Hirsch, J. (2002), *Herrschaft, Hegemonie und politische Alternativen*, Hamburg.

Holm, A. (2001a), "'Behutsame Verdrängung' am Helmholtzplatz: Ausgrenzung im Aufwertungsgebiet. Trinker, Punks und Obdachlose im Zangengriff von Polizei, Sozialarbeit und Quartiersmanagement", in: *Berliner Mieter Echo* n. 286, 8-10.

Holm, A. (2001b), "Ausgrenzende Einbeziehung - Flexible Kontrollstrategien am Helmholtzplatz", in: *Berliner MieterEcho*, n. 288, 8-9.

IHS gGmbH (2000), "Selbstdarstellung der IHS Beschäftigungs- und Qualifizierungs gGmbH", Ms. (unpublished) Berlin.

Jessop, B. (1997), "Die Zukunft des Nationalstaats - Erosion oder Reorganisation? Grundsätzliche Überlegungen zu Westeuropa", in: Becker, St., Sablowski, Th., Schumm, W. (Eds.), *Jenseits der Nationalökonomie? Weltwirtschaft und Nationalstaat zwischen Globalisierung und Regionalisierung*. 50-95, Hamburg.

Jessop, B. (2000), "Globalization, Entrepreneurial Cities, and the Social Economy", in: Hamel, P., Lustiger-Thaler, H., Mayer, M. (Eds.), *Urban Movements in a Globalizing World*, 81-100, London/New York.

Jessop, B., Peck, J. (1998), "Fast Policy/Local Discipline: The Politics of Scale and the Neoliberal Workfare Offensive" (Paper presented at the Annual Conference of the Association of American Geographers, 25.-29. March). Ms. (unpublished), Boston.

Krätke, St., Borst, R. (2000), *Berlin. Metropole zwischen Boom und Krise*. Leske + Budrich.

Kury, H. (Ed.) (1997), *Konzepte Kommunaler Kriminalprävention. Sammelband der 'Erfurter Tagung'* (Kriminologische Forschungsberichte, Bd. 59), Freiburg/Brsg.

Lanz, S. (2000), "Der Staat verordnet die Zivilgesellschaft", in: *Widersprüche*, Heft 78, 39-51.

Lemke, T. (2000), "Neoliberalismus, Staat und Selbsttechnologien. Ein kritischer Überblick über die governmentality studies", in: *Politische Vierteljahresschrift*, Vol. 1, 31-47.

Lindenberg, M. (2000a), "Zwischen sicher sein und sich sicher fühlen. Kommunale Hilfsdienste als Geburtshelfer für verdichtete städtische Gemeinschaften?", in: *Widersprüche*, Heft 76, 37-49.

Lindenberg, M. (2000b), "Kommunale Hilfsdienste. Moderne Schutzengel?", in: *Neue Kriminalpolitik*, 4, 8-10.

Mahlberg, L. (1988), *Gefahrenabwehr durch gewerbliche Sicherheitsunternehmen*, Westberlin.

Mayer, M. (1987), "Staatsknete und Neue Soziale Bewegungen", in: Kreuder, T., Loewy, H. (Eds.), *Konservatismus in der Strukturkrise*, 484-504, Frankfurt/M.

Mayer, M. (1997), "Berlin - Los Angeles. Berlin auf dem Weg zur 'Global City'?", in: *ProKla*, 109, 519-543.

Nitz, G. (2000), *Private und öffentliche Sicherheit*, Berlin.

Nogala, D. (2001), "Ordnungsarbeit in einer glokalisierten Welt - Die neue Mischökonomie des Polizierens und der Polizei", in: Fehérváry, J., Stangl, W. (Eds.), *Polizei zwischen Europa und den Regionen. Analyse disparater Entwicklungen*, 184-222, Wien.

Ottens, R. W., Olschok, H., Landrock, S. (Eds.) (1999), *Recht und Organisation privater Sicherheitsdienste in Europa*, Stuttgart.

Pohl, G., Schäfer, C. (1996), *Niedriglöhne. Die unbekannte Realität: Armut trotz Arbeit*, Hamburg.

Ronneberger, K., Lanz, S., Jahn, W. (1999), *Die Stadt als Beute*, Bonn.

Rose, N. (1996), "The Death of the Social? Re-figuring the Territory of Government", in: *Economy and Society* Vol. 5/No. 3, 327-256.

Rouhani, N. (2000), "Hundedreck ist ein politischer Stoff. Über das Leben mit Hunden und Haltern", in: *Frankfurter Allgemeine Zeitung* 4. April 2000 (Lokalteil Berlin), BS 1.

Schuller, K. (2001), "Eine Illusion zerbricht: Aus eigener Kraft kann Berlin kein leuchtendes Metropolis werden", in: *Frankfurter Allgemeine Zeitung* vom 23. Juni 2001, 3, Frankfurt/M.

Schuster, W. (1998), "Kommunale Kriminalprävention. Der Stuttgarter Weg", in: Innenministerium Baden-Württemberg (Ed.), *Fachkongress Kommunale Kriminalprävention*, 19-24, Stuttgart.

Senatsverwaltung für Arbeit (Ed.) (2000), *Berliner Arbeitsmarktbericht 1999/2000*, Berlin.

Senatsverwaltung für Arbeit (2001), *Hilfe zur Arbeit nach dem BSHG in Berlin 2001*. Ms. (unpublished) Berlin.

Shearing, C. (1997), "Gewalt und die neue Kunst des Regierens und Herrschens. Privatisierung und ihre Implikationen", in: Trotha, T. v. (Ed.), *Soziologie der Gewalt*, 263-278, Opladen.

Simon, T. (2001), *Wem gehört der öffentliche Raum? Zum Umgang mit Armen und Randgruppen in Deutschlands Städten*, Opladen.

Strukturpolitische Expertenkommission (1992), *Auf dem Weg zur Wirtschaftsmetropole Berlin*, Berlin.

Veblen, Ernst (2000), "Workfare - wenn auch der Sheriff vom Sozialamt kommt...", in: *Berliner MieterEcho*, No. 279, 20-21.

Wieking, K (2000), "Der beste Freund von vielen Feinden umstellt. Im Gegenwind der öffentlichen Meinung", in: *Der Tagesspiegel* vom 10 Januar 2000, 11, Berlin.

Endnotes

[1] Berlin lost most of its industry and headquarters to the currently thriving southern regions of Western Germany.

[2] The radical destruction of the East German industrial core was most severe in Berlin. Some scholars claim that the early 1990s' industrial policy in Berlin was informed by revanchist intentions of Western policy makers (Krätke/Borst 2000). In this view Berlin suffers doubly from the consequences of the Cold War.

[3] More than that, in the early 1990s the local government was confronted with federal devolution politics leaving the City of Berlin (as well as many of its citizens) with a reduced budget. For example: In 1997, the federally funded programs for job creation (Arbeitbeschaffungsmaßnahmen, ABM) were available only for 13,000 participants, compared to 36'000 in the year 1992 (see Senatsverwaltung für Arbeit 2000).

[4] The financial crisis, accentuated by the crisis of the Berliner Bankgesellschaft, complicated the fiscal situation furthermore. The city-state Berlin is currently indebted by around 46 billion Euro, resulting in a daily net interest of more than six 6 million Euro: "an amount that would be sufficient to finance one thousand ABM-employees for one year", as the Frankfurter Allgemeine Zeitung recently observed (Schuller 2001: 3).

[5] Salomon and Anheier, together with the Institute for Policy of the Johns Hopkins University, for the first time attempted to "register the Third Sector quantitatively in a social-economical survey and [...] analyzed it on an international comparative level" in 1997 (Anheier u.a. 1997: 9).

[6] For private security agencies see: Mahlberg 1988; Ottens, Olschok, Landrock 1999; Pitschas 2000; Nitz 2000; for communal crime prevention: Kury 1997.

[7] Berlin - following the Expert Commission on 'Public Duties' set up by the former SPD/CDU-Senate - entered into a contract with private security agencies. For more details on the (re)structuring of state and federal police see: for Berlin: Eick 1998a; for Frankfort on the Main: Ronneberger, Lanz, Jahn 1999, Beste 2001.

[8] Eastern nonprofits are a result of deindustrialization processes led by a body of the German government known as the Treuhandanstalt, which was active at the beginning of the 1990s. During the early 1990s, industry plants have been 'abgewickelt' (the special term for: 'ruined') by the Treuhandanstalt (THA, established to 'reconstruct' East Germany's industry). For the remaining workers so-called 'holding companies' have been established, out of which the nonprofit organizations originate (Eick, Grell 1996).

[9] To compare: Altogether, 16,000 persons have been employed in ABM and similar measures on the second labour market (Senatsverwaltung für Arbeit 2000).

[10] It is also true that the local state alone would not be in a position to maintain essential parts of the local infrastructure (e.g. infant-schools, homes for the old, sanitariums), nor be able to mobilize the still-growing number of long-term unemployed and welfare recipients.

[11] Besides, the employment services send 900 unemployeds out of whom 300 are pre-selected by the nonprofit-organization. The one-year employment and the parallel-basis training are financed through public money.

[12] Confrontation was highly aggressive between dog-keepers on the one hand and mothers with little children on the other, because from the latter point of view dog-heaps mark 'no-go-areas' for their kids. Both groups established citizen associations, both appeared before the public with spectacular events (Wieking 2000: 11; Rouhani 2000: BS 1).

[13] The integration of a commercialized Quartiersmanagement and a - with regard to its procedure-logic - commercialized ABM-security-agency, moreover, refers to an important shift: The emphatic Gemeinschafts-definition coined by Ferdinand Tönnies - one will find Gemeinschaft "where ever people are connected in an organic way through their own intention and affirm each other" - does not carry the same resonance today. Taking care of other people no longer emerges from reciprocal dependency and solidarity among the Gemeinschaft-members, but calls for the "paid off fortitude to care" (Lindenberg 2000a: 48, translation, ve).

[14] Similarities are striking, if one draws a parallel to the strategy of the Deutsche Bahn AG, which first started its 3-S-Strategy (Sicherheit, Sauberkeit, Service; security, cleanliness, service) through repressive strategies followed by an in-part-integrative strategy (Eick 2002c, 1998b).

[15] Starting salaries in the cleaning-service are at 7,20 Euro, private security agencies pay 4 to 9 Euro before taxes per hour, which is equivalent to a disposable income of 600 to 700 Euro (2001).14 hours shifts, (absent) qualification, non-guaranteed and unhealthy working conditions are common.

[16] Note should be made of the fact that a multitude of scholarly colleagues actively participated in the development and implementation of concepts like the state programs for 'disadvantaged quarters' (for instance in Hamburg and Berlin), the federal-state-program 'social city' (Bund-Länder-Programm 'Soziale Stadt') or the communal crime prevention programs.

[17] The Berlin Quartiersmanagement, as shown above, knows no bounds and describes, in all seriousness, restrictions for migrant(families) to move into specific housing estates (Eick 2001a) and restrictions for alcoholics, punks and homeless to gather in specific urban districts (Holm 2001a) as 'integration'.

1.5

TEXT.......................................Ahmed Allahwala and Constance Carr
PHOTOS.......................................Constance Carr

Alternative Urban Publics: Between Repression and Emancipation

Who has the power to make places of spaces? Who contests this? What is at stake?
(Gupta and Ferguson, 1992)

This paper starts with the premise that it is not possible to build public spaces free of socio-economic, socio-cultural, socio-sexual dishomogeneity in the context of current capitalism and its differentiating and flexibilizing modes of production (a supposition that many liberal theorists counter), and aims to explore the existence, function and importance of alternative publics inside the urban territorial boundaries of Berlin.

The Neglect of Place and Space.

Numerous studies have already shown that members of marginalized or subordinate groups (e.g. women, blue-collar workers, visible minorities, the homeless) prefer alternative public spheres to existing conventional or mainstream public spaces - arenas of public congregation and consumption defined and controlled by the majority. Nancy Fraser (1993) named these spaces, "subaltern counterpublics", parallel discursive arenas in which alternative or oppositional interpretations of identities and needs can be articulated and realized. Historical examples of such "counterpublic" spaces are those of the American feminist and gay liberation movements of the 1960s and 1970s. In Berlin, many social groups and political movements have been relegated to secondary or subordinate status, and would benefit from counterpublic spaces.

Classical theories of the historical development of the public sphere - one has to think only of the path-breaking work of Habermas and Negt/Kluge - do not take its spatial dimension into consideration. Space and its capacity to structure is the object of almost no critical discussion. Space in these theories is perceived as a mere "container," a location or physical structure that hosts a particular form of public action and deliberation. Aside from this functional view of public space, the question of the structuring capacity of space is largely absent from the debate. Meanwhile, studies - especially feminist ones - have shown that public space as it is viewed and analyzed in classical studies is not fully open and accessible. In fact, it is argued that these spaces were/are deliberately and systematically exclusive, often to the disadvantage of women and socially-marginalized sectors of society (Landes 1988; Ryan 1990). Therefore, the constitutive principles of public space, of "non-rivalry" and "non-exclusivity," have to be taken more as a normative ideal than an actual accomplished fact.

Lefebvre (1991) argued that spaces and places are not public merely because architects and planners designate them as such. Rather, it is the social interaction within a given space that makes it public. Public space is *lived* space. Public spaces, therefore, cannot be seen as culturally neutral, offering equal and indiscriminate opportunities of articulation to all forms of cultural expression. In fact, public spaces materialize and exist in and through cultural institutions, as well as in and through the socio-cultural geography of urban territories.

In Berlin, in the event of a demonstration, public spaces (that exist in the predetermined designated sense) are altered. The area is sectioned off and controlled by police to the extent that demonstrators may be required to show their passports upon or before entry to the rally, and/or submit to random body searches. Demonstrations are also prohibited within a radius of 1km from the Capital City´s Headquarters *(Bannmeile)*, and these measures effectively silence demonstrators and/or alternative voices.

These regulations, however, do not prevent opposition thought. Instead, counter movements simply occur elsewhere. Notices and flyers are pasted on lamp posts or stapled to bill boards. Meetings are held in private homes or offices. Gatherings or festivals take place in courtyards or neighbourhood streets.

Der Reichstag.
Public spaces for communication and interaction...or not.

As public arenas continue to be equated to places of mass consumption and communication, the relationship between public and space is lost. Humans act in relation to others present in the same space, and therefore, their actions cannot be isolated from the presence of "the other". Every action plan is connected to a perception and is spatially oriented. In this context, space does not have a particular size; rather, its parameters are defined by a particular negotiation and definition process. The distinctions between public and private spaces, as well as the categorization practices that make these distinctions possible, are an integral part of the process of societal change. Thus, negotiation and experience take on a key role in the structuring of space (see Wöhler 2000).

Urban public spaces are socially produced and as a result, are often places of contention. The usual winners in the struggle for the social production of space are the players who control and possess capital power (economic, cultural and social). This process of interaction and the influence of the uneven distribution of power are central negotiating positions in the construct of space. Dominant spaces express social conventions and articulate the cultural representation of an (allegedly universal) social order. A meaning or sense is given to every space. A simple normative organization of space undermines this process of representation.

Poster for Antifa, LuftransACTION, and Frauen Fest

The photo above shows a wall in Friedrichshain plastered with poster advertisements for political events. Two of the posters advertise a concert/action of the Antifa, another advertises a demonstration against a German airline, and the third advertises a women´s festival.

The Antifa (short for antifascist action) is one of Germany´s most radical movements against the extreme right. Their primary goal is to obstruct attempts by the extreme right to circulate their materials, teach their propaganda and generate further support. For reasons of security their identities are not willingly publicized, and their discussions are kept guarded.

In this realm of counterspace there are also discussions of immigrant politics. Whether it is the simple indignity of negotiation with a racist bureaucrat at the "foreigners office" *(Ausländeramt)*, or months at a time spent in a "deportation jail" *(Abschiebeknast)* without reason, or government sponsored deportation with co-operating and profiteering airlines, the politics and ethics of this daily routine of asylum seekers, refugees or immigrants remains a protest seen only at the margins.

The third poster shows that, just as the feminist movements in the United States did in the 1970s and 1980s, young women in Germany also gather at counterpublic parties to unite, chat, eat, sing, and exchange experiences that situate and relate their sex/gender or sexual/gender orientation to the urban space around them.

Power, Space and Identity: from Fragmentation and Contrast to Interdependence

Identity and space are mutually constitutive and can only be understood and analyzed as relative to one another. Cities, in their multifaceted social spatial forms, set the context for the freedom of expression, and articulation of various identities (Massey, 1997). One can therefore conceptualize the flexible, changing relationships among identity, difference, space, place, and power within the urban context, implying that one must study identity and social space together. Social spaces, then, whose structure reflects social relationships, cannot be seen as power-free; nor can power be mistaken as an independent external entity ready to oppress, suppress or repress other identities. Instead, power becomes a construct (just like identity) expressed and lived in and through a certain spatiality (*ibid.*).

If we assume that 'city' is a multitude of discourses in a relatively closed whole, or one that forms a relatively closed entity, the question remains whether or not it is possible for one to define herself within an urban space amidst its material, cultural, social and political discursive formations.

The strict dichotomy between private and public spaces is an increasingly insufficient categorization of space because of the ever-emerging mixed spaces that one may designate as either semi-public or quasi-public: such are emerging "postmodern" spatial phenomenons of "gentrification" and "disneyfication" - processes that commercialize and culturalize fundamental living areas such as housing and recreation. In these cases, participation in such public spaces becomes ever more dependent on the participant's possession of economic and cultural capital.

To counter the unevenness of social spaces, space must lose its supposedly transparent, or quasi-objective character and assume a more hybrid one. One might call this process, an "Entgrenzung" (de-limitation/border crossing), or de-habitualization of the public spheres. [2]

Das ist unser Haus, schmeißt doch endlich
Schmidt und Press und Mosch aus Kreuzberg raus!

So sang the beloved punk-folk band *Ton Steine Scherben,* in resistance to the developers that posed a constant threat to the squatters living in the district of Kreuzberg, during the eighties. It translates, unfortunately not so rhythmically, to "That is our house, throw Schmidt and Press and Mosch out of Kreuzberg, once and for all!"

After the fall of the Wall, it wasn´t just the planners and the prospectors who dug up the landscape. Many westerners skipped across the border into the abandoned tenement housing of the former eastern districts of Mitte, Prenzlauer Berg and Friedrichshain, looking not necessarily for low rents (they had those in the west, too) but for large empty spaces to build counter-culture and community. At this time more than 30 squatter settlements rose up. Of those, approximately 5 still remain today. About one third have been "legalized" and the remaining "cleaned out" *("geräumt")*. 'Wagon' settlements seem to have had a greater success of survival than the tenement squats that suffered intense renovation pressure. [1] Wagenburg at Treptow (below) still survives. Gentrification pressure in this eastern district is, however, minimal.

The Tacheles

Standing at the heart of the district of Mitte is the famous Tacheles. Once an abandoned and severely damaged building during DDR rule, then a squatter´s settlement during the 1990s, it is now a centre for the arts - or as cynics say, a "cultural Tra-la-la."

The series of photos shows the Tacheles after the renovation that began in the fall of 2000. After the window panes were put in, the concrete structures around the window were sanded and moulded into a somewhat more polished representation of the rough and gritty, bombed-out look it had before.

Social Spaces and Class

Public spaces are constructed in isolated locations defined by institutions, forms of communication, and cultural practices. Therefore, an analysis of public space must refer to the structure of social space. Bourdieu (1995) described the social sphere as a multidimensional space of fixable points. Every actual position is part of a determinable multidimensional system of co-ordinates, whose value corresponds to relevant variables, while participants are distributed across the board according to their share in the relevant forms of capital. Classes are formed when a multitude of individuals are placed in a similar position within the social sphere (*ibid.*).

Grasping and comprehending the social world calls for an investigation on how participants of a particular space imagine and define their surroundings, both collectively and individually. Further, it requires an understanding of how these conceptualizations were created, re-created and ultimately identified and categorized. We agree with Bourdieu's assertion that political struggles - including the struggle for the social production of urban spaces - are struggles towards the recognition of the social world and the processes of categorization that influence and define it. Change can therefore only be achieved through the identification, deconstruction and reconstruction of dominating social perceptions articulated through space and spatial practices.

First, however, it is necessary to identify how and why particular categories of social groupings attain dominance and others remain suppressed. According to Bourdieu (1995), prevailing categories of perception result from the incorporation of supposedly objective structures. The social world, then, is produced as a result of the distribution and character of symbolic systems.

Each social arena is characterized by a continuous classification process. Bourdieu (1995) discussed the objectification of particular interpretations of social realities. The enforcement of specific categories of perception through objectification can be realized and understood as a dominant or even hegemonic discourse. By incorporating the quasi-objective structure of the social world, power (im)balances become embedded in the minds of all players, and this reinforces and reproduces the dominant patterns of social organization and stratification. In order to escape being accused of fatalism, progressive opposition movements need to detect power imbalances, and articulate and enact alternative interpretations of the social world.

Berlin flaunts itself as a multicultural city. The Senate chief official of Foreign Affairs *(Ausländerbeauftragte des Senats)* boasts that Berlin is host to "436,182 registered citizens of non-German nationality from about 190 different countries." Absent from this self-congratulating statement, however, is the fact that these individuals do not carry German passports, and therefore have restricted rights. These populations, too, are concentrated in the western districts - and not in those of the East (Häußermann and Kapphan, 2000; Hermann, Imme and Meinlschmidt, 1997).
It has been suggested that the uneven distribution of "alien populations" is a result of the different histories of the former east and west Berlins - that the DDR permitted fewer foreigners (with the exception of refugees from other communist nations, eg. Vietnam), while the former West admitted more. It is, however, striking that the distribution did not change after re-unification.

Für
DEUTSCHE
sind die
etablierten
Parteien
nicht mehr
wählbar!

Unabhängige Nachrichten • Postfach 40 02 15 •
W-4630 Bochum 1. Kostenl. Probeexemplare anfordern!

Perhaps, however, the reluctance to settle in the eastern districts should not be so surprising, given the not uncommon presence of (not always neo-) Nazi thought. The illustration, left, shows a piece of Nazi-propoganda found in Prenzlauer Berg. It reads, "For Germans (capitalized), the established parties are no longer adequate."Aside from the fear of the extreme right, non-Germans face a government that struggles with the concept of "integration" - a discussion that focuses primarily on the central question of what it means to be German.

Figures on the right were postcards distributed by the German government. One could find them in bars and clubs; they supported the revised immigration laws that came into effect January 1, 2000. Until this date, many landed residents (including their children born on German territory) did not have the right to hold a German passport and enjoy the privileges associated with it.

The flip side of the postcard, right, reads:

Citizens with foreign passports:
Speak German. Think German
Dream German

Notice also that the woman is not wearing a hijab, as do thousands of women walking the streets of Kreuzberg or picnicking in Berlin´s Görlitzer Park. Equally ambiguous in its meaning, the larger fish illustrated in the second postcard says, "I find integration good," while the trapped fish says, "not I!"

The change in the German immigration law marked a major breakthrough in policies that were characteristic of (and by and large still are), a "migrant-friendly nation/welfare state," [3] (Wsevolod,1997) - policies that grant citizenship to individuals with a particular bloodline *(jus sanguinis*), while they permit residence only to non-Germans who will later leave or be deported.

Defining and classifying the social world is a collective act in which all players participate, in some form or another, in identifying and defining their particular part within the whole. For Bourdieu, each social arena in which this process occurs could be conceptualized as a show-place for an open struggle for legitimization. This process of identification enjoys relative autonomy in comparison to other forms of social power, and it this relative autonomy that alternative political movements must take advantage of. The possibility to call into question traditional arrangements that are usually simply accepted opens political spaces for social transformation (Bourdieu). Economic, political, social or cultural power become, then, the symbolic power if they manage to be recognized; if the power has, so to speak, the power to be able to be misjudged as power.

Towards a Radical Opening of Marginalized Spaces

Berlin has now spent a little more than a decade in reunification, a process that it was hoped would amalgamate and integrate the west into the east and the east into the west, creating a new, whole city out of the formerly segregated, divided one. However, this process has generated new forms of fragmentation. There are now a new set of stake-holders and holders of capital power - patterns that create and sustain new forms of repression.

In the end, the question (and therefore, the outstanding political project) remains whether or not a political project of a critical discourse that can transform the recognized socio-spatial hegemony is possible - one that critically challenges existing structures and allows lived social spaces for the emancipation of marginalized groups, not just in the foreground, but also in deliberate realms of counter publics that counteract, counterpose, counterweigh and counterbalance assumed existing hegemonies, discourses and identities.

References

Berg, R. (1998), "Islands in a Cold Urban Space – Wagenburgen in Berlin", in: Wolff, R., Schneider A., Schmidt Klaus C., Hofer A., and Hitz H. (eds) *Possible Urban Worlds: urban strategies at the end of the 20th century*, Zurich: Birkhäuser Publishers.

Bourdieu, P. (1995) [1985], *Sozialer Raum und "Klassen"*. Frankfurt/Main: Suhrkamp.

Bourdieu, P. (1987) [1982], *Die feinen Unterschiede: Kritik der gesellschaftlichen Urteilskraft*. Frankfurt/ Main: Suhrkamp.

Fraser, Nancy (1993), "Rethinking the public sphere: a contribution to the critique of actually existing democracy", in Robbins, B. (ed) *The Phantom Public Sphere*, Minneapolis: University of Minnesota Press.

Gupta, A. and Ferguson J. (1992) , "Beyond 'culture': space, identity, and the politics of difference", in: *Cultural Anthropology*, 7, 1, 6-23.

Habermas, J. (1990) [1962], *Strukturwandel der Öffentlichkeit*, Frankfurt/Main: Suhrkamp.

Häußermann, H., and Kapphan, A. (2000), *Berlin: von der Geteilten zur Gespaltenen Stadt*. Opladen: Leske & Budrich.

Hermann, S., Imme, U., and Meinlschmidt G. (1997), *Sozialstrukturatlas Berlin 1997: Eine Disaggregierte Statistische Sozialraumanalyse*, Berlin: Senatsverwaltung für Gesundheit und Soziales.

Isajiw W. (1997), "Introduction: ethnic heterogeneity, conflict and the dilemmas of social incorporation at the year 2000", in: W. Isajiw (ed). *Multiculturalism in North America and Europe: Comparative Perspectives on Interethnic Relations and Social Incorporation*, Toronto: Canadian Scholar's Press.

Landes, J. (1988), *Women and the Public Sphere in the Age of the French Revolution*. Ithaca: Cornell University Press.

Lefèbvre, H. (1991), *The Production of Space*. Oxford: Blackwell Publishers.

Massey, D. (1997), "Space/Power, Identity/Difference: Tensions in the city", in: Merrifield, A. and Swyngedouw E.(eds) *The Urbanization of Injustice*, New York: New York University Press.

Negt, O. and Kluge A. (1973), *Öffentlichkeit und Erfahrung. Zur Organisationsanalyse von bürgerlicher und proletarischer Öffentlichkeit.* Frankfurt/Main: Suhrkamp.

Ryan, M.P. (1990), *Women and the Public: Between Banners and Ballots, 1825-1880.* Baltimore: Johns Hopkins University Press.

Sassen, S. (1999), *Guests and Aliens*, New York: The New York Press.

Ton Steine Scherben (1972), "Rauch Haus", in: *Keine Macht für Niemand*, Indigo Records.

Wöhler, K. (2000), "Zur Verräumlichung von Öffentlichkeit", in Faulstich, W. and Hickethier K. (eds), *Öffentlichkeit im Wandel: neue Beiträge zur Begriffsklärung*. Bardowick: Wissenschaftlicher Verlag.

Endnotes

[1] See Renate Berg´s "Islands in a Cold Urban Space - Wagonburgen in Berlin" for more about wagon living.

[2] Bourdieu (1987) defined the habitus of a society as a set of limits that structures social behaviour

[3] Wsevolod contrasted this (primarily continental European) model of immigration policy with other forms, such as the American "melting pot" approach, or the Canadian "pluralist" approach.

1.6

TEXT................Ingo Bader
PHOTOS................Ingo Bader

Subculture: Pioneer for the Music Industry or Counterculture?

Music industry is an important sector of Berlin's urban economy. During the 1990s, the riverside of Berlin-Friedrichshain was a key-place in the development of club culture and the Berliner underground scene. Kreuzberg, an adjacent neighbourhood located on the other side of the river, could also be seen as a focal point of counterculture, made famous in the late 1970s and early 1980s by bands like Einstürzende Neubauten, Ideal and Nina Hagen. The temporary use of de-industrialized areas by subcultural and clubcultural pioneers, and the role of subculture as part of the resistance against the city's neoliberal project will be discussed here.

Although Berlin has suffered an economic decline and its vision to develop into a Global City has failed (Scharenberg, 2000), the city has recently attracted global players from the industry of cultural production - the music industry, in particular (Krätke, 2002). The city's most important music industry cluster is a waterfront development area called Media Spree, where the new German headquarters of Universal Entertainment Inc. moved to from Hamburg in July of 2002, located in a former cold-store for eggs. Neighbouring this site, in 2004 MTV Germany is also scheduled to move in (into a former port office). In this area, port warehouses have been turned into lofts for offices and studios and will soon be combined with high rise office buildings and an enormous multi-function entertainment arena constructed by a media and entertainment giant, Anschutz Entertainment Group.

Mainstreaming Counterculture

Next to the Universal building stands a sculpture created by Olaf Menzel called "13.04.1981". When it was erected in 1987, it caused a great scandal. Threatening letters and a badgering press campaign eventually forced the artist to leave the city. After the sculpture was removed from its public space due to pressure from the mayor, the real-estate company Wert-Konzept Unternehmensgruppe asked for it and placed it next to the building where the headquarters of Universal is located today.

The story behind the scandal was that Menzel was a known sympathizer of a group of left-wing radicals, the so-called "Autonomous" coming from West Berlin in the 1980s. His sculpture was created as a memorial to a demonstration that was sparked in response to the popular press's false reports of the death of Sigurd Debus, an imprisoned activist from the militant "Red Army Faction" on hunger strike. Demonstrators smashed 200 shop windows of businesses located in the then centre of West Berlin (Kurfürstendamm). The sculpture depicts relics of the riot.

The positioning of this memorial symbolizes the reasons for MTV's and Universal's decision to move their German headquarters to this location. Both companies try to take on the subcultural flair of this city district, and aim to appeal to new urban middle class that is not long attracted to standardized mass culture, but instead prefers an atmosphere produced by small innovative bands and labels and a lively bar scene, along with legal and illegal clubs.

Subculture in Berlin

In Kreuzberg, as well as in other inner city districts of West Berlin, a brisk sub- and counterculture of Punk, Industrial and German New Wave (Neue Deutsche Welle) evolved out of a subcultural mix of social movements in the late 1970s and 1980s. Squatters, community activists, gays and rebellious students all contributed to this specific mix, and a network of small labels, studios, disk jockeys and organizers was formed. The only multinational corporation that influenced the local music scene at that time was Bertelsmann (BMG) which owned the legendary Hansa Studios that launched stars like David Bowie (Connell and Gibson, 2003).

At this time, the position of west Berlin as an "island" and the then peripheral position of the lower working-class and immigrant district of Kreuzberg led to the decline of the district's economy. It was not a focus for developers. The large number of abandoned warehouses and buildings provided squatters with the opportunity to use them as clubs, bars and community centres. This counterculture defined itself as a branch of the resistance against major redevelopment projects. Examples of this kind of reuse are the alternative cultural centres UFA Fabrik in Tempelhof, Regenbogenfabrik, and the SO36. When the Wall fell in 1989, further opportunities for illegal or cheap land use opened up in East Berlin. Because of constantly changing ownership and administration systems, tracking of this activity was nearly impossible.

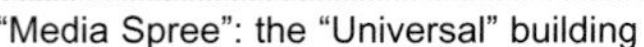

"Media Spree": the "Universal" building

The MTV furure site

In the German Democratic Republic, many abandoned industrial areas in the inner city were not cleaned up or rebuilt. Many apartments remained vacant. Moreover, the old tenement districts of Friedrichshain, Mitte, and Prenzlauer Berg were not redeveloped, and former administration offices were left empty. In addition, buildings close to the Wall were often not used and their ownership was uncertain. After the Wall was torn down, the quick transition from the highly subsidized Fordist economy of the divided city to post-Fordist capitalism led to the deindustralization of both east and west Berlin in only a few years. In east Berlin these developments were furthered by the Treuhand [1].

In the districts of Prenzlauer Berg and Mitte, the eastern underground [2] united with people from west Berlin who had moved to the East after the fall of the Wall. Small clubs and bars, often organised in apartments or basements, dominated this scene. In the Friedrichshain squatter scene, Punk experienced a revival. However, the most important musical innovation of the post-unification period in Berlin was the arrival of Techno music and the rave scene. Techno soon grew into a mass movement in the early 1990s.
Besides the temporary "living-room clubs," the most important venues were the old warehouses in east Berlin. Low rents and spaces available for temporary use enabled the creation of experimental music, and the ambience of abandoned buildings perfectly complemented this kind of music and partying. Furthermore, because some clubs operated illegally, their location changed constantly. This created an adventurous searches for sites, yet another peculiarity of Berlin Techno [3].

Initially, the club scene began in the eastern part of the inner city, with clubs such as the UFO and Planet (both located in the Köpenicker Street). Later, some clubs appeared in the wastelands located at the site of the former and future Potsdamer Platz - an area that was vacant after the Wall was torn down. Such clubs were, for example, the E-Werk, located inside a transformer station, and the still-existing Tresor, constructed inside the only part of a former department store that remained standing after World War II - the company vault [4]. Other smaller and temporary clubs, such as Kunst & Technik, the WMF and the Schlegel Club, were also influential.

Between Commercialisation and Repression

Unlike the alternative music subculture of the 1980s, the Berliner Techno scene was initially apolitical. "Raves took place largely in post-industrial landscapes, transforming rundown warehouse sites into timeless, de-localised and de-realised spaces, where obsolete industrial infrastructure was juxtaposed to state-of-the-art technology to create a surreal, almost virtual world - a fun factory." (Richard and Kruger, 1998). In addition to being a "fun factory", greater product differentiation within the wider music industry also helped pave the way towards commercial success for this subculture. Firstly, Techno received a great deal of commercial hype as awareness of the scene flowed into the mainstream. Secondly, as club culture became legalized, club managers were faced with rising costs. The result of these two processes was a large influx of money into the scene, causing its commercialisation. Well-known examples are techno-star Marusha and the famous yearly summer Love Parade. The city's private-public advertisement agency [5] quickly used the Love Parade for the "festivalization" and marketing of the city's image. At the peak of this development, in 2001, more than one million ravers came to the Love Parade. Indeed, it was the largest event in the city's tourist industry. In this respect, The Love Parade fitted well into the vision of a neoliberal city.

In Berlin large, sophisticated clubs were not popular. The city's club culture, instead, was characterised by local organizers, a hard 'n' heavy sound, an industrial atmosphere. Clubs situated in temporary-use spaces, (sometimes the space would only be available for one or two nights), was also a central identifying characteristic. "Bicolage" (Hebdige, 1979), the collage-like combination of items, often in the style of 1960s eastern modernism, gathered up in the locations used as clubs and bars, was typical of the "Berlin style" during the 1990s. These items were taken out of the context they had in the former use of the club locations.

After the gradual gentrification of Mitte (around 1998), the scene moved back to and concentrated in Friedrichshain, the area that lies between the Eastern Railway Station (Ostbahnhof) and the Eastern Port (Osthafen), where Media Spree is now located. This area had once been an important part of the city's infrastructure. However, in the last decade the inner city port had lost its importance. The freight station was once an active node in trade with eastern Europe. After reunification, however, several structural changes occurred that caused the decline of this area. Economic connections to Russia were broken off as a result of Berlin's new position in the global economy. Much of the transport and communication infrastructure was shifted to the outskirts of the city in the period of post-Fordist restructuring.

Furthermore, in the first years after unification this area was physically disconnected from the restructuring of east Berlin because it is completely surrounded by barriers, such as the memorial relic of the Wall called Eastside Gallery at the Spree riverside, railroads, and the freight station.

In the end, the enormous abandoned buildings made for good club locations. The first club to open in this area was the gay and lesbian disco, Die Busche, which had already opened up in East Germany. In 1998, the Maria, the Deli and the Ostgut opened as the first Techno Clubs. The Maria opened in a former mail delivery centre that was built in the style of east German modernism. This club combined Techno with a wider range of Berlin's electronic music. Berlin's label Kitty-Yo is a well-known example of this kind of experimental electronic music. In January 2002, it had to close because of the Media Spree development project, but was able to reopen at the location of the (now former) Deli which was evicted because it did not have permission to operate as a club. The Ostgut was opened by organizers of illegal gay S/M-parties with up to 2,000 people, called Snax Club in 1998. It developed into a strange mixture between this gay S/M scene, the Techno club scene, and kids from the suburbs. Mostly Berlin's typical hardcore Techno, but also innovative House music was played. Like the Ostgut, the Casino is also located in a warehouse in the former freight station, and the nearby Non-Tox is located in what used to be an old grain mill. Attention from big developers was first drawn to this area after a major exhibition, the Körperwelten [6], which took place in the former mail delivery warehouse. In recent years, many clubs have closed because of redevelopment initiated by the Anschutz Entertainment Group.

There is, however, another history of the 1990s Berlin underground. After the closure of the "Temple of Gabba" (industrial Techno music), a club called the Bunker in 1997, and the exclusion of music that does not fit into the Love Parade's mainstream marketing concept, a more radical voice from the Berlin underground arose. The Hate Parade (later in 1998 renamed the Fuck Parade) was initiated as a protest against the commercialisation and sell-out of subculture, as well as against the "cleaning" and restructuring of the inner-city districts. In addition, still there were parties in temporarily occupied spaces, where music from the non-commercialised subculture was played, as well as others organized parties that merged art and rave in public spaces. These ideas were based on a guerrilla-like use of public space that created a "temporary autonomous zone" which "[liberated] an area [...] and then [dissolved] itself to re-form elsewhere, before the state can crush it" (Bey, 1991). Examples are the collectives Querilla, Reclaim the Streets, re:z, which organize events at different locations - public spaces, squats or temporaly occupied locations.

Subculture as Revaluation

As is often found in the process of gentrification in residential areas, subculture pioneers are also playing an initial role in the redevelopment of abandoned industrial areas. Club culture brought these areas to public attention. Unlike the gentrification process, however, displacement does not occur, because the affected areas are already out of use (although displacement effects may occur in adjoining residential neighbourhoods). The media industry, in particular, profits from the image created by subcultural pioneers, because this image helps create a feeling of cultural authenticity that is readily marketed to the new urban middle class. However, it is not just the image of a place that is important. The development of a music production infrastructure (such as sound studios) and expansion of gastronomic services are also critical components of the media industry.

The clubs and their organizers do not protest against this process. Rather, in 2000, an alliance of Berliner clubs was founded called the Club Commission. It was intended to link various interests and coordinate marketing. The Club Commission acted as a guild, insulating the interests of the established clubs from the more radical ones.

While the primary goal of the more commercially oriented actors was profit, the counterculture defined itself by temporary use and movement. During the 1980s, the subculture stood in opposition to the predominant culture of the economy. Nowadays, subculture is an important part of the lifestyle of the new urban middle class. Clubs like Maria, managed by individuals with a leftist intellectual background, may very well be the same places where new multimedia enterprises are born. This means not only the production of a new urban life style, but also that subculture now has direct links to the cultural production industry.

Subculture has become a laboratory for new styles that can keep up with shortening product cycles. It supplies the industry with well-educated professionals, and it functions as an independent part of an enterprise network. The independents have given up their opposition to the industry, but meanwhile have challenged and changed the industry's structure, because they are more flexible and represent authenticity. Low Spirit Recordings GmbH, the record label behind the Love Parade, is formally independent but it distributes through Universal Music. Enterprises like Universal have comparatively few professionals and a lot of work is outsourced to independent companies or freelancers. To support and sustain this kind of network, proximity is crucial, because of the importance of friendship bonds and personal relations (Scott, 2001)

Media Spree - a Local Cluster of the Global Music Industry

Creativity plays a key role in the production process in the cultural production industry. For that reason, there are limited opportunities for standardisation. Acreative urban milieu is a necessary prerequisite for a production network like the so-called 'Third Italy' (for instance, Benetton) and the recruitment of specialised employees.

Moreover, the symbolic of place is important. The manager of MTV Germany, Catherine Mühlemann, explained why MTV is moving from Munich to Berlin, "MTV and Berlin have much in common. Both are creative, both are young, both boil over with living energy, both are always new and always different. Both have international appeal." (Senatsverwaltung, 2003, author's translation). This celebrated image is produced by subculture situated in this cluster. It can be argued that Universal and MTV transform subculture into a commodity. Music and cultural products in general are not only sold as products, but also as lifestyle, as a feeling of authenticity, and as a hyperreality.

Berlin's government has pinpointed music and the cultural industry as one of the few key service industries where the city has the capacity to be part of a global network. However, real-estate interests and the city's development policies are about to displace the special Berlin music scene in the inner city area. Thereby they tend to undermine their own economic visions - to be a capital of cultural production - which do not go uncontested.

References

Bey, H. (1991), *T.A.Z. The Temporary Autonomous Zone, Ontological Anarchy, Poetic Terrorism*, New York, Automedia
.

Connell, J. and Gibson, C. (2003), *Soundtracks: popular Music, identity and place*, London, Routledge.

Hebdige, D. (1979), *Subculture: The Meaning of Style*, London, Methuen.

Ingham, J., Purvis, M. and Clarke, D.B. (1999), "Hearing places, making spaces: sonorous geographies, ephemeral rhythms, and the Blackburn warehouse parties", *Environment and Planing* D 17: 283-305.

Krätke, S. (2002), *Medienstadt - Urbane Cluster und globale Zentren der Kulturproduktion*, Opladen, Leske + Budrich.

Richard, B., Kruger, H.H. (1998), "Ravers' paradise?" in Skelton, T. and Valentine, G. (eds.), *Cool Places, geographies of youth culture*, London, Routledge.

Scharenberg, A. (2000), *Berlin: Global City oder Konkursmasse? Eine Zwischenbilanz zehn Jahre nach dem Mauerfall*, Berlin, Karl Dietz Verlag.

Scott, A. (2001), "Capitalism, cities, and the production of symbolic forms", *Transactions of the Institute of British Geographers* , 26: 11-23.

Senatsverwaltung für Wirtschaft, Arbeit und Frauen, Referat Medien, Informations und Kommunikationstechnologien (2003), *Klänge der Großstadt - Musikwirtschaft in Berlin*, Berlin.

Endnotes

[1] After reunification, the Treuhand was the semi-official institution managing the privatization of state property of the German Democratic Republic.

[2] In these districts, there was a mix of artists, students and dissidents as well as subcultural bars before the fall of the Wall.

[3] To compare with Great Britain, see Ingham et al. 1999

[4]"Tresor" is the German word for "vault".

[5] It is called Partner für Berlin. It was founded by the city's government in the attempt to develop Berlin into a Global City.

[6] Körperwelten was a mixture between art and scientific presentation, where dead corpses preserved with synthetic resin were exhibited.

Brussel / Bruxelles: Tale of a Fragmented City

Photo sequence in front pages of this chapter by Manuela Conti / ogi:no knauss

2.1

TEXT..Eric Corijn, Stefan De Corte and Walter De Lannoy
PHOTOS ....PTTL-archives

From a Multicultural and Fragmented City Towards the "Mediterranean" Capital of Europe?

The Brussels Region is one of the richest regions in the European Union, but almost 40% of its residents live in deprived neighbourhoods. And this is but one of many contradictions in this city. For historical, cultural and political reasons Brussels is more segmented and more fragmented than many other cities. This is at the same time a source of wealth and a challenge. The wealth lies in its great diversity. The challenge is to translate this diversity into a mobilizing project where everybody finds a place. To make such a project work, Brussels has to wrest itself from a swampy historical past and a paralyzing institutional context. But the absence of a clear and strong image gives this city exceptional chances to develop a flexible identity in the light of globalization and the process of European unification.

With special thanks to Karen Thaens, Bob Colenutt, Richard Milgrom, Myriam Stoffen and Richard Wolff for helping out on the translation of this text. This is a modified version of a text published in Corijn, E. & De Lannoy (eds.) (2000), *La qualité de la difference - De kwaliteit van het verschil.* Brussel, VUBPress.

The Past Divides

There are few elements in history that anchor Brussels to a strong tradition. The Belgian 'revolution' of 1830 was not led by a self-conscious bourgeoisie with a well-established cultural hegemony. The capital of the rather artificial state Belgium is not the seat of a flamboyant cultural and intellectual tradition. Here the palaces of kings and courts of justice are more imposing than those of the nation. There are no popular historical characters. The local architecture oscillates between neo-Gothic and neo-Classic depending on the (catholic or liberal) political colour of city and state government. The short period of Art Nouveau reflects the success of private entrepreneurship rather than that of enlightened leadership.

The linguistic history of this city also conceals the deep historical roots of culture. Well into the 19th century Brussels was a Flemish-speaking city in the province of Brabant. In less than three generations the city was 'Frenchified' under impulse of a movement of capital concentration, which drew the French-speaking bourgeoisie from Flemish and Walloon cities to the capital. Popular immigration from Wallonia and the Frenchification of the Flemish middle-classes in search of upward social mobility fuelled this process. Undoubtedly, French is the 'lingua franca' in Brussels, but it does not represent any clear-cut cultural identity.

The lack of bourgeois leadership was not filled by modern popular culture as the labour movement hardly had any impact on urban development. Brussels has always been marked by its commercial and service functions, by its petty bourgeoisie and the state apparatus. It was alternately governed by Catholics and Liberals. The Social Democrats of this city have always been rather liberal. The lack of the sort of local working-class tradition, found in many big industrial cities, has also hindered the integration of immigrants, who remained strongly tied to their ethnic roots.

Brussels lacks an urbanistic project. The city centre is a concentration of imitation and what is locally called 'façadisme'.[1] On top of this comes the destruction of the urban tissue by modernist projects: the North-South Railway Junction, the preparations for the Expo '58 World Exhibition, the demolition of the 'Maison du Peuple', the Manhattan project in the Quartier Nord, many office and car-park projects realised during the sixties and seventies by the locally renowned developers Van den Boeynants & De Pauw, and last but not least the developments created by the European institutions.

Giving a new impetus to the city is not an easy task because of maladjusted institutions. The Regional Government is a part of the federal state, depending on 19 municipalities which correspond with an equal number of political 'baronies', all sharing responsibility for the spatial reproduction of social inequality. Moreover, the Brussels Region is under the cultural authority of the Flemish and French communities which deprives it of the political right to develop a city-based cultural policy (see further).

Real-estate investments next to Midi-Station | Street-wise mobility planners | Preparing for the King's venue

The maps show the socio-economic characteristics of Brussels residents, and illustrate the very large contrasts in wealth and housing conditions between the deprived parts in the 19th century neighbourhoods (situated around the historical centre) and the rich neighbourhoods in the south-eastern part of town. These unacceptable contrasts are even more painful if we know that they are matched by striking ethnic differences. As such, the urban dynamics of Brussels are trapped in its historical and institutional restrictions and there are insufficient social and cultural coalitions to provide counterbalance. Overcoming its many fragmentations is one of the main challenges for future developments.

A Small Global City

In 1968 the Brussels population peaked at 1,079,181 residents in its 19 municipalities. In the following 24 years the Brussels Region experienced a continuous population loss. Any change in the Brussels Region population during the last thirty years has been strongly determined by migration movements. The urban exodus of the Belgian population was responsible for the declining number of residents. Since 1992 the number of residents has stabilised at about 950,000 mainly due to international immigration and a decrease in the mortality surplus of the Belgian population. The reinforcement of the international position of Brussels after the European Summit of Edinburgh, the expansion of the European Union to 15 countries in 1995 and the large size of Brussels families from a Mediterranean background all play important roles in balancing the population loss.

The ongoing suburbanisation at the fringe of the city has expanded the area and number of residents well beyond the limits of the 19 municipalities of the Brussels Region. This wider 'city region' is composed of a densely built urban part (the morphological agglomeration) and a surrounding area (the banlieue) that does not look very urban but depends heavily on the city. The morphological agglomeration consists of 36 municipalities (including the 19 municipalities of the Brussels Region), with a total of 1,356,208 residents (2002). Another 404,574 residents live in the surrounding banlieue. So the 64 municipalities of the wider city region counted a total of 1,760,782 residents in 2002. Unless otherwise mentioned, we consider only the 19 municipalities (the Brussels Region) in this chapter. Notwithstanding its important international role - Brussels could easily claim to be a World City - we have to bear in mind that it is in fact rather small in size.

Brussels Institutions

Brussels is an urban region with maladjusted institutions. Its institutional framework is derived from the Belgian federal state structure and not from urban dynamics. The city region is divided into a central 'Brussels Region' and a periphery located in Flanders and Wallonia. The Brussels Region is one of the three regions in the federal state in charge of territorial affairs (infrastructure, economy, mobility, housing, etc.). The Brussels Region is led by a parliament and a government. That is why Brussels is led by a minister-president, the chair of the regional government.

Personal matters (education, health care, culture, etc) are dealt with by the country's linguistic "communities". As Brussels is a bilingual city, these cultural matters are taken care of by both the Flemish and the French community, with their local dependencies. The Brussels Parliament is divided into two parts to deal with these questions, and each part has its executive body. The two communities do not have much in common and operate in the city with their own policies.

The Brussels Region is thus governed by different state structures: a regional government, a Flemish executive, and a French executive, each linked to its respective communities. Moreover, the territory is divided into 19 municipalities each with their legal autonomies, e.g. municipal schools, cultural policies, social work, etc.

The institutional organisation contributes to the segmentation and the fragmentation of the city, although it does not enhance integrated development schemes, on the other hand it does allow for multiple initiatives and alliances.

Fewer Residents, but more Households

Notwithstanding the decrease in the number of residents, the Brussels Region has witnessed an increase in the number of private households. Between 1970 and 2000 they increased from 448,673 to 468,899 reflecting smaller average household sizes (2.39 persons in 1970 and only 2.03 persons in 2000).

The declining household size goes hand in hand with a considerable increase in the number of single-person households. Their share in the total number of households grew from 32.8% in 1970 to 50.1% in 2000. Single-households are mainly located in the central part of the city, where there is a good supply of small apartments. In the city centre (the Brussels 'Pentagone') and near the Avenue Louise, several neighbourhoods include more than 70% one-person households. The reduction in household size also reflects an increase of non-traditional households like one-parent households and unmarried couples. In 1970 married couples with or without children accounted for 53% of all households. In 1991 their share was already down to 37%. To further 'stabilise' the Brussels population or - as intended by the Regional Development Plan - to increase the number of residents, it will be necessary to increase the housing-stock and to create a residential climate that is attractive for a range of household types, both with and without children.

Foreigners Save the City

Over the last 30 years the composition of Brussels residents by nationality has changed dramatically. In 1970 the population consisted of only 16.1% foreigners. By the beginning of 2000 they had increased to 28.5%. This figure would be even higher if we took into account the number of immigrants that changed their nationality to Belgian (52,246 between 1987 and 1996). The Moroccan population is by the far the biggest foreign group (62,278), followed by the French (34,497), the Italians (28,951), the Spanish (21,442) and the Turks (18,386).

Analyses of the residential distribution of the most important groups of foreigners show a clear link between location and socio-economic position. Two patterns clearly emerge:

- on the one hand, the foreigners of Mediterranean origin (Magreb included) live mainly in the central part of town, with the biggest concentrations in the 19th century belt near the city centre. Due to their low income, these households have limited access to the housing market and are 'forced' to look for neighbourhoods where 'relatively' cheap housing is available. The residential pattern of this Mediterranean group reflects their deprived position in Belgian society;
- on the other hand, foreigners from north-western Europe (and also Americans, Japanese and Scandinavians) who belong to the highest income groups in the city, and consequently have a wider access to the most attractive neighbourhoods. They live more spread out over the city but, with a clear preference for the richer south-eastern part of town (municipalities like Woluwe, Uccle, Auderghem, Ixelles and Watermael-Boitsfort).

Apart from these two fundamental residential patterns some nationalities prefer particular neighbourhoods. For example, the Turkish population is concentrated near the Chaussée de Haecht and the Germans near the Park of Woluwe. These particular zones of concentration are caused by cultural factors like the feeling of concordance, shared language, religious habits or region of origin (e.g. the Turkish population), but also the location of work (e.g. the Germans, most of whom work in the European district) and of international schools (Japanese and Americans).

We want to make clear that although zones with significant concentrations of foreigners exist, it would be completely wrong to label them as ghettos. First of all, the term ghetto has a particular connotation of mono-culture and isolation, referring to the Jewish neighbourhoods in medieval towns. In Brussels hardly any neighbourhood exists where one nationality represents more than half of the population (except for the Belgian residents, of course).

And in most of the ethnic neighbourhoods many different nationalities live together. For example, in Old-Molenbeek, where Moroccans make up the dominant group, you also find many Turks. The same goes for the Turkish neighbourhood at the Chaussée de Haecht, where many Moroccans and Italians live as well. The ethnic neighbourhoods in Brussels are clearly multicultural neighbourhoods. Certainly if we take into account that the different nationalities do not form homogenous groups but show considerable cultural differences according to whether they represent first, second or third generation immigration.

Culture, Multi-Culture and Urban Culture.

Culture is a battlefield in social structuring. This is a daily experience in Brussels, given its particular institutional and linguistic structure and the existence of strong racist parties. The existing cultural mosaic is, however, not fully represented, as illustrated by two examples: more than one third of the population does not have political rights, as suffrage is only granted to Belgian and EU-citizens, thus unevenly distributing the population “that matters” over the city. Secondly, a city with more than 100 nationalities and dozens of languages is culturally structured into two communities, according to the two dominant nations *under construction* in the Belgian federal state (French and Flemish). Government figures and data focus only on these two “communities”. In reality more than 41 % of the households in Brussels are culturally mixed and multilingual. These intercultural practices do not have any institutional expressions. There is a deficit both in the recognition of a number of cultural identities and in the opportunities for intercultural urbanity. Brussels lacks urban politics and is over-determined by its state structures.

Old Belgians and Young Immigrants

The age-structure of the Brussels population today differs little from the national profile. But the figures hide important differences between the age-structures of the Belgian and the foreign populations - the foreign population is much younger. In 1997 the Belgian population comprised 27.4% elderly people (60 years or older) compared to only 9.3% in the group of foreigners. More then a quarter of the foreign population is under 20 (26.3%), compared to only 21.9% within the Belgian population.[2] Young people are strongly present in the central part of town (the Pentagone) and in the surrounding 19th-century belt in Kuregem (Anderlecht), Old-Molenbeek and the older parts of Schaerbeek, Saint-Josse-ten-Noode and Brussels. Not surprisingly, these are also the neighbourhoods with the highest percentage of foreigners. Other neighbourhoods with high percentages of young people (mainly Belgians) are to be found at the edge of the city (‘villa’-neighbourhoods in Uccle and Woluwe-Saint-Pierre).

Some of the neighbourhoods in the central part of the city have recently undergone ‘rejuvenation’ thanks to the immigration of young adults. These young adults (‘starters’ on the housing market) prefer to live in the central part of town, close to numerous urban facilities, where small and cheaply priced housing is available. In some parts of the city this causes ‘gentrification’ (e.g. near the Dansaertstreet in the city centre, some neighbourhoods in Saint-Gilles, Etterbeek and Ixelles).

The Central Part of the City Impoverishes, the Banlieue Enriches

The suburbanisation of the middle and high income groups and, less important, the concentration of the poor results in the impoverishment of the central part of the city and the enrichment of the *banlieue* (outskirts of the city). In 1963 the average individual income in the Brussels Region (19 municipalities) was 60% above the national average. In 2001 it was 10% below the national average. Fewer residents and lower incomes affect the fiscal base of the Brussels Region and reduce the possibilities for a (necessary) redistribution of wealth. Measured by average income, the municipality of Saint-Josse-ten-Node is the third poorest in the country (the average individual income was only 52% of the national average in 2001). The municipality of Lasne, situated south-east of Brussels within the wider Brussels periphery, is the second richest municipality in the country. Within the Brussels Region the municipalities of Watermael-Boitsfort, Woluwe-Saint-Pierre, Auderghem and Uccle are the richest, forming a cluster of rich municipalities in the south-eastern part of town.

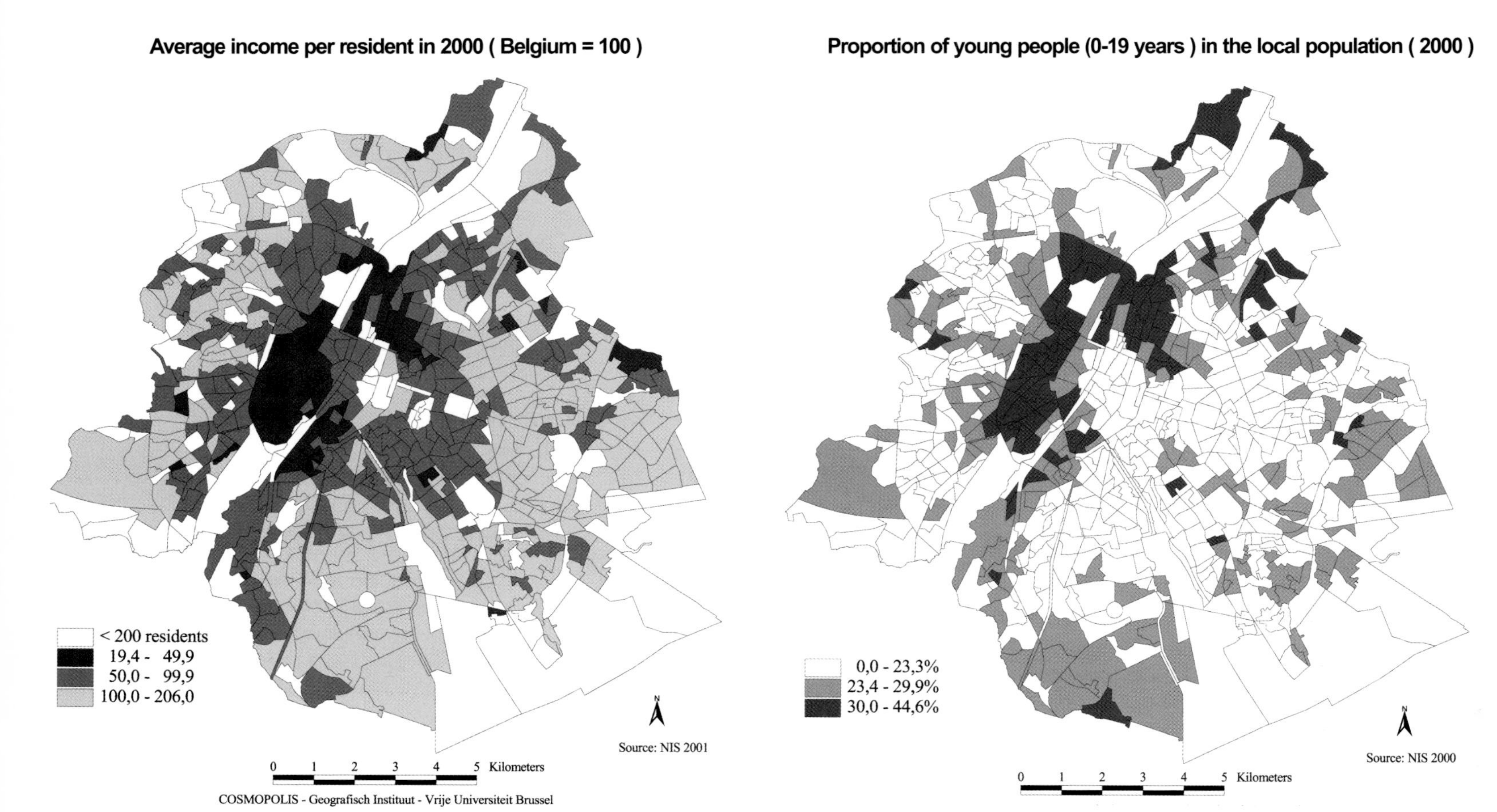
Average income per resident in 2000 (Belgium = 100)
< 200 residents
19,4 - 49,9
50,0 - 99,9
100,0 - 206,0
Source: NIS 2001
0 1 2 3 4 5 Kilometers
COSMOPOLIS - Geografisch Instituut - Vrije Universiteit Brussel
Proportion of young people (0-19 years) in the local population (2000)
0,0 - 23,3%
23,4 - 29,9%
30,0 - 44,6%
Source: NIS 2000
0 1 2 3 4 5 Kilometers

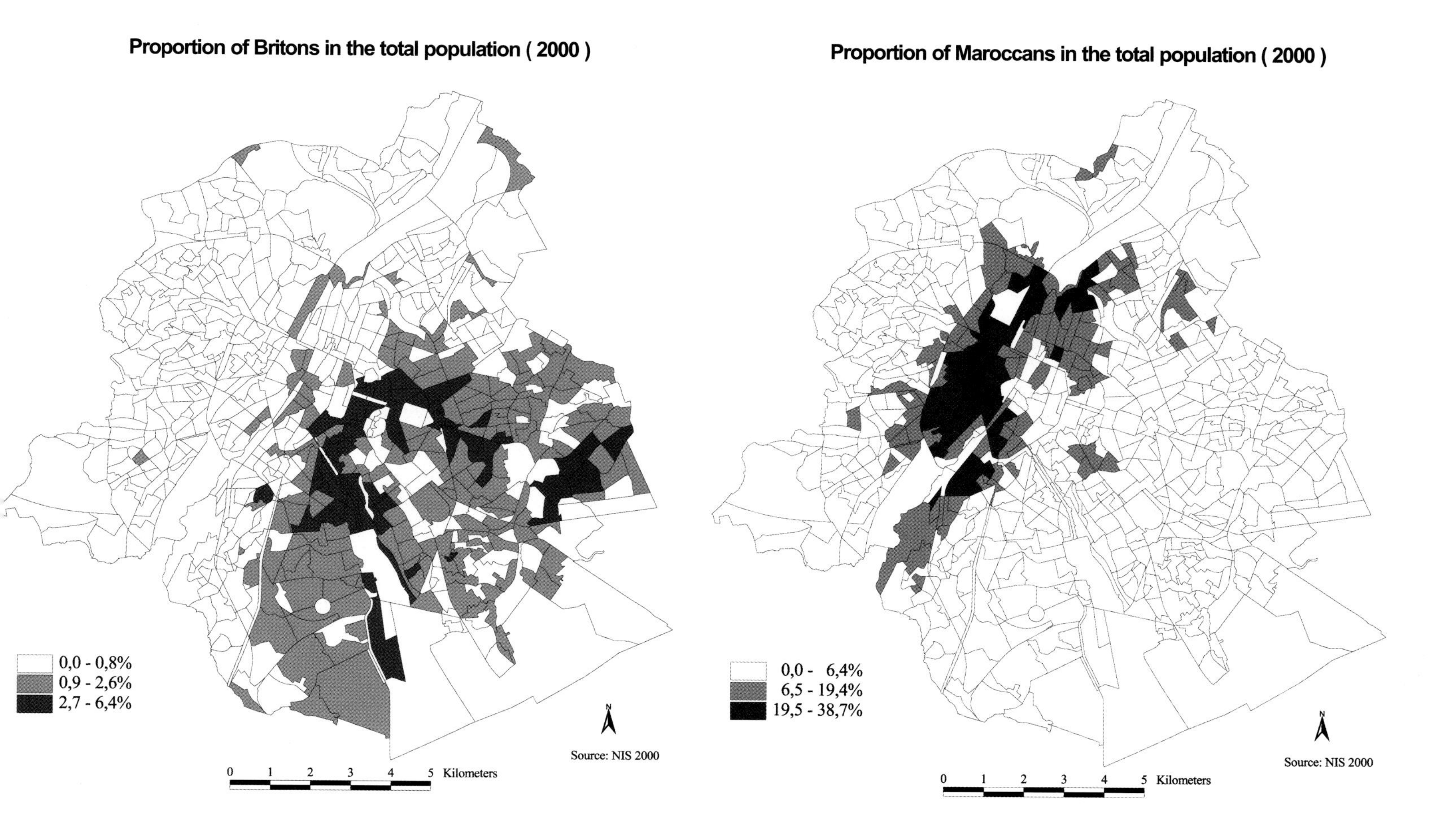
Proportion of Britons in the total population (2000)
0,0 - 0,8%
0,9 - 2,6%
2,7 - 6,4%
Source: NIS 2000
0 1 2 3 4 5 Kilometers
Proportion of Maroccans in the total population (2000)
0,0 - 6,4%
6,5 - 19,4%
19,5 - 38,7%
Source: NIS 2000
0 1 2 3 4 5 Kilometers

Nearly 40% of Brussels Households Live in Deprived Neighbourhoods

In recent years several researchers have pointed out the very troublesome situation in Brussels concerning poverty and social inequality. Various social indicators show a progressive process of polarization and point towards an increase in social inequality. The percentage of households with an income below the poverty-line is estimated to be 16% of all Brussels households. The share of the Brussels population that lives in a state of social insecurity is estimated to be 30%. Although it is one of the richest European regions (measured by Gross Domestic Product) in 2000 the Brussels Region had about 70,000 unemployed, with an unemployment rate of 14%.[3] This was due to the poor education of many of the residents of the deprived neighbourhoods, and the fact that half of the jobs in Brussels are taken by employees living outside the Brussels Region.

The spatial concentration of social problems in the Brussels Region has been shown over and over again. One hundred seventy-eight statistical wards are labelled as 'deprived', and together they house nearly 40% of all Brussels households.[4] The spatial distribution of these deprived neighbourhoods almost totally corresponds to the western part of the city-centre (the Pentagone) and the 19th-century belt that surrounds it. Not all of the households in this part of town are poor, but they live in an unfavourable material and social environment. In this part of the city we often see an accumulation of problems: bad housing conditions, high structural unemployment, low quality education, many school drop-outs under 18 years of age, lack of job prospects for school-leavers, emergence of all kinds of criminality as survival strategies (drug dealing, car theft,...), while there is no sign that the local authorities have far-reaching neighbourhood-development and town-renewal programmes. Most of these areas house many foreigners, who are often targeted as scapegoats. The problems in these neighbourhoods are often 'criminalized'. In other words, the neighbourhoods are portrayed in the media as dangerous, without taking into account the interrelationships of the various existing problems.

The economic crisis and the restructuring of the labour market have strongly decreased the possibility of upward social mobility of residents of deprived neighbourhoods. The new higher-skilled jobs in the service sector are not accessible to the low-skilled residents of these neighbourhoods. Moreover, foreign youths have less success on the labour market (position and unemployment) than their level of education would warrant. Globalization of the economy, the greater mobility of capital and the conseguent competition among cities has increased social displacement on the housing market.

In Favour of a Dynamic Urban Project

It is clear that Brussels is in need of an integrated approach, combining a concrete social-economic policy to eliminate harsh inequalities with a cultural project to support the construction of an intercultural identity.

In our opinion deprived neighbourhoods are in desperate need of a broad and long-term programme of neighbourhood development. The specific circumstances of different neighbourhoods must be taken into account in order to find the specific combination of initiatives and strategies that need to be employed for each neighbourhood. Physical renovation of housing and public spaces, as well as social renewal and economic initiatives, should be a part of this. Cultural initiatives can also play an important role in neighbourhood development. A dynamic cultural policy should rise above the communitarian approach and try to develop a multicultural identity for Brussels. To achieve this kind of urban cultural policy, initiatives that are visible and attractive to the population are necessary, as well as the construction of public places where people of different cultural backgrounds can meet. It goes without saying that the participation of local residents is needed to elaborate strategies for neighbourhood development. And it should also be obvious that non-Belgian population groups in deprived neighbourhoods need to obtain political rights equal to their Belgian neighbours. A broadening of voting rights is therefore necessary. More than one third (37.0%) of the inhabitants of these neighbourhoods are young people (0 to 24 years old) and 37.9% of them do not have Belgian nationality (2000). For the sake of the city's future and from a viewpoint of social justice, it is important that a positive perspective on the future be created. The availability of decent and affordable housing can be ncreased by greater governmental influence on the housing market. A considerable expansion of the social housing market seems necessary. This could partly be achieved by new construction, and partly by socialising the residual rental housing stock. In addition, the government could try to obtain more influence over the private rental housing stock by giving greater importance to tenant organisations, and the establishment of social rental agencies would be a good start.

These measures could be accompanied by giving rent subsidies to people in the lowest income groups. Today the private housing market is dominant: whereas 50% of the population qualify for social housing, the offer only covers 8% of the housing market. Moreover, the growing importance of the city as the capital of Europe has triggered speculation that has reduced the stock of cheap housing even further. Today, for three quarters of the population, housing is a real problem.

Finally, it is clear that strategies of neighbourhood development and urban policy in general, however desirable and indispensable, can offer only a partial solution in fighting poverty and discrimination. Urban policy cannot influence general developments on the labour market, which is more than ever internationally determined. Without structural measures the unemployment rate will not be solved by the labour market alone. Measures like shorter working hours and redistribution of labour, or the introduction of a universal allowance (basic income) will have to be discussed. Finally, financial redistribution between Brussels and its surrounding regions is necessary, especially given the fact that more than half of available jobs are taken by people living out of town. People pay taxes where they live, not where they work.

Capital of Europe *à la* Mediterranean

To meet these challenges Brussels should take advantage of the opportunities offered by globalization. The international role of the city has the potential to generate the means necessary to compensate for the lack of redistribution within the federal state. Therefore, the city's image abroad has to be improved. The presence of European institutions is not experienced as a positive factor, but rather as the locus of a bureaucracy that issues many regulations in a rather undemocratic way. The city image has to be transformed from 'the location of European institutions' to a capital city of Europe. That is the conclusion of an international taskforce comprising Umberto Eco and Rem Koolhaas. The image of Brussels is thus closely connected to the image of the European unification process itself.

One cannot deny that European integration is market-led. Despite all efforts through regional development funds, and other mechanisms of financial redistribution, regional inequalities persist. The economic dynamic in Europe is dominated by a strongly industrialized core area, the 'Blue Banana' between London and Milan, which places Southern and Eastern Europe under pressure of a core-periphery duality. This has an influence on cultures and life styles as well: the standards of the (Protestant) north-western core tend to replace the Mediterranean way of life, which as nobody can deny, contains a lot of "Europeanness". After all, the historic core of European culture lies in the south, and many standards for the quality of life have been developed there. So, besides a democratic deficit, the European unification process is also experiencing a cultural deficit. Without a cultural and social project, the unification process will not find the necessary popular support. Europe has to project an image of 'the good life', and we doubt that this can derive solely from the productivist model based on a Protestant work ethic. It is in this sense that we value the fundamental contribution of the Mediterranean way of life.

Representing South-African housing

Celebrating the European Union at The Grand Place

Tyres going wild at the Palais de Justice

Training new mobility skills

It is remarkable that in several European cities the tension between North and South has been reproduced in the cultural oppositions between indigenous and foreign population, between rich and poor. In Brussels this is particularly striking. For this reason the construction of a multicultural identity for Brussels should accompany the construction of its position as the capital of Europe. To obtain this, Mediterranean culture can no longer only be associated with social and economic deprivation, but has to be associated with the historical source of European culture and its qualitative values of good living. The presence of large Mediterranean populations in Brussels should be positively valued as an irreplaceable contribution to the city's role of European capital.

Furthermore, an urban project implementing the ambition to become a European capital has to be based on the multiple "marginalities" of the city. Brussels lies at the border between German and Roman cultural territory. In its own history it went through significant cultural transitions. It is a place that has both many global elites and a large Mediterranean popular base. The city's image should be built as a positive cultural *métissage* (hybridization). Urban cultural politics in the perspective of the development of a true European cultural city, can be part of fighting segregation and positively integrating all existing cultural elements. To rise above the Belgian national question and build a platform for a new Brussels identity foreign residents have to play a central role for Brussels is a city of foreigners. A positive integration of the Mediterranean cultural elements would offer guidelines for urban design, the development of public space, cultural programming, etc.

Such a cultural re-imaging of the city is but one aspect of the struggle against existing segmentation and fragmentation. If we want to obtain a more integrated approach, we will have to abandon numerous traditions, habits and concerns to achieve a mobilizing project. Apart from social, economic and political elements, this project should represent a radical choice for urbanity. This has to be reflected in a new urbanism and an integrated socio-economic development programme, should contain a positive image of "good urban life". For this, the contribution of every single population group is necessary.

References

Corijn, E. & D. Kavadias (1994), *Brussel 2002. Een Delphi-onderzoek.* Brussel: VUB (research report).

Corijn, E. (1996), "Cultuurbeleid, wijkontwikkeling en burgerschap", in De Decker, P., Hubeau P. & S. Nieuwinckel (eds.), *In de ban van de wijk.* Berchem: EPO, 181-192.

Corijn, E. (1997), "Brussel scheef bekeken", *Vlaams Marxistisch Tijdschrift*, vol. 31, n°4, 6-8.

Corijn, E. (1999a), "Ville et convivialité démocratique", in: *La revue nouvelle*, vol. 109, n°1, 76-81.

Corijn, E. (1999b), "Can the city save the world?", in: Nauwelaerts, M. (ed.), *The future of the past. Reflections on history, urbanity and museums.* Antwerpen: Musea Antwerpen, 85-103.

De Keersmaecker, M.L. (1998), "Staat van de armoede in het Brussels Hoofdstedelijk Gewest. De opbouw van sociale indicatoren", in: Vrancken, J. et al. (eds.), *20 jaar OCMW.* Leuven: Acco, 79-101.

De Lannoy, W. & C. Kesteloot (1990), "Het scheppen van sociaalruimtelijke ongelijkheden in de stad", in: *Werkgroep Mort Subite*, Barsten in België. Berchem: EPO, 143-178

De Lannoy, W., Lammens, M., Lesthaeghe, R. & D. Willaert (1999), "Brussel in de jaren negentig en na 2000: een demografische doorlichting", in: Witte, E., Alen, A., Dumont, H. en Ergec, R. (eds.), *Het statuut van Brussel/Bruxelles et son statut.* Brussel: Larcier, 101-154.

Kesteloot, C. (1996a), *Atlas van achtergestelde buurten in Vlaanderen en Brussel.* Brussel: Ministerie van de Vlaamse Gemeenschap.

Endnotes

[1] Façadisme is derived from the French word 'façade' (front of a building). It refers to the reconstruction of a building by demolishing it, except for its historical façade. During the 1990s it became common practice in Brussels. It could be seen as the post-modern answer to the 'destructive' planning practices of the 1960s and 70s.

[2] These figures have somewhat changed over the last few years. In 2000 the share of elderly people within the foreign population reached 10.4% while the share within the Belgian population decreased to 25.5%. The most remarkable evolution is that of the young population. The Belgian population now compromises 23.7% of young people (0-20years) compared to 22.7% within the foreign population. This is probably due to the change in policy regarding nationality at birth and change of nationality at 18th birthday.

[3] The national unemployment rate was 7% in 2000, and the European unemployment rate was 8.7%.

[4] In 2000 the Brussels Regions counted 636 statistical wards with more than 100 residents.

TEXT....................Stefan De Corte and Christine Goyens
PHOTOS....................PTTL-archives

Neighbourhood-Contracts: Towards Participatory Planning?

The Housing Question and Town Renewal: the Debacle of the Past

Brussels authorities have recently put a lot of faith in regeneration programs called 'neighbourhood-contracts' (*contrats de quartier*) to fight urban deprivation, poverty, neighbourhood decline, social exclusion and many of the other social issues mentioned earlier. These have become the most important instruments of urban regeneration since they were launched in 1994. Despite their important shortcomings, they are light-years ahead of the programs we have known during the 1970's and 1980's. At that time there was a lot of bravado about tackling the housing-question. The amount of housing in need of renovation was estimated at 200,000 units of which 40,000 were in acute need of major work and 30,000 were derelict (Brussels has about 450,000 dwellings). The so-called 'housing-block-renovation' [1] of that time was aimed at promoting low-cost renovation (a concession made under the pressure of many neighbourhood groups who strongly opposed the modernist clearance policies of that time) and at promoting social housing (Brussels has less than 8% social housing and no rent aid for an estimated 16% of the population living below poverty-line). The outcome of two decades of renovation programs was shameful: between 1986 and 1998 a total of 1628 dwelling were renovated or newly constructed. Even if we add the 1,500 dwellings realized within the only other major scheme [2], we still are far from the estimated 40 to 70,000 dwellings that needed urgent care.

With thanks to Katrien Dosogne, Eric Corijn, Mark Trullemans, Reinoud Magosse and Bob Colenutt for their critical reading of earlier versions, their constructive comments and additional information about the neighbourhood-contracts. Thanks to Richard Milgrom for the English corrections

This debacle is to be understood in the context of the spirit and political constellation of that time. It was before Brussels got a proper regional government that could impose a policy adapted to its needs. Municipalities could choose freely if they wanted to get subsidies out of a national fund that was available to all municipalities in Belgium. Many of the Brussels municipalities did not bother, since they showed little interest in the declining parts of their territory. Most of these 'deprived neighbourhoods' housed a majority of foreigners with no right to vote, depriving local politicians of an important incentive to act. And most of these municipalities have a pie-like shape, making it rather easy for local politicians to divert their political attention (and public funds) away from the poor neighbourhoods near the city-centre towards the more peripheral and wealthier 'Belgian' parts of their municipality.

Schaerbeek residents visiting the Regional Administration

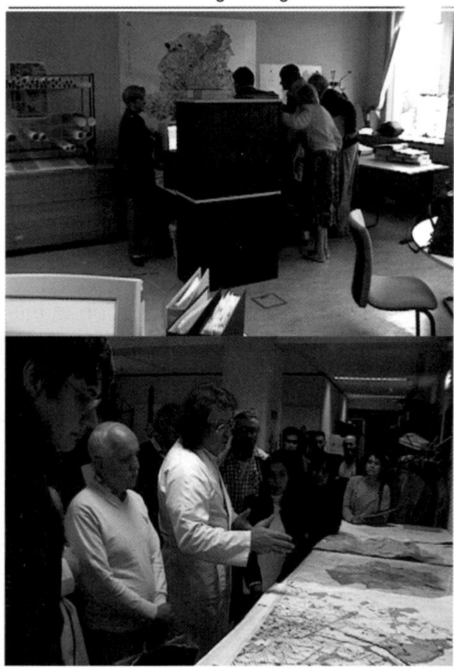

How maps are made to be readable without specialisation

Changing Urban Policies: New Authorities, Social Unrest and Political Rights

Many things have changed since then. First of all, there was the founding of the Brussels Region at the end of 1989. In the first years of its existence the regional government (at the time dominated by the Social Democrats) had the will to 'plan' the future of Brussels. One of the most important achievements in these founding years was the establishment of the first 'Development Plan'. Within that same context new regeneration programs were set up, of which the 'neighbourhood-contracts' are the most important. It is even the case that some activists from the neighbourhood movements became cabinet members in the regional government, or were taken up into the new regional administration or consultation bodies, adding a grass-roots touch to politics.

A second significant turning point was related to the riots in the spring of 1991. For the first time Brussels experienced large-scale street protests, triggered by the tense relationship between the police and local youth. A rather banal traffic infraction exploded into several days of rioting and looting, including an attack on a classy discotheque.[3] It did not take much political or social insight to link these uprisings to the social problems mentioned earlier on. The fact that most of the 'deprived' neighbourhoods are located in the 19th-century belt surrounding the city-centre (i.e. within two kilometers of the Grand Place) made regional and local politicians very susceptible to this matter. They did not have the relative 'luxury' of combatting social unrest in the *banlieues* at the edge of town (as for example, in Britain or France), but they were faced with it right at the heart of the city. This triggered off policies both at the level of more sophisticated policing (which does not necessarily mean less repression) and more attention for neighbourhood regeneration. It was within this context of social upheaval that the neighbourhood-contracts were drafted.

A third important element was the increasing number of foreigners changing their nationality (their official citizenship) and thus obtaining suffrage. Especially at the municipal level, this started to have an impact, with the local politicians showing more interest in the 'deprived' neighbourhoods and their residents. Again, we can not say that this has changed urban policy in a fundamental way, but the renewed political interest is certainly welcome and could have a positive effect in the long run.[4] This is not to say that we agree with the political refusal to give non-European citizens the right to vote (a national policy matter which is being actively debated today). Urban citizenship should not (only) be defined by formal membership to a nation-state, but should include full political rights in the place one lives and works, whatever one's nationality.

A New Integrated Approach to Regeneration

It was within this context that the regional government launched its new regeneration program in 1994 with the rather misleading name 'neighbourhood-contracts'. If we expect this to be a 'contract' between the community of a 'neighbourhood' and other stakeholders (of which the political authorities are the most important) then we will be disappointed. In reality the 'contract' is between two authorities, i.e. the municipality and the Brussels Region. This came about as a reaction to the disastrous outcome of the preceding decades of regeneration. Because of the strong position the municipalities hold within the Brussels political framework, the Region wanted to make sure that its regeneration program was implemented. A contract with the municipality seemed to be the best solution, forcing the municipality not only to execute the program, but also to do it within a given time limit. However, this does not mean that the local residents are not involved. We will turn to this issue further on.

The neighbourhood-contract scheme will soon be 10 years old, and it has undeniably scored some good points. Some of the shortcomings of the first years have been ameliorated. A total of some 30 contracts have been or are about to be completed, and especially in recent years, the program has gained momentum. Although only 483 dwellings have been renovated or newly constructed, this number will grow as many other contracts are completed, and new ones are due to start soon. Perhaps more important than the quantitative achievements are the qualitative shifts the neighbourhood programs introduced. Notwithstanding all their shortcomings, it must be admitted that they offer a more integral approach that mixes aspects of 'housing', 'living environment' (*cadre de vie*) and 'social development'. But this should not blind us to the fact that only by increasing today's efforts several times over can we expect a long-term impact, given the extent of the social and housing problems discussed above.

Geography is a military science: The conquest of Brussels

Too Many Bricks, Not Enough Participation

Although they have good intentions and have been relatively successful, the neighbourhood-contracts have shortcomings. One of the major problems is their exaggerated concern with 'bricks and mortar'. Although each neighbourhood program consists of a wider set of interventions and serious efforts are made to have a more integrated program, most of the money goes into real-estate and the physical upgrading of public space (3/4 of the total budget). The political authorities seem unable to broaden the heritage of the previous period of town renewal to include more participatory processes. Neighbourhood decline is still directly associated with the physical decline of buildings and public space. We do not deny that these issues are important, but there is more to it if you want to solve the social and economic problems faced in these neighbourhoods. We will turn to this matter later, but first we want to point out three shortcomings: the first has to do with timing, the second with follow-up and the third with the practical side of participation.

1) Experience teaches that there is a problem with the timing of the initial program. The municipalities have 10 months after approval by the regional government to put together a base-dossier. This consists of an analysis of the neighbourhood (local economy, social situation and physical condition) and includes the main development lines, the objectives to meet and the projects to develop. It has to include consultancy of the different stakeholders in the neighbourhood. Most of the municipalities have not enough qualified staff, and quite often hire a private consultant to do this job. Several months can pass between the approval of the neighbourhood-contract and the start of the survey, leaving little time to elaborate a base-dossier built on a profound knowledge of the neighbourhood, let alone to involve the population. On average, not more than 3 to 4 months are left to involve the CLDI and the AG (see frame).

2) Improvements in public space are proposed and discussed with residents and users who might not be the same in several years time. And the residents that intervene in these meetings are not necessary the ones that will be using these spaces. In short, participation at this level can not taken for granted and demands a very open and flexible process. Numerous spaces will be created or upgraded, financed by the neighbourhood-contracts, without planning for the follow-up. Who will be responsible? Who will take care of these spaces? Formal structures to guarantee the future management and up-keep of these spaces are lacking. They should be specified during the neighbourhood-contract, in collaboration with municipal services and political authorities. The authorities responsible for the future of these public spaces have to take part in the projects to make sure that they are included in future budgets and policy-making.

What are Neighbourhood-Contracts?

Neighbourhood-contracts or 'Contrats de Quartier' ('Wijkcontracten' in Flemish) are today the most important regeneration instruments in Brussels. They were launched in 1994 by the regional government and consist of 'contracts' between the several municipalities and the Brussels Region.

Each year the regional government puts together a list of neighbourhoods that should get funding within this framework. The choice is based on the physical state of buildings, the decline of public space, the number of abandoned buildings and vacant plots of land, the quality of housing and some social indicators like unemployment and dependence on social welfare. So this program is completely targeted at what is officially called 'deprived neighbourhoods' and is geographically limited to the poor neighbourhoods of the city-centre and most of the surrounding 19th-century belt.

A neighbourhood-contract covers about 12 housing blocks on average. So the name of this program is somewhat misleading, because it only partly matches a neighbourhood. Consequently, some neighbourhoods have several of these contracts. Each neighbourhood-contract consists of 5 sections (the locally notorious 'cinq volets') consisting of:

1) social housing to be realized by public authorities either through renovation or new construction (volet 1);
2) middle-class housing built by either private or public authorities on private land that is taken into long lease by the municipality, using it themselves or renting / selling it below market price to attract private developers (volet 2)
3) housing realized by private developers of which a part is taken on long-lease by the municipality and rented as public housing and a part is rented or sold by the developer on the market (volet 3);
4) interventions in public space - renovation or new construction of sidewalks, roads, road crossings, squares, new lighting, greening etc. (volet 4);
5) neighbourhood infrastructure like sports, children's, and community infrastructure (playgrounds, sport fields, halls,...) and local economic and social initiatives like the relocation of people affected by the construction program, participation, local employment schemes for local residents, etc. (volet 5);

People who want to gain access to the public and middle-class housing realized in a neighbourhood-contract have to match certain income criteria, and priority is given to local residents.

A neighbourhood-contract spans a time period of 4 years, extendable by two years to enable the contract to be completed (only used to finish larger construction sites). To increase quick visibility, interventions in public spaces have recently been speeded up (projects should now be realized within 2 years, extendable by one year)

The 4-year period of the neighbourhood-contract is preceded by a preparatory phase of 10 months. Within these ten months the municipality should put a base-dossier together, agree on a program and start the participation process. Most municipalities use consultants (most of them are either planners or architects) to draw up the base-dossier. This includes an overview of the 'physical' state of the neighbourhood (buildings and public spaces), the planning situation (inventory of different land-uses and other legislative plans) and an analyses and diagnosies of the social and economic 'vitality' of the neighbourhood. This is the basis for putting a draft program together, including possible projects, a list of the buildings and spaces involved, the annual timing and financing of the programs, an overview of the real-estate market with a list of measures to prevent speculation, measures to preserve the architectural heritage,...

The participatory process involves public neighbourhood meetings (Assemblée Générale or Curtly AG) and the creation of a participatory body (Commission Locale pour le Développement Intégré or curtly CLDI). Three public neighbourhood meetings should take place during the preparatory phase of ten months, followed by two meetings each year during the execution of the neighbourhood-contract (4 years). The public meetings discuss the findings and proposals of the Local Commission for Integrated Development (CLDI). The CLDI consists of at least 22 members, of which eight are representatives of local residents and two represent either schools, neighbourhood or local business associations. Most of the rest are representatives of local and regional institutions (municipality, social services, Brussels Region, the Flemish and French communities,....). All the meetings are presided over by the municipal mayor. All these bodies and meetings have consultative power; final decisions are taken by the municipal council and are approved by the regional government.

The preparatory phase is concluded with a public enquiry that includes a public hearing. Several local and regional authorities make up the public enquiry commission, which 'hears' spoken or written complaints by residents, associations, shopkeepers, local businesses. This is also an advisory body with no decision making power.

The Brussels Government has launched 32 neighbourhood-contracts since 1994, of which 10 are finished or will be soon. A total amount of 289 million Euro will be spent on these 32 neighbourhood-contracts, which run until 2007 (2009). Half of this budget (52%) is spent on neighbourhood-contracts that are completed or will be completed in 2004 (2006).

3) The numerous meetings of the participative bodies wear out even the most motivated residents (8 meetings a year for the CLDI, 2 meetings a year for the Assemblée Générale, see frame). We notice that most of the residents leave the board of the CLDI in the second year. It also seems hard to attract young people and women to become members of the CLDI. The motivation of the residents to stay on the board depends strongly on the content of and the way in which the meetings are run, that is to say how clearly, transparently and coherently the political representatives, the coordinator and the local associations communicate to and inform the residents. There is also a need to extend the functioning of the consultative bodies beyond the time limit of a neighbourhood-contract. Most projects are realized rather late, very often in the 2 years following the 4 years of the neighbourhood-contract. This phase of realization is not included in the working of the CLDI (there are no meetings anymore because no coordinating staff is available)

It is obvious that these weaknesses have to be overcome to make the neighbourhood-contracts perform better. But there is more at stake than just fine-tuning and increasing the general scope of the regeneration effort in Brussels. There has been a major policy-shift away from social concerns in regeneration. During the 1970s and 1980s there was at least more 'talk' of generating public housing and local social services through neighbourhood regeneration (but with very poor results as we showed earlier). Nowadays Brussels seems to follow the general trend of relying on the market by attracting private capital and middle-class families to deprived neighbourhoods. Buzz concepts like 'improvement of the social mix', 'positive trickle-down effects', 'public-private partnership' and the like are used over and over again to label today's neighbourhood regeneration.

We could write a long critique on this policy shift, a critique that is probably familiar because it has been formulated before within similar contexts and because it is applicable to many cities around the world today. We could also dwell on the poor performance of public-private partnerships within the neighbourhood-contracts, or we could underline the dangers of gentrification induced by these regeneration programs. But we prefer to look ahead and explore a little further the potentials of this program. After all, Brussels now has a device for neighbourhood development, there is legislation in place, money is being spent within this framework, participatory bodies have been created, municipalities take it seriously and there is a slow but steady tendency to upgrade and fine-tune this program. To raise this to the level of sustainable social neighbourhood development requires at least two things: thinking in terms of (1) neighbourhoods and (2) more participation.

Can Neighbourhoods Save the City?

We think that Brussels is in urgent need of an urban project (een stadsproject - un projet de ville). The strong fragmentation and segmentation of the city has created an amalgam of political, social and cultural institutions that all have their own agendas. The day to day politics of this city are the product of the power relations among these different actors, quite often resulting in very predictable outcomes but also producing many unexpected coalitions and free zones of action (see Cosemans in this chapter). On the one hand the absence of absolute hegemony within this power game opens possibilities for activists and social movements which other cities can sometimes only dream of. At the same time this laisser-faire attitude leaves it to the 'hidden hand of the market' to regulate society. A lot is tolerated in Brussels, as long as the borders that make the capitalist city go round are not decisively crossed. Once you pass this line, the real forces take over and it is surprising how quickly, coherently and firmly authorities take action. This has been experienced on several occasions by the local squatter movement, the free transport activists (Collectif sans Ticket), defenders of the 'sans-papiers' (Collectif de résistance aux expulsions et aux centres fermés and the Ambassade Universelle), i.e. those who fundamentally question basic categories of capitalism like property rights, privatization and nationality. The combination of anti-systemic movements and the existing free-zones and liberties in this city is not self-evident.

One of the scales of regulation could be the neighbourhood. We will not discuss here whether this is the 'right' or 'only' scale or whether globalization puts other scales in the forefront. In any case neighbourhoods are a level of proximity. The mental construction of cities should include such neighbourhoods, i.e. discrete places with a history, with their problems and potentials, with futures. And it is exactly about these futures that we should be thinking and talking. What concerns us should be more than the general targets to meet for housing, employment, traffic,... which you find in the Regional Development Plan. It is not enough to split it into figures and targets at the neighbourhood-level (although this would be very welcome). Imagining a neighbourhood is a collective process whereby the different stakeholders position themselves in the urban fabric as a whole. It is not so much about planning levels, about the (artificial) divide between bottom-up and top-down planning. It is rather about the negotiation of a vision common to the different stakeholders, who are anyway in interaction and contribute to urban dynamics. It is the construction of more self-reflexivity. This is of course not conflict free. It takes place within a network of uneven power relations. It involves struggle.

One of the first things at stake is the limits (the delimitation) of neighbourhoods. Brussels claims to be a city with more than 100 neighbourhood committees (most of them voluntary or temporary organisations), which would make you suppose that we do know our neighbourhoods. But that mental map is mainly determined by the scope of action and the thematic origin of the neighbourhood committees. In fact, neighbourhoods are not conceptualized in Brussels, either by the neighbourhood organisations or by the local government. The new neighbourhood-contracts suggest that the local and regional authorities could do better, but a close look at the delimitation and contents of the neighbourhood-contracts teaches us otherwise. Most of them cover not more then a few housing blocks, with a too disparate shape and a too small size to be labelled neighbourhoods. The act of delimiting a neighbourhood-contract is often restricted to the bureaucratic act of mapping the different buildings, plots of land and public spaces that should be included in a specific neighbourhood-contract and drawing a line around it. There is hardly any interest in social practices. In most cases we can barely speak of a 'meaningful entity', large enough and with sufficient coherence to become the location for negotiating the future.

We highly favour including neighbourhoods in the mental construction of Brussels. Not because we believe that neighbourhoods are more important than, say, families, municipalities, regions, countries or the global scale. The background against which our lives are projected is still that of a capitalist city within a globalizing world. But just skipping 'scale' is no guarantee for more progressive actions or outcomes. Moreover, it could prevent a mediation between private and public and contribute to maintain 'consumer democracy'. Neighbourhoods have been left to the traditional parties and the extreme right to develop a populist and essentialist rhetoric. The New Urbanism in the United States defends a very conservative view of urbanism through its concept of the neighbourhood. Defending the neighbourhood level as a scale of regulation is not necessarily thinking in terms of 'local community', of a sort of extended family, of the locus of 'Gemeinschaft'. Cities have become (or maybe always have been) so diverse in their composition that it would be a reduction of urbanity to approach neighbourhoods as communities. It is not by mapping the urban 'communities' that the different neighbourhoods will reveal themselves to us (certainly not in today's network society, where our social relationships are spread out over space more widely than ever before). Neither will it be by the physical structure of this city. Market-led development has given the city a rather 'organic' structure with very few planned and/or distinct neighbourhoods. Defining the different neighbourhoods in this city will consequently be a social process, the outcome of which has to be negotiated.

For several reasons we think that neighbourhoods and neighbourhood development opens up paths for possible progressive action and projects. Within the context of the globalizing world of today, neighbourhoods may become important nodes of social action. Proximity and involvement might be necessary to deal adequately with the highly diverse and multicultural character of today's urban societies. As Sandercock has written elsewhere in this book, if we want to escape the repressive, silencing practices of the modernist past we should have the right kind of participation. Brussels offers a lot of opportunities for this. First of all, the whole debate about neighbourhood and neighbourhood development is not dominated by a particular group, a social organisation, political party or a particular view on this matter. This leaves the debate open. Secondly, legislation has been enacted that channels money to neighbourhoods for regeneration purposes. Although there is still a lot to do, important first steps have been made. Maybe the neighbourhood-contracts as such cannot be turned into full-scale neighbourhood development, but they offer an important starting point towards a broader discussion about the future of this city and its people.

From Consultation Towards Participation

The last matter we turn to, and perhaps the most important one, is that of participation. Participatory democracy is first of all about sharing power! One of the main critiques of the existing neighbourhood-contracts is that the participatory bodies (with resident representation in the CLDI, see frame) have only consultative capacities. The final decisions are taken by the municipal council or the regional minister, not by the CLDI. This has frequently led to frustration, with residents resigning from the commission because their decisions were overruled. Perhaps these advisory bodies should be made full participatory bodies, with a right to share decision-making and a participative budget. This of course opens a question about the composition of the CLDI and the accountability of the representatives. At present they are appointed by the municipality without a clear policy or rule. The first phase of a neighbourhood-contract should include a search for and a selection of talented members who can be part of the CLDI.

We are surprised how important decisions like the physical delimitation of neighbourhoods are kept out of the public debate. Defining the territory for social action is an important first step in neighbourhood development and should be part of inclusive participation. On top of this, residents and users of the city are confronted with many 'policies' in their neighbourhood, involving different political levels and different administrations,which have dissimilar, partial and sometimes contradictory plans for the area. Streamlining these different policies should be a simple, straightforward and obvious act. But in reality this seems extremely hard to change. Although it opens possibilities for the unexpected and for the development of free-zones (which some of us like so much), one of the aims of a neighbourhood-contract should be to overcome these disparities.

There is not only the problem of defining physical borders and streamlining existing policies, there is also an important issue about whose knowledge gets included into the diagnoses of a neighbourhood. We mentioned before that some groups are underrepresented in the CLDI, like local youth and women. It is obvious that this has to change, but even if that were the case, there is still the issue of knowledge production. The conceptualisation of a neighbourhood is very much done by 'experts' and 'professionals' whose languages, categories and conceptualizations have become the standard on how to look at neighbourhoods. This leaves many other kinds of knowledge outside the picture, with silencing or even repressive results. Inclusion of these 'hidden voices' should go beyond 'consultation' or - what has been tried in Brussels with the Four-Cities project [5] - education of residents to match the standards set by experts and professionals. This means that we search for other ways of grasping, representing and communicating these hidden voices. This is why we expect a lot from inventive ways to do, so which are often artistically inspired or use alternative media. This is the real challenge of a participatory policy. This is the path of neighbourhood development we should take in Brussels, and maybe the neighbourhood-contracts are a good starting point.

References

De Corte, S. (1996), "Wijkontwikkeling met wijkcontracten? Stadsvernieuwing in Brussel", in: De Decker, P., Hubeau P. & S. Nieuwinckel (eds.), *In de ban van de wijk*. Berchem: EPO, pp.209-217.

De Corte, S. & W. De Lannoy (2001), "99 keer Brussel: een woontypologie", *Brusselse Thema's 7*, Brussel: VUBPress.

Delloite and Touch & Aries (2001), *Bilan van de wijkcontacten 1994-2000*. Brussel: Brussels Hoofdstedelijk Gewest.

Endnotes

[1] Opération de rénovation d'îlots

[2] Between 1986 and 2001 a total of 1523 dwellings were renovated within the regeneration program called 'Opération immeubles isolés'

[3] The classy discotheque les Bains/Baden used to be a municipal swimming pool and Turkish bath which closed down and was sold by the municipality of Forest (Vorst) for financial reasons. Located in the middle of the very working class neighbourhood Saint-Antoine, near the South Station, it was a source of conflict between the richer suburban customers and the local youth (to whom entrance was often refused). After the riots it was abandoned until a few years ago, when a group of artists and activists squatted the place. It has now become an important alternative arts centre (Les Bains::Connective) which is part of the scene Marie-Eve Cosemans describes in her article in this chapter.

[4] Some Brussels municipalities do already experience the political effects of the change in nationality of many foreigners. The most striking but rather exceptional example is Sint-Joost-ten-Node where 51% of the municipal council consists of 'new' Belgians.

[5] The Four Cities Project (1999-2001) involved an interchange of residents from the cities of Brussels, Dublin, Belfast and Liverpool with the aim of 'forming' residents in 'participation' and exchanging local experiences between the different cities. This program was supported by European funding (Interreg II) and resulted in a good practice guide.

2.3

TEXT .... Marie-Eve Cosemans
PHOTOS .... PTTL-archives

In the Ground: Convivial Culture in Brussels

Brussels is not commonly thought of as a lively cultural city. This impression is not due to the absence of cultural initiatives, but has more to do with the lack of a coherent cultural policy, caused by the political fragmentation of the Brussels Region.

However this may be, there are in fact some very visible cultural initiatives. And besides these, there are dozens that are far less visible, the ones that do not enjoy prestige and large audiences.

Some may call this "underground"... For me, it's daily life. Despite the fact that I spent lots of time in basements, I would not call this underground culture. I don't suppose many groups consider themselves underground, because they are not about conscious isolation. For sure there's a lack of accurate vocabulary to define this kind of group, but on their part ther is also at times a lack of efficient communication and a clear profile. We could also call these less visible initiatives "informal culture", which refers to cultural (in the broad sense of the word) initiatives which are not institutionalised, hardly recognized by government, and mostly aim at a bottom-up approach to projects and their context. There are other terms in the running, such as "projets émergents" ("emerging projects") referring to their recent and urgent character. In Amsterdam they are "vrijplaatsen" ("free spaces", which is not limited to physical space) and in the academic world Edward Soja has coined the term "third spaces" for similar phenomena.

Diverse as the words we choose for them may be, there are a lot of things these groups and initiatives have in common. More important still than the activities as such, often situated in the artistic-cultural domain, but also touching on questions of work, asylum or neighbourhood development, are their organizational structure and way of functioning. Structure, the search for an appropriate structure or in some cases the absence of structure (sooner or later compelling groups to start searching actively for a fitting structure)... As a consequence, these groups develop new and "own" organisational forms which ban all formal hierarchy. I consider the latter to be one of the essential features of these initiatives, along with openness, networking, and social engagement. Some other characteristics are autonomy, eclecticism, conviviality and innovation.

An interesting "case" in Brussels is Cinema Nova. Nova is an actual cinema; it's a physical place in the city, located at some hundred meters from the Grand Place, but it's also a mental place: a crossroads and a meeting place. At the same time, Nova can't be situated out of the context in which it operates: the commercial film world, the cultural field and the urban context.

The project "Cinema Nova" started in the autumn of 1996. It was a so-called "projet d'urgence" ("emergency-project"). The challenge was to build in a short time (some months) a place for films, which would specialize in non-distributed work. A place that wouldn't give in to commercial demands and that would participate actively in the urban context. The idea was one year of experimentation.

Some dozen volunteers started to clean, build and renovate an abandoned former cinema that until then served as storage space for office equipment. The bank which owned the building agreed on the free use of the place. For residents of other capital cities, this may seem at least a bit weird, but at that time Brussels was a kind of ghost city with lots of empty buildings (the so called "city cancers") and neighbourhoods where people would rather not live. In the mid nineties, the first signs of change became visible, a city revival set in. The year before the start of Nova, a coalition of organisations and urban activists occupied an empty block of houses threatened with demolition and speculation. (Hotel Central). Thanks to this action, this kind of problematic captured public attention.

Back to Cinema Nova. From the beginning Nova promoted itself as a real Brussels project that wanted to be "neutral" in the politico-cultural domain. Brussels is officially a bilingual city (French and Dutch-speaking, but in reality there are many more languages spoken, of course!), where culture is a matter of the two official communities: the Flemish and the French communities. Producing culture in Brussels means automatically making a choice for one of the two communities, who each have their own policies. Not making this choice means self-isolation, because neither community will claim you as theirs. Nova refused to make this choice, and this is an element that still influences its position, e.g. financing (mainly subventions, because it's a non-commercial project).

After one year a very positive balance could be drawn. So the project was carried on, after the buildings' owner consented to extend the agreement. Meanwhile the building was sold to another company, with whom the agreement was re-negotiated. A monthly rent was introduced, but an extremely low one, in exchange for a yearly noticeable contract.

Another element, with which Nova was confronted right from the start, is that of voluntary work. As long as Nova was a one-year experiment , no one made a problem of unpayed work. The commitment was logical and the enthusiasm very great. But more important than the voluntary engagement is the non-hierarchical aspect, which is central to the project. The statutory form Nova took was "association sans but lucrative" (the most common form for a non-profit organisation in Belgium), but the "management form" was non-hierarchical. This is still the case: there is no director, no business manager or staff. It's a collective that is open to everyone: today you are in the audience, tomorrow you may be fellow-worker.

This kind of 'flat' structure has its own logic. Other collectives experience nearly the same development processes and dynamics. Whereas in the beginning the non-hierarchical aspect equals lack of structure, during the development of the project it becomes a search for an adequate structure, fitting the functioning that has developed organically and spontaneously; a structure that is open, that able to follow the fluctuation of voluntary involvement and individual motivation; a structure that can easily accept new people and is able to communicate efficiently internally and externally.

Another aspect you see clearly in Nova its eclecticism. Of course it's a cinema, of course there are daily films shown. But there's more. There are concerts, there's sometimes an expo, and a film can provoke a debate... This eclecticism goes well beyond the programme: Nova is a place to meet. Lots of individuals and groups recognize its attitude and commitment, and they see Nova as a crossroads for other creative initiatives in the city. In this sense Nova can be compared with social centres in southern European cities, without this role being formalised or claimed.

At this moment, June 2003, Nova has already survived more than 6 years, thanks to the voluntary involvement of dozens of people who open the cinema, take care of administration, find hidden copies, etc. Cinema Nova can count on a growing recognition in Belgium and outside. The search for an appropriate way of functioning is of course not evident. The structure has to be (re)invented constantly. Who takes decisions? A what meetings? Are the fellow-workers aware of this? How to communicate efficiently? Cinema Nova is a balancing exercise between the informal and the institutional field. Recognition grows, but at the same time lots of questions remain open, partly linked with the future of Brussels as a cultural city.
www.nova-cinema.com

Some Other Initiatives in Brussels are:

PTTL
PTTL or Plus Tôt Te Laat is a collective of artists and unemployed people, what works out of the unemployment office of Sint-Joost-ten-Noode (Brussels). Not interested in hierarchic structures, these bilingual activists organise art interventions in public spaces, such as this local dole office, since 1998. Not supplying information passively to the inhabitants, but pretty much involved in questioning the social field from a cultural prospective, they are active in participation side of neighbourhood contracts, where they struggle for real participation (for example via the video medium).
pttl@netcourrier.com

Universal Embassy
A network of people active in the struggle for the rights of homeless and immigrants started the Universal Embassy. It wants to transgress different domains and bring together citizens attracted by the idea of universality. They opened an abandoned embassy where people without papers can live on their own and function autonomously.
http://www.universal-embassy.be

Vox
Vox is a "media activist" collective formed around a common interest: video. The aim is to make videos with "another view on society". Contrary to traditional media, where information passes via several "intermediate stages" operating as filters, Vox wants to give direct access to audio-visual tools to individuals and groups. Vox is a collective that exists in meetings that take place every first and third Wednesday of the month. These meetings are open for everyone.
www.vox-video.be

Housing action next to the European Parliament

Inner garden

Albert desperatly building a house himself

Unemployment office at St-Josse

Les Bains::Connective
Les Bains::Connective is an 800 m² laboratory for creative activity. Home to long-term residencies in the fields of music, dance, visual arts and botany, it also welcomes short-term and one-off proposals by individuals or groups keen to participate and invest in the life of the Connective. They are established in the former Forest public baths. The building is a project in itself, an architectural experiment in renovation and rehabilitation. It is a social and cultural meeting place, where visitors and members of the local community and the wider public are encouraged to become involved, to "connect". This approach is based on the principles of inclusion and participation.
www.bains.be

Collectief Sans Ticket
The "Collective without Ticket" in Brussels is a network of users of public transport that united by the will of making this public service an instrument of collective emancipation, recomposition of ways of living territories, and provoking a real bottom-up process. They intervene in public spaces and they practise civil disobedience as well as research and debates.
http://cst.collectifs.net

43°
No. 43 rue des Chartreux, a building located in the centre of Brussels, had been empty for quite a long time. In November 2000 some organisations approached the building's owners, who were quick to show interest in the proposal. Finally, a rental agreement was concluded for a period of two years. The building was baptised No. 43 and the occupiers (consisting of small scale organization ranging from architects and comic strip artists to hip hop initiatives) assumed responsibility for its renovation. The common meeting room is used not only by the organisations which have taken up space in the building but by many outside organisations as well. The programme includes all kinds of activities, but mostly meetings, conferences, concerts and exhibitions.
http://www.citymined.org/article.php3?id_article=7

City Mine(d)
City-Mine(d) is a production room for social-artistic projects that stimulate the liveability of the city. Established in 1997, their objective is to support, initiate and/or produce projects of a socio-cultural nature, mainly in open public spaces in areas and neighbourhoods characterised by problems typical of a large city, such as poverty, exclusion, weak identity, etc. The organisational structure is flexible, network-oriented, rhizomatic and the activities are temporary.
www.citymined.org

BruXXel
BruXXel was a temporary combination of interests and ideas for Belgium's presidency of the EC (2001). By bringing together lots of different people, and occupying the empty train station "Gare de Léopold", situated next to the European Parliament for 4 months, the initiative BruXXel was present in an active, artistic way in Brussels, and more precisely in the European neighbourhood in Ixelles (Brussels). The station was a symbol of the speculation problem in this neighbourhood, which lots of residents have been forced to leave. At the same time, BruXXel was active in the so-called other-globalisation movement, organising different kinds of meetings and debates all around Europe, and participating in the street-party during the Summit of Laken (December 2001).

Manu and Bernard installing a crashing-down-dishes-machine at the unemployment office

Go-kart race at the Palais de Justice

Cycling action in front of the Stock-market

TEXT..Tristan Wibault

The Universal Embassy

The Universal Embassy settled in the deserted building of the former Somali Embassy. The Universal Embassy brings together individuals conscious of the discrimination produced by the national identification. The Embassy is an emergency housing, a meeting place, a representation... for undocumented people fighting for regularisation. The Universal Embassy aims at mutual aid and, consequently, autonomy !

june 2003 **special edition**

PAPIER

Logbook - Universal Embassy - Bruxelles

We settled here in 2001. At that time, the place was unhealthy and unliveable. There was no water, no electricity. The rooms were full of rubbish, dirt and dust. We had to fix and clean everything. We have worked together to make this place liveable. We receive food from the food bank once every month, and nowadays we even have a vegetable garden. Even though I'm unemployed, I don't want to work illegally, because it is too risky. I eat everyday, sometimes with friends, sometimes thanks to the food bank and sometimes I receive a little bit of money. That is the way we live our lives.

Joseph

When I get papers, I wanna be a star! Albertino

The people who get caught by the police are those who are going to encounter the police. When you do something wrong, you take the risk of encountering the police. Me, I am doing nothing wrong. I'm not stealing. I don't go inside shopping malls. If I don't have any money, I do not enter a shopping mall. I don't want to be noticed. I give you an example: once a friend told me to meet him inside a shopping mall. For a few minutes I waited for him inside. But he did not show up, so I took the bus and left the place, because I didn't want the police to notice me.

Abdelwahab

If the law permits anybody to take residence in the community of their choice, then the community loses an integral relation with its inhabitants. If the right to oppose the residence of undesirable members doesn't exist anymore, one cannot anymore ask the community that to ensure a fair relation between individuals. This, for Georg Simmel, is the reason why the state took charge of the poor. This problem is now taking place on a planetary scale.

Migrants without protocols, 'the undocumented' are moved by the evidence of the right to have rights. Their movement's autonomy calls for a new relation between the individual subjet to the law and the productive subject. Today, supernumeraries of the biopower, they live transnationally, reinventing diasporas without original breakdowns and forming multiple solidarities and exploitations networks where generations, settlement and transit mix.

DECLARATION OF THE UNIVERSAL EMBASSY

12 December 2001 - extracts

The 'person without papers' is a pariah, s/he has nowhere to feel at home. S/he reveals clearly the inanity of our conception of citizenship, where the roads of inclusion cross those of exclusion. The users of this passage are creating a common world. Universal Embassy intends to trace the political expression of this common world.

Globalisation jostles the scales. Historically, rights have been linked to nationality, and nationality to a territory. Nation expresses a community of destiny. The community to come is planetary. Territory, borders are the prerogatives of police. Repression is the only political potentiality to realize itself. An undercurrent runs through our world, it is technical, financial, ideological. The everyday life of the human myriad is subverted. Work, housing, food, displacements, time... have changed their dimensions.

The local is the global on a small scale. Paradoxically, a possible political expression germinates in the local. This is the inhabited space. Cities are perpetually recomposing themselves, they are evolving into an inter community without majority group origin. Urban diversity is a world to live. Political reclaiming of living space is a constitution of the self and of the collectivity. Citizenship is not the establishment of rules independent of practices made by participation. This practice means searching for the common within diversity. It situates itself before governorship.

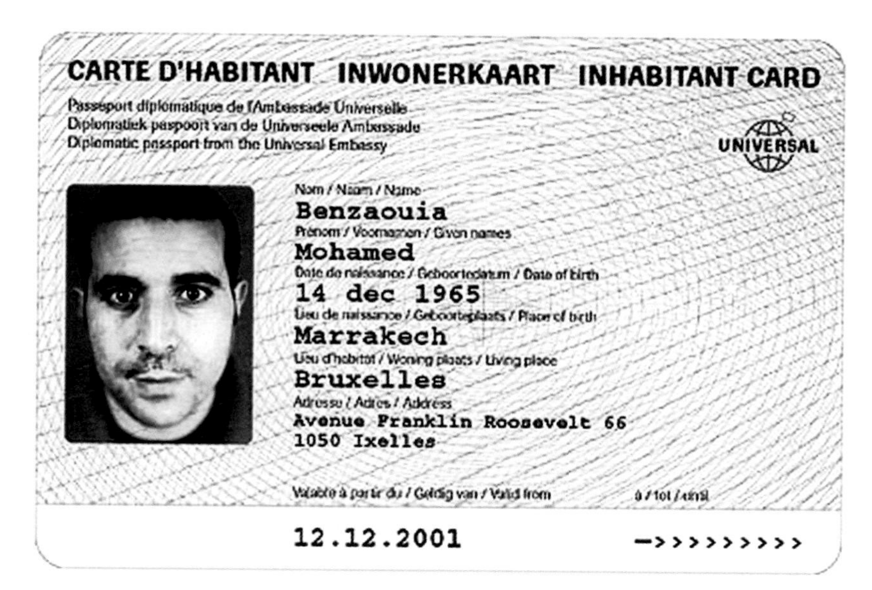
CARTE D'HABITANT INWONERKAART INHABITANT CARD
Passeport diplomatique de l'Ambassade Universelle
Diplomatiek paspoort van de Universeele Ambassade
Diplomatic passport from the Universal Embassy
UNIVERSAL
Nom / Naam / Name
Benzaouia
Prénom / Voornamen / Given names
Mohamed
Date de naissance / Geboortedatum / Date of birth
14 dec 1965
Lieu de naissance / Geboorteplaats / Place of birth
Marrakech
Lieu d'habitat / Woning plaats / Living place
Bruxelles
Adresse / Adres / Address
Avenue Franklin Roosevelt 66
1050 Ixelles
Valable à partir du / Geldig van / Valid from
à / tot / until
12.12.2001
->>>>>>>>>

passport of the Universal Embassy

This passport is delivered to the inhabitants and the *sans papier* who come regularly to the Embassy. This is a document of adhesion to the principles of the Universal Embassy. Then the 'undocumented' develop its use.

The postmen are satisfied with this document as a proof of identity.When Rashid decided to visit a cousin in Germany, he left with a copy of the registration of his file in the Ministery, and a copy of his Universal passport. In case of control, he wanted to have something to talk about.

Once in the Embassy, we met a lot of people we didn't know before. I've lived in the Universal Embassy for two years now. I have learned a lot of things here, because some activities are being organised: French language courses, English language courses, cultural exchanges between inhabitants and the visitors, parties. I don't want to forget the students of the university that try to be on our side when it gets difficult. Also, I will bear in mind the people who come from abroad to meet us and share our sufferings, or to work on the problems that immigrants are encountering. It is important that we all support each other and work together to achieve the same goals, because if we lose each other's confidence, we'll lose everything.

Youssef

Thanks to the work of the inhabitants and the volunteers, the place we occupied became the Universal Embassy and didn't stop welcoming people without official documents. Everybody can come here and help the inhabitants and we want to be able to share what we have. We multiply acquaintances to break the solitude. The people who come to talk and listen are moral supports. Today the Universal Embassy is well-known. It is represented in discussions, debates, and there is even a website. But it has to continue to grow through the inhabitants. Everyone has to appreciate the value of this building, what it is and what it represents, and take care of a place that is much more than a place to sleep.

Joseph

I will never forget the 31st of November 2002, the day when the police invaded our house, at 7 am, during the Ramadan month. This day will leave a scar in my heart because it frankly showed me the real face of the Belgian democracy. The police handcuffed us and numbered us from 1 to 14. We then had to remain kneeling for about three hours. Why all this? Nobody knows. Since that day, no one in the Embassy feels safe. Even the children are traumatised. When the local policeman comes to inform us about something, the kids are really afraid. Everybody is frightened. Fear has become our shadow, it moves with us, wherever we go. Personally, I had never been so afraid before.

Youssef

Nevertheless, I feel happy that a place like the Embassy exists because it gives the opportunity to pass on important information, to organise ourselves and to exchange our experiences. The unity of the inhabitants seems to me essential to move forward. As long as there is unity, we'll be able to carry on. We have to be aware that every individual act of the inhabitants can have repercussions for all the others. We hope that the future inhabitants will not let the project fall apart. We have to hold on. Also, it is important that in case our personal situation improves, we continue to involve ourselves in the project to make our experience useful to others.

Betty

The Embassy

It is true that we have often worked in a state of emergency, but when looking at the outcome, you see it was worth while. In the first place, we have maintained ourselves throughout time (nearly two and a half years) and we have succeeded to build up solidarity between us. What is more the Embassy has given a meaning to our lives that were at different levels broken by the constraints of our clandestine and precarious circumstances. Even if the Universal Embassy is not as visible as the occupation of the church in 1998, it is still a signal which calls out beyond the absurd question of 'papers'. It asks fundamental questions about universal projects, even if it seems utopian.

Mohamed

Justice and human rights, they don't exist, or at least, I don't believe in them anymore. Some people are being arrested with dozens of kilos of heroin or cocaine and they go to jail for only two months, but we, the "sans-papiers", we are being imprisoned for months, or even years. We are being treated like dogs. During the police raid, when we had to sit on our knees for three hours, handcuffed, guns pointed at us, a police officer told me: "Marc Dutroux will fuck your kid"

Moumou

TO BE WAKEN UP BY THE POLICE

The Embassy constitutes itself in an evolving process. It works on the basis of meetings and exchanges to define its own universality. It rearticulates the symbols of the state and the missions of an embassy far from the idea of a fixed constitution. Each manifestation of representation is a new materialisation of the process. The void of the "sans-papiers" becomes the motor to interrogate the weight of the history of our conception of citizenship.

Tarik, two weeks before he gets his papers

I'm addressing myself at the judicial institutions and to the judges. We aren't animals; we are human beings, like the judges who condemned me. All I have done, I did for my son and to be able to feed my family. At present, it is 13 years that I live without papers and I am suffering because I want them to give me back my son. Do you think it is fair to separate a child from his father, to wilfully deport him far away from his son? What laws tolerate that? I want my papers and a right of residency to be able to retrieve my son and to have a quiet and normal life. I want to work. I am not a public danger.

Moumou

While these identities are naked on the face of nationality, they can become a place of recomposed universality on reaching the crossroads. The Universal Embassy attempts to move forward in this passage: from a naked identity to a universal identity to be constituted. To go beyond the negative affirmation and sow the seeds of constituent desire. To leave the obligatory state mediation in order to bring back a direct drive for a transnational law. Like any Embassy, it is a representation, but without a state being represented. The represented is to come. Its inhabitants, the undocumented, the new pariahs of the free world, are contesting by their acts a citizenship consanguineous to nation. By interfering in the outlines of state representations, the Embassy is locally abolishing the border limit. Its inhabitants are the ones already there, locally present in the world.

Universal Embassy
66 av. Franklin Roosevelt-1050 Brussels
email: info@universal-embassy.be
www.universal-embassy.be

Two years ago, I spent two months in the centre for illegal immigrants of Vottem (near Liège) and recently I spent one month in the prison of Saint-Gilles, here in Brussels. And always for the same reason: attempts to expel me. In my opinion, the prisoners who are in jail live in better conditions than the foreigners who are living in the centres for illegal immigrants.
The objective of the raid was to destroy the Universal Embassy, because there are people without papers who are organizing themselves; people without papers who are talking, telling about their sorrows, telling what is happening to them in their daily lives. The objective was to destroy that voice.
After we all had been interrogated and our fingerprints had been taken, most of the inhabitants were released with an order to leave the territory within five days. Three people have been detained, and I was one of them. They told me that I had already received four orders to leave the territory before and that I was still there. I was detained for one month in the prison of Saint-Gilles before being released on the 1st of January 2003, and of course not without receiving my fifth order to leave the territory within five days.

Albertino

Abdelwahab on the 1st of May 2003

Center for illegals of Vottem

Trying to see someone

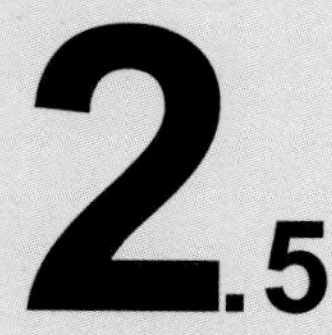

TEXT ....Myriam Stoffen
PHOTOS ....PTTL-archives

The Zinneke Parade - An Artistic Citizens' Parade?

As an artistic and social experiment, the Zinneke Parade claims that art and creation cannot be left behind closed doors. The parade presents itself both as an expression of and an experiment in living together in diversity in the city of Brussels, formulating an artistic language that fits in seamlessly with current urban cosmopolitan development.[1] The following is a brief outline of the main issues of the project.

1.The Birth of a Brussels Popular Event - Bruxelles/Brussel 2000

The story of the Zinneke Parade starts during the preparations for the programme of 'Brussels, European Cultural City', in 2000. Various ideas emerged about having some kind of Brussels street festival created for and by the citizens. Each of the cultural projects proposed shared the desire for a widespread, active participation of residents in close collaboration with artists. Three proposals were put forward in 1997: the creation of a Brussels carnival (Brussels does not have its own carnival); a project called "Bridges for the Pentagon" (an artistic, architectural project aiming to link the city centre -which is pentagonal- to the 19th-century belt around it through the construction of five symbolic bridges); and an idea to set up cultural 'development poles' in the various neighbourhoods of Brussels. What these different projects shared was the desire to break down the multiple boundaries that mark our western society and the city of Brussels in particular. It was considered paramount that the resulting event should celebrate the cultural diversity of Brussels and be constructed across linguistic, social, economic, political, ideological, educational, geographic... divides. Several brainstorming sessions ensued, in which, for instance, local and international experts in street art shed light on the project.

The term "Parade" emerged at some point, considered to be a better alternative for 'carnival'. There was a clear desire to distance the event from any form of carnival-like folklore that only puts forward one or more cultural origins. Instead, the organisers looked for a more dynamic, fluid mode of expression intended to embody the aspects of evolution and hybridity in identity. The most powerful and coherent name for the event suggested was "Zinneke", the nickname for a resident of Brussels, referring to the Zenne, the Brussels river that is covered nowadays, but in which mongrel dogs, not very pure in origin and also called "Zinnekes", were often drowned.
The basic philosophy behind the Zinneke Parade was to realise a 'collective creation', a huge artistic walking extravaganza with citizens, artists and partners from all walks of life sharing the same ambitious goals and willing to do this in a spirit of close co-operation across traditional divides. Throughout the process, the active participation of residents of the different (often dubbed "difficult") areas of Brussels was crucial, as well as the collaboration with artists from different disciplinary backgrounds. Local actors of all kinds (social, cultural, educational, whether or not organised or institutionalised) were asked to climb on board and to involve themselves wholeheartedly in the creation of a contemporary urban event. After all, the ambition was also to merge fragmented initiatives and consequently create synergies through a common project. The Parade was meant to show and celebrate the hybrid identity of Brussels in a resounding manner while aspiring to express a recognisable artistic unity at the same time.

In order to be faithful to the love for the city that the project radiates, it was also crucial that the parade not contribute to those phenomena considered a blight on the city, air pollution and noise in particular. This resulted into two deliberate restrictions: no combustion engines and no electric amplification. This meant that all exhibits in the Parade should be pushed, carried, or pulled and that the music should be acoustic, a cappella or amplified in a natural, creative way. In keeping with the philosophy behind the project, preference was given to collective group work rather than to individual performances so as to place the force and symbolic power of gathered human energy firmly in the spotlight. In order not to "affect the creative potential of the citizens of Brussels", no uniformity was required in the way the hundreds of Zinneke projects would take shape; "artistic multiplicity would determine the unity and quality of the Parade".[2]
The structure of the Zinneke Parade was inspired by the same principles: artists and producers were selected in five areas of Brussels, in which projects would be set up through a close collaboration between residents, organisations and artists. These five so-called 'development zones' (later on called 'Zinnopoles') functioned at the same time as starting points for the five parade sections which joined each other on the central boulevards of the city on Z-day.

Once the philosophy, the basic principles, the methodology and the organisation were clear, the project of the Zinneke Parade could go into its preparatory phase. This period was crucial: residents of Brussels and elsewhere were to be given the possibility to collaborate with other residents, associations, organisations and artists in order to contribute to the event that would be the Zinneke Parade. For months and months in the years of 1999 and 2000, thousands of people invested an innumerable amount of time and energy into sharing emotions, fantasies, fears and dreams with people they had never met before. Furthermore, what happened during the creation phase of the Parade in the different neighbourhoods was miles removed from the traditional model of "The association works with its own members or target group, on its own premises and with its own means".

The first Parade, in 2000, was based on the theme of the city in all its aspects: the rebirth of the city, the re-claiming of the city, the re-emergence of a sense of unity within the city, the connections between neighbourhoods through old and new networks, the city's cultural diversity... In May of that year, more than 4,000 participants from all over Brussels and beyond (Belgium or abroad) seized the central boulevards of the city. About two hundred associations and organisations and more than one hundred artists organised and assisted numerous workshops in all possible disciplines (choreography, dance, music, theatre, circus, dressmaking, construction, etc.). Beyond all expectations, the public showed up in massive numbers in the boroughs as well as the city centre to watch and participate in the spectacle.[3]

A dangerous street-barbeque

And forbidden too

2.Zinneke Parade, Take Two

The Zinneke Parade injected a breath of fresh air into Brussels. For many people who had assisted or participated in the Parade, the event could not remain a flash in the pan. One could say that the parade had held up "a mirror, in which the reflection was globally positive".[4] The question of the project's autonomy, which had already arisen during the period of the project's conceptualisation, needed to be addressed. A feasibility study was carried out at the beginning of 2001. A decision by the Brussels Regional government (department of neighbourhood revitalisation) to invest both in terms of financial and human support allowed the project to continue under its own steam towards a new Parade in 2002. During the preparatory phase of the second edition, a co-ordinating network for the local partners in the five Zinnopoles was further developed in order to guarantee the sustainability and local embedding of the project.

In May 2001, the second edition of the Zinneke parade was given the green light. The majority of associations, organisations and institutions of all kinds that had collaborated for the first edition was willing to invest in a second one. Some decided not to continue (whether or not temporarily) if the organisational, financial and time requirements seemed to outweigh the benefits. New participants showed up. Once again artistic projects started taking shape in different parts of the Brussels district (mostly in the less privileged areas) and other places in the country or abroad. Workshops were inspired by the theme of "Zinnergy", thus focussing on "synergies, on flows of energy that meet and enrich one another, on the realisation of joint projects, on diversity".[5] A year later, despite all expectations and restricted means, even more participants showed up on the boulevards (more than 4,300).

Nowadays, the Zinneke Parade is a biennial event, aspiring to be a contemporary, urban, hybrid, artistic parade. As such, it is only the cherry on the cake, the result of a process in which contemporary artistic endeavour goes hand in hand with local creativity. Zinneke seems to have become indelibly woven into the Brussels landscape and might soon face the difficult challenge of contributing to the creation of a new cultural, urban and popular space.

3.Eulogy for Brussels' Lunacy? Culture in Action

In a nutshell, the Zinneke Parade is (1) an artistic event, (2) built by the residents of the different neighbourhoods of Brussels, (3) in co-operation with a local network of associations, organisations and schools, (4) through an intensive process of encounter, collaboration and creation with artists, (5) resulting in a parade in the public space.

The formula of such a project seems to appeal to an actually existing need in urban environments where rituals have disappeared. The Parade 'citoyenne' might be the contemporary emergence of a new ritual. By means of a few key words, we would like to try to grasp the phenomenon and sense its limits and possibilities.

(1) An urban project
It is no coincidence that cosmopolitan Brussels is the place where the Zinneke Parade was born. The city combines tremendous cultural diversity with important vocational and occupational diversity.

The *cultural diversity* of the neighbourhoods of Brussels is, on the one hand, the result of the different and ongoing migration waves that sway to the rhythm of economic, social, political developments, both on a national and international level. On the other hand, it is a feature of every metropolis that its inhabitants maintain a relatively high degree of mobility. The final result is an extremely mixed urban population that does not live in homogeneous ethnic areas (or ghettos).[6]

It is exactly this variety, also on the neighbourhood level, that feeds, changes and time and again renders the existing diversity of the city more complex. In everyday life, this reveals itself in a great diversity of values, attitudes, fantasies, perceptions and interpretations, expressions, (symbolic) sense making, languages and behaviours, in social groups as well as in individuals. In everyday Brussels life, this means that cultural heterogeneity has become the norm. For a district like the Brussels Region, squeezed in a political straightjacket imposed by the two important language communities of the country, this remains an extremely ambivalent situation which leaves little room for an integrated and coherent urban policy.

The *vocational and occupational diversity* of Brussels should not go unnoticed either. Brussels boasts numerous political and administrative institutions as well as companies within its borders, amongst which a large number of international organisations. Not all these institutions or corporations are endowed with a thorough sense of the multifunctionality and the dynamics of the urban environment they settle in.

Traditional economic and political strategic arguments, however limited, often decide the choice of location and manner of establishment in the city. Speculation is rife. It is obvious that this situation has far-reaching consequences for social and urban development, and therefore also for the social cohesion and sense of dynamics in numerous areas, especially in those neighbourhoods where descend diagnoses and dynamic development projects are few and far between.
The city as a political and economic centre also generates a daily stream of commuters to and from the office, which constitutes another type of mobility. To this day, Brussels' streets and avenues are still dominated by cars and leave scant space for cyclists and pedestrians. The public transport system is without doubt far from visionary, whatever it purports to be.

Furthermore, residents and visitors (work, leisure, tourism) use the city in different ways. This complex tension between inhabitants, workers and passers-by, each with different interests and desires, lies at the heart of the enormous diversity in the way the city is perceived and given shape.

These, and numerous other aspects that are typical for a metropolis and for Brussels in particular, are often an important breeding ground for conflict, resistance, and subsequent quests for alternative, more coherent ways of imagining living together in the city. It is not surprising that more and more cultural actors develop initiatives that raise precisely these ambivalent issues by addressing the numerous divides and by launching projects that build bridges across the existing institutional boundaries.

If we take the cohesion between the different dimensions of this cultural, functional and occupational diversity for granted, no part of the urban reality as such falls outside the interest of this new vanguard of, what might be called, cultural activists. The Zinneke Parade should be seen as a staging of this diversity in Brussels and of the contradictions it brings along in everyday life. Through the preparatory process and the final parade, the urban quality of life is addressed from an angle other than that of social poverty or safety. Moreover, the parade is a moment of public expression that allows each of the participants to encounter, show and exchange artistically encoded messages with an audience that is not necessarily familiar with the metropolis, powerful messages that show the force and quality *of la différence*.

(2) Power to the imagination
Inhabitants of the different boroughs and neighbourhoods are invited to claim the right to express their own creative individuality and sense-making in a language comprehensible to everyone during the preparatory phase of the Zinneke Parade, which starts one year before the actual event. Individuals, groups, organisations, artists show up with ideas inspired by the global theme. These ideas are then locally gathered, discussed, transformed and joined with other projects through the artistic co-ordinators and finally result in a project which forms an artistic unity called 'Zinnode'. Numerous workshops are set up to give shape to the entire range of imaginative projects. As such, "the Zinneke Parade appeals to all artistic disciplines and crafts, so that everyone, whatever their origin, knowledge or skill, finds a place to suit their ambitions".[7]
In places where many of the participants perceive to have only a limited understanding of and control over their everyday environment, the Parade seeks ways to question and unsettle the dominant relations of power and sense-making. This is done on the basis of an exchange that is not meaningful in terms of traditional trade relations. In other words, the Parade tries to give meaning through cultural action and participation rather than through consumption and labour.

Enabling residents to participate

Different kinds of camerawork for the parade

Looking for identities

The desire for a collective imagination is also fuelled by the realisation that the different cultural forms of expression and life-styles are not equally visible and documented in our society. To the degree that culture can be considered to be the space of meanings, values and symbolic structures, whether or not shared, it is likewise the space of social structuration and thus bearer of societal differentiation - read inequalities. We might wonder which differences in the participation and expression of each human being in all aspects of (public) life are considered to be acceptable. When do these differences reflect inequality, exclusion, oppression, injustice ? It is s a big topic, but questioning the limits of it means as much as questioning the limits of our democracy.

'Giving a voice' to cultural minorities often means that people are addressed in terms of their traditions, rather than for their actual and contemporary reference schemes. This adds up to a problematic reduction in the complexity with which identity is approached (of individuals, groups, places). In the Zinneke Parade, one of the issues raised is to what degree tradition can hinder openness towards the unknown and the foreigner, and to what extent it can form a basis for new exchanges and confrontations. Through the process of encounter and creation, the Zinnekes explore this notion of diversity and *métissage* far removed from a folkloristic notion of tradition.

As has been mentioned before, an important role in the Zinneke Parade is put aside for artists who can stir and channel the imaginative powers of Brussels' residents. Some consider them to be plumbers working with the social tissue, vital for our society. The commitment of the artists working in the Parade cannot be reduced to simple artistic terms. Their involvement is crucial when it comes to the exchange of knowledge and skills, research into new creations (whether or not through traditions), often resulting in works of art with an enormous cultural potential. These artists guarantee the translation of the participants' creativity into artistic forms and modes of expression, which is surprising and constant. How meet each other and create together is one of the common challenges the artists collaborating on the project need to address.

(3) A Parade by virtue of co-operation and encounter
The Parade is a 'collective creation'. The Parade offers a free zone for collaborations and encounters that might otherwise not take place. Participating inhabitants, associations, centres, schools and artists start to generate new urban networks in their own modest way. Amateurs, professionals, generations, social groups, areas, nationalities, etc... meet. As such, Zinneke wants to stem the tide of hate or exclusion on the basis of identity, contribute to the fight against racism and counteract community disputes as they arise in Belgium and in Brussels in particular.

However, collaboration does not mean avoiding conflict. The idea is to consider conflicts as quintessential for a confrontation between different opinions, values, perceptions, interpretation schemes and habits. From this point of view, confrontations and conflicts become portals that allow us to question ourselves, our references, and our society in a critical manner. These kind of experimental juxtapositions should help us to deepen our ideas.

(4) The neighbourhood as a space for lived-in diversity
One of the questions raised is how people can live together within such great diversity. Living together, sharing the same space, is not possible without common references. But that which is considered 'common' cannot be described in terms of a homogenous cultural identity that should appropriated (the classic integration model, or assimilation model), nor should one isolate one self within one's own traditions. If Zinneke stands for *métissage*, the concept of cultural heterogeneity cannot be translated into a succession of carefully delineated cultural identities or particularities. On the contrary, each individual is the bearer of a complex, hybrid history and develops an identity in constant flux through his or her social practices. Every identity is, as a consequence, condemned to an unavoidable hybridisation.

This means that interaction and exchange are important in order to explore common references (and thus differences as well). The place where people live is probably an important basis for this exchange. This place can be a concrete site, a neighbourhood for instance, as well as a symbolic or imaginary space, not limited to an actual physical space, where interests, desires, ideas are shared. During the preparatory phase of the Parade, numerous shared places are created in which exchanges and conflicts occur. On the day of the Parade, the city centre and the areas in the Zinnopoles become partially shared (mental) spaces.
The local context is therefore of great importance in places where meaning is created through collective projects, places/spaces which are concrete but at the same time symbolic.

(5) The conquest of the public space
The Parade offers an opportunity for the resident to reclaim the city. During repetitions and on Z-day neighbours, spectators, participants and their creations are on the streets, seizing the public space. The urban space, thus physically re-appropriated, becomes the space of encounter (mental appropriation). The public performance as well as the artistic language of a parade allows the participants to return the event-as-a-common-experience to the other residents of the city.
Interesting questions that are related to the use of the public space as a space for free expression arise: What is tolerated? Is there a legal tendency to safeguard public areas more and more? The Zinneke Parade makes a case for an open space...

4. End Note

The most important challenge for projects such as the Zinneke Parade is probably to avoid becoming a mere folkloristic event. If the project loses the essence of its combativeness and drifts away from its experimental nature as a human, urban, artistic laboratory, Brussels will lose an emerging popular contemporary ritual. The Parade should not evolve into another city attraction. This means that development of the project should be continued along each of the axes mentioned above. And there is still a long way to go. Numerous areas of tension remain, for instance between socio-cultural workers and artists (whose ideas on mediation and creation are not always compatible), or on the policy level, which still suffers from fragmentation and segmentation, especially in matters of culture and urban development. Numerous questions are still insufficiently addressed: which diversity is represented and which is not? what kind of artistic expression and artistic practice is favoured ? what is a so-called social artist? what part of everyday urban life is documented? how is tradition mediated ? do we truly succeed in transversal action? which urban utopia does each of us stand for? do networks really create new social cohesion? how do the projects integrate and cope with confrontation and conflict? what kind of local embedding is preferable? does a thing like an open, evolving, common identity through diversity truly exist? These are just some of the interesting reflections a project like this generates.

Therefore, to be continued ...

Endnotes

[1] It goes without saying that this Parade is not an isolated case : in France, Ireland, Luxembourg, Germany and the UK similar manifestations have seen the light, even though each of them has its own particularities.

[2] First Charter of the Zinneke Parade, Brussels, 1999.

[3] Official figures released mentioned 300,000 spectators - a figure which is difficult to verify, but is probably a bit of an overestimation. All of this confirms the unexpected success of and enthusiasm for the event.

[4] D'Haeyer A. (2000) "Un bel exemple de parade citoyenne - A bout portant." In *Le Soir*, 19 December 2000. Interview with Michel Crespin, urban régisseur and founding director of the Centre national de creations des arts de la rue in Marseille.

[5] MagaZinneke, 5, May 2002, p. 11.

[6] See "Brussels: from a multicultural and fragmented city towards the Mediterranean Capital of Europe ?"

[7] MagaZinneke, 5, May 2002, p. 11.
Draft - Zinneke Parade, artistieke Parade citoyenne - maart 2003 - p. 9

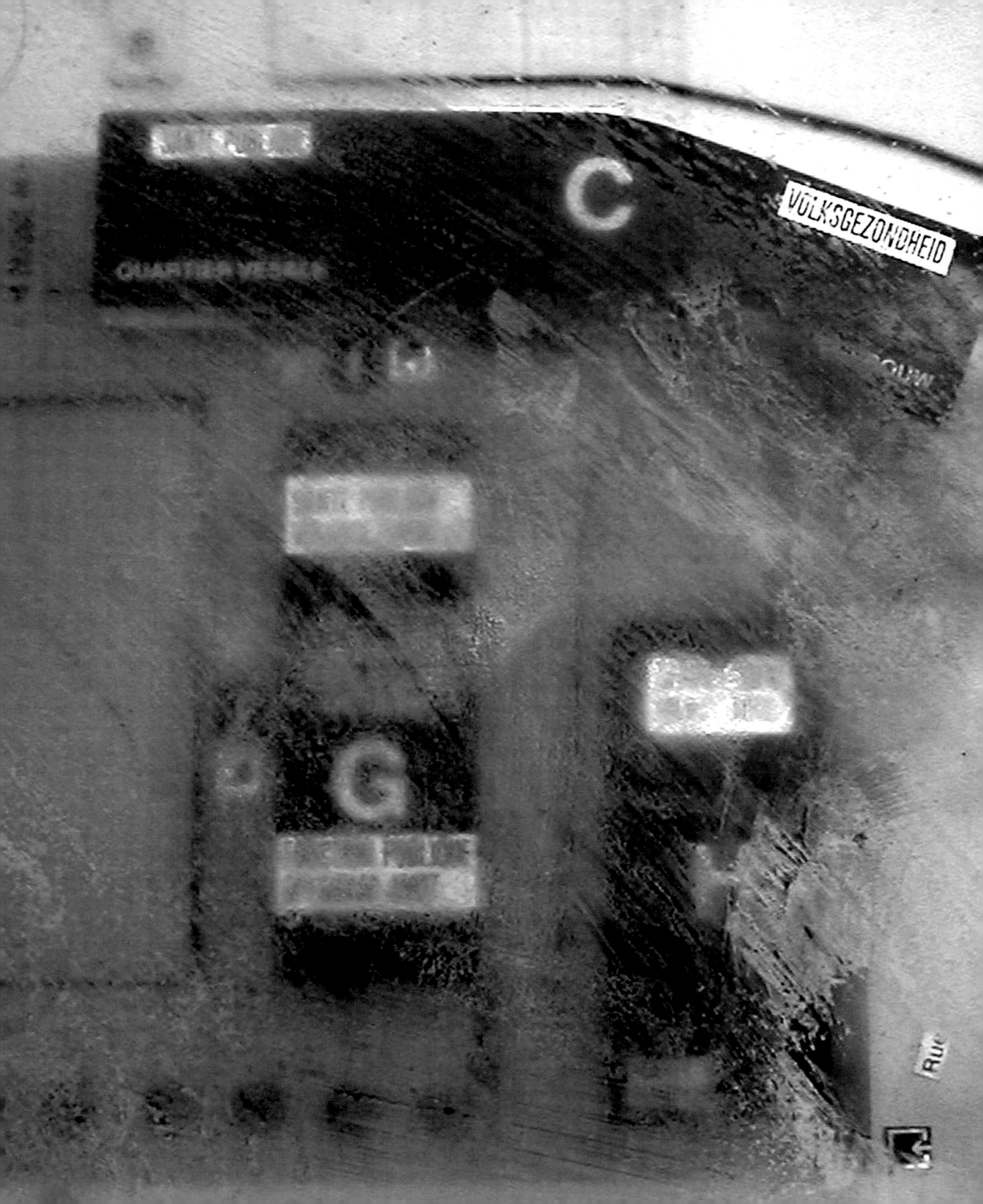
VOLKSGEZONDHEID

Firenze Insurgent City

Photo sequence in front pages of this chapter by ogi:no knauss

3.1

TEXT..............Giancarlo Paba
TRANSLATION..............Syd Migx, Kate Shaw
PHOTOS..............Ogino knauss

Contested Places: Stories and Geographies from Another Florence

With its population made up of two categories of people, those who do business and those upon whom they prey, the city has only a painful life to offer the young person who goes there to learn and study; for sooner or later anyone who lives there, whatever his constitution, becomes disturbed and is eventually deranged and destroyed by the city, often in the most deadly and insidious manner. The extreme weather conditions have an unfailingly irritating, enervating, and sickening effect on the inhabitants, an effect which is compounded by the devastating influence of the [...] architecture. Anyone who is familiar with the city knows it to be a cemetery of fantasy and desire, beautiful on the surface but horrifying underneath. Whoever goes there to learn and to study [...] soon discovers that this city, renowned the world over for beauty and edification [...] is in truth nothing but a chill museum of death, open to every kind of disease and depravity [...]. What was at first a place of natural beauty and matchless architecture soon becomes a vile and impenetrable jungle of human viciousness, and when he goes through the streets they are no longer filled with [architecture] but with the moral filth of those who people them.
Thomas Bernhard, *Gathering Evidence: A Memoir*, Vintage, London, 2003, pp. 77-79.

This invective by Thomas Bernhard quoted in the opening remarks was aimed at Salzburg. It would need very few corrections to make it fit Florence. Florence also could be defined as “a squalid device for making money and yet more money out of the exploitation of beauty”. For many of its inhabitants, both newcomers and long-time residents, it generates material suffering and conflict. The deadly atmosphere – an unholy communion of environmental devastation and horrible climate – renders the place noxious. The contrast between downtown and suburbia shows the device to be lying and double-faced; the dominance exerted by commerce and money makes it cynical and cruel; the exploitation of ancient culture, and the crisis of contemporary culture makes it sterile and dull; mental and material avarice make it, more often than not, hostile and unwelcoming.

As in Bernhard's Salzburg, the Florentine public scene reflects the physical and environmental decay of the city: indifferent governance, sheriffs and enforcers, barkers and couturiers, film directors and fat, ‘has-been’ former ‘alternative singers’, sclerotic theatres, farces that recycle TV shows. All these contribute to producing a fossilized cultural environment, where there is no place for courage to experiment or critical discrimination. The perverse ‘beauty machine’ of Florence, the ‘cold museum of death’, is represented in the city's maps and guides. Inflated in images and stories, it offers ‘rooms with a view’ with conventional, banal sights; a terminal flood (but a desert of meaning) of Florence to the world.
Our research goes beyond this aspect of the city's arts and cultural trade to address the reconstruction of another geography of Florence: an interstitial, hidden, fluid, mutating, active, dense, creative counter-geography of a different Florence, a budding, emergent city inside of and counter to the existing city.

We often define Florence as an insurgent city. Some explanation of the meaning of this expression is necessary, and of the term ‘insurgent’ in general. A few years ago, James Holston (Holston 1999) designated as "spaces of insurgent citizenship" those areas subordinated to the planned, modern domination of the city. According to Holston, these "include the territories of the homeless, the networks of migrants, the neighbourhoods of gay communities, the self-built suburbias ..., ganglands, fortified condos, places of self-production, squatters' settlements, the suburban encampments of foreigners, sweatshops and the so-called areas of new racism" (Holston 1999, p. 167). Holston considers insurgent all spaces in which there are practices "disturbing the modern city's established history". For our purposes this overstretches the term, lumping together as it does places of creative opposition with new exploitation and decay. Closer to our perspective is the terms used by Leonie Sandercock in a recent issue of the magazine *Plurimondi*, edited by her (Sandercock 1999). Sandercock defines “insurgent planning practices” as initiatives of planning and resistance opposing the existing city (its organisational and power structure) and building the first positive devices of an alternative, different city. Friedmann links these initiatives to the dynamics of expanding citizenship, to a progressive widening of democratic spaces (Friedmann 1999). New citizenships create a fecund, pluralistic context, a bona fide multipli/city, in which concrete, achievable forms of utopia become feasible and lay the ground for humans to achieve their full potential.

The term insurgent has older resonances, in particular in the thought of the early nineteenth century Scottish planner Patrick Geddes, and in the derivation of the concept in the writings of Lewis Mumford. In Geddes it is possible to find a sort of insurgent urbanism: an idea of city transformation capable of setting "the forward movement of life" in motion, "its insurgence and its expectancy". "Insurgence", Mumford wrote, is in fact "the ability to overcome, through power or cunning, through plan or dream, the forces threatening the organism" (Mumford 1959, p. 83). Both individual and collective insurgent practices are biological and existential before being political; to us they are the basic exercise of the right to live and the right to the city on the part of its poorest and most deprived inhabitants. Insurgence, in this Geddesian-Mumfordian sense, is the very movement of bodies within the city, of the organisms that yearn for survival and hope for the future. Molecular movements: the trajectories of bodies in the city's public scene, in pursuit of life and happiness and similar movements: the interaction between bodies that are mutually supportive, solidarity within shared work and friendship; and organized networks of resistance and action: the rooting of new communities within the space, the process of building or transforming places and settlements.

Our stories bring together living practices of new citizens, little daily anthropologies, histories and micro-histories of individuals or groups. To use another Geddesian metaphor, we are reconstructing a web of life, a new grid of life, of new citizenships expanding within the territories of Florence. Insurgent city does not mean subversive or revolutionary city (neither in Florence nor in any other Italian city these days, whether we like it or not). It is, however, a field of force, tensions, desires, projects, expectations. It is the whole of finite or partial transformative actions, of small realized utopias or simple acts of survival, manifestations of struggle and resistance, of individual or collective achievements, of diffused micro-powers ("thousands of tiny empowerments", to borrow again from Sandercock). Insurgence is not antagonistic action, algebraically negative, a mechanical overturning or challenging (and simultaneous legitimizing) of the established social (and spatial) order. Insurgent social practices are the outcome of positive, constructive collective aims. Practices on a different level, on thousands of different levels, impervious and indifferent to the traditional world of political struggle and ideologies. Unpolitical practices to some degree, and perhaps because of that, the only politically effective ones.

The Perspective Space

The original intent of the research project was to create a real city atlas of Florence's new social morphology. There are many ways of conceiving an atlas. One of the classic ways is to lump together compact, well-defined images of all the established knowledge regarding a certain portion of the world or society. In this way, the atlas fixes the known territory, the *terra cognita*, in a unitary, shared pattern. This mode of representation presupposes unity and stability and an unequivocal point of view. It implies that the time exploration is over, and that the sanctioning function of command and ownership, implicit in every geography, prevails over knowledge and action. In the end, this type of atlas is a homogeneous product, defined according to scales of representation, in a linear correspondence between the language of graphic symbols and the universe of 'real' phenomena. But how could we reach such a safe and fixed representation of Florence's mutating citizenships and their ever-changing relations to space? In short, we could not: this was not an option. However, there is another way of understanding the concept of atlas. 'Maps' and narratives - iconographic and topographic tales - fill up with tracks, with provisional signs; they swathe themselves in images and suggestions that make inroads into unknown territory. The atlas gives temporary validity to the path a route follows, almost as though it were a flight log, as opposed to the map of a peaceful Baedeker. This type of representation remains close to the things represented.

Our task was complicated by the fact that object of representation was precisely the world of the insurgent city: the city of freed subjectivities, of expanding and moving citizenships, a fluid and dynamic field of acting agents and initiatives. The materials to be represented were not made up of objects but by an interweave of human relations: new intra-subjective relationships having difficult and conflictual relations with the organizational and morphological structure of the city. We considered the possibility of a pluralistic, polymorphic, de-centralized atlas that might represent 'the perspective space' of the emerging city in its extension and its complication, an atlas of voices and relations, of routes and testimonies.
An indication by Pierre Bourdieu, contained in a volume which we used as model for ours (but whose quality we can barely begin to approach) guided us along the way: "To understand what happens in places ... moving people separated by everything else closer together, forcing them to cohabit, both in ignorance or in mutual incomprehension, in conflict, latent or patent, with all the suffering thus derived, it isn't sufficient to address each of the points of view in a separate way. It is also necessary to compare them as they are in reality ... to illuminate, through the simple effect of juxtaposition, the outcome of the clash of different and antagonistic visions of the world; i.e. in some cases, the tragic, born of an uncompromising clash between irreconcilable points of view, equally founded upon some social reason" (Bourdieu 1993, pp. 14-15). New urban geographies are "difficult to represent and to think" and require a multiple, complex representation: "to abandon the unique point of view, central, almost divine, in which the observer often gladly collocates him/herself, ... in favour of a plurality of perspectives corresponding to the plurality of points of view". At the end of our attempt, the answer to this question is open still: is the disorder of the material presented in our work simply the result of the limits of our capacity to conduct and interpret our research, or does it represent precisely the space of the perspective we have tried to investigate?

Effects of Place

Another aspect of the study created difficulties. Our intention was to arrive at a physical, even architectural and morphological description, of the alternative, emerging city. Not just to tell tales and collect testimonies, but to represent the transformations, to capture the new spatial figure of the city — the insurgent territory of Florence, the physical grid of a new geography. We thought that in the social energies deployed by the new citizenships the capacity for transformation of the city could be discovered, and we wanted to represent the results of this capacity. In reality, we found that the universe of emerging subjectivities is not yet capable of producing organic, structured change within cities. The movements are the origins of punctual modifications, of micro-transformations, at times depositing only symptoms of presence, signs marking a track. Therefore we have surveyed only the phenomena which are identifiable, to borrow once again from Bourdieu, as the "effects of place" of the new collective actions (Bourdieu, 1993)). Taking into account the many different ways of carving out public and social space, we have tried to record a wide field of the effects of place generated by new social practices on the Florentine territory. These include changes in use and function; re-signification of buildings and public places; creation or re-creation of collective places; the 'colouring' of urban space (from aerosol art to modifications in urban décor, to the sights and sounds of social life, markets, passing presences, etc.); the reconfiguration of urban times (the different patterns of night, the operating rhythms of the city); the occupation and reoccupation of built and non-built spaces; self-managed restoration work on housing; participatory projects; alternative occupations of the airwaves and non-material space; self-managed forms of 'renewal'; and in some cases the creation of real 'social building sites' for the city's transformation (such as the Isolotto in former times, and nowadays the Piagge area), capable of clearly and significantly affecting the city's organization. A gauge of the effects of place by the new citizenships might be summarized as the extent to which urban space has become contested space, place in dispute; in particular this regards public spaces, squares, streets, open spaces, parks and gardens, marginal and connective areas, abandoned buildings and vacated areas. These are places where different options of use and expectations in the city are being contended: Homi Bhabha (Bhabha 1994, pp. 101-102) calls them "third space", interstitial, in-between spaces, within which differences are articulated and life is negotiated, and existence agreed upon and played out.

The choice of topic and the way this research has developed has influenced its form, forcing a change from our initial intentions. The contents of this often figurative research are created from surveys, from partial focus on particular issues, contacts with and explorations of the city's movements. The content is often made up of discourses concerning small episodes, micro-phenomena, and sometimes also by inquiries into more complex phenomena encountered during our exploration of the city and its social space. The materials presented here are made up of many things and are mixed among themselves: iconographic material (photos, maps, drawings, diagrams, interpretative sketches), oral stories, interviews, narratives.

From Resistance to 'Social Building Sites'

Potentially, the list of acts of resistance is endless – everything from foot-dragging to walking, from sit-ins to outings, from chaining oneself up in treetops to dancing the night away, from parodying to passing, from bombs to hoaxes, from graffiti tags on New York trains to stealing pens from employers, from no voting to releasing laboratory animals, from mugging yuppies to buying shares, from cheating to dropping out, from tattoos to body piercing, from pink air to pink triangles, from loud music to loud T-shirts, from memories to dreams – and the reason for this seems to be that definitions of resistance have become bound up with the ways that people are understood to have capacities to change things, through giving their own (resistant) meanings to things, through finding their own tactics for avoiding, taunting, attacking, undermining, enduring, hindering, mocking the everyday exercise of power.
(S. Pile, M. Keith, eds., *Geographies of Resistance*, Routledge, London/New York, 1997)

A few comments are necessary to explain the content and articulation of different sections of the research project. Two, often intertwined, types of narration can be found. A number of themes run through the text through the contributions and interviews, repeated and re-examined from different perspectives. More specific aspects of the research use more traditional means of reporting, in the form of small essays or critical reconstructions. Images and quotes from the interviews constitute a sort of narrative infrastructure, meant almost as moments of reality guiding the reader to different parts of the book. I will review the contents by overview, so to speak, pausing at those aspects that I personally find most interesting. An orderly, hierarchical classification of the actions and movements researched is impossible. In the 'other' city, not one single ideal or project comes from above. It would therefore be wrong to list urban movements and projects or rebellious actions in any order of importance or meaning. Many small actions repeated can have greater affect on urban space than a single large organized initiative. In reality, one of the most relevant features of the world we have explored is precisely this mix of significant things and their unforeseeable emergences in different places around the city – in a simple individual biography a politically organized squat or the transformation of a building or a neighbourhood.

The threatening profile of a city hostile to the expansion of new citizenships is in the background of all the urban explorations represented. We call it the gated city: the forbidden city, under surveillance, a city that rejects and withdraws in its attempt to harness and contain alternative urban energies. It is the city of enclosures, fences, barriers, gates, access codes, remote control of time and space, of privatisation and surveillance of public space. It is the city that discriminates and pushes to its edges, the city of ethnic cleansing on the main commercial streets, of social cleansing along the banks of the river Arno. It is an architecture of fear that consolidates itself as such, through spatial control devices both large and small: a paranoid, security-obsessed vision of urban life opposing the very substance and *raison d'etre* of the idea of city.
The first dimension of the opposition to the city-fortress is therefore that of resistance. The "arts of resistance" are the weapons of the poor, a sort of "infrapolicy of the powerless" (Pile, Keith 1997, pp. 89-91). To hide, to dissimulate, not cooperate, to disobey, to feign ignorance, to live off one's wits: the arts of survival constitute a range of spontaneous and informal activities, needing no coordination nor planning, a form of "Brechtian or Schweikian class struggle" (Pile, Keith 1997, pp. 89-91). Even in the more mature, planned and transformative movements, resistance constitutes a foundation and a starting point. It is on the basis of resistance and rebellion, often individual and lonely, sometimes organized and intentional, that even high hopes of concretisation rest. Resistance to control and the positive organization of survival are deployed especially within public space, in the city's contested space par excellence.

We have examined these collective spatial challenges in a few sensitive places: the squares, the social hangouts of the inner city; the railway station and zones of commerce and transit; and the streets themselves. We have recorded the positive signs of these challenges, the micro-transformations and the processes of reclaiming collective space (multiethnic squares, coloured streets, etc.) In particular we have attempted to draw up map of the inhabitants who have come from far away, the 'foreigners' and migrants.
To live and keep on trying to live by 'insurgent living practices', paraphrasing the expression by Sandercock which we began with, means in this instance to be forced at the same time to resist and to change the city. Life isn't guaranteed to this category of unwanted citizens, their existence hasn't quietly crystallized in houses around the city. For migrants, continuing life is still a goal, not the natural starting point, and is a project in and of itself. To live means to secure a shelter, to furnish a collective space for survival, to ensure the satisfaction of basic needs, to adapt the structures of consumption and commerce, to seize the possibility for movement and communication, to tackle the problems of employment and training, to affirm the right to a family and children, to face the problems of leisure, to have not only bread but also roses. It is as a consequence of this gradual process by which the lives of migrants take root that the effects of place accumulate and the city is reshaped, transformed, coloured.
The lives of migrants are never linear or commonplace. Complex and contradictory biographies: resistance and capacity to create life projects, behaviour patterns considered unorthodox and desire for normality, individualism and solidarity. What comes out is, at the same time, discomfort and adaptability emerge, cunning and entrepreneurship, along with an appreciable cultural level, with knowledge of other cultures and of other languages far superior to that of most 'ordinary' citizens. In some cases, the life-stories cross a sort of wild zone, the border territory of the city, placed on the edge, and sometimes beyond it, of regulations and laws: third space, wild zone, again, oblique spaces, hybrid, ambiguous, such as queer spaces, the 'wrong' spaces of free sexual practices. New geographies of desire and bodily freedom of the body are formed, often balanced on the threshold between self-expression and self-exploitation.

An important part of our research is dedicated to the geography of occupied sites in the city, of real-estate liberated by groups of homeless citizens, of vacant or abandoned factories and areas that have become complex places of the alternative, emergent city. I would like to underline here the open, unforeseeable, unplanned character of these experiences, to the point of being unpolitical in the sense I explained earlier. I think this is important, for instance, in the via Aldini squat, given the complex character of the experience: the hopes, the internal relations, the meeting of different lives and cultures, the mixing of ages and expectations, the appreciation of collective feeling and work albeit amid many difficulties and contradictions. Florence's social centres are very different from one another both in the way they are conceived and in the way the meaning of their experience is lived as they are in many other Italian cities; here, however, they are more radically hostile to the power structure of the existing city in the material, daily, existential content of the occupations. The insurgent aspect is, therefore, in "Geddesian": the insurgency lies in the collective life of that moment, the energy unleashed, the direct experience of change.

A Partial and Plural Research

The images and the stories of our research were born of compelling, albeit partial investigations. Our choice of tools depended on the moment, perhaps causing some confusion and risk of approximation: intense, participatory interviews, more dense than the average question-answer format, highlighting some aspects (they were dialogue-interviews and thus with a high degree of subjective interaction-interpretation); 'critical reconstruction of cases' conducted from deep down; sometimes participatory observation in the traditional sense, complicated by a high degree of personal involvement, as in the case of urban explorations; action research (as in the case of the neighbourhood lab at the Piagge, still in progress), where the researchers actively worked with the projects and their implementation. In many cases, the researchers were part of the situations described, or they have become so. At times, parts of the report assume a form of self-description. The point of view expressed is never neutral; rather it is invariably influenced by a relationship with the subjects of the research. Many developments arose out of our research from unforeseeable outcomes of interaction with the subjects, as is demonstrated in many of the interviews. The dialogue-interviews have been re-worked and double-checked with the interviewees, in a mutual, circular process. The group of the researchers itself constitutes an example of the multiplicity of perspectives and horizons of an insurgent, alternative city. The researchers involved hold diverse opinions, some have a point of view coming from within the movements, almost conspiratorial; others have a more detached, not fully convinced point of view. The materials deriving from this difficult weaving of sensibilities and positions are therefore differentiated amongst themselves, even contradictory at times, but we preferred this sort of presentation to a reduction or amalgamation of the process of work. It seems to us that the articulation of the many voices and languages within the project group is itself a representation of the plurality of voices, attitudes and hopes coming from the part of the city that we have tried to study and understand.

References

Bhabha H. (1994), *The Location of Culture* New York/London: Routledge, 101-102.

Bourdieu P. (ed.) (1993), *La misère du monde* Paris: Seuil,

Ellin N. (ed.) (1997), *Architecture of Fea*r, New York: Princeton Architectural Press

Friedmann J., "Claiming Rights: Citizenship and the Spaces of Democracy", in: *Plurimondi. An International Forum for Research and Debate on Human Settlements*, 2, 1999, 37-46, 287-303.

Friedman J., "The Good City: In Defense of Utopian Thinking", in: *International Journal of Urban and Regional Research*, 2, 2000, 460-472.

Fyfe N.R. (ed.) (1998), *Images of the Street: Planning, Identity and Control in Public Space*. London/New York: Routledge

Holston J.,(1999) "Spaces of Insurgent Citizenship" in J. Holston, ed., *Cities and Citizenship*, Durham/London: Duke University Press, 155-173.

Mumford L. (1952), *The Conduct of Life*. London: Secker & Warburg

Mumford L., "Mumford on Geddes", in: *Architectural Review*, 108, 1950.

Pile, S. and Keith M. (eds.) (1997), *Geographies of Resistance*, London: Routledge

Sandercock L. (1998), *Toward Cosmopolis: Planning for Multicultural Cities*. Chichester/New York: John Wiley & Sons.

3.2

TEXT..Lorenzo Tripodi
PHOTOS..Ogino Knauss

The AbroGATED City

In drawing an atlas of the insurgent city, our initial aim was to identify the counter-geography of a hidden, “other” Florence. But the *effets de lieu*, “place effects”, the object of our attention, appeared insignificant at first glance, too small for urban-scale research. We were concerned that only isolated cases of sporadic unconventional relationships with the territory could be reported, rather than more complex, configurational, aspects. Hence, our first step was to sketch an outline of what we called *"la città cancellata"*, a phrase that in Italian signifies both *erased* and *barred,* which well expresses the simultaneous subtraction of a role, and the material closing of spaces by means of gates, chains and tools of surveillance. Starting from this standpoint, it was then possible to define an insurgent entity what was trying to escape, defy, or deny this configuration of economic rules, policies, borders, and control devices. What follows is the result of this critical view of the city, based mainly on the observation of visible transformation processes in the public spaces of Florence, and takes the form of a journey across the inner city.

With thanks to Laura Colini and Donald Bathgate for helping out on the translation

The Separation of the Inner City

Entering the city's historical centre, evident signs of a change of state can be seen. Surveillance cameras, policemen and municipality surveillance corps abound, there is but limited access to cars – multifarious devices betray a process of virtual reconstruction of the city walls reversing the move to reconnect the urban tissue which had taken place with their demolition during the 19th century. Even the check-points and electronic gates are installed where ancient city gates stood. Inside this confine, the city is heavily structured for and conditioned by the flows of international tourism.

The tourist economy progressively redesigns the inner city, transforming it from a nodal point of social life into a place of representation. The formal elements of the city are now totally separated from the dynamics that generated them. Somewhere between a "renaissance theme park" and a mall dedicated to Italian *bon goût,* Florence participates in the process of *disneyfication* already described in the last decade as a pre-eminent evolution of American urbanism (Sorkin, 1992). And it is quite ironic to note that while the *Italian Piazza* was once an idealized model for the renewal ideology of urban centres all over the world, the same places inspiring this model are being quietly subverted and polluted by this process. The characteristics of sharing, proximity and conviviality that created "public space" (in the widest sense), are turned into mere consumerism. *Come and taste the atmosphere of the Italian Piazza*. No matter that the interaction forms that built this civic arena are no longer possible, thanks to the effects of this intense interest. Indeed, the perverse power of tourism should be acknowledged and analyzed for what it is - one the most powerful factors in the process towards capitalist globalization.

Conservative Transformation?

While in the past the debate on the evolution of contemporary cities has been shaped by the opposing forces of transformation and conservation, the one often referred to as an American pragmatic and innovative attitude and the other, a more prudent European one, to preserve heritage, Florence's example seems to defy this easy classification. Here, it can be observed that the reason for no change often hides a surrender to the changing environment, in the sense of the dominant economic and political trend. Although the institutional control on the formal aspect of the city is very strong – you cannot even change the colour tone on your house's facade - the city is being significantly conditioned by global factors. Social life is attracted elsewhere by better opportunities, housing is granted for transitory use, and *façadistm* marks total restructuring and rebuilding of interiors for the creation of even more, new commercial spaces.

Changing Public Space: from Place of Contact to Space of Exposure

If the dynamics which redefine the set up of most contemporary cities are to be the defining yardstick, Florence has emphatically entered in the age of *symbolic economy* (Zukin, 1995). The city no longer produces either goods or even lively cultural interchange, but provides a particular frame of atmosphere and personal security to the intercourse between global passers-by and global goods. In this process, public space is redefined as a crossing space and as a space for representation, denying and erasing the concept of a space for contact and mutual exchange.

A significant number of the city's public spaces is taken up by museums; explicit rules of behaviour are posted in piazzas and loggias and enforced by police, security guards and sanitation workers. Metal gates close the loggias off and steel spikes appear everywhere to stop people from sitting down. The environment has been quietly redesigned for a continually moving flow of transient visitors. While benches have been thinned out and become rare, the municipality is increasingly releasing concessions to restaurants and bars to set up tables and build open air structures on public property. Besides being a form of privatization of the public space, this is not a traditional attitude for Florence, though it sits easily with a certain stereotyped idea of Italian Open-Air Life. Often these concessions are released in the frame of explicit public order policies, such as is the case of Piazza S. Spirito.

Institutional schizophrenia: the soon revocated prohibition to seat.

"Pacification by Cappuccino" [1]

While most public spaces are becoming expensive *locales* for tourists or are being strictly monitored, the need for social spaces is on the rise and is becoming radicalized. During the summer months especially, young people gather in the few *piazzas* that remain outside this expropriation process. Emblematic is the case of piazza S. Spirito, a beautiful square in the San Frediano neighbourhood which despite the gentrification process, maintains a strong popular character. In recent years, S. Spirito has become one of the last remaining places where youngsters and students can feel at ease, for them to meet and stay until late on the steps and benches of this starkly, scenic square. But the lack of space produces an excessive concentration of people and needs, with obvious collateral effects like noise, drug dealing and loitering. The authorities' response to this situation, instead of increasing the availability of proper space for civic life, was restrictive and repressive. (Rispoli 2002)

A special daily task force, composed of sanitation workers and police, "cleans" the square every night at midnight with jets of water and disinfectant - how symbolic this disinfection-removal of the city's sociality, treated as though it were unhygienic - dispersing the people chatting on the steps. This, obviously generated a certain nervous turmoil to which repressive police action ensued. At the same time, the whole central area of the square has been bequeathed to an association formed by the owners of cafes, bars and restaurant around the piazza, to manage an expensive open-air bar, with obligatory table consumption. The association provides a daily programme of entertainment the doubtful cultural quality of which is just enough to arouse public interest.

The Reinvention of Tradition

The sale of public spaces to open air cafes, restaurants and bars is only one example, and perhaps not even the worst, of a growing "reinvention of tradition" process. The entire commercial interface is being transformed by what the guest's expectations are. Brand new "ancient" bakeries, "old" *hostarias* and ice-cream parlours flourish as exhibition oxymorons - shameless in their contradictions. Hotels and restaurants are renamed with references to historical figures. Furnishings are redesigned in a vernacular style that attempts to appear traditional: this phenomenon radically redefines the uses of the city according to standards demanded by the international customer. At the same time, many commercial licences have been issued for new franchise enterprises: money shops, laundromats, internet access-points – and all sorts of services on offer to the temporary visitor – spread all over the inner city territory.
It is interesting to note that while the general political trend is to reduce the powers of most public sector welfare-oriented bodies, municipalities like Florence are making strenuous efforts to concentrate their initiatives on intensive economic exploitation of public areas through the privatization of control functions (governance). The main scope of the city government has become that of managing the incomes deriving from the productive activities of regulated access to (former?) public spaces. The increase of temporary flows and traffic creates a new labour market: the car-park attendant cooperative, car-removal attendants, private guards, all of which have grown into a more than secondary economic sector, and from which paradoxical effects arise: taken to an absurd extreme, when the income from parking fines becomes the biggest contribution to a city's budget, traffic no longer is a problem to be solved but a precious resource to be safeguarded.

Insurgency Signals

While exploring the "erased and barred" city of Florence, our attention was also captured by dissonant signals: acts, behaviour and signs pointing out emergent and alternative relationships with the urban space, resistance to the changes and the evictions, new forms of aggregation, interaction and communication; events that trigger innovative perceptions of space, new meanings modifying the values of places in community geography. Between the surveyed behaviour the use of walls and other urban surfaces stands out as a means to communicate and complain. A texture woven of small acts, often indeed illicit, but nevertheless able to narrate the still remaining discontent, the indignation, the obstinacy of voiceless minorities. These manifestations have an important place in the saturated spaces of the city, where land value heightens the level of control and conflict, but where communication capacity is higher, thanks to the combination and density of criss-cross trajectories. Inscriptions, flyers, graffiti, tags, banners: volatile texts, scratches that leaves traces, are covered, reappear, faintly stratify and fade, but nevertheless leave a glimpse of a fighting flutter of vitality.

Welcome to merchandise country, showcase heaven, paper pin-up covered streets, postcard landscapes, festivals and parades of corrupt artists and false prophets. Welcome to profit city, to the shiny plasticized culture, to the "buy and run" sociality and take-away experience, to selective entertainment.
Welcome to the city of the refined loan-shark, the urbane freemason, pseudo-enlightened education chancellors and hospital overlords, hypertech nippo-idiots, illustrious dollar-greedy shopkeepers, and frustrated super-cops.
LUMINOUS SIGNS CALL FOR FOOLS!!!!
Our time is too precious to spend in desolate school and university corridors, in streets and squares controlled round-the-clock, in dormitory-neighbourhoods between boredom and shopping malls!!! They won't succeed in shutting us up in a cathode-ray tube! We squatted in via Maragliano. The powers attempted to use force to clip our wings.
THEY FAILED!
We are wealthy bearers of a different sociality aiming at direct participation for the fulfilment of our needs and flee from the commercialization of minds and bodies.
WE ARE STILL HERE!!!
We still need a place where contamination of experiences and projects is possible, a place to share tools, knowledge and skills to set free our hopes of achieving an alternative to this paper-money-city. Every day we move within the inner city, in streets and buildings of an environment that does not belong to us, forced by study commitments, precarious jobs and channelled amusements.
We want to conquer a space to communicate and to be communicable.
We need to carve out a slice of the centre of this city, because whether we like it or not, this is where we live most.
2001: THE ODYSSEY FOR SPACE CONTINUES....

PUBLIC MEETING IN PIAZZA SS. ANNUNZIATA

References

Rispoli Francesca (2002), "Piazza Santo Spirito", in: Paba G. et al. (eds) (2002), *Insurgent city. Racconti e geografie di un'altra Firenze.* Livorno: Mediaprint, 24-31

Sorkin Michael (ed.) (1992), *Variations on a theme park. The new American city and the end of public space.* New York: Hill and Wang

Zukin Sharon (1995), *The culture of cities.* Cambridge, MA: Blackwell

Endnotes

[1] The definition comes from Sharon Zukin . A typical example is the case of the Bryant Park Restoration Corporation in New York city. *op.cit. p. 28 -38*

3.3

TEXT...Giovanni Allegretti
PHOTOS ....Giovanni Allegretti

Urban Transgression Beyond the Geography of Transgressive Spaces

Frigidity is mostly the consequence of social factors [...] *it may originate from fears of various kinds, from everything that represents the price of civilisation* [...] *It is the typical synonym of a sclerotic culture, inflexibility in the unyielding forms of civilisation, of a culture that is nearing its end.*
(Sandor Márai, *Divorzio a Buda,* 1935, Adelphi 2002)

Is Florence a Frigid City?

In the light of the hospitality that a large part of the city gave to the participants in the European Social Forum (ESF) in November 2002, such a brutal definition would seem to be unjust. Indeed, in certain ways the ESF was a turning point for the city, demonstrating the continuity that exists between today's city and the traditions of hospitality (both institutional and informal) that have characterised its social fabric in the past. And the importance cannot be denied of the Community of Isolotto, the research foundation named for the architect Michelucci, ARCI, and the FIOM-CGIL trade-union having produced and distributed the bilingual book, "Florence: Traces of Another History" to all participants at the Forum, for in this book there are to be found the memory of several 'hospitable places' in the city bearing the clearest traces of a Florence open, progressive and capable of integrating differences within the stratifications of its urban space. All of this does not prevent Florence, in its daily life, from also showing another face: the face of a city afraid of being assaulted, a city that puts a cautious distance between itself and the differences that impinge on it. As one so-called non-European guest-resident remarked during the course of a survey that enriches with real-life experiences a study carried out by researchers from the Department of City Planning of the University of Florence in the text "Insurgent City":

ORGANIZZIAMOCI
CONTRO
LA REPRESSIONE
SINDACATO
VENDITORI
AMBULANTI
IMMIGRATI
„3 febbraio"

In some ways each of us (foreigners) is transgressive. Perhaps because we are coloured in a city made up of grey and brown stone, or because we stay on in the city while foreigners are assumed to be simply passing through here. Their passing is so rapid that not even public toilets have been provided...

It is true - in Florence, the foreigner is often interpreted as a transgressive presence. No scientific investigation is necessary in order to affirm this: one needs only to live in the city as a resident in order to experience it personally on a day-to-day basis. For this reason, perhaps, the foreigner is regarded with a certain detachment, even by those who make their living from foreigners.

This is true above all for the so-called non-Europeans. Above all, but not only. Even many of the students in the Socrates programme end up feeling rejected by the place that they had dreamed of for such a long time. And so they often meet together, at their parties at language schools or American universities, in their bars, in their discos, in their Irish pubs or in their Brazilian cafés. Their separate spaces perpetuate the tradition of the English-speaking communities of the last century: 'a world apart'. Only that today, this 'parallel circuit' also has a 'virtual anchor': *www.studentsville.it*, the English-speaking site for young foreigners who become temporary Florentines. It provides information for those who want to participate in the city's life, even without being fully integrated into its human fabric. Luckily, not all of Florence rejects them, but at times the rejection encountered is sufficient to create a rupture.

Non-Europeans are more likely to be kept at arms-length. This is because their everyday life may seem transgressive when it is interpreted as a 'contamination' of the purity of traditions or of consolidated spaces. This is not necessarily a racist attitude. It is a distance which the ancient city places between itself and its new inhabitants.
For the most part, this type of transgression is involuntary, but it cannot be denied. It arises above all from the differences that are noted in the use of public spaces. For example, the difference seen in the by-now familiar figures around Piazza della Repubblica, who attract groups of people that obstruct traffic from the surrounding streets. They are mostly street artists, who bring back a bit of the chaos that was familiar to this area before the large popular market in the severe 19th-century square was demolished. They are the 4 'graffiti artists' and spray painters (2 Romanies, one Egyptian, and one Spaniard), the Iranian Charlie Chaplin, the Serbian and Polish mimes, the Peruvian and Slavic orchestras, the Chinese weavers of paper grasshoppers and their colleagues who 'embroider' the names of passers-by translated into oriental languages. Currently, the Municipal Council – which has always been opposed to improvised, multi-functional spaces – would like to move them away from there, to exile them to a 'specialised' space, perhaps far from the town centre, such as Piazzale Michelangelo. It would not be the first time: this has already happened for the non-European street vendors ....

Equally transgressive is the group of South-American families who meet and dance on summer evenings in the same Piazza della Repubblica, to the music provided by the little orchestra of the Café Paskozski. Without paying, because the street belongs to everyone – at least up until now.

Equally transgressive are the groups of young South Americans who, with a car radio and four loud-speakers, manage to carve 'squares to meet' out of the parking-lots where streets widen, which all true Florentines would be ashamed to call 'squares'.

Transgressive are the Albanians who build their cardboard houses under the bridges and those who sunbathe in groups, stretched out on old boxes in the Station Square, or in the garden in Viale Strozzi – especially on days when the 'high society' of the Pitti Immagine trade fairs are close-by.

Transgressive are the non-European women of the 'Nosotras' Association who, with the 'Paladar' multi-ethnic catering centre, have breached the implicit regulations of the world of 'culinary purity' and single-specialisation, preferring to mix the dishes of many different countries together into an original culinary 'melting pot'.
Transgressive are the Peruvians of the village of Settignano or the Filipinos of the Church of San Barnaba near the San Lorenzo market, because their religious processions continue to wind through a city where the great Easter religious celebration has by now become a mere tourist attraction. The same is true for the informal football games of the Singhalese in Piazza Indipendenza. By now, the squares considered the 'jewels of Florence' are only used officially for sport events like the 'football in costume' matches that have become a mere tourist attraction. The piazza where they take place, Santa Croce, is devastated by ghastly metal bleachers that are also utilized for tens of other performances, with the result that residents are deprived of the main neighbourhood square all summer long.

Transgressive are the Senegalese along the *lungarni* [streets along the banks of the Arno River, *ed. note*] who, as a protest and to protect themselves – after two years of patiently waiting for a municipal authorisation that has never arrived – have begun to open up large colourful umbrellas with which to protect their legally-authorised merchandise from the sun and rain. Only by forming themselves into a cooperative have they finally nailed the Municipality of Florence to its responsibility to build a small multi-ethnic market, a promise that has been under discussion since 1995.

And also transgressive are the Chinese when they put their fish out to dry on the fences between the houses of San Donnino, or when they cook their fried specialities and are accused of making the air in the district almost impossible to breathe. Better to leave the monopoly on contaminating the air with the smell of fried food to MacDonald's, as the people living around the MacDonald's in Via Cavour know all too well…

Often, however, the transgression that is perpetrated in the urban spaces becomes voluntary, because it is seeking attention, it is trying to remind distracted passers-by of something. It wants to re-introduce the 'outside world' into the city, so that its culture and its tradition of hospitality remain alive and are not transformed simply into a 'Renaissance Disneyland'. Thus, the Eritrean community that passes silently through the historic centre to remind us about the war with Ethiopia is transgressive; or the Palestinians who, under the 'Peace Tent', try to prevent us from becoming hardened to the tragedy of the Middle East. Transgressive is the Somali community that camps out in tents in Piazza Duomo to remind us of the drama of the failure to recognise the need for reuniting families.

Transgressive are the 200 Romanies who – guided by their association, 'Amalipè Romano' – stop traffic in front of the Prefecture and – sitting on the ground – celebrate a prayer vigil for a child who has died in a fire at the concentration camp for gypsies called 'Il Poderaccio'.

And transgressive are the 50 non-European citizens of the 'Housing Movement', who not only squat under-utilised buildings (and – if left to their own devices – try to put self-reclamation into practice), but in the middle of August 2002 had the courage to organise a sit-in in front of the Spanish Consulate out of solidarity with the 400 Algerians who had been violently deported from the Iberian peninsula.

Equally transgressive are the non-European citizens of the Street Vendors Union, because they 'usurp' the name of a formal structure for their informal union, which is fighting for the free circulation of merchandise on the street.

Transgressive is the Islamic community which voluntarily welcomes Florentines to its mosque-garage in Via Ghibellina, and one day hung up a sign that said: *For solidarity with the Somali community, from now on Friday prayers will be held in the Tent in Piazza Duomo. All the faithful are asked to join us there.'*

The Senegalese community is also transgressive, and not just because it holds demonstrations in Piazza Signoria or hunger strikes in Piazza Duomo, where it exhibits placards in four languages as a 'resource' for explaining its problems to the numerous passing tourists. But also because it remains vivacious and vital, even if it is very small, while it has become the most Florentine of non-European communities – to the point of having recently been the promoters one of the few in-depth policies to have emerged from the annals of the city's local government.

Strange: indeed, it is usually the less lively communities that are the most 'Florentinised' ones. Like the Iranians who – in order to celebrate their New Year – no longer take to the streets as they did 30 years ago, but now rent the halls of the Hotel Sheraton alongside the A1 Motorway. Thirty years ago, they were the ones who made the San Lorenzo market a place of welcome and belonging for non-Florentines.
As a well-educated representative of an African community observed synthetically one day:

Your city is a little like Benozzo Bozzoli's Chapel of the Magi: it represents an inter-religious council, but the faces of the guests who arrive from far away are those of the Medici family. Already then, perhaps, guests were more welcome when they took on the faces and customs of the Florentines….

But are the manifestations of diversity really transgressive in regard to the city spaces that they occupy? Perhaps not really, since many of them succeed in retrieving the memory of the historically-consolidated – and recently lost – significance of various of the city's public spaces. Or perhaps they are transgressive precisely because of this: because they place consolidated patterns of use in doubt, and restore historical depth to the significance of the city's public spaces.

Were the Senegalese transgressive when they threatened to appeal to all the Muslims and black people in the world to boycott the American film '*Hannibal II,*' which had 'purged' them from several scenes filmed at the Ponte Vecchio after pressure brought to bear by the local Jewellers Association? Perhaps not. They were only reminding Florence that the Ponte Vecchio once used to house businesses that were more similar to pedlary than to the goldsmith's art, and that there is no sense in wanting to preserve a postcard image of the city that does not correspond to reality. Thus, director Ridley Scott was immediately obliged to re-integrate them in another scene in the film. But perhaps he did so only because they had touched the sensitive spot of an economic boycott.

Are the gypsies transgressive in their annual street celebration of the '*Festa of Romany Pride*', when they dance in the street and throw garlands of flowers into the river? After all, in celebrating their diversity, they remind us that we have a river that once 'housed' activities that were a vital part of the urban space, while today it seems almost 'wasted'.

Did the family-members of peaceful Chinese families use the city's spaces in transgressive manner when in '95 they staged a protest at the Trespiano cemetery because they feared that their funeral customs were not being respected? Certainly not, because the 'final' spaces – those dedicated to 'rites of passage' – have always been delegated to representing collective memories and different traditions, 'condensing' the identities of every religious or ethnic group into a visible, permanent form.

Were the Somalis transgressive when, out of protest, they set up their tents and prayed to Allah in an improvised mosque in Piazza Duomo? Perhaps not: even the Bishop who lived over their heads praised them and supported their battle by offering them connections to the power and water systems. After all, the controversy over their prolonged presence stimulated Florentine journalists to reconstruct the history of the square and its statuary, in discovering that this square had played a secular and inter-religious role ever since the late Middle Ages ….

Was the Senegalese community being transgressive when it held its night-time assemblies under the Porcellino Market in order to attract attention to how small its official premises were? After all, it rediscovered the important role that the Florentine markets (first of all, the Straw Market, and then San Lorenzo) played in the 'integration of foreigners' during the past century.

And the same goes for the groups of Somalis and Albanians who meet outdoors in the evening in Piazza Santa Maria Novella, thus transforming it into the real 'multi-ethnic heart' of Florence, which all public demonstrations having as their theme the integration of foreigners in the city leave from. Do they contribute to the square's 'loss of identity' – as the flyer of a municipal convention on the restoration of the *parvis* in front of the Church put it – or do they, on the contrary, rediscover its ancient significance as a square that has always been used for multi-cultural encounters, as an ancient marble plaque on the façade of the Hotel Minerva recalls?

It may seem paradoxical, but it is perhaps the gypsies, i.e. the nomads, who are the most transgressive among Florence's new inhabitants: the ones who protest because they want to stay here, while they are still treated as 'people of passage'; the ones who built the experimental village of Guarlone, where they can remain close to their own customs and ways; the ones who – in the working-class district of Le Piagge, in the far outskirts of the city – have 'dared' to design the project of a small camp for families, which they mean to construct themselves. Their transgression – after 15 years spent in the dismantled shacks on the river bank – was to want to stop and live in the city which by then they felt a part of. Many of them have been forced to leave. And the 'District Laboratory' for the recovery of the working-class settlement of Le Piagge – which had dared to re-propose their construction project – was substantially scuppered by the authoritarian planning board of the local administration. After all, as an Albanian mason, who has lived and owned his own business in Florence for more than 10 years, observed:

Today, to be politically correct, everyone uses the term 'migrants'. [But this] overemphasises the idea of passage, of something temporary, while many immigrants come here to stay […] *In many places, we foreigners are given the right to pass through but not to stay* […] *If you look at the advertisements, there are entire buses that publicise telephone cards to call 'home' in far-away countries. There are ads in many languages* […] *This is intelligent, because immigrants are the main passengers on buses.* […] *Work is available; as they say, flexible work, for people who fit in, who stay on for two or three years and then leave. But there is no housing. Because houses mean staying on. And it is a cause of fear to think that foreigners come, stay on, live in a different way, pray in a different way, have their own celebrations, with their own music* […] *It would be easier to have all tourists or American students, as there are in Florence: they come, they spend money, they leave, and not even shop-keepers have to be nice to them. Two people who stay on (an Italian and a non-European) cannot ignore each other; sooner or later they need to talk to each other. And if you are in contact with someone and talk to them, then you change. Both of us change.* (sic)

A Counter-reading of the Traditional 'Transgressive Spaces'

In interpreting transgression within this perspective, we also change our way of regarding those spaces which are traditionally indicated as 'transgressive' because they house activities that are legally out-of-bounds, or at any rate go beyond what current moral codes accept as 'normal' in spaces open to the public.

Can we say, then, that these spaces show a higher degree of transgression than is traditionally recognised for the activities carried out there? Perhaps. And this is due to the fact that these activities interfere with the system of empty urban spaces through informal processes of appropriation and privatisation which 'mark' the territory and create 'zones of influence' superimposed on the traditional use of open spaces. New informal 'planning' links are 'de facto' occupying places that by right belong to the collectivity, at times transforming the language of prevarication and violence into 'internal regulations' that must be respected by everyone within the 'separate worlds' that created them.

These 'additional links' often colonise the spaces variably following a time differential. In fact, their dominion comes into effect above all in the 'kingdom of the night'. The 'spatial divisions' are therefore not visible to the naked eye, but can often be sensed intuitively, inferred from external clues - above all, by the change in the people who can be found there. It is as if a more refined form of transgression, deriving from the 'distorted' ways of using open spaces, were superimposed on a more 'banal' and almost 'standardised' one (carrying out an activity that would not be tolerated in the light of day).

The drug-traffic subculture in Florence is an example of this 'double transgression' in that it deals in illegal goods but also because, if we consider it from a bird's eye-view as a network that exploits public spaces, it is marked by a strong 'territorialisation' tending to superimpose its foreign subdivisions onto the city's physical spaces. This foreign geography is mapped out according to a logic that follows the contiguity of the native countries of the drug-pushers and to hierarchies in some cases already existing in those countries, or else is 'inherited' from former dealers who have chosen or have been obliged to abandon the Florentine 'market'.

However, not all of the city's space seems to be 'compartmentalised' with the same degree of rigidity. Above all for soft drugs there are areas with more 'fluid' margins, places whose availability is not certain from one year to the next, where it is not possible to know how long one will be able to work there undisturbed. In the past, these places left room, if not actually for free enterprise, at least for more 'extemporaneous' initiatives.

Obviously, the 'geographies' to which these illegal practices anchor themselves are fluid, as they have to adapt to changes in 'external' conditions. But these sudden variations in the 'surrounding conditions' are perceived more quickly by some than by others. And so, the image of certain places can remain fixed in strange ways. As an example, police living in the former Hotel Magnifico at Peretola recently captured two Albanian delinquents who had taken refuge there after being pursued. The Albanians still had in mind the image of the hotel as a refuge for clandestine persons and drug-dealers, which it very often was up to the year before, during the long period when the building works that turned it into lodgings for police functionaries were suspended.

In contrast, the unauthorised street vendors and 'windscreen washers' who wait at the city's traffic lights do not have 'binding networks' for the assignment and management of day-time work on the street. The most plausible explanation, therefore, for the fact that the same persons tend to work at a given traffic light is the existence of a sort of 'right of primogeniture' ('first come, first served'). This margin of autonomy (and, therefore, of disorganisation) has both good and bad points. For example, it does not provide for mechanisms of 'compensation' in case something goes wrong (such as streets being closed to traffic for public works or other reasons, traffic lights being replaced by roundabouts, etc.), and the 'displaced' workers, left without a pitch, have to find their own alternatives. However, mechanisms of 'inheritance' and 'transfer' of the spaces (either free of charge or at a price) exist in the form of 'territory ceding'.

It is interesting that with the passing of time several informal categories of workers have undergone a sort of '*job upgrading*' that has often involved entire communities, which have gradually disappeared from the street to move on to other occupations – thanks to informal word-of-mouth networks and direct 'calls'.

For example, the Poles who presided over the traffic lights as windscreen washers at the beginning of the 1990s have completely disappeared from their posts. They have been replaced mainly by North Africans and Roma. However, the term 'Pole' as a synonym for 'windscreen washer' has remained in common use.

Lastly, some fleeting observations should be dedicated to the night-time activities linked to the sex trade in Florence's public spaces. Florence lived for over 20 years with the fear of the 'monster', a homicidal maniac who killed several couples of lovers in isolated spots in the surrounding countryside. This threat caused a particular evolution in the sexual customs of Florentines, in their search for the safety and protection that seemed guaranteed by staying in groups, so as not to feel isolated and vulnerable.

Thus, along with the preferred choice of closed spaces (private houses, hotels, the first 'swappers homes'), the phenomenon of semi-collective exploitation of secluded open spaces has arisen. Even today, therefore, there are peripheral or badly-lighted places (the open spaces along the viale dei Colli or the narrow street below the Church of San Miniato, for example) where at night fixed or casual couples withdraw in cars parked one next to the other, blanking off the windows with newspapers. This semi-collective use – goodhumouredly tolerated even by the police – represents a typically – though not exclusively - Florentine 'transgression' of the rule of complete isolation that are in force elsewhere. It often carries with it 'complementary' uses of these semi-protected areas: condom-sellers and groups of local adolescents who play practical jokes at the expense of the couples.

A more articulated network of spaces closer to the city centre describes the 'queer geographies', which in Florence are characterised by 'personalised exploitation' of the territory (freer and more variegated for gay males, more secluded and stable for lesbian groups). Despite the fact that the 'self-made' maps and guides compiled by the homosexual communities indicate the spots where meeting places (bars, discos, shops, theatres, saunas, squares or parks) are to be found, the procedures that determine how these places are frequented tend to expand beyond these 'anchors', creating 'fluid', 'flexible' geographies of use open to sudden change. This makes it possible to use – temporarily or permanently – 'alternative' spaces if the traditional ones become dangerous or inaccessible.

As in other urban realities, in Florence the network of 'queer' spaces is well-articulated and differentiated. It corresponds to a microcosm of differences that are not limited to the groups operating at the most 'visible' level, which offer hospitality and engage in political activities to advance demands and provide services. Various geographies of non-communicating homosexual aggregation seem to exist, parallel and autonomous worlds that tend to come together almost by chance only on the occasion of highly important political or social happenings. Or – in contrast – on lighthearted, festive or 'trendy' occasions, often having to do with the world of fashion or with certain 'cult' theatres like the Comunale [Florence's concert and opera hall, *ed. note*] the Limonaia, the Rifredi).

In recent years, the capacity for 'wider involvement' of initiatives at first meant the rapid increase in participation by the homosexual community in initiatives created around 'themes' in spaces generally frequented by heterosexuals. With an ironic approach to '*hetero-compatibility*', gay groups have often rigorously selected only these improvised initiatives, often rejecting others aimed towards a gay clientele only to take advantage of its spending power. In this, the gay community adopts '*hetero rules*', i.e., using the various 'venues' casually, without no care for the needs of the users, such as *relaxation, spontaneity of use* and *hospitality.* An interesting feature of the queer geographies is, moreover, their extreme sensitivity, vulnerability and instability, which at times result in individuals moving with unexpected rapidity from one territorial 'anchorage' to another. This happens on the basis of a 'geography of glances' made up of sensations and changes of mood linked to an almost 'hypersensitive' perception of how genuine are the welcome and good-feelings offered to gay/lesbian groups in the places they frequent.

More steadily 'anchored' to the territory, instead, is the network of hidden places for nocturnal homosexual encounters, which follow a clear logic of localisation and 'visible invisibility' (the Cascine Park, the large square at the stadium, several lay-bys along the motorway). They often function as centres for contact with individuals (such as many non-European gays) who do not participate in the spaces of 'visible social relations' in Florence.
Differently from elsewhere, in Florence the geographies of queer encounters do not tend to take possession of unused border territories (the far outskirts, abandoned areas, etc.). At most, they use 'weakly structured' places that have multiple uses during the course of the day. In this sense, their degree of 'transgression' does not go much beyond the transgressive activity to which the encounter may possibly give rise, since the 'new' uses to which the public space is put are not fixed or exclusive.

The same is true for the activities of male prostitution, although on the whole prostitution tends to superimpose on urban spaces 'heavy' territorial divisions which affect networks of both public and private spaces. The fact is that in Florence there seem to exist 'different degrees of freedom', according to who the subjects are that offer themselves or are offered to the clientele, and to their sex .

Territorial sub-divisions in the form of 'lots' ('virtual' pieces of the territory rigidly respected for those who are 'inside the milieu') are valid above all for female prostitution, except for the so-called 'old ladies' in the historic centre. This rigid apportionment is instrumental for the collection of the 'tolls', which are in proportion to the desirability and centrality of the beat, and as the basis for whatever change and territorial reorganisation are made necessary by increasing danger or urban 'pressure' on the territory. Thus, if the unwanted disappearance of a place from the 'map of exchange' forces female sex workers to move from one zone to another, they can identify the new collectors and be inserted within a network of renewed relations of 'price-controlled competition' with other colleagues. The minute organisation of the territory into zones of influence generates a saving mechanism of 'compensation' during the 'hotter' periods of attention from the police or politicians, taking advantage of the substantial lack of interest shown by official programmes to eliminate prostitution in closed spaces, which is in fact the largest and most remunerative slice of the Florentine 'business'.

'Insurgent' phenomena are often connected with the 'Slavic' prostitutes, who are often 'slaves' dragged onto the streets and 'managed' like objects by pyramidal joint ventures that collaborate in the administration of the territorial 'spaces' and the 'services' provided within them). This is in contrast with the indigenous, prevalently female, management that characterises much of the prostitution of African origin (Nigeria or Cameroon), which even opens up prospects for passing from 'employee' to 'self-employed' work. It is no coincidence, therefore, that precisely among the Nigerian night-time workers it has recently been possible to witness the development of interesting, albeit corporative, forms of united action, or even rare events like an informal 'strike' against the excessive number of requests for unprotected sex. This was proclaimed in 1995 in the streets of Calenzano, where most low-cost prostitution is found, having been expelled from the gentrified city-centre. Here preference is now given to prostitution in flats or in the high-powered cars of male and female night-workers who crowd the ring roads from the Fortezza da Basso to Piazza Beccaria every evening. In reality, nobody has as yet succeeded in verifying whether the strike did in fact take place. In any case, the vast echo of the initiative in the local papers attained its purpose - the message reached many potential clients.

Today another interesting phenomenon is taking place within small evangelical religious communities founded and supported thanks to the commitment of groups of Central-African female night-workers. As described in the words of a Nigerian cultural intermediary employed in programmes aimed at the rehabilitation of ex-prostitutes set up by the Co-operative CAT: is a 'reaction insurgent practice', sorting out from a distorted and negative use of the territory:

There is a reciprocal utility between the pastor and the congregation, since these women survive within their work and keep their balance thanks to their faith and the idea of pardon. This has determined strange mechanisms that arise precisely in a field like the Church, which is in general directed from on high and works through commands that are, or at least pretend to be, divinely inspired, to which the faithful conform. Here, no. It is as though the women who follow these sects had elaborated their philosophy from below. It is as though they said, forcefully, "you'll be in trouble, priest, if you do not keep silent or if you contradict us. Don't talk to us about sin, but only about pardon. Just pray for us and for our souls; we will manage our lives by ourselves." This is interesting, because they change the characteristics of how faith is approached, and how ecclesiastical hierarchies are constructed.

Is it possible to think that reactions like these represent 'acts of rebellion', a sort of constructive transgression in contrast with phenomena in which 'transgression' against socially-accepted rules for the organisation of activities in the city's territory can be seen as distorted, unjust, excluding and therefore, in the end, negative?

.4

TEXT..Camilla Perrone
PHOTOS ....Camilla Perrone

Urban Geographies, Coloured Networks, New Social Practices

Re-placing Difference [1]

The city swings between celebrating and encouraging values of difference, and repressing and regulating them. In this oscillation the matrices of difference had slowly gained and defined new urban spatial dimensions. Mental measurements, physical lengths, human geographies, cultural colours had built scenarios of difference, spaces of cultures, geographies of another Florence; they had defined a new viewpoint of the urban space and told stories of cities far from the “traditional memory” that traps Florence within an image of identity no longer adequate for the complex nature of the “new city” which yearns for change.
To whom does the city of difference belong?

Events, stories, tales, urban adventures reveal issues of identity and gender, build up scenarios of change and spaces for cultures, put into play new inhabitants who overturn the rules of urban space, highlight borders, tell fragmentary tales of a distant city: the city of differences belonging to those who interpret resources of space and of borderline cultures creatively and who draw new urban geographies. To identify and recognize the difference and to tell about and give a space to the diversity were the two complementary and diachronic paths of this itinerary that its creators followed through another Florence. On the one side, an analysis of the factors through which an attempt was made to give space and recognition to the forms of difference; on the other, the affirmative action by the new inhabitants who were telling of other possible places, setting viewpoints and building the insurgent city.
The urban adventures which follow, and the parts of the city, then, represent important elements in the building of another Florence. They are parts of the story of places of the city that have already become something else, but surely also the fundamental components of a matrix of change that will draw new urban scenarios.

New Inhabitants: the City and the Foreigners

The first aim of this itinerary in the city of Florence was to listen to the voices coming from the borderlands of the multicultural city, of those who are marginalized and spread out over the territory. Voices from physical and mental places of the urban edges of the city, of the borders of the social space, both economic and political; voices of those who are turning their marginality into a creative affirmation; voices of outsiders, of the excluded immigrated population, able to conceive and build a new identity, redefine their position within society and transform its structures little by little. Every culture lives through contamination, uprootings and new rootings, of real "identity projects" (following an expression of Manuel Castells [2]): the insurgent practices we are about to tell of are indeed the daily stuff that builds up new projects of identity, the group of actions that allows anyone to "take him/herself to the other side of something" [3].

The 'Immigrants' Public Space: Contended Space, Borderlands, *Terrains Vagues*

It is possible to interpret the public space of Florence, inhabited, crossed over, lived in by the immigrants, as a borderland. The word border "holds within itself the substantive front; the frontier is a front to, is turned towards (against) something, towards (against) someone. This front is moving, it could continuously transform itself: the frontier is an artificial construction, it arises from aspirations and expectations of a community, which is to say from social rather than geographical motivations" [4]. The concept of frontier seems then to be suitable to represent the places of the public space where the often combined actions of old residents, together with those of newly arrived outsiders, changes the semantic and social code of the city and also, partly, the morphological one. The frontier is something continuously evolving "it's a vague zone, it's difficult to set, it's difficult to represent; more than a line it is rather a band of undefined dimensions, a place where it is possible to take refuge, and at the same time where it is possible to exchange goods and opinions, where meetings can happen in any way." [5]
The borderlands are those places where the implicit agreement of anonymity gives everyone the opportunity to express his own right to belong and "build a place" with objects belonging to his cultural reference which, whenever they are introduced into a free zone, give it a symbolic mark. Stations are borderlands, places of passage where everyone is temporarily a stranger, without an I.D. and at the same time free to be themselves.

The characteristic function of a borderland is to unify rather than to divide [6]. Although current meaning is similar to borderline or line of separation, its meaning has shifted in time and now a frontier is something which indicates or makes visible meeting spaces, places where different societies can meet and different cultural forms of life maintain contact, rather than a line of separation. To separate and unify at the same time is a conceptual paradox. In order to comprehend something that unifies and divides, we must think of a sort of no-man's land placed between two spaces each of them occupied by a social group or culture with a separate life-styles. Despite the distinction and the differences that characterize the two social groups or cultures, the exchange and reciprocal fecundation between cultures Ernesto Balducci [7] talked about take place in the metaphorical no-man's land.

The ideal form of frontier is the one experienced as an interactive space where every group tends to compare their own life models with others' and adapt to the needs of the cultural and social environment.

The term frontier brings to mind the place where two diversities face each other. So if the frontiers are the "face to face" of two cultural bodies it is necessary for them to have a place to be the "filter and the stage of the difference" [8]. And in order for them to be at once filter and separation, the place where two identities face each other, it is necessary that the frontier must not be clean cut. In this way the frontier appears as a common realm of differences, a fluid moving space, a stage for insurgent, emerging, rising forms of existence.

Places of Outsiders: Transformation and Colourings

The borderlands par excellence are markets, places for filtering and sharing, where the dominant condition is equality of outsider-ness: the meeting between two or more identities is possible when differences are nullified. Places for praying or producing are also borderlands.

The market area allows the dynamic or even casual interaction, physical or barely perceptible between ethnic groups and people of different cultural and geographical origins. The market is by nature multiethnic, open and, tolerant. It contains an intrinsic "misunderstanding" that makes it possible for different cultures to face each other and be tolerant, perceiving how their differences enable them to accept misunderstanding as a social pact.

The territory affords many opportunities to thousands of forms of commerce and to the relations and interactions they produce. The market receives the user in different and irregular ways, as in the case of informal commerce. The "ethnic corridor" we are familiar with, which winds along the central streets of Florence with its goods on show in small stalls or laid out on blankets, offers an alternative to the formal market and the urban parade of shops. Its locations are not chosen by chance. In Piazza San Lorenzo, for example, improvised cardboard stalls are to be found together with authorized ones in front of the entrances and exits to the central market, on street corners, at crossroads. These locations are chosen not only as advantageous selling points, but also in the attempt to avoid police checks and conflicts with local sales people. These are the sites where tourists stop and pass most frequently, such as the stairway leading to the Church of San Lorenzo and the street of San Lorenzo itself.

The San Lorenzo neighbourhood is possibly the part of the city where the changes that have occurred are most striking, thanks to the wealth of new life styles and of commercial activities that the phenomenon of immigration has introduced. It is a district almost completely re-inhabited by newcomers. Time after time, native Florentines have fled the area, to be replaced by students, tourists and foreigners, in successive waves of repopulation. Thus, both living quarters and the ways the new inhabitants find to assure their survival, to earn a living, have been significantly transformed. Today San Lorenzo is a colourful neighbourhood that lives according to ways and means, and even times, different from the rest of the city. It's a neighbourhood mostly inhabited by African immigrants who have adapted the shops abandoned by their original owners and set up food and fashion shops selling goods from their native lands, phone shops to facilitate communication with families left behind, African style hair-dressers and so on.

The nearby central market has been a determining factor in the "re-production" of the surrounding space. It seems as though the whole marketplace, with all its social and symbolic significance, has expanded into the surrounding city area, affecting the streets and the people. The market-place represents the oldest expression of how an urban community takes root at the same time as it provides evidence of the meeting of diverse cultures. To the Africans who live and work in that area, the adaptation of the market to their rules and times is an expression of how the appropriation of space is made possible by the relationship to enacted activities, the social links that have been forged, and the living spaces won.

Thus, the San Lorenzo neighbourhood is once again a lived-in area, and not one occupied merely for reasons of survival and trade. It has become a place for both informal and formal commerce, where steps along pedestrian walk-ways, places where streets widen, and the market square itself are places where people meet and develop relationships. The character of every corner of the neighbourhood is being transformed: they have become passageways and spots where people stop for a brief chat during the day and longer encounters at night. The neighbourhood has, then, become a spontaneous laboratory for multiculturality, fostering the growth of self-awareness and the reacquisition of the urban space.

There are basically two kinds of ethnic markets in Florence: the one in the San Lorenzo district, rooted and relatively structured, which encourages new life-style activities through concentration and imitation; and the one found along the streets of the city centre along the Arno River and on the Ponte Vecchio. The latter is an improvised and transitory market, hardly recognizable by foreigners, but more frequently found irritating by native Florentines.
The entire outlying productive area around Florence, comprising the historic boroughs of Brozzi and San Donnino and the bordering municipality of Campi Bisenzio, represents the most significant example of the 'colouring' and transformation of a production-based urban space. The Brozzi area and the neighbouring Piagge area south of the Via Pistoiese represent a sort of borderland of the Florentine outskirts that is particularly complex, urbanistically speaking [9]. North of this area is the development of Osmannoro, one of the city's most important centres of industry and commerce, comprising a structured network of warehouse and storage facilities, wholesalers, and small manufacturers - a sort of gigantic anti-city within Florence.

In this area immigration assumes two very different characters: the Chinese community in the Brozzi area is has a clearly structured character, product of a well-defined immigration project marked by organized work practices and residential stability. On the other hand, the Rom and Albanian communities are more "casual", characterized by spontaneous and "informal" life styles that depend on day-to-day survival strategies.
The Rom settlements, whether spontaneous and therefore illegal or organized in areas provided by the municipality and therefore legal, are structured according to five actions that could be identified as the ingredients of a sort of insurgent urbanism [10] of the Florentine outskirts: occupying an area, drawing a borderline, structuring individual dwellings, finding ways to build an active sense of belonging within the specific social context, claiming rights. The act of establishing and clearly marking a borderline separates and defines the group ethnically, distinguishing between what is the next person's place and what is an "out of place" in the urban context (the Rom's place); but at the same time that physical borderline, made of wire fencing, gates or corrugated iron, allows them to define a place and control it, to "invent an area and enclose it, marking it with elements that clearly show its dimension, form and functions. It aims to make a clearly recognizable statement of both what belongs and what is excluded. [...] behind the fence one can expect shelter and protection and if necessary also defence." [11]

At the same time, in a process of evolution, the old historic neighbourhoods on the via Pistoiese have been gradually abandoned by native Florentines and occupied by Asian communities, mainly Chinese, who have turned the lower floors of houses into textile and leather factories. The Chinese are spread out over the outer metropolitan area following a logic based on the local economy. They have inserted themselves into a specific productive sector and have renovated it. Nonetheless, it's not possible to talk about a real Florentine Chinatown as the nature of the settlement and its distributive practices make it impossible define the Florentine Chinese settlement in this way.

The Chinese community's dwellings are located close to production sites, allowing the most efficient use of resources, especially time. This has resulted in a slow but continual transformation of the urban and residential spaces involved.

What is happening in the neighbourhoods of via Pistoiese and Brozzi is a process of replacement of the old inhabitants with new ones. Second generation Chinese families invest a considerable part of the capital gained in buying housing, turning the "old neighbourhood" into new urban areas dense with social and urban events introduced by novel lifestyles, and by the colouring of public space. The squares of Brozzi and San Donnino have become meeting points for the community during certain hours of the day, and particularly on Sunday afternoons. Chinese men, together with their little children or grandchildren frequent the local coffee shops. The yards and areas in front of the houses have been turned into home extensions, following typical Chinese customs. The Brozzi's square flowerbeds, fenced off to avoid people stepping on them, become safe places to stop for a chat on Sundays. Here men are found seated in circle to re-enact the tea ritual. Thus, the community slowly takes possession of places, through quiet urban practices, micro-transformations of both open and closed spaces, and modifies their symbolic significance. It occupies squares, streets, and courtyards, filling them with sounds and smells; it frequents bars and shops, spreading the colours of its own culture over the public space.

The Speech of Differences in the 'Borderlands'

Along our route we encountered several spontaneous micro-systems that give colour to the urban space. They can be discerned at a distance, but cannot really be experienced without walking through them. Within these micro-systems it is possible to identify new ways of living, positive signs of survival and small affirmative actions that are able to develop intelligent, articulate identities.
The search for and creation of a public space to spend one's free time with relatives or members of one's ethnic group, building barracks along the river bordering the Piagge, claiming the right to have an interpreter at the immigration office, all these are insurgent living practices. Most significant of all is the web of work relations and the use of space created by immigrant women. One such insurgent practice is that of the oriental women who in the evening become itinerant vendors of handmade silk scarves along the streets of the city's centre. Another insurgent practice, less visible from outside but more differentiated internally, is characteristic of Philippine women, and often by African men and women, based on the care of children and the elderly made possible by a network of relations often going back to their place of origin. An anomalous living practice, but also a form of resistance and demonstrating the will to survive against all odds, is that of the Nigerian immigrant women who autonomously manage their part of the prostitution market, safeguarding the prostitutes' living conditions while creating the opportunity to build a new life in the new country.

Behind this sort of *insurgent-scape* [12] is the background of a metropolitan reality that has changed tremendously in recent years precisely because of the issue of foreigners, with immigration coming from a growing number of nations. Each of them, individually or in groups, acts within the urban space to change it by designing different geographies of use: geographies of informal living (the Rom and Albanians who live in barracks and shelters in the city's western outskirts); urban geographies of defence (the occupation of streets in the city centre for unauthorized street-vending on the part of the Senegalese); the network of geographies of needs (Somalis requesting assistance from local institutions); polar geographies of social relations (the occupation of central areas carried out by Somalis and Philippines); geographies of production (the work experience of the Chinese who have taken over a whole productive sector in the industrial areas of the Florentine plain); geographies of individual survival (the adaptation and first settlement of Albanians); and so on.
Sometimes these living practices, carried on in urban spaces, initiate genuine processes of physical transformation of these spaces; in other cases they are merely "colouring" processes.

Endnotes

[1] The title is borrowed from Fincher, R., Jacobs J. M. (eds) (1998) *Cities of Difference*, London/New York: The Guildford Press. The concept is reformulated in this work in a different way.

[2] Castells M. (1997) *The Power of Identity*, Malden, Massachusetts: Blackwell, pp. 6-8.

[3] Zanini P. (1997) *Il significato del confine,*Milano: Bruno Mondadori, p. 61.

[4] op. cit., p. 11.

[5] Ibid.

[6] Fabietti U.(1995) *L'identità etnica*, Roma: NIS.

[7] Balducci E. (1992) "La dialettica tra identità e alterità", *Testimonianze*, n. 334, p. 26.

[8] La Cecla F.(1997) *Il Malinteso*, Roma-Bari: Laterza

[9] Paba G. (2000) "Il territorio delle Piagge come risorsa fisica e sociale della città di Firenze", in C. Marcetti, N. Solimano, *Immigrazione, convivenza Urbana, conflitti Locali*, Firenze: Fondazione Michelucci, Angelo Pontecorboli Editore, pp. 28-32

[10] Holston J. (1998) "Space of Insurgent Citizenship", in L. Sandercock, ed., *Making the Invisible Visible, a Multicultural Planning History*, Berkeley, Los Angeles, London: University of California Press,

[11] Zanini, P., cit. p. 57.

[12] The coining of this term out of the words *insurgent* and *scape* follows the same criteria used by Appadurai to semantically set the five dimensions of global culture fluxes: *ethnoscapes, mediascapes, technoscapes, financescapes, ideoscapes*. Cfr. Appadurai A. (1996) *Modernity at large*, Minneapolis; London: University of Minnesota Press,

3.5

TEXT....................Marvi Maggio
PHOTOS....................Manuela Conti

Rights and Fights. Urban Movements in Florence

The City of the Capitalistic Market

Florence is a city of contrasts, conflicts and contradictions. The social division of space is evident. A gentrification process has progressively expelled the working classes from the town centre, which has assumed a markedly bourgeois character: luxury housing, shops, hotels, banks, offices [1].

In Florence real estate values are among the highest and most speculative in Italy – the price of housing varies from 3,400 Euro per square metre in the most exclusive areas, to 2,650 in the centre and 1,700 in the outskirts. The absence of accessible prices in the rent market forces even those who can ill afford it to buy a flat, with the result that in 1991 60% of the population were owner-inhabitants and only 34,4% tenants. Needless to say, for those who cannot afford to buy a house, the situation is difficult indeed. The 12,000 publicly owned flats are all assigned, with 5,500 families on the waiting list, and there are 6,920 evictions of tenants pending. The price paid by Florence for being an important tourist and university town is a significant under-the-table rent market, with prices as high as 350 Euro for a place in a shared room. There are 30,000 out-of-town students but the "Agency for the Right to Study of the University of Florence" offers fewer than 1,000 places. The demand for public housing is also on the increase because of the growth in immigration - the Town Council of Florence calculates that in the year 2000 the number of legal plus illegal immigrants was 60,000.

Instead of devising and enforcing a collective public plan for the urban area and surrounding territory, the centre-left administration, who won the 1999 elections, has taken on board almost every proposal made by private real estate enterprises and construction companies (including FIAT, Baldassini & Tognozzi, Pontello), just as previous municipal councils had. In so doing, it actively favours the exploitation of space for economic interests, a process in continual expansion which also involves many decayed industrial areas close to the city centre, with the result that the "dangerous" working classes are pushed further and further outwards to the city's outskirts.

Memories

Nevertheless, Florence is something more than a bourgeois town or a shop window for tourists: it has deep-rooted anarchic and communist traditions, resistance to fascism and trade union and social strife. The widespread diffusion of "Case del Popolo [Recreation and Leisure Centres, run by the Italian Communist Party]" and Mutual Aid Societies, although still considerable, represents only a pale reflection of that past. Florence was a protagonist in the social and urban struggles of the seventies and the 1977 Movement: struggles in the workplace, for the right to housing, for social services, for a "quality of life" measured by the satisfaction of the right for everyone to have "not only bread but roses as well", and by the elimination of all discrimination and exploitation.

These memories explain the extension, maturity and lucidity of some of the urban movements present in the city today, and who also benefit from the high level of planning and organizational ability developed by the many of the participants in the movements of the seventies who have not lost their wish to contribute to building a fairer, more egalitarian and creative world, run through self-government.

As in the rest of Italy, Florence, too, saw a radical break at the end of the seventies: all the movements of the extreme, revolutionary left were hit by harsh political repression, with trials, inquisitions and imprisonment. This was not for any alleged connection with the armed struggle, but simply because of people's radical social and political aims: the pernicious "single thought" predominated inspired by Thatcher and Reagan-style liberalism. Despite this hostile institutional and political environment, the eighties were marked by the spread of the movement against nuclear power plants, which caused them to be shut down all over Italy in 1987.

2003. A "Housing Struggle Movement" demonstration against the privatization of Florence's social housing patrimony

One of the protagonists of this movement was the "Centre for Antagonistic Communication", an autonomous Communist group started up in 1982 and located in via di Mezzo, in the Santa Croce neighbourhood, the same location where, until 1981, "Lotta Continua [Communist Struggle]" had had its headquarters until it disbanded. It was inside this building that in 1985 Florence's the first social centre was born, the "Chiricahua Tribe", at once pub and venue for social gatherings, concerts and theatre performances. Here some of the proposals of the 1977 "Movement of the Circles of proletarian youth" were taken up and re-elaborated once again - the struggle for the enjoyment and production of culture; the right to creativity; the spread of self-managed neighbourhood social centres fostering collective organization and decision-making, and the experimentation of new modes of social relations that do away with one-man leadership, sexism and in general all the destructive, dominant social and economic models of social interaction. The beginning of the eighties saw the growth of self-produced music and fan-zines outside the capitalistic market, as well as the birth of anarchist punk. The "Florentine Anarchic Movement" (MAF), that had its headquarters in a squat taken over in 1979, in via Panico behind the central Piazza della Repubblica, became a meeting place with a wine bar and meeting rooms. "Chiricahua Tribe" and "MAF" were where some of the participants of the squatter's movement met and developed the "Self-Managed Social Centres": the "Indiano", located in the Cascine park (1987-1990); the "South Florence Self-Managed People's Centre" (1989 - present); the "Self-Managed ex-Emerson Social Centre " (1989 - present); the "Villa" (1994-2000). From the "Centre for Antagonistic Communication" (today called "the Tuscan Antagonistic Movement") were born the "Spartacus Self-Managed Sports Centre", the magazine "Antagonistic Communication" (1991 - present), the "Housing Struggle Movement" (1990 - present), the "Ex-Emerson Social Centre ", and the "Social Trade Union" (1999 - present).

Urban Movements: Housing and Social Spaces

The Florentine urban movements represent the answer to the social contradictions and inequalities produced by the process of urbanisation that characterizes our times: shortage of housing at prices accessible to people with low incomes, functional and spatial social segregation, privatisation of public spaces and their transformation into commodities, lack of social and public services, destruction and pollution of the environment. How effective these movements are depends on their capacity to single out particular issues that tackle specific contradictions concretely and directly, at the same time as they keep in mind an awareness of the economic, social and institutional processes that are at the root of today's urban problems. These contradictions and social-spatial injustices are evident to all; what differentiates diverse interests and social/political groups are how they evaluate and conceptualize these injustices, and how they think they can be overcome. The methods of struggle chosen and the characteristics of the concrete, positive, emergent answers given depend directly on the analysis carried out and the prospects which manifest themselves, whether they be social transformation, no-future, or the search for a unique individual solution. The concrete practices located in the territory materialise, verify and modify the social and political hypotheses that produced them: the realisation here and now of an alternative to what already exists becomes a fragment of "new worlds under construction". As the Tuscan Antagonistic Movement maintains: "they make the prospect of a social alternative understandable and achievable".

"...material practices are the measuring point precisely because it is only in terms of the sensual interaction with the world that we can reconfigure what it means to 'be' in the world" [2]

"...Material practices are not the only leverage for change, but they are the moment upon which all other effects and forces (including those within material practices themselves) must converge in order for change to be registered as real (experiential and material) rather than remaining as imagined and fictitious" [3]

The "Housing Struggle Movement" was born in Florence in 1990, as a consequence of the increase in rents and the growth in real estate assessment and exploitation which dramatically worsened the housing problem. Its purpose is to guarantee the right to housing for everybody through direct action, self-organisation and self-management. Through its activity it aims to promote the social cohesion all those involved in the housing question and who want to link it to the struggle for a social alternative to the capitalist system. The practice of squatting unused empty buildings and defending tenants threatened by eviction is part of a comprehensive general struggle against those who are responsible for the housing problem: land and real estate owners, real estate entrepreneurs and state institutions. The demand made by the movement to the city administration and the state, is to requisition vacant houses, prosecute landlords who indulge in under-the-table rent practices, increase the supply of public housing and stop the process of privatization of state buildings and properties which, at the moment, even involves public housing. The movement has the aim of setting the construction of structures independent of the profit-dominated market rules, as the squatted houses are, within a struggle able to attack the comprehensive dynamics of social contradictions, so as to find shared, collective solutions instead of selective, individualistic ones.

Therefore, together with squatted houses there are demonstrations, symbolic squattings of places like the Cathedral, the Town Hall and Piazza della Signoria accusations and protests against real estate entrepreneurs; street performances about the right to housing. This is a way to draw the attention of the whole town to the aims and social practices of the movement, to gain solidarity and broaden citizens' support in the struggle for the right to the town.

Nowadays the movement counts some 400 people and it self-manages 11 squats, of which 3 are privately owned while the others are owned by state bodies and are in the process of privatisation, including houses, factories, schools and offices. It involves singles, couples, families, out-of-town students and immigrants, united by neither being able to afford housing at market prices nor to gain access to public housing. From 1994 the movement began to include immigrants in the squats, and they have since become the majority of squatters; they come from Somalia, Eritrea, the Maghreb: Libya, Algeria, Morocco and Tunisia, and Serbia, Rumania, Poland, Albania and China. Therefore, it is no coincidence that the movement is in the forefront of the struggle against "temporary detention centres" for immigrants and the Bossi-Fini law that links "stay permits" to work contracts, but favour free circulation for everybody.

To achieve its aims, the movement carries on a struggle against the capitalistic real estate market and urban land rent, but also against local public administrations that actively support the economic exploitation of the territory. It is a hard struggle, made up of evictions and court cases but also of the hopes, life-projects and aims of squatters and activists, the joy of finally having a roof above your head, a place you can organise in relation to your needs and where you can keep your things, a place for creative self-renewal, where you and your children can live your lives. The over ten-year history of the Housing Struggle Movement, is the history of decades of houses squatted and evicted of being clubbed by policemen; of suffering at having lost your home and of the anger provoked by eviction and by seeing your possessions thrown in a rubbish bin by armed men; of charges and trials for illegal squatting, street blocks, resistance to public officials in the course of the eviction of squats and defence of tenants from eviction.

The geography of squats is constantly changing, although some of them have lasted over time. At the beginning of the Nineties the squats were located in central areas and in privately-owned properties left vacant for speculation; later squats involved publicly-owned properties and decayed industrial areas located in more outlying parts of the city. Even if the movement has undergone a process of gentrification involving central areas, it has also been able to challenge the social division of space: the house in Via Aldini is in a high-value, quasi-central area, and the owner, the Local Health Administration, would like to sell it for financial reasons; the one in Via Incontri, owned by the Army Red Cross, is in the hills of the Careggi area, among villas and medical buildings.[*ed. note*: Careggi, Tuscany's main hospital, is named for the hillside it occupies] Today the headquarters of the movement is in Via Palmieri, in the Santa Croce neighbourhood, and nearby, in Via Pandolfini (2002) an empty hotel has recently been squatted. And it is in the town's historical centre that in all these years the movement has defended hundreds of tenants threatened by eviction.

Since 1993, to guarantee squatters permanence in their homes, the movement has proposed to the Town Council to legalise home renovation done by the squatters themselves, so that they become tenants by contributing to the reconstruction of the non-structural parts of buildings, while the Town Council bears the cost of structural ones. For the movement this sort of autonomous renovation is a model solution to the housing problem, since it is rooted in inhabitants' participation in planning, building and management, and in the reutilization and "recycling" of territorial resources otherwise destined to be pulled down or to remain unused. Nevertheless, up to 1998 there was no real answer on the part of any of the local administrations that came and went over the years, whatever their political orientation.

After that year, negotiations have begun more than once, but have always collapsed. In spite of the high social value of the proposals and the achievements of the Housing Struggle Movement, the Town Council is very hostile towards it, and until now has not been at all receptive to the idea of taking advantage of the innovative planning capabilities existing in the vast social sector involved.
Parties and dinners open to the citizenry are very often organized in squats to favour social interchange. The movement aims to create a "House of Culture" in the squat in Via Pergolesi, where it will be possible to exchange and produce culture, and where immigrants and other inhabitants of the town can meet and talk together.

"OMME, students and non-stable workers for the right to housing" (2001 - present) also adopts the practice of self-management and squatting, and collaborates with the Housing Struggle Movement, but it is aimed at a specific age group. In 2002 it consisted of four squat houses, but at the beginning of 2003 the only one left is the oldest "Cecco Rivolta" in Via Dazzi (2000 - present), located in the foothills of Monte Morello. It also acts as a meeting place and has a pergola, a view of Florence and an urban vegetable garden. The house "Soqquadro", squatted on 13 April 2002 and evacuated on 3 December 2002, was located in the caretaker-house of an empty villa in the hills south of the River Arno, and defined itself as an "artistic/housing community" that aimed at "overcoming the housing problem and the lack of spaces for contemporary art and culture". Now it is looking for new spaces.
"OMME" was born out of the "Network Odyssey for spaces" (2000-2001), that also included secondary school students, but which split from it at the end of 2001. The Network had formulated proposals for teaching and communication, music, theatre, video and computer sciences. Its opposition to urban transformation led to demonstrations, and in March 2001 to the squat of a decayed industrial area in Via Maragliano, in the Novoli neighbourhood, called the "Bandone". Here the Network intended to practice social relations founded upon direct participation in responding to one's own needs, against "the transformation of body and mind into commodities".
Evacuation took place after only three months. In November 2001 the Network squatted what had been the "Cherubini Conservatory of Music" located in the heart of the town centre in Via Bufalini, behind the Cathedral. They wanted to create an Info-shop, but were evicted on 10th January 2002 with significant recourse to "the forces of law and order". At this point the Network broke up because of divergent views among its members regarding the kind of relations to be held with the local administration and on social/political priorities. "OMME" went on with its activities, while others started to take up temporary, symbolic squatting: in December 2001 they occupied the empty National Theatre, located in the centre, for two days, and in the Spring of 2002 for three days they occupied a sector of the Cascine Park, giving concerts and performances.

Today there are two squatted Social Centres in Florence: the "Self-Managed South Florence People's Centre" (CPA) and the "Self-Managed Ex-Emerson Social Centre", which offer meeting places free from the logic of profit and consumerism . Both were born in 1989, during the spread of Social Centres all over Italy, and both have occupied decayed industrial areas, taking an active part in the debate on their re-utilization that was then under way, affirming the necessity and the right to use them as urban social resources to be treasured and exploited instead of earning land rent and promoting real estate exploitation. The factory sheds proved wide enough for many uses and adequate to host new activities when the need emerged over time. The squatters have set in motion a process that has given new interpretation and new meaning to a space formerly used for financial exploitation; they have turned it into a place of encounter, cultural and artistic expression, and social and political initiative. This is a collective production: self-renewal happens by following transformations that occur in layers over time which aims at creating new places for encounters and social activity. Murals cover part of the outside walls and a large part of those inside. By claiming the right to use spaces outwith the philosophy of capitalism, such "illegal" occupations rescue them from speculation, at least temporarily.

The possibility of not being evacuated then depends on the strength of the pressure put on the municipality by the owner to regain his property and redevelop it; on the political choices of the Town Council and the Police Force/Ministry of Interior; and on the social power that the squatters are able to exert.
The (CPA)"Self-Managed People's Centre" started as a place for neighbourhood encounters, to establish collective practices and explore new processes, and share the social spaces. The two main interests are, on the one hand, cultural and artistic production - music, cinema, video, theatre; on the other, political activity, which mainly takes the form of internationalist solidarity. Its history has been dogged from the beginning by having to defend itself from the evacuation requested by the owner, the Coop supermarket chain, to develop a new shopping centre. The CPA held out until its eviction on 28 November 2001; today its old headquarters have been pulled down for redevelopment. After a few weeks its activists squatted an empty school in Via Villamagna, where their activities could start up again. There, it hosts dinners, concerts, theatre performances, films, book presentations, meetings and assemblies. It has a library and a documentation centre.
The "Ex Emerson" squat, occupied by activists of the "Centre for Antagonistic Communication", was born as a place in the territory "where the chain of dominion is broken and we once again set out to overcome social, architectural, racial and economic barriers". In 1993 it was evacuated from its first headquarters, not far from the FIAT decayed area in Novoli, and immediately occupied it present site, also a decayed industrial area. Nowadays it houses the weekly meetings of the social centre, meetings of the "Tuscany Antagonistic Movement" and of the "Town and Territory Monitoring Body"; there are the headquarters of the "COBAS", an independent, grass-roots trade union, as well as of the "Social Trade Union" a library, an exhibition room, a sports hall and a rehearsal room for musical groups. It organizes concerts, performances, readings, parties and self-financing dinners , as well as projections of movies on social and historical issues.
Together with the "Tuscany Antagonistic Movement", it organises meetings and assemblies about issues like "the Endless War", the urbanisation process, the Porto Alegre Social Forum, social movements, and the conflict between capital and labour. The "Tuscany Antagonistic Movement" and "ex-Emerson" have promoted and participated in committees against refuse incinerators, electronic pollution by mobile phone antennas, genetically modified food and against the environmentally destructive infrastructures for the new national High Speed Train line. Together with the "Housing Struggle Movement" they participate in "no-Global" demonstrations and encounters.

These are all fragments of new worlds under construction…

References

Harvey, D. (1996), *Justice, Nature and the Geography of difference.* Oxford UK, Malden USA: Blackwell Publishers Inc.

Comune Network, *Progettare Firenze. Materiali per il piano strategico dell'area metropolitana fiorentina*, Firenze: Edizioni Comune Network, ottobre 2001.

Endnotes

[1] The Florence area population is 600,000: 378,000 in Greater Florence and 224,000 in outlying municipalities.

[2] Harvey, D. *op.cit*, p.93.

[3] Ibid, p.94

3.6

TEXT........ Anna Lisa Pecoriello
TRANSLATION........ Luigia Padalino
VIDEO STILLS........ Manuela Conti

Planning Stupidity and Children's Intelligence

Children: from Protection to Indipendence

In Italy, just as in the rest of Europe, a number of experimental projects with children's participation have been developed over the years, which are specifically aimed at creating child-friendly cities, in the firm belief that "a city good for children is a better city for everybody".

The child seems to have become a sort of "quality parameter" of urban life, indeed the only one on which everyone seems to agree in this era of advanced social fragmentation and criticality of shared values.

In extremely simplified terms, children are seen as being naturally good and spontaneous, defenders of nature and therefore natural allies in the battle against unsustainable city development. This, however, does not take into account a point Mauro Giusti underlines: "Children and young people are increasingly assuming points of view and behaviour patterns that anticipate those of adults" and because of the domestic segregation and excessive media influence to which they are subjected, they are increasingly becoming "bearers of virtual and sweetened images of the city" (Giusti 1998)

In order to block this process it would be much better if "children were put out to play in the street at an early age", in order to restore to them city spaces, and give them the freedom to play the games that childhood uses to build its relationship with reality.

This, however, means revising the image of childhood in need of protection which has been created and fostered in the western world, and giving children independence, free from adult control. It also means shifting some of the "weightings" that work within the areas of society that wield power, towards favouring a social category which is domineered, numerically a minority, unproductive and with no means of exerting political pressure: children.

The adult world often finds it very difficult to encourage and accept children's real desires for what they are instead of what adults would like them to be because, as Frönes says: "Although adults are influenced by the social order... children offer living examples of the real limits of this order, of its potential destructivity and of its fragility. Children, even if only temporarily, exert anarchist tendencies...they are carefully instable, systematically subversive and un-restrainable".

Taking this consideration as a starting point, a "mildly interactive" attitude is needed in the process of getting children's participation and involvement in the participatory projects, (Giusti 1998), an attitude that enables one to listen and translate, and begin reciprocal learning projects (otherwise children, just like adults, end up becoming victims of banal stereotypes). In particular, we must be ready to accept the consequences of the involvement of children who, potentially, are "one of the many forms of insurgent citizenship which, in the abstract circuits of the metropolis, are always trying to impose the reality of the radicalism of their collective bodies" (Paba 1998).

Perhaps it is because of the difficulties typical of the child-adult relationship (which is always asymmetrical) and because of this potential subversiveness in spatial hierarchy (typical of the way children relate to the space around them) that many of the experiments in participatory projects which have been attempted over recent years have shown rather disappointing results. They have failed to innovate the way space is produced and, worse still, they have merely brought about exploitation of children by politicians and local administrators who, without even putting any children's requests into practice, have taken advantage of the attraction, positive image and unanimous approval that appearing to champion children's rights always brings.

In this way, the following is a perfect example of both children's ability to tackle an analysis of their living environment with great competence, underlining the banality with which it was planned and also the extent to which children are exposed in participation processes in which there is no intention of accepting their requests, as well as the danger they run of becoming tools in the hands of others.

The Participatory Project Workshops with the Children and the Young People of the Piagge District.

In the Piagge district, a growing part of the western outskirts of Florence where there are serious social, environmental and urban problems, working with children was part of the activities of participatory projects included in the Council Contract promoted by the City of Florence to restore two buildings of public housing of the so called "Le Navi" complex and the surrounding spaces.

In the Council Contract, the start up of a "neighbourhood workshop" as a place for developing the participatory projects with the people who lived there was entrusted to a group of researchers from the University of Florence. Furthermore, in the first phase of analysis and creation of a scenario of shared developments, associations and local residents' committees (also from areas outside the one being restored) were involved. Debate on open spaces was introduced by the video "A journey in the Piagge" produced by the children of a junior high school together with people working for the "neighbourhood workshop". The video, which shows and describes some significant aspects of the area, highlights problems and lack of resources of the open spaces that make the stereotyped image of the Piagge as a place of degradation even more complex and less likely its earmarking for re-qualification.

In fact, the images filmed by the children portray unexpected usage of some public spaces (car-parks used as meeting places, spontaneous use of the space around the houses instead of those *ad hoc* which lie abandoned, extensive, largely underused green areas with low correspondence to real needs). A workshop on open spaces was launched with the cooperation of the children living in the Navi complex at the same time as the projects involving adults. The Navi complex suffered from a marked social stigma being the symbol of the degradation and difficulty of living in the suburbs. Many children are in social service care but this kind of social intervention is uncoordinated which often raises competitive tension amongst the social cooperatives sharing the so-called "hardship cake").

Moreover, many of these interventions, instead of attempting to reintegrate "difficult" children into their territory, end up moving them to specialised institutes where they get involved in expressive and educational activities. The Navi car parks are often occupied by the buses that take the children to school, the institutes, or the summer centres, etc. Many children have discovered their own "Council" through the activities of the project workshop and the hidden resources they have brought into play have become immediately apparent. First of all, it is not true that there are no children's parks at the Piagge; indeed there are too many, but they are all of low quality. The spaces are too big and alike. In the enormous grassy areas around the Navi there are signs of previous development projects which have become submerged by weeds and equipment in a state of total abandonment. Most of them were play areas for children, but the children now put them to very different use, and some improvised structures have been added to them by groups of youngsters (for example, a football pitch).
In their work, the children have also taken pains to draw the paths beaten spontaneously across the grassy areas which are always different from the abstract few tarred pedestrian walkways.

The difference between the planned and the spontaneous indicate how distant the former is from the everyday needs of the people who live there. Interaction with the new open space project, still under development by the Council ERP offices, will also become very difficult, despite the apparent commitment of the Council Contracts. In fact, the open space project was committed to a number of earlier developments which allowed only certain pre-defined structures of a mostly standard playground/recreational-area type: a small square, a kiosk, a multi-functional play area, a children's theatre, mini-golf. Inhabitants could chose different combinations from among these as long as they did not exceed the budget limits. The work with the children completely overturns this pre-ordered options system and leads to a much wider view of the playground which either goes beyond the mono-functional playground or else radically changes its meaning.

In the drawings the children have done, for example, the need clearly emerges to reclaim a relationship with the river, which is denied by the railway line, on which they imagine bridges and boats where once the Brozzi "ship" existed, a ferryboat whose story they have uncovered by interviewing the descendants of an family of longstanding residents who still live on the river and who used to cross it by boat. Or they rediscover a marsh which has become hidden in an abandoned area among houses and buildings and which has become an environmental micro-system, and a source of continuous sensorial stimulation and curiosity to know more. Water appears in the gardens, in the form of ponds and fountains of different shapes, almost all designed to allow the children to get wet or to throw water at each other (behaviour unacceptable only in Italy but common enough in northern Europe).
The vertical is preferred to the horizontal (on the two existing artificial little hills, they even planned a sort of "observation tower") and, above all, they view play as an activity for transforming space, a vision recalling the model of the adventure playground and that of the urban farm (including the erection of little huts, farming, picking flowers and fruits and breeding animals etc).

When the results of the open space workshop were submitted to the adult inhabitants of the district and the associations that work with the children, the comments were: "How strange, the world has gone backwards instead of forward; these children who could have so many modern structures and games, want to play the way I used to when I was a child!".
In fact what the children had emphasized here too was the redundancy of the nature/city dichotomy and its replacement by a blend of the two as well as the overlapping activities of production and learning. This general concept is unfortunately often incompatible with planning which limits itself to the old logic of standard residual collocation in which structures are kept separate one from the other and all look the same and serve the same purpose as those just a short few hundreds meters away, where there are no problems in their fulfilment, maintenance and management because they have already been planned from the beginning.

Contact with the children's work has brought about some improvement in the open space project now in the process of realization (for example in the designing of the paths or of the more individual or public specificities of some elements in greater accordance with their surroundings of which children are highly aware) although this will not modify the planning of the playground nor will it help to identify the complexity of its nature.

In the final project the pre-defined structures such as the multifunctional playgrounds remain despite the fact that, during the presentation of the project for restoring the Navi district (in the presence of Florence's mayor, the councillor responsible and the inhabitants), the children had been invited to talk about their wishes.

The definition that Roger Hart would give of the kind of participation reserved for the children is "tokenism": the children had a purely decorative role in the presentation; only a representative chosen at the last minute could speak. They were, however, awarded a t-shirt for their participation!

Moreover, the management of the Council workshop was entrusted to others because the relationship with the person previously carrying it out had become problematical. Participation of the inhabitants in the Council Contract is thus relegated to a mere handing down of the project results together with the technical decisions taken elsewhere. In just a very short time, all the efforts made by the many associations who work with children of the district to get them involved in a process of direct communication with their "little consumers" which could have led to a much more effective and co-ordinated action (also towards preventing hardship, and education toward legal and active citizenship), has been lost.

The children of the Piagge, who, thanks to the workshop had got to know each other, had learned to play together and had re-discovered their territory and the desire to look after it all together, are taken back to their buses and the places of their "re-education".

References

Frönes I., cit. in Holloway S.L., Valentine G. (2000) *Children's geographies*, London and New York:Routledge

Giusti M.(1998) "Imparare da altri sguardi: i bambini nella progettazione del territorio", in Magnaghi A., *Il territorio degli abitanti*, Milano: Dunod

Paba G. (1998) *Luoghi comuni, La città come laboratorio di progetti*, Milano: Franco Angeli

3.7

TEXT ....Gabriele Corsani

Insurrections in the History of Florence

It would be misleading to call Florence rebellious given that the last real revolt, the "Tumulto dei Ciompi" (Tumult of the Ciompi), dates back to 1378. This was a remarkable event that marked the end of the 14th century, awakening strong civic passion in response to the decline of the city which had begun with the bankruptcy of the Bardi and Peruzzi banks (1341). This is all in the distant past, but it was an event with far-reaching repercussions, not only on the subsequent, history of Florence, but also on that of Italy as a whole and beyond, since it was effectively the most impressive uprising of 14th century European pre-proletariat" (Rutenberg, 1971). A century later there was another important revolt in the city. On 26th April 1478 the final act of the Pazzi conspiracy was enacted: Giuliano de' Medici was killed in Santa Maria del Fiore while his brother, Lorenzo, found refuge in the sacristy. The population, who had remained faithful to the Medici family, assembled and proceeded to loot the houses and buildings belonging to the families behind the conspiracy.

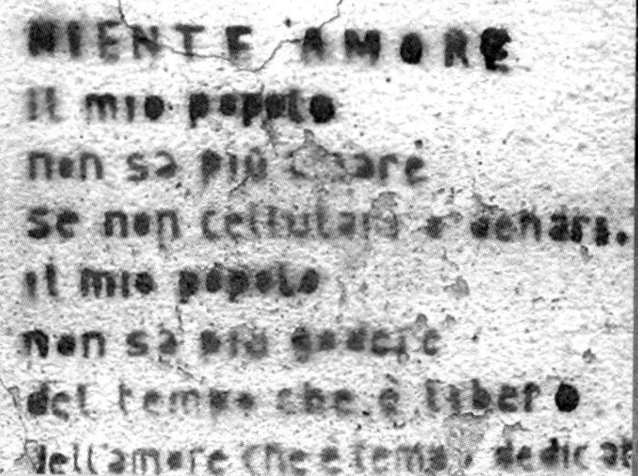

Between 1496 and 1498, Girolamo Savonarola launched a *ante litteram* Fourier-style venture. Hundreds of young boys, many of whom were already running wild, were grouped together in squads and, fired by moralising zeal, went about calling on people, often aggressively, to repent for the many sins the city as a whole was committing. This brief yet intense phenomenon highlighted the precariousness of the social and economic reality, especially considering that the population of Florence at the time was little over 70,000. Capturing Savonarola was later to be the reason behind the assault on the convent of San Marco on 8th April 1498, led by the "Compagnacci" (a grouping inspired by the Epicureanism of Lorenzo the Magnificent), which led to his being hanged and burned at the stake on the 23rd May that same year. On that occasion, the general population also sided against Savonarola despite having supported him on previous occasions.

The popular riots which, on 26th April 1527, brought the "regency" of Cardinal Giulio de' Medici to an end and restored a republican government for the last time, were noble in aim and effective in outcome. Once the Medicis were finally restored to power in 1530, the remainder of the 16th and the whole of the 17th centuries witnessed nothing more rebellious than intentions. Opposition to the oppression took the form of participation in religious brotherhoods rather than more direct forms of political militancy.

The peaceful decline of Florence was interrupted by a small revolt towards the end of the 18th century on 9th June 1790, notable for its having taken place at night. It was one of the reactions to the free-trade reforms imposed by the Grand Duke Pietro Leopoldo, which were, however, much more severely felt in other parts of Tuscany. This small-scale urban interlude was orchestrated by the oligarchy against the person held responsible for the free trade legislation, the talented economist Francesco Maria Gianni. The mobs attacked his house along with those belonging to some others, giving the impression of being "more recalcitrant than daring". As Gianni also commented: "Truly popular revolts against a system of legislation are usually directed towards the whole Ministry, so how can it be explained that all the other ministers … were spared … and only I was attacked?" (Gianni, 1848).

The young John Ruskin who visited Florence in the spring of 1845 was unfavourably impressed by the behaviour he saw in the city: "The square is full of listless, chattering, smoking, vagabonds, who are always moving every way at once" (letter to his father, 17th June 1845). Ruskin gave a detailed description of what he considered to be so detestable from an aesthetic viewpoint, a true affront to the secular sacredness of an environment which was still almost completely medieval. In point of fact, he had grasped, albeit in part, the essence of a city in which the preponderance of its role as an administrative centre, while relying heavily on craftsmanship, produced an imbalance with consequences similar to those of contemporary British industrial cities, but on a smaller scale. There was no a true uprising in Florence in 1848. Even the Guerrazzi dictatorship, the most extreme expression of the temporary government which made Grand Duke Ferdinando III flee to safety, was only short lived and was overthrown by a peasant revolt instigated by the big landowners. In 1848 urban unrest was much more violent, for example, in Livorno, the liveliest Tuscan city at the time and, more particularly, in 1849, when Austrian troops intervened to quash the revolt.
The "revolution" in Florence took place a few years later. This was, in fact, the term used to describe Grand Duke Leopoldo II's abdication on 27th April 1859. The most notable event of that day – once it was certain that the Grand Duke had left Florence – was the march from Piazza Barbano (now Piazza dell'Indipendenza) to Piazza della Signoria, while Florence's bourgeoisie rushed to display the tricolour flag from their windows.

The brief, single riot which took place on 6th June 1861 had its roots in the political climate of the period immediately following national unity and the disquiet among the lower middle classes. The evening procession around the cathedral in the week after Corpus Domini (*ottava del Corpus Domini*), included a number of aristocratic nostalgics who, preceded by liveried servants with torches, marched brandishing the decorations of the house of Habsburg-Lorraine, that of the deposed Grand Dukes. In particular, it appeared that these people were displaying ill-concealed satisfaction, which was unbecoming as well as offensive, considering that Italy was then in mourning for the prime minister, Camillo Cavour, who had died that day in Turin. The crowd began to riot. The immediate flight of the group targeted by the crowd and the pleas for calm, marked by cries of "Viva l'Italia", made by Giuseppe Dolfi, an influential popular leader, avoided the situation getting out of hand. The National Guard was, however, forced to intervene.

Mikhail Bakunin settled in Florence at the beginning of 1864. He joined the Freemasonry and made contact with political exiles as well as with Italian and European progressive democrats, many of whom lived in the city. He founded *Fraternité Internationale*, the blueprint of how to achieve the socialist and anarchic phase of his doctrine. The result of so much activism was, however, disappointing and, in June 1865, he moved to Sorrento. He did not find Florence a suitable place for preaching revolution. There is, however, one interesting episode connected with Bakunin's Florentine sojourn. A young professor of Sanskrit, Angelo De Gubernatis, "one of his first novices ..., initially made a violent break with the academic and bourgeois world but then, horrified by Bakunin's nihilism and the ruthless rules of conspiratorial discipline, quickly retracted in a finale which had shades of both mystery and romance: he married Bakunin's charming cousin, who he had met at the maestro's home." (Masini, 1969). In fact, the greatest obstacle that hampered the opposition of Florentines to power in those years was the individualism they applied to political struggle, even in the most extreme case of insurrections. This was also linked to autonomist demands, as expressed in one of the many auspices, at the end of 1868: "We will see Palazzo Vecchio / With its old flag / The red one, the true one, / Not the intolerable Tricolour." (Conti, 1950).

From an economic point of view, the 1870s and '80s were bad because of the difficult situation in general, aggravated by the whirlwind beginning and, particularly, the equally sudden end of Florence's role as capital city (1865-1871). The ensuing financial crisis led to the bankruptcy of the City Council (1878). The central government's slowness and frugality in granting aid - which was morally due - was in response to a parliamentary crisis fuelled by Tuscan Members of Parliament in March 1876, as well as by the Florentine politicians' aspirations of administrative autonomy. It is certain that Florence's cause was not helped by the bomb explosion which, on 18th November of the same year, 1878, caused four deaths and several people being injured during a parade marching to the royal anthem along Via Nazionale, which was being held as a gesture of solidarity with King Umberto I, who had been wounded in an attack in Naples.

The turn of the century was marked by a significant change in political opposition which witnessed an increase in its associative capabilities, and which shifted its main point of reference to the International. Florence is "the city which could then be considered the capital of the International in Italy, in terms of mass demonstrations, conflict and tension, and political and organisational awareness". (Masini, 1969) This situation led the anarchist, Errico Malatesta, to decide to move to Florence at the end of 1882. Here, a year later, he began publishing his newspaper *La questione sociale* and, the following year, he published two important theoretical pamphlets. However the results did not meet his expectations.

In 1891, out of a total of approximately 180,000 inhabitants, 72,000, 40% of the population, were classified as being poor. This potentially explosive situation together with the bleak general economic prospects, laid the bases for the riots and strikes which took place in the years which followed (1896-98), which were then triggered by the spiralling increase in the cost of living. Then, the straw workers in the outlying countryside (the "trecciaiole") also joined the dispute, and this led to a real unification between the urban and the rural agitation.

Rainer Maria Rilke spent the spring of 1898 in Florence. His Florentine diary grasps the feeling of unease in the city: "In the days in which I left Florence, groups of rebellious boys were throwing stones at the Loggia dei Lanzi". Initiatives such as these were more petty vandalous than rebellious, and was an indicator of disquiet under the surface, and unexploded revolt (Luperini, 1973), which could be felt in the city in those years. This climate also influenced a number of men of letters, such as Giovanni Boine, Carlo Michelstädter and Dino Campana.

An important event occurred at the beginning of the 20th century. In 1902, the first general strike took place in Florence, preceded by a series of partial strikes. This was a very important demonstration, second only, in Italy, to the one held in Turin in February of the same year. The fact that comparison with a city which was one of the country's primary economic centres, the western point of the "industrial triangle" was possible, highlights the importance of the Florentine protest. It did not last long (from 30th August until 2nd September) but it was quite intense, due to the unanimous participation of the workers despite the numerous arrests made every night. It was indeed so intense that the Interior Minister sent troops on summer manoeuvres in the Mugello area (around 30 kilometres north-west of Florence) to the city, and gave the Prefect peremptory instructions: "The main squares - Duomo, Signoria, Santo Spirito oltre l'Arno, Indipendenza - must be occupied by at least one battalion each. Heavy cavalry patrols should move throughout the city." (Ballini, 1975).

In the early part of the 20th century a more traditionally individualistic and anarchist type of conflict emerged, characteristically perpetrated by the "teppista" (hooligan), one example of which was the young artist Ottone Rosai in the years following the First World War. Basically rebellious, and one of the first fascists, he was later unable to identify with the narrow-minded, philistine bourgeoisie which supported fascism, and turned to expressing his disappointment for the failure of the renewal process, which was compounded by long-standing, unresolved disagreements. He lacked a steady income, despite the early success of his paintings, and had stronger roots in a neighbourhood than a particular domicile; he loved visiting the city by night and was a loner by necessity. Over and above this particular example, isolation can generally lead to a progression of the "teppista" from potential rebel to misfit and, finally, to a bizarre character, personifying being "against everything", an attitude now popular as a general principle of the history of the Florentine people. Amongst the literary expressions of this more or less sterile rebellious stance are some of the tirades of Giovanni Papini, such as the slanderous pamphlet "Contro Firenze passatista" (Against a die-hard Florence) or the unseemly insult in verse about the banality of Piazza Vittorio (now Piazza della Repubblica). Vasco Pratolini was the only writer to describe the heroic deeds of proletarian Florence in the first half of the 20th century in several of his novels. A significant part of *Metello* (1955) is dedicated to the strikes of 1902 and the protagonist's role in the building sector. *Cronache di poveri amanti* (1946) describes the grim climate surrounding the rise and establishment of fascism (note the episode of the murder of "Maciste", the communist blacksmith, in the square in front of the Church of San Lorenzo). In *Il quartiere* (1944), the protagonist is the district of Santa Croce, riddled with the tensions and lacerations of the final stages of fascism which foreshadowed the Resistance; the beautiful finale illustrates the effects on the social structure of the demolition which began in 1939 in the heart of the novelist's birthplace.

Although strictly speaking outside the subject, the events which occurred during the final stages of the Second World War merit a brief comment. On 11th August 1944, Florence gained the distinction of freeing itself from Nazi and Fascist oppression before the arrival of British and American troops, and the significance for the entire country of the organisational ability displayed by the Comitato Toscano di Liberazione Nazionale (Tuscan National Liberation Committee) is well known. It is also true that there was no actual insurrection: the involvement of the people was manifested in a quite limited way. It was more a flare-up of initial enthusiasm than actual participation in the military actions which went on throughout the month of August in the northern part of the city (Fiesole was liberated on 1st September).
One singular episode of an environmental nature occurred during that period: it is said that the pigeons abandoned Florence during the most difficult times and returned *en masse* right after the city was liberated.

In the post-war years, two forms of religious opposition emerged. Their paths were different and both had a notable effect on the social community of the city. There was, of course no real and proper revolt, but rather very strong opposition. As a source, I refer here firstly to the reflections and works of Lorenzo Milani and, secondly to the Isolotto community.

In the former, the opposition began in the early years (1947-1954) of Father Lorenzo Milani's (1923-1967) ministry as a young chaplain. He spoke out critically in a compelling book Esperienze Pastorali (Experiences in Ministry), about the serious predicament of Christianization in a rural district on the outskirts of Florence, San Donato a Calenzano, during the time of the crisis of traditional agriculture, which was based on share-cropping, and the consequent move of the workforce to the textile industry in nearby Prato. The book provoked consternation in the Holy Archiepiscopal Institution, when it was published in 1958, four years after his ministry had ended. Towards the end of 1954, when the old parish priest died, disagreement among parishioners deprived Father Milani of the post and caused his removal from San Donato a Calenzano, and his banishment to a remote mountain parish, in S. Andrea a Barbiana, on the northern slopes of Mount Giovi, in Mugello, to the north-east of Florence. Remaining faithful, and not only formally, to the Church which had condemned him to total isolation, Father Milani responded with a truly revolutionary initiative: he set up an extraordinary school for children, whose parents were farmworkers, open all year round. Its main aim was to give the children concrete knowledge in reading, writing and spoken skills which would provide them with the necessary tools for moving into the modern world from their own one which, up to then, had been far from the developing civilized social community.

The ideas of work and teaching methods, together with the disapproval of the class-based discrimination in traditional schools, are to be found in the *Lettera a una Professoressa* (Letter to a Teacher, 1967) written on behalf of the "Scuola di Barbiana" (school in Barbiana): the book acquired world-wide fame, also because it was published in coincidence with the warning signs of '68. "Letter to a Teacher" remains a milestone for pedagogy and sociology from the 60's pointing to what was in decline, and Experiences in Ministry is an incomparable prophetical work

The community of Isolotto is linked to the council house neighbourhood of the same name built by Ina-Casa Constructors in the early 1950's – it was inaugurated at the end of 1954 - in the western suburbs of Florence, on the left bank of the River Arno opposite the Cascine Park. Despite the lack of infrastructure, the new district has remained the most successful of the new additions made to Florence from the 50's to the 70's. It established strong community cohesion, surprisingly so considering the inhabitants came from completely different places and backgrounds. Around the figure of the parish priest, Father Enzo Mazzi, the community became involved in a reflecting on issues of loss of faith-liturgy relationship, the improper use of the faith, etc aimed at bringing the church back to the social community. The community customs, typical in those years, from the assemblies to the vigils, have a strong and lasting power to create participation and remain an exemplary model to follow. The community of Isolotto is still in contrast with the Florentine curia. Furthermore, the events of '68 and in the religious world, the developing maturity of movements like Dutch theology and the theology of liberation in Latin America give the Isolotto experience an international aspect.

To conclude this brief review, mention should be made of the student uprisings of '68 which were particularly lively and saw considerable participation, especially in the Faculties of Architecture, Literature and Philosophy. With regard to the Faculty of Architecture, indeed 1968 can be considered the birth date of some of the present day trends in the teaching of city and territorial planning.

References

Gianni F.M. (1848), *Memoria sul tumulto accaduto in Firenze il dì 9 giugno 1790*, in: *Scritti di pubblica economia*, Firenze: Niccolai, I, 209-266.

Tumulti in Firenze la sera del 6 giugno 1861, ottava del Corpus Domini; storia contemporanea, Firenze: Tipografia della Minerva, 1861.

Il Ponte, anno I, n. 5, agosto 1945, dedicato a *La lotta clandestina e l'insurrezione di Firenze*. .

Conti E. (1950), *Le origini del socialismo a Firenze* (1860-1880), Roma, Rinascita.

Il Ponte, anno X, n. 9, settembre 1954, numero monografico su *La battaglia di Firenze*, nel decimo anniversario.

Milani L. (1958), *Esperienze pastorali*, Firenze: Libreria Editrice Fiorentina.

Capitini Maccabruni N. (1995), *La Camera del Lavoro nella vita politica e amministrativa fiorentina (dalle origini al 1900)*, Firenze: Olschki.

Scuola di Barbiana, *Lettera a una professoressa*. Firenze: Libreria Editrice Fiorentina, 1967.

Masini P.C. (1969), *Storia degli anarchici italiani da Bakunin a Malatesta*. Milano: Rizzoli.

Comunità dell'Isolotto, *Isolotto 1954-1969*, Roma – Bari: Laterza, 1971.

Rutenburg V. (1971 - ed. russa: 1954), *Popolo e movimenti popolari nell'Italia del '300 e '400*, Bologna: Il Mulino.

Luperini R. (1973), *Letteratura e ideologia nel primo novecento italiano*, Pisa: Pacini.

Ballini P.L., "Lotta politica e movimento sindacale in Toscana agli inizi dell'età giolittiana. Lo sciopero generale di Firenze", in: *Rassegna Storica Toscana*, anno XXI, n. 2, luglio-dicembre 1975, 243-295.

Spadolini G. (1977), *Firenze mille anni*. Firenze: Cassa di Risparmio di Firenze.

Istituzioni e società in Toscana nell'età moderna, Atti delle giornate di studio dedicate a Giuseppe Pansini, Firenze, 4-5 dicembre 1992, Roma, Ministero per i Beni Culturali e Ambientali, 1994, voll. 2.

London Un-Contested Capital?

4.1

TEXT..Michael Edwards
PHOTOS..Al Deane/Boris Baggs

Introduction

In this chapter we have a dilemma: many of the changes which are happening in London are not being effectively contested: systematic opposition to the dominant economic and political trends is absent or very weak as the new millenium begins. Yet we know of dozens or hundreds of oppositional activities and alternative projects (and are ourselves involved in some of them). How has it happened that effective resistance to corporate interests has been so thoroughly weakened in a city which has often prided itself on strong grass-roots organisation? This is one main theme of the chapter.

Just as resistance and criticism are fragmented, so is our own commentary on it, but we think that the passages which follow paint an accurate picture - partly because they are so fragmented.

In another sense, however, London is in a state of constant contest as individuals compete for jobs, for over-priced housing space, for a seat in the tube, for room to drive or park on the streets, for a good school for their children, for a place which feels safe from crime and to meet a host of other urgent needs. Corporations compete for operating space (driving commercial rents up and smaller businesses out); investors, domestic and foreign, compete for the limited stock of real estate (pushing values up and yields down) and one of Margaret Thatcher's dreams is coming true as we re-create the class of private housing landlords. Poor and middle-income people (and a lot of public services like schools and universities) survive in ever-decreasing amounts of space. And at the level of community action, localities are in competition with one another for pots of government money for "urban regeneration".

In this contested battle for public money, the prizes go to the localities which can present themselves as most deprived, but also as best organised to use the money and to account for it in a time-consuming and energy-sapping ritual of output-measurement. We are all forced into these multiple contests, whether we like it or not. In this sense London is truly a contested city but the contest is a divisive and wasteful one orchestrated by the state.

Tony Blair's "New Labour" government, elected in 1997, implemented its pledge to create a new London metropolitan government, filling the vacuum left after Margaret Thatcher abolished the Greater London Council (GLC) in 1986. The new authority is structured on a rather north-American model with a strong directly-elected mayor and a parallel elected chamber with powers of scrutiny and budgetary control. It is well-known that New Labour lost control of this new creature when it refused Ken Livingstone the right to stand as the Labour Party candidate for mayor. He stood as an independent candidate and won in the year 2000. This felt at the time like a victory for the left, like a warning shot across the bows of the New Labour regime. But it has been a mixed blessing, as we shall see and leaves the red-green spectrum feeling partly abandoned.

London: some Description

There are many Londons and many descriptions. This one is about the economic and social geography.

This introduction tries to sketch the main elements of what has been happening in London in the last few years. We have written as though we were addressing someone from far away and hope we have done it without seeming to be condescending to those who already know the story well. And because we do not normally sit back and give an account of our condition like this, we are not quite sure of ourselves.

"Uneven development" is a very helpful way of thinking. The results of uneven development are strongly apparent in London and its surrounding region. At the global scale, London (or at least its financial institutions and wealthy residents) sucks in a very large share of the world's income and wealth - which is thus controled here in the most internationally-oriented financial centre on earth. It is also one of the most cosmopolitan cities and international migration now contributes strongly to the growth of its population.

Within England and the wider United Kingdom (which includes also Wales, Scotland and the province of Northern Ireland) the South East continues to be the overwhelming concentration of high-income people, growing economic sectors and heavy investment. It is the destination of choice for migrants from many parts of the country, especially people coming to study or to start their careers.

Within the city and the region too, we experience dramatic - and sometimes growing - inequalities. Some localities prosper, with high-income residents, healthy investment flows, strong tax base and good services, while other localities concentrate poverty, overcrowded housing, unemployment and ill-health. While these local inequalities are severe by national and perhaps by some European standards, we do not have the extreme forms of large-scale ghetto common in the USA: most electoral wards contain a variety of ethnic groups. The strongest concentrations of people of uniform ethnic origin and class position are in some white suburbs on the edge of Greater London and in the luxurious 'countryside' and small-town settings of the green belt and of the outer region. See fig 1 which comes from the best and most recent book on the geography of London.

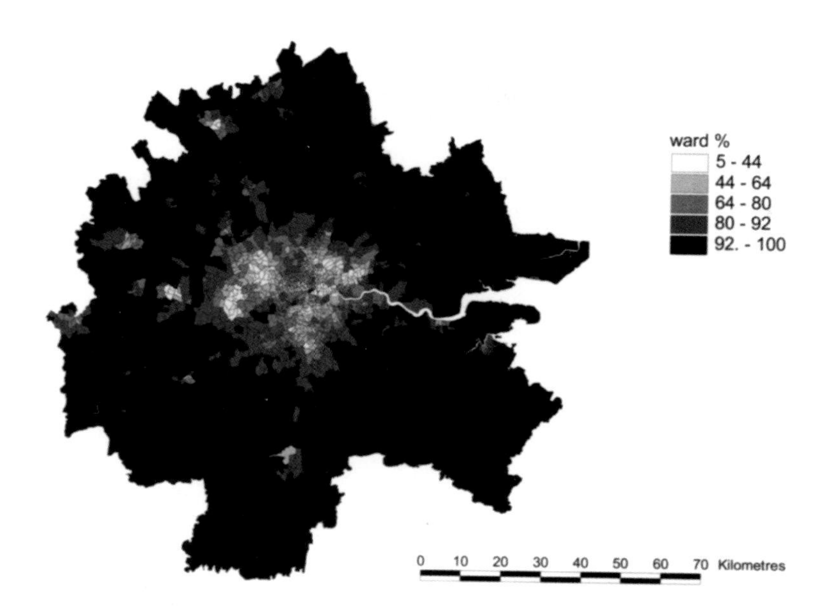

Fig 1: Percentage of population white, 1991. Source: Buck and others 2002 p 43 from the 1991 Census.

London: Interpretation

London is the subject of rival interpretations.

There is a neo-liberal view of the London situation in which its is seen as a success story of de-regulation and enterprise. It generates high incomes, strong growth of measured GDP (especially in finance and business services) and attracts strong flows of migrants - many of them highly qualified - who want to take advantage of its universities or its labour market to develop their careers. It has a unique concentration of cultural activities, a rich collection of outstanding new architecture, the core of music production and many jobs in government, consultancy and research of a kind which do not exist outside the capital. While competition for space is intense (and reflected in high costs for housing and business space), the market offers choice and automatic regulation of the pressures: those households and firms which do not want to afford London can (and do) move away to cheaper regions. The main aim of policy should be to keep the growth going.

An alternative view we might call "growth with redistribution". It shares the satisfaction with London's wealth and dynamism but points to the inequality of British society and the extreme version of that inequality which is found in London.

Those holding this view note the steps which the Blair government has taken to reduce inequality nation-wide through establishing a minimum wage, supplementing (or subsidising) low wages through negative taxation (Working Families Tax Credit) and helping many non-working households back into the labour market. It is accepted that these policies will not be enough to cope with London's needs because of the high cost of housing, so some of the extra growth generated in London must be re-distributed to compensate. In particular, property developers must be required to make some of the space they construct available as housing for low- and middle-income housing. However growth itself is not a problem - indeed it is essential because it represents the expanding wealth and income which can be used to solve problems. Thus all the investments which seem to be wealth-creating for London need support - additional airports and runways, more radial railways, the National Stadium, a bid for the 2012 Olympic Games. If we tried to limit the growth, these people claim, investors and employers would go away. And the key actors in finance and business services would not go away to poorer regions of the UK but to 'our competitors' New York, Tokyo or (worst of all) to Paris, Frankfurt or Amsterdam. This view of London seems to be the dominant one, shared by many segments of the business community and by mayor Ken Livingstone and his advisors.

Our more radical / critical view emphasises the fact that the way in which our growth takes place is itself the source of many of our problems. Specifically we argue that the very high incomes and wealth-concentrations found in London are generated through the impoversihment of others: of low-wage employees around the world and in London. The prosperity of the rich is made possible partly by the low pay of catering staff, domestic servants, public service workers and others within London. Furthermore the rich have a disproportionate effect on the prices and rents for housing, with the result that low- and middle-income people get less for their money than they would elsewhere. The national minimum wage, which may be adequate in the average British region, is a poverty wage in London. For those living on pensions or other welfare benefits, the same applies: what is an adequate income nationally is a poverty income in London. These special problems of London help to explain why national policies addressing poverty do not work effectively in London. The policy implications of this analysis are necessarily structural: the need is to modify or transform the structures and mechanisms which produce the problems. Proposals cover a wide range, from a root-and-branch resistance to contemporary global capitalism to interventions designed to strengthen the labour maket position of low-earners, socialise land and property markets and foster growth in sectors other than finance and business services.

This classification of views about London into three is an over-simplification of course, and may do less than justice to the position of the Mayor. He has fought two major battles in London which are quite remarkable: one victory and one defeat. The victory has been implementing the central London congestion charging scheme, which he pushed through against intense opposition from many car and business lobbies and in the face of sustained attack from London's only local newspaper, the right-wing Evening Standard. In the event this scheme has been a huge success, cutting central area congestion by 30-40%, speeding up buses and taxis, improving conditions for cyclists and pedestrians. This has been a very astute political move, demonstrating that a cheeky, stubborn, insistance on a good idea can change the world and confound critics.

Equally to his credit, Livingstone has also fought very hard indeed to persuade the British government to abandon its partial privatisation of the London Underground system through a 'Public Private Partnership' - PPP. After the total fiasco caused by the privatisation of the British railways, it should have been a relatively simple matter to force the abandonment of a similar scheme for the tube, and on this issue Livingstone had much wider popular and media support -including even the Evening Standard. However the business forces behind privatisation, and the neo-liberal ideologues in the Blair government were strong enough to defeat Livingstone: the PPP is being implemented during 2003.

In many other spheres, too, the Mayor has been a radical force - supporting gay and lesbian rights, developing broadly-based cultural strategy and offering leadership on the Iraq war and other international issues.

However the infant London administration does not (or not yet) seem to be the focus for a wider diffusion of democratic activity. The traditional politics of Labour and other parties is in serious decline, Trade unionism in London is relatively weak. Grass-roots and community politics have not blossomed to fill the vacuum. One element of explanation must be that Livingstone is an 'independent' mayor, not the candidate of a party. He is thus cut off from the organised support network which would be expected - and which he could call upon 20 years ago when he was Labour leader of the GLC.

Despite all this, there are elements of optimism within the left in London. Fragmentary, and often very localised, autonomous movements proliferate, the defence of social housing by tenants is very strong in some areas and the anti-war movement is powerful, very multi-ethnic and representative of all age groups, including many young people otherwise alienated from formal politics. The largest anti-war demonstration of February 2003 brought millions onto the streets of London (one million or three million, depending who you ask) and that was by far the biggest mass demonstration in British history.

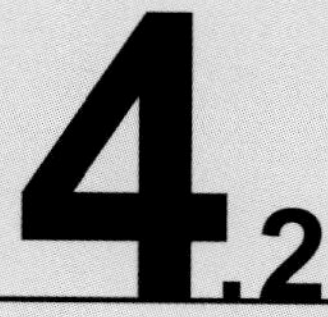

TEXT....................Louanne Tranchell
PHOTOS....................Al Deane/Boris Baggs

ACTION for Equality

With the election in 2000 of Ken Livingstone as Mayor of London we got back our voice which had been stifled since the abolition of the London metropolitan government in 1986. With that voice there came a new City Hall on the south bank of the Thames next to the Tower Bridge; an Assembly of regional representatives; the "spatial development strategy" (the London Plan); a whole raft of strategies on environmental improvements, economic and social frameworks, a lively website (www.london.gov.uk) and a busy cultural calendar. London is focussed again, motoring, with Ken at the wheel!

This new energy and sense of direction has reached many of the groups and individuals of London, many of the layers and the neighbourhoods. Yet there is clearly a contest taking place in this capital "world city" between Central Government and the Greater London Authority (known as the GLA). The New Labour administration which came to power nationally in 1997 promoted the legislation that returned this London tier of government, but they also worked hard to block Ken Livingstone from office. He was successful eventually as an independent and he promptly took on New Labour over the privatisation of the tube system, and laid out his stall with his distinctive and popular style. He and his diverse and clever teams are in a hurry: a four year term flies by. This Mayor himself is a natural insurgent.

The City Hall style is an asset to Londoners. Good publications along with lots of events. A full agenda with public debate and contentions. At a stroke, the Mayor makes a demand for 50% "affordable housing" in all housing planning applications. Very soon the driver is paying the £5 "Congestion Charge" in the centre of London and a whopping £100 fine if they drive in a bus-lane. Certainly the pigeons are feeling the pinch. (Ken who is famous for keeping newts, is determined to reduce and control the pigeons in Trafalgar Square.)

Unprecedented expansion of transport systems including another controversial bridge in East London. These are strategies to vastly improve public transport, reduce congestion, improve air quality, and create and manage high quality public spaces. Over the next five years the Mayor aims to create or upgrade 100 public spaces in London. The first ten projects have been identified across London; Trafalgar Square and Parliament Square Gardens are almost completed. Ken explains simply "I have always enjoyed walking through London's streets, squares and parks" - and you believe him and most of us join him.

Trafalgar Square, the Mall and Jubilee Gardens have hosted thousands of Londoners for the Millennium, the Golden Jubilee (of the Queen) and a whole range of cultural feasts including Chinese New Year, St Patrick's Day and Diwali. The Mayor has made over thirty reports to his Assembly describing the wonderful tapestry of communities and neighbourhoods that he has visited or supported. He has appointed a set of advisors and ambassadors to specialise in links with Londoners and their priorities. The problems continue, even increase, but the paths to solutions have been carefully made, and more resources and people assembled to tackle them.

Central Government is also pumping resources and "targets" into strictly defined local areas of "deprivation". It takes local people some time to swallow the fact that where they live has this negative "tag", but in some of the regeneration areas there are soon new facilities or training opportunities and "ways into work". There are mantras repeated on "social inclusion" "neighbourhood renewal" "new deals for communities" "Sure Start" "youth at risk" "crime reduction" and most of these are delivered through complex partnerships where the "grass-roots" have to fight their corner.

There is a good line in "carnival", from the tiny street party to the colossal Notting Hill Carnival, the culmination of August every year, now coming up to its 40th anniversary Many of the Mas(querade) artists, the steelpan orchestras, the lantern makers, the "face-painters", the mural and banner painters, the performers, dancers, DJs, soundmen, are now experienced, talented and original. The groups are not overt "rebels"; they apply for grants and stick to the criteria for the most part, but the tradition remains strong. They symbolically take over the streets to witness their identity in Britain. In the good fun that is generated, lies the ballast of "troubles" for the Irish, or slavery, colonisation and refuge for the many black communities in London.

The high profile rebels today are common to most leading cities and are in the anti-globalisation movements and social forums. London has a number of inventive and committed groups: the "Critical Mass" of cyclists who meet each month and cycle slowly along the streets of central London; "Reclaim the Streets" who are mostly young with street bands, costume and swift running with silky banners; "Campaign Against Arms"; "Friends of the Earth"; "Greenpeace". There are still a few raves, big parties, green fairs and "beach parties" at low tide by the Festival Hall. The "Stop the War" campaign and the big march were unforgettable events. London received thousands of marchers (the whole of Victoria, Park Lane and Knightsbridge were a coach-park), but there were thousands of Londoners there too. The banners were so witty, the bands brilliant, hundreds of children as well as elders, loud and shy, novice and old-hand and even the police were well behaved. It was crushing that the nightmare and the carnage in the "cradle of civilisation" still went ahead. The surface "price" is expressed in the concrete blocks around the Parliament building and the need to frisk people going into City Hall and public buildings.

It has been evident in the "Examination In Public" of the London Plan that there is much competition for space, land and quality of life. Can the neighbourhoods thrive and a world city grow? In central London even when the office market is "soft" - developers still make applications for office/hotel/retail/luxury housing because these permissions increase the land value and the planning authority looks on this as potential "economic development". The usual contest is between the developer's profit and useful local amenities and the London Plan cannot help much in that struggle. There is competition for road space, green belt, waterfront sites. Will the big developers support local facilities, residential moorings, allotments, rich-mix culture, refugees and newcomers like community-based developers in the Social Enterprise and Development Trust movements? There is a new "front" between security and liberty in the "terrorism" framework. There is the old "front" of objectors versus people enjoying themselves: youth, noise, festivity, alcohol, cannabis, parking, the 24hour economy.

The TUC (Trade Union Congress) and the HQs of most Trade Unions are in London. Since 2000 there has been a marked shift to the left with the result of each election for TUC General Secretary.

In this very wasteful city, 2003 is the first year of the London-wide penalties on landfill (a substantial tax per tonne) making waste-management more of a priority. 2004 is the year of wheel-chair access when all public buildings should have completed their adaptations according to building regulations. The Race Relation Amendment Act 2000 (RRAA2000) now requires local authorities and institutions to identify how they can deliver an "equality" service to all in their care - the duty is now on them to draw up a strategy, not just a state arbitration over abuses. We have no plans to join the "single currency" yet but London will make a bid for the 2012 Olympics which will impact on Lottery funding for other Londoners.

There is an interesting "change" being steered by English Heritage and London Tourism. The new slogan is "An Historic City for a Modern World". Instead of red (buses, phone and letter boxes, guards summer uniform) - there is a shift to silver (bridges, Canary Wharf, the wheel- the London Eye). Objectors poured scorn on the London Plan for its lack of care for "heritage, historic buildings, views, a sense of place". London is led to believe that it has a buoyant economy yet almost every locality has a recent- sometimes a dramatic-loss of a local swimming pool, sports field, football club, nursing home, local butcher, baker or hardware shop, post office, nursery school, community centre. There are pressures on local services from the supermarkets, from new technology, and some local council seek to improve their facilities through the mechanisms of doubtful financial partnerships (PPP PFI). These are issues that raise large turnouts in local meetings and widespread exchange of expertise via locally based websites, press and radio -with some successes.

Local Action for Equality is a constant process. Some of the most serious social conflicts are in the towns and cities outside London where the British National Party (of the extreme Right) has gained several local council seats, often boosted by inept management of local regeneration schemes. London has a developed a skill-base of tolerance, especially among the young, supported as a core value in both the statutory and voluntary sectors There is wide acknowledgement among institutions and faith groups that this is not optional, and that it is a necessary strength. There is "prejudice" as in any settlement and that is a personal flaw, but "discrimination" is a crime; not only dangerous harassment and assault, but all forms of denial of equal opportunity.

2003 is the 10th anniversary of the death of the teenager Stephen Lawrence, stabbed at a bus stop by a group of racist youths. His parents fought a long battle with the police and the state, which brought about a public inquiry that led to big shake-ups in how all staff are trained in the Metropolitan Police and other public institutions. The Mayor has dedicated the annual "respect" festival (London's biggest and best free anti-racist and multicultural festival) to be held at the Dome to the memory of Steven Lawrence who wanted to be an architect.

The Emerald Centre

by Joyce Wade

The Emerald Centre was refurbished and re-opened as community centre in 1986 with funds from the local council and the Greater London Council (GLC - just before it was abolished). It is located on the central island site, that is over the tube station in Hammersmith Town Centre.

There is a hall with 350 capacity and a planted front garden. It is a popular venue for classes, rehearsals and events. Groups and tutors run their own sessions; organisers run their own events. The Emerald Centre has been managed by the voluntary organisation Hammersmith Community Trust since 1987; I have been the centre manager for the past five years.In the early years it was subsidised by grants but in my time it has been self-funding. It is especially important to the local Black communities for family, carnival fund-raising and other social events. For anniversaries and birthdays; engagement and weddings; re-unions and graduations; funerals and commemorations; blessings and namings.

It is also used by many groups who need space to practice physical skills: traditional English Morris Dance sides and groups who train in martial arts; young performers, start-up theatre and dance groups. Meetings and conferences are held in the Emerald Centre and 'umbrella' events in Refugee Week, Black History Month, May Day and the local Borough Festival. Carnival Arts, stone carving and other workshops are held in the hall and out in the yard. London Transport owns the site and there have been a series of short leases with the understanding that this site will be redeveloped to complete the town centre scheme. We have now received notice that London Transport only want to do an 'interim' scheme, for 5-10 years. Hammersmith Community Trust has consulted widely with users and has worked up a replacement scheme with other partners.

The fortunes of this town centre development have been up and down. London Transport were too deeply 'in the red' to develop a scheme designed by Norman Foster in 1980. They teamed up with the Dutch developer Bredero who went bust in the 1990 property collapse. They sold on to Slough Estates who then sold to the Walt Disney Co. Ltd in 1995.Walt Disney Co. Ltd were granted planning permission for two buildings, only one of which they built. The second included a planning gain agreement to make space for the replacement of the Emerald Centre. They have now sold their remaining strip of land back to London Transport who have said that they intend to expand the bus station, which they chose to build on the first floor level. We have hundreds of users who are now asking for support for this popular community facility. There is disbelief that a UK public body will not honour a similar agreement which was entered into by a US global corporation.
We have more ways to network now with e-mails and mobile phones; there are more 'neighbourhood strategies' and 'social inclusion' frameworks to point to; there are some dedicated funds and the lottery (if the Olympic bid does not claim it all). Most of all, there are the growing numbers of young people and our new generation that need this kind of facility to keep their parties and train their skills. This is the kind of place which is the right size and status in which to meet, learn and celebrate - and it is reassuring to us as parents and elders that we can go on growing together.

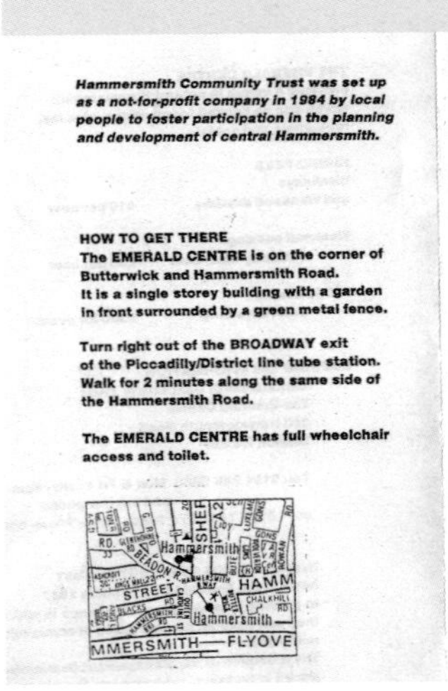

Hammersmith Community Trust was set up as a not-for-profit company in 1984 by local people to foster participation in the planning and development of central Hammersmith.

HOW TO GET THERE
The EMERALD CENTRE is on the corner of Butterwick and Hammersmith Road.
It is a single storey building with a garden in front surrounded by a green metal fence.

Turn right out of the BROADWAY exit of the Piccadilly/District line tube station. Walk for 2 minutes along the same side of the Hammersmith Road.

The EMERALD CENTRE has full wheelchair access and toilet.

Emerald Centre

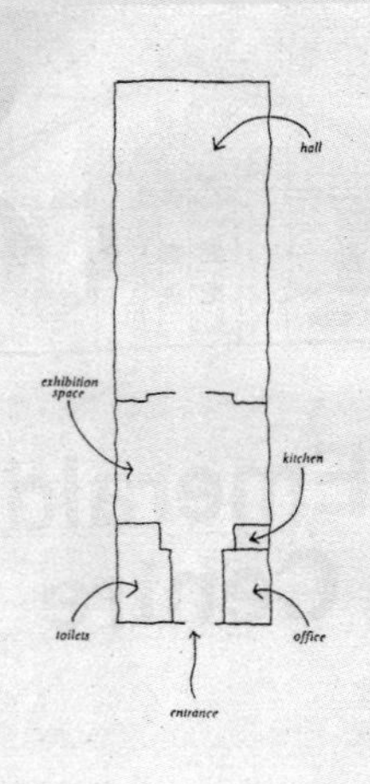

Joyce Wade and Judith Pierre at Emerald Centre

170.171

Hammersmith and Fulham Refugee Forum

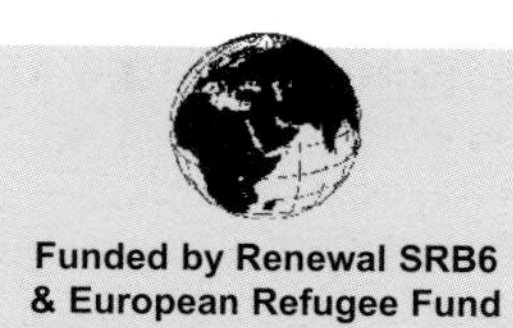

Summary Report by the Co-ordinator, Ayar Ata
To: Open Forum Meeting on 19 September 2002

Funded by Renewal SRB6
& European Refugee Fund

The Forum was launched in November 2000 after several months of preparation work by local refugee community groups and by close involvement and practical advice from the Hammersmith and Fulham Community Law Centre. I am employed by the Law Centre to work as Co-ordinator of the Refugee Forum. The following is a short report covering our activities and progress since October 2001 when I started my work.

In March 2002 the Forum managed to organise its first Annual General Meeting which was very well attended and successful. The first elected Management Committee with twelve representatives from local refugee groups and three from local advice agencies, including the Law Centre, helped the Forum to shape a sound and strong structure designed to help the refugee organisations take leadership roles on issues of importance to them.

In line with the strategic role of the Forum as an active, representative voice for the refugee community, the Forum Management Committee set up different taskforces: Housing and Welfare, Health, Training, Immigration and Legal, Finance and Personnel. These taskforces will address specific issues and problems facing the refugee community and also develop partnerships with other relevant agencies in order to improve communication and exchange of information among all parties, for the benefit of refugees and asylum seekers in the borough.

The Forum's main areas of work are:

• Fundraising: The Forum has helped five small groups to raise over £300,000 toward the operating costs of their offices, employing staff and organising community events. There are tow aspects of capacity building for refugee community organisations: one is resources and the other is training. For many small groups with little experience and often no resources, apart from their willingness and effort to help others, they also need training to learn about how to run a voluntary group or a charity in this country. However, before doing anything some funding is required and to successfully fundraise it is often necessary to demonstrate that you are trained and have some office space. It is the famous catch 22, is it not? We have been working with some organisations to overcome these challenges.

• The Forum has made over 100 outreach visits between October 2001 and September 2002 to refugee community organisations, providing face to face advice, information and practical support, for example, about fundraising. These visits have been important in establishing and maintaining a strong link between the Forum and its members. They have also provided groups with an opportunity to communicate their needs and interests more directly. The goal of this type of action research has been to identify the problems together and try to find the best way to deal with them together. The key aim is to work with groups rather than for them.

• One practical outcome of these visits was to identify some of the training needs of groups. As a result, a 10-week customised training programme entitled: Organisational Management and Active Citizens was planned and delivered with the help of Community Liaison of Hammersmith and Fulham Council, regenasis and the Volunteer Development Agency. As well as management, the course covered housing, benefits and immigration rights. Quoting from the feedback forms many participants were very satisfied with the above course, saying, " I learned new things". Some went on to attend the assessment day at Hammersmith and West London College and asked for further and more advanced training. One student has applied to East London University to study a degree course on refugees and migration in the UK. The Forum organises regular "Open Forum" meetings at which representatives from both voluntary and statutory agencies can discuss issues of concern to refugees and asylum seekers. This is an important achievement for us because many different people are able to and show increasing willingness to talk and listen to each other. This is an essential first step toward creating a real and meaningful community partnership, with a real chance given to community groups to speak up and feel included in the process of local decision making. The agenda of the meetings are well considered, providing groups with direct control over who is invited and who talks for how long. Of equal importance is the notion of accountability of the Forum MC to its members meeting where full reports are given.

• A very successful Refugee Week event organised in June 2002 by Forum members. Over 100 people attended and enjoyed this local community celebration. Three local refugee organisations, Kurdish Association, Fulham Somali Women's Group and the Somali Women's Support and Development Group jointly organised the event, which was the first time Kurdish and Somali groups came together to work on the same project.

• Refugee Forum workers and volunteers, including the members of the Forum Management Committee, have attended many networking meetings and presentations have been made to different statutory and voluntary agencies. Mulat Haregot, chair of the Forum MC and a member of the Law Centre MC, gave a presentation to regenasis board, a local Regeneration agency working with Hammersmith and Fulham Council. He successfully raised the profile of the Forum as an umbrella organisation representing refugee community in this borough. I made a similar presentation to Council workers and officers with the aim of helping refugees access job training. Many participants admitted that they knew nothing or very little about the existence of refugee community organisations, showed appreciation for their contribution to the wider community and expressed their interest in working with refugee community organisations in the future.

• The Forum looks ahead with confidence.

The Management Committee held several successful meetings this summer, the following action plan agreed:

1) Completing legal and administrative paper work, including registration with companies house, opening a separate bank account and fundraising.
2) Finding a suitable office space in the Hammersmith area
3) Organising a policy day and relevant training for MC members, the policy day is arranged for 3rd October 2002 at Palingswick House.

Residential Boats and Moorings on the River Thames

by Clive Wren

Inquiry into the planning application for: Proposed Moorings/ Land east of Riverside Court, Nine Elm Lane, London SW8

These are the final comments of the appellant:

1. This stretch of river is lined with wharves. Although many are disused, the principal function of the river is still as a navigable waterway of which adequate and safe moorings are an essential part. The appellant contends that moorings are an appropriate use of the site and that the developments would neither destroy the open character of the river nor result in the loss of an identified local view.

2. Not only is there a lack of mooring facilities on the river, but also of sites where moorings can be provided. As the River Thames Society and Thamesbank point out, much of the riverbank has been redeveloped for luxury flats and riparian owner consent is generally unavailable. Also, unless there is a provision at the planning stage, such development makes it difficult to access and service moorings adequately.

3. There is no prospect of moorings being developed between the appeal site and Nine Elms Pier or between the appeal site and Vauxhall Bridge because the river bank is occupied almost entirely by apartment blocks. The proposed moorings would occupy a tiny proportion of river frontage along this stretch: the rest would remain completely open.

4. Groups with experience of these types of development (the River Thames Society, Thamesbank, the Residential Boat Owners Association, and the Hammersmith Community Trust) agree that the proposed moorings would enhance the special environmental quality of the riverside at this location.

Suggested Conditions:

The appellant would have no objection to any of the conditions suggested by the Council should the appeal be allowed.

Objection 1: The proposals take account of any invertebrate communities in the foreshore by supporting boats and pontoons on ribs of ballast-filled bags and by creating additional areas in the terraces where they could live undisturbed. There would be no significant reduction in available food for fish or in the fish population as a result of the proposals. The moorings would provide shade and shelter for fish and food in the form of weed growth on the sides of the vessels and structures. It is well know to waterway users who enjoy watching wildlife that moorings attract fish and birds, including shy ones such as the heron, kingfisher and yellow wagtail.

Objection 2: The proposed moored vessels would be unlikely to cause significant scour or siltation.

Objection 3: The proposals are designed to maintain the Statutory Flood Defence Level of 5.41 m OD. A higher level of flood defence could be accommodated if required. If the appeal is allowed, this issue would be dealt with in the application to the Environment Agency (EA) for Land Drainage consent, and in details pursuant to Condition 3 as suggested by the Council. The moorings would afford a safe landing place in the event of a flooding incident.

The Environment Agency's conservation duties apply equally. It is significant that they do not object to the proposals on grounds concerning natural beauty and amenity.

The EA's encroachment policy does not take account of the fact that residential boats are also used recreationally in navigation - many people can only afford to own a boat because it provides them with a home. Residential moorings also enable facilities for visiting boats to be provided and enhance security and safety on the river and the riverbank.

TEXT...Penny Koutrolikou

Grassroots Activity in London - New Perspectives

The spring months of 2003 have been extremely eventful for London. Furthermore, summer is almost here and with it, along come the summer parties, festivals and other events that change the common perception of London as a stressful working city. On the other hand, what took place in London in the last few months, while the 'war against terror - chapter 2003' was unfolding in another continent was something - or even better some things - which suggests a transformation of a long standing defeatist attitude towards action and participation that had dominated the English political scene, putting people and politics together or against each other, but mainly in action.
Community participation and action has been an old established tradition in England, for many years. Voluntary and community associations and groups were thriving and they actually were able to influence decisions. Until recently, part of this attitude - and probably an important part - disappeared into disillusionment with politics and action, mainly due to the events of the Thatcher period. Since then activity has been mostly very muted.

In a global city such as London, with hectic lifestyles, long costly travel distances and constant flows, it seems reasonable that people tend to associate themselves with those they work with and places where they live. Alongside its broader image, London is an extremely localised city - even more so when we look to the more deprived areas / boroughs where distance, time and cost intensify the local focus. Ironically, as in most other cities, these are the areas that are extremely important in the national regeneration and development agenda and where most of the capital investments and programmes which make up 'urban policy' take place.

Within these vast regeneration and development initiatives, incorporating dozens of organisations, companies and schemes, what has come up as being crucially important is the role of the community. Community participation and involvement has been recognised as one of the key elements through which success would be assured. What exactly was (and is) meant by that, to what degree the community is allowed to participate or be heard, and even more, which communities are encouraged to participate and which are not, were questions that remained outside the agenda. Especially when delivery agencies realised the potential of using community consultation as a device through which 'communities' are persuaded that they have been taken into consideration.

The multi-level and intricate maze of regeneration in London works in accordance with the highly localised character of the city and the structures of the community, voluntary or collective associations. Similarly, the collapse on one level of great ideologies and actions in favour of more locally or non-governmental collectives and actions is strongly visible, and increasingly so in the late 1990s and earlu years of the new century.

While 'politics', in the common formal perception, have been severely damaged along with traditional forms of action and intervention from what is termed the 'community', several other forms of information dissemination, debate and dialogue have arisen, not necessarily new but with different focus, aims and praxis. These forms reflect a broader transformation that engages and acts locally while still carrying a broader vision, and is especially based upon the co-operation and networking beyond structured and absolute boundaries. This is a transformation which has been highlighted under the banner of the anti-globalisation movement, but which also exists very locally. Under this spectre, one case that seems to vividly reflect these characteristics while actually managing - at times - to put forward actions and changes that affect a locality or London in general, is the case of Urban75, especially of its bulletin boards.

Although quite a famous website, or, to be more precise, e-magazine, the impact Urban75 has had during the last few years is not widely known. It influence extends over the reality and events of its locality-Brixton-but also over broader London issues. In its own words

"urban75 is the bewildering obsession of Mike Slocombe who has single-handedly run the site since 1995, ably assisted by a small collection of contributing chums. With an independently accredited hit rate of over half a million individual users per month, urban75 is one of the most popular sites of its type on the web. It serves up a non-mainstream viewpoint on a wide range of issues including environmental action, rave culture and civil rights, as well as offering essential drug information, rave rants and resources, cartoons, short stories, a popular photo gallery and, of course, "the most useless games on the web" (USA Today). The site also runs some of the liveliest bulletin boards on the web. Despite its popularity, urban75 remains resolutely non commercial and carries no ads, banners or cheesy sponsor tie-ins."

For a website and an e-magazine created for football fans as a response to the Criminal Justice Act, it has grown much larger than expected. Urban75 obviously is not the only popular e-zine in the UK Internet scene and is not the only one that deals with issues ranging from drugs, to football, to politics to DIY or that host bulletin boards. But, it is definitely important, especially for the bulletin boards that have managed to have an impact on contemporary situations. From even the first visit to the bulletin boards, one has the feeling of entering a collective. The themes vary and so do the 'forums' within them. Still, inside each discussion topic, inside each 'forum', there are some prevailing characteristics: the sense that some people feel close to each other, the realisation that a certain form of network exists where everyone can participate-even as a visitor. The network is adequately open so that first timers do not feel outsiders, and it can also exist beyond the web. The discussions and debates that take place, range from advice for housing, life and current events for newcomers to concerns and information about current situations and actions to be taken in response.

OK, one might say that up to now, nothing has been extremely new or important so where is the point?

The crucial point is when the discussions in the bulletin boards escape the web and are transformed into actions. Within the last couple of years examples of such events were many. Being strongly rooted in a locality, namely Brixton, concerns about the future of the area, the problems that exist and which confront people, the lifestyles that exist and can be enjoyed, and a broad dissemination of information and knowledge, come high on the discussions. Brixton is already a famous and infamous place, facing serious problems along with substantial investment and development while also being constantly on the verge - if not in the centre - of gentrification processes and tension. All these are reflected in the bulletin boards - not only as observations and opinions but also as information, experience and advice or action.

There is a strong concern about gentrification, about people being 'priced out', about different lifestyles overtaking the place through their money, about increasing tensions. These concerns, for a change, are articulated not by academics but by people who actually experience the changes in their lives and reality. Similar worries are expressed regarding crimes, especially drug related ones, in an area that carries a strong stigma of it. At the same time, worries are also expressed about police and police reaction to this or to perceived crime. Even more, grounded in the area's tradition, there has been a strong reaction against racism, especially when expressed in policies and attitudes of big club and bar owners. Chained ownership of entertainment and the changes it provokes by pricing out other local businesses and lifestyles is another recurrent and strong issue.
For each of these issues and events happening, there has been a strong discussion, information exchange and influence over decision-making in several ways. The major stakeholder of the night time economy has been drawn to participate in these discussions regarding accusations about racism in his clubs. Opposition to his take-over and expansion in the area is currently on-going regarding a planning application recently put forward to which resistance is growing - although private interests are strong. Similarly, another night businessman was put into the bulletin boards to answer accusations of somebody being drugged in his club - and actions were taken.

An issue with even greater impact and influence for Brixton, was the debate triggered around a chief police commissioner and a programme going on at Brixton last year regarding the temporary decriminalisation of use of cannabis. The programme and the police commissioner were heavily criticised by some - which led to his removal from the post - while local residents mainly insisted on having him back. A strong debate took place in the bulletin boards, with this police officer answering and that, amongst other actions, led to his re-instatement.

At the same time, a lot of information and local knowledge is offered to new arrivals in the area, while also, transcending the virtual to the real: meetings (mainly for socialising) and parties often take place, providing an actual place and opportunity for people to meet and interact - if they choose to do so.

All these cases refer mainly to the bulletin boards regarding Brixton and London. Other information on events and actions is disseminated through other forums, each acting as a network connecting people to groups or actions, or distributing information and local knowledge. In each of them, the sense of collective / collectivity-and not necessarily of community-is strong, along with a sense of people caring enough and being prepared to act and to escape apathy.

These issues might seem trivial in the broader perspective of change in a city such as London.There are a lot of awkward questions.
What is the importance of some actions or resistance taking place in Brixton while the overall picture is just slightly transformed?
At another level, certain questions arise, regarding the dangerous exclusion of those whose access to the Internet is limited or none.
Is there another danger too, that the relative de-politicisation that attracts people to the bulletin boards and sites is also potentially damaging to the development of democracy by putting formal politics and organised actions right off the agenda (although it provides information about these as well).

The success of the bulletin boards of urban75 depended on several features, some general and some specific to the reality of London. On an immediate level, its success depended upon a critical mass of people being there and taking upon themselves to defend the boards against other people attacking them with offensive or accusing material. What attracted this critical mass of people to these particular boards could be broadly summarised under two headings. Firstly the sites have a charachetr which is not overtly political and that attracts many people for whom 'politics' is associated with formal organisations, rigid agendas, established ideologies. Many people simply do not want to be associated with organisations which are 'political' in this sense, however radical they may be.
Secondly, the mixture and diversity of interests in the whole site works as a main attractor from the beginning. The discussions in the forums also reflect this diversity between the people who participate in them - diversity of age, ethnicity, background and social circumstances - especially highlighted in the area forums.

Because of the nature of the bulletin boards, the conventional anonymity provides the necessary first step for those willing to participate but not confident enough to do so in person. Moreover, the diversity of the people involved and the indeterminate structure of the forums (both in theory and in meetings) means that more people from diverse backgrounds are involved. This, by itself, creates a critical mass and a network connecting to several other networks with which each participant also identifies him/herself.

In a large city fragmented into small and diverse localities and complicated transport, united mainly under the 'London' image and through work relations and 'big' events or 'disruptions', local knowledge, actions and networks that expand beyond localities are crucial - especially when they come face to face with corporate interests. Due to London's role as a world city and to the intense domination of corporate interests over ideologies and governments, it is extremely hard for counter-opinion to be heard - unless on a local level. There are several levels and several needs to be addressed both by organised actions, activists, non-governmental organisations and local people. The examples that manifested themselves through the forums of the bulletin boards highlight a form of action beyond what is commonly perceived as 'political action' They are also examples of a transitional political reality

The ability to transcend (local or strictly political) boundaries and create affiliations, networks and co-operation with those sharing some common beliefs and ideas (rather than forming separate, isolated blocks that each fight their own battle) along with the ability to operate locally and globally is one of the current features of political action that has intrigued and has been subject of questioning, especially through what has broadly been named as the 'anti-globalisation' or 'anti-capitalist' movement. Under its banner, a lot of different collectives and groups have been put together and have acted together; groups from institutional politics, NGO's, radical action, and so on. Without claiming that this transition is new, it is one that keeps happening on different levels all around the world. In some way, urban75 partially reflects this transition, along with the power that local action might have. It is a process that hasn't ended yet. It is still ongoing in several places. If someone is interested in the small locality of Brixton, or even sometimes London , they can pay a visit to www.urban75.com and perhaps join in.

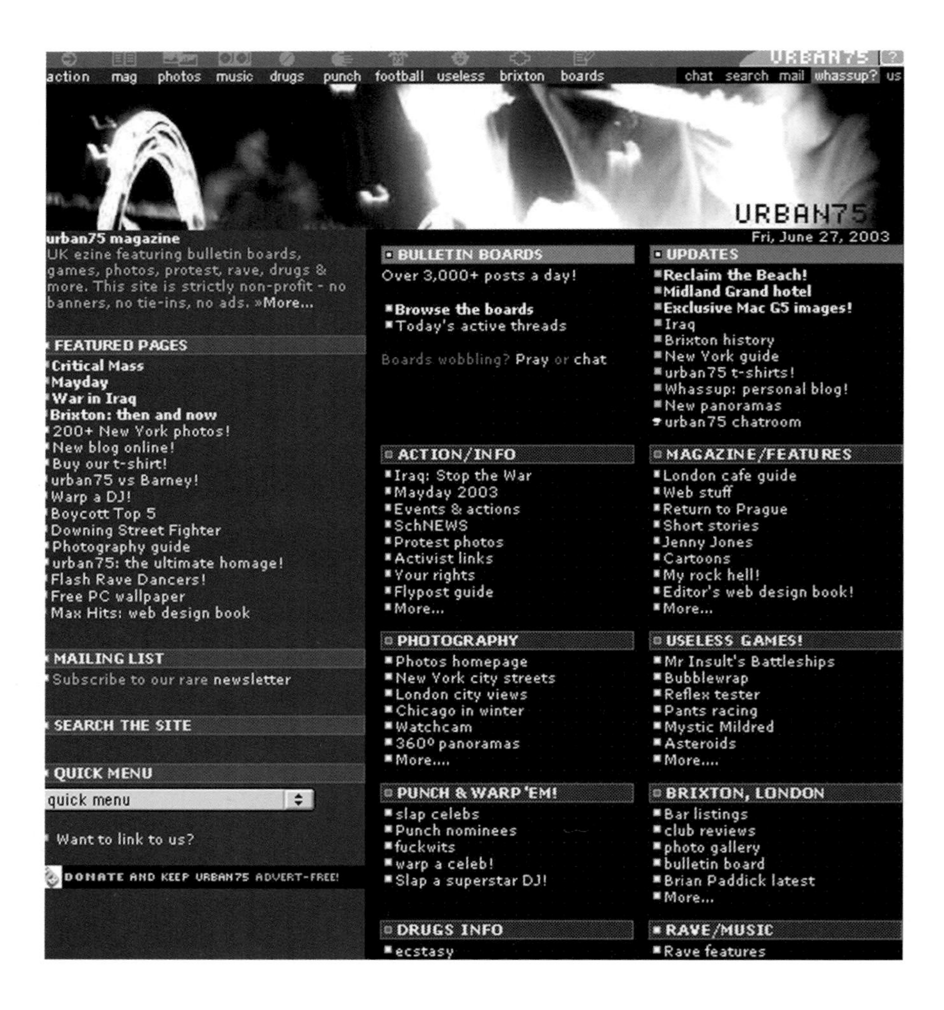

TEXT..........Michael Edwards
PHOTOS..........Al Deane/Boris Baggs

Wealth Creation and Poverty Creation: Global-Local Interactions in the Economy of London

London is at an important stage: after 15 years of de-regulation and weakened democratic institutions it is grappling now with a new government structure (outlined by John Tomaney 2001) and the preparation of new strategic plans (see Doreen Massey 2001).

The focus here is on the interaction in London of markets for land, housing, commercial property, transport and labour - markets which can be instruments of innovation and dynamism but which can also be instruments of exploitation and inequality. It is argued that London's draft strategic plans have not yet got the measure of this dualism, indeed they stand to benefit real estate interests, established owner-occupiers and the financial sector, at the expense of poor and middle-income people and at the expense of the less glamorous parts of the economy which make it robust and which offer the best chances of employing poorer people of all ethnic groups.

This section of the London chapter examines the relationship between international and local processes in London. It formed the basis for objections made at the Examination in Public (public hearing) on the Mayor's Draft London Plan in April 2003. An earlier version was published in 2002 in the journal CITY (vol 6, no 1).

Global position and the capture of value

It is so hard to say, nowadays, where economic life takes place. The stores in London's West End are stacked with clothes, designed perhaps in Italy, London or New York, cut and made up in China and the Philippines from textiles woven in Turkey or Pakistan, on machines from Italy or Germany. They arrive by air freight at Heathrow, in aircraft made in Seattle and Toulouse, and reach the store via warehouses in the periphery of London. On arrival they are sold by workers from inner and outer London (and some from far beyond) to customers from across the world and across the nation. Such stories are so familiar that we become blasé about them - and about the flows of income and wealth which correspond to such an extended system of industrialisation.[1]

A city captures, for a while, certain stages and moments in these processes - in this example London has design, retailing, some transport and a share of the resulting income and wealth. But the income and wealth does not show up in proportion to the contributions by workers in each country. As more of the world's activity comes to be dominated by the corporations which orchestrate and finance production and marketing (at the expense of firms and workers which carry out the operations), so we find more of the income and capital accumulation showing up as the 'product' of these dominant corporations and companies. Their offices are highly concentrated in great cities, along with the financial companies which handle the transactions. Part of London's role as a 'world city' is to be a place where such wealth appears to be created: the productive work is done all over the world but the surplus value created across the world shows up in the 'value added' statistics for London.

In some respects these relationships are nothing new. David Harvey in the last INURA book reminded us of a much earlier account:

"The bourgeoisie has through its exploitation of the world market given a cosmopolitan character to production and consumption in every country. To the great chagrin of reactionists, it has drawn from under the feet of industry the national ground on which it stood. All old-established national industries have been destroyed or are daily being destroyed. They are dislodged by new industries, whose introduction becomes a life or death question for all civilised nations, by industries which no longer work up indigenous raw materials, but raw material drawn from the remotest zones; industries whose products are consumed not only at home but in every quarter of the globe. In place of the old wants, satisfied by the productions of the country, we find new wants, requiring for their satisfaction the products of distant lands and climes..."
Marx and Engels, *The Communist Manifesto*, 1848
(partially quoted in Harvey, 1998).

When Marx and Engels were writing, however, it was perfectly clear that inequalities and exploitation were endemic within metropolitan capitalism: exploitation was clearly local as well as global. What has changed is our capacity to see that the metropolitan economy - the London of today - is both a fabulous producer of new products, new processes and new wealth and a powerful system for producing and transmitting inequality, not just across the world but within the urban society itself. This failure to understand is a threat to our capacity to plan and act collectively. If we had a better grasp of the underlying social and spatial relationships we would be halfway to changing them - so we could have some of the benefits without so much of the inequality and inefficiency.

For the last 3 years London has had, once again, an elected metropolitan government: an assembly and a mayor (Ken Livingstone), charged with producing 'strategies' for the economy, transport, culture, environment and spatial development (Edwards 2001; Tomaney 2001). Some of these 'strategies' are creative and radical documents, grounded in good analytical work and extensive participation - those on Culture and (to some extent) on Poverty Reduction. Some of the mayor's most important actions have been major challenges to the neo-liberal orthodoxy. His greatest campaign has been to prevent the British central government from going ahead with the privatisation of the infrastructure of the London Underground network. On this issue he fought extremely long and hard, gathering support from most Londoners, from many business interests and even from the reactionary local newspaper the Evening Standard which has a monopoly of the London market. All these efforts have in the end been defeated by the combined weight of the finance and construction companies (and their supporting lawyers and accountants) who stand to benefit and by the intransigent neo-liberalism of forces within the central government wich held the power of decision.

The other major project the mayor has been pursuing is the introduction of road pricing in central London. This scheme covers the city core of shopping, government and office activity - roughly the area inside the Circle Line and east of Hyde Park. Vehicles entering, or moving within, this zone between 0700 and 1830 except Sundays must pay a charge of £5 (just over €7) on each day. There are exemptions for public buses, taxis, emergency crews and a narrow group of others, including LPG vehicles, and there are big discounts for people living inside the zone. The charge really does seem to have deterred enough drivers (30% - 40% traffic reduction is reported after 6 months) to reduce congestion radically and enable buses to run at improved speeds, and thus better frequencies.

Since all the congestion in central London was caused by the tiny proportion of travellers who used their cars to drive into or through the centre, most users of the centre have been clear gainers, and those who could claim to be losers are very few. The detailed evaluation reports are not released yet but the public response seems to be satisfaction and euphoria: the mayor has shown that it is possible to push through something which had never been done before, do it quickly, and confound his critics. On this battle there had been strong opposition from retail and private transport lobbies and from the Evening Standard - ever a champion of liberty when it is the liberty to drive.

London thus has a mayor (sometimes supported by the Assembly) who is willing and able to fight some tough progressive battles on behalf of Londoners.

However there is a grave risk that the crucial economic and physical plans may be grounded in a dangerously neo-liberal understanding of the London situation and may thus fail to achieve, for its citizens, the egalitarian aspirations which the mayor and senior politicians espouse.

The aim of this text is to sketch an account of London's economic life which challenges the prevailing wisdom and to suggest ways in which the authorities should act differently. It is paradoxical (and may be reassuring to senior politicians) that the proposed shifts could work in favour of many business interests, as well as reducing impoverishment, exploitation and social exclusion.

There are many ways of thinking about the city. Here it is viewed through a discussion of the main markets which intersect in any city - the markets for labour, for transport and for land and buildings (including housing). This emphasis on markets is appropriate because a new feature of our society - and the UK has been rather in the lead - is a much greater reliance on market mechanisms for distributing what used to be public services: transport, housing, health, recreation, and energy.

Furthermore, markets are increasingly important in determining who gets access to the best of those services which remain universal and 'free': in particular, the housing market rations access to the best schools while the 'internal market' has changed the running of health and social services, universities and colleges in a search for efficiency, competition and 'choice'.

The combined effects of these processes are not understood, either for UK cities or internationally. The paper thus outlines some of these forces as they operate in the case of London, emphasising the problems which arise from the 'successful' operation of markets just as much as those flowing from market 'failure'. To explore these forces fully would be a major research programme, and the need for it is urgent.

Market societies, and the capital which drives the dynamism of markets, are constantly changing, producing new innovations, new surges of growth and accumulation and, although they typically distribute wealth and prosperity to many, they ensure that poverty remains the reality for a significant proportion of the population of many cities. My argument here is that London should be seen as a social system which produces poverty, just as it produces wealth, and that a lot of this impoverishment is avoidable.

Rapid change in market conditions occurs at global, continental and local levels, and within the city itself. Disparities between regions and within them remain severe and in many respects are worsening. Income differences between men and women, between social classes and between dominant ethnic groups and some minority ethnic groups remain stark and demonstrate the existence of inequalities within predominantly market economies. Within the London region many people are experiencing unprecedented prosperity; they can benefit from buoyant markets for labour, property and many goods and services while others have to compete in these markets with the odds stacked more sharply against them.

The international context

Whether or not 'globalisation' is a useful concept, we are clearly witnessing the extension of capitalism into new territories-what Hardt and Negri (2001) call the expansion of 'empire' - to include the former Soviet Union, the Middle East and Asia. The violent and destructive absorption of these new areas is proceeding fast, policed and implemented partly through pliant states, partly through enforcement action on the less-pliant states via the World Trade Organisation (WTO) (e.g. the assimilation of China) and partly through indirect trade with areas where states have failed. Events since September 11 2001 are clearly accelerating this process - indeed many would argue that the main aim of western policy just now is to press forward in the subordination of the whole globe, with central Asia next in line.

These events take place against a difficult economic background. One particular problem of the world economy in recent years has been its dependence on the long-run US trade deficit to make good the demand deficiency in the rest of the world, to keep the rest of us employed (Brenner 1998) and to prop up the profitability of the world's swelling mass of capital investment. This is a second important factor for us to bear in mind, especially when we think of the vulnerability of the UK and of the London economy to external shock: however robust the EU and the UK claim to be, this dependence on the USA cannot be ignored.

A third international dimension is the peculiarly strong role of foreign direct investment in the UK: both inflows and outflows of direct investment are extremely large, both absolutely and relatively to GDP. We are a remarkably open economy.

Is there a "London Economy"?

The concept of 'an economy' is a tricky one. It used to be clear enough at a national scale, especially for an island nation, with the bulk of activity taking place internally, and with international transactions linking the nation to the outside. If records are good enough we can construct national accounts. This is beginning to pose problems for the national economies of Europe as the single European market settles down and cross-border trade within Europe becomes ever harder to identify. The problems are much worse for any city, even the most clear-cut and well-bounded city region, where at least some key economic relationships lie within the region. Within a well-bounded city region it is plausible to think about supply-demand interactions in housing and labour markets. Greater London, however, is still defined on the 1964 boundary - roughly the area within the Green Belt (within the M25 motorway) - so the cross-border flows of income and of daily labour are huge and the housing market extends its influence 100km or more in all directions.

But the London Plan covers only Greater London, a somewhat arbitrary chunk of the activity of the region and of the nation so that is what this section concentrates on.

Measured activity within the London boundary

We have about 7.4m residents (Figure 2) in Greater London, of whom about half are economically active (GLA 2001, 9). There is a net inflow of commuters across the Greater London boundary of about 700,000, adding about a fifth of the workforce. (Labour Force Survey quoted in LDA 2001 24; ONS LRC GoL 2000)

The structure of activity, as conventionally measured in official statistics, is subject to all manner of reservations. GDP of course measures only recorded activity, not the mass of "cash-only" transactions with which we are so familiar: the whole drug market, a great deal of small construction, repair, cleaning and personal services and probably quite a lot of retail and catering work. GDP also omits (by definition) the environmental and other external effects of recorded activity. Furthermore, it handles non-market activity (like schools, universities, health, museums - which adds up to a large part of the London economy) on the basis of the costs of their inputs, rather than the value of their outputs; which leads to gross under-estimation of the value of public service work. Unpaid domestic and voluntary labour are of course omitted too.

The measured economy is demonstrably one in which finance and business services are dominant, contributing 39% of London GDP from only 32% of its employees (Figure 3). The numbers employed in these sectors have doubled in the last decade, despite mechanisation and labour-shedding in routine banking and insurance. Interestingly, the manufacturing sector in London is just as productive in terms of GDP per worker: it's a small sector in size but manages to be dynamic and flexible enough to survive, even in the face of the high costs which it confronts in London.[2]

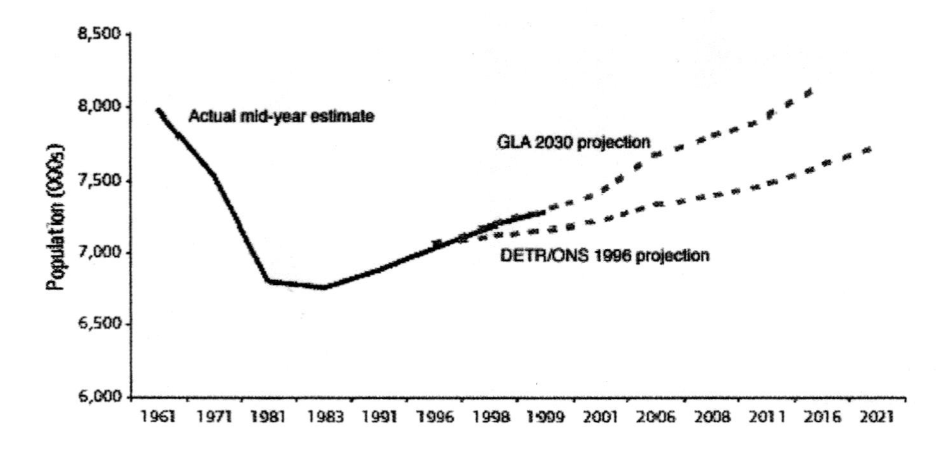

Fig 2 Greater London population since 1961 and projections to 2021
Source: (GLA 2001 fig 3).

At the other extreme we have distribution, hotels, catering and many other services which contribute far more to employment than they do to GDP. In other words they are low productivity, labour-intensive activities - and hugely important: a quarter of working Londoners are engaged in shops or hotels or catering; a further quarter in public services.

Recent years have seen a very patriotic, almost 'gung-ho' approach in descriptions of the London economy, led by agencies whose job is to promote inward investment, but often echoed by consultants and researchers. We thus hear a great deal about the innovation and creativity of the economy, the overwhelming popularity of London as a visitor destination and gateway, the ability of its markets to dominate various international exchange processes and so on.[3]

What is obscured by that perspective is the dual character of London as simultaneously a wealth machine and a poverty machine, as sets of relationships which produce exploitation and deprivation as surely as they produce growing net outputs. We should probably be glad that the Economic Development Strategy as revised last summer does include passages which acknowledge at least some of the problems, and all the latest Mayoral documents do contain some re-distributive measures.[4] However my contention is that the mechanisms which produce our dual character remain effectively hidden. This is partly because - as market relationships - they are widely viewed as in some way 'natural'.

The extension of markets

The extension of market relations into ever wider areas of urban life further obscures the underlying relationships: in the days when the city council allocated housing sites the issues were clearly political; now that market criteria are seen to rule, the issues are the de-politicised ones of 'viability' and 'financial feasibility', abstracted and presented as unquestioned realities. Who are we to challenge these? The decision-making techniques for 'feasibility testing' are now taught to students of planning as part of their 'technical' courses as though they were as value-neutral as forecasting heat loss through a wall.

The 'extension of market relations' sounds abstract and perhaps a bit fussy. But the last two decades have seen so many - individually small - changes in how goods and services are distributed that we are in danger of missing the massive cumulative impact. Stephen Graham has showed how the liberalisation and privatisation of telecommunications have led to dramatic polarisation in access to information between affluent and powerful groups and those in conditions of 'advanced marginality' whose access may actually be getting worse (Graham 2001). With Simon Guy he has made similar analyses for the other network services on which we all depend like water and energy supply (Graham and Guy 1995). In the transport field, Londoners are much more exposed to market forces than are citizens of other European capitals because ticket revenue has to bear a much higher proportion of public transport costs. These changes are relatively easy to understand, once the analysis is done: we are moving in each case from state provision to market provision, the rich do better, the poor in most cases worse.

Another set of changes, however, is more complex. It arises where access to scarce commodities is effectively rationed through some other market. The important instance in London is access to what is perceived as 'good' state education. State education is free of charge to parents of children up to age 18, but of very variable quality between schools and between neighbourhoods. Until the Inner London Education Authority was abolished in the late 1980s, much effort and money was spent in trying to equalise standards of schooling across the inner areas of London. Since then, standards of schooling have diverged and parents with motivation and money have increasingly sought to improve their children's chances by living close to good primary and secondary schools. This individualistic competition for scarce and privileged access to education is now powerfully affecting house prices, just as competition for high quality environments has always influenced them.[5]

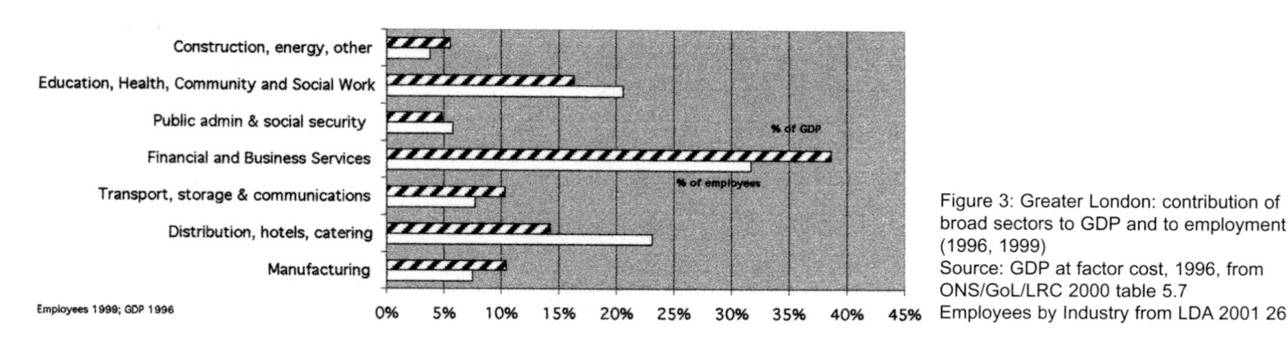

Figure 3: Greater London: contribution of broad sectors to GDP and to employment (1996, 1999)
Source: GDP at factor cost, 1996, from ONS/GoL/LRC 2000 table 5.7
Employees by Industry from LDA 2001 26

The Key Urban Markets...

Markets for labour

We could characterise our labour markets in London as very rich and diverse in the range of jobs and workers, very flexible (for employers), highly unequal in their pay patterns and not good at the internal housing or reproduction of the labour force. Greater London is dependent upon large flows of labour from outside the boundary, where reproduction conditions are quite different: cheaper housing areas are available further out (notably in Essex, east Kent, north Buckinghamshire and Bedfordshire) and it is to these areas that many inner Londoners have migrated in a moderate version of the 'white flight' afflicting many US cities. In these outer areas schools are often perceived as being better and the products of these schools seem to compete well in London's labour markets.

In another sense too, London depends upon labour raised and educated elsewhere. It is a heavy recruiter of skilled staff from many other parts of the world-the EU, the old Commonwealth and the third world (Mogridge 2000).

Alongside those who prosper in the London labour market, however, large numbers of ethnic minorities and of poor whites are effectively excluded from employment, or from progressing in their careers.
The economic geographer Ian Gordon has drawn attention to what he describes as a 'bumping out' of working class people from jobs through the availability and recruitment of more highly-qualified (often "over-qualified") migrants, students and young graduates to fill positions which they would historically have expected to occupy-in catering, hotels, secretarial work and many other fields (Gordon et al 1997; Gordon 2001, Buck et al 2002). This form of exclusion must have effects similar to those of discrimination by employers and would thus be hard to distinguish from it.

A contributory factor in London's dys-functional labour market is undoubtedly the 'benefits trap'. For very many people of low or moderate earning-power living on social benefits it is hard to find employment which pays enough to justify taking employment and thus going 'off benefit'. The difficulty and delay in getting back 'on benefit' after a period of employment are a further disincentive. For many people in London, benefits can be higher than the national average because of the level of transport and housing costs (discussed later in this paper). It is thus entirely rational for such people to work just the limited part-time hours permitted under benefit rules, or to do some un-recorded 'cash-in-hand' work to supplement their benefit. Government policies to relieve poverty through getting people into employment thus face a major resistance in the London context. For many people they just do not work.

Though not just a London problem, our contemporary 'flexible' employment patterns tend to be very bad for the sustainability and reproduction of the labour force: Linda Clarke has recently shown how damaging has been the effect in the construction sector of the shift to casual sub-contract labour on the sustainability of a skilled labour force, on productivity and on safety (Clarke forthcoming). Similar problems are evident in the maintenance and operation of the railways since privatisation, recently dramatised in the film Navigators written by Ron Dawber and directed by Ken Loach. More generally Richard Sennett has written of the damaging effect on social cohesion and solidarity of the shift to flexible working and insecure careers (Sennett 1998).

Markets for transport

A full discussion of how the London transport system is working is beyond the scope of this paper. Certain features of the current situation are, however, integral to my argument, linking global forces with local outcomes.

First of course the airports. We have been hearing for decades that London must grow its airport capacity rapidly or risk loosing its 'hub' functions to competitor cities - Amsterdam, Frankfurt or Paris - with consequential effects on the whole economy of London. This has, of course, been the main thrust of the evidence given by British Airways and BAA (the former British Airports Authority, now privatised) to the recent public inquiry into the proposed new terminal 5 at Heathrow. The same boosterism and appeals to patriotism are echoed in the publications of the City Corporation and London First. Now we find it as a lynchpin of the Mayor's strategies (GLA 2001; LDA 2001; TfL 2001). This is a classic case of spatial competition producing bad outcomes: Hotelling demonstrated in 1929 how competing ice-cream sellers tend to cluster in the middle of the beach to avoid losing market share to their competitors: customers in remote parts of the beach would just have to walk (Darnell 1990). The rational alternative (for customers and for the environment) which has the ice cream sellers spread around the beach is simply not a stable outcome which market competition could produce.

In the airport case what we clearly have is a strong combined interest of the airport operators and their entrenched airlines in strengthening the domination of the world's hubs. This works at the expense of second and third order cities to reinforce uneven development. Aeroplanes can fly from any point to any other point and should thus-like cars-be able to contribute to more even development at a European and world scale. However, the market imperative for long-haul airlines is to capture intercontinental flows through maximising feeder connections and this throws all these benefits away: it is as though all car journeys in the UK had to pass through a city centre and then out again.

Not only do people in remoter regions have a worse service: they also pay more since the intense competition which drives prices down is only on the routes between main cities. Correcting for this sort of malignant tendency of markets is just what supra-national authorities should exist to do but in transport, as in international trade, the EU and other potential regulators do precious little to undermine the vested interests which conserve the status quo.

There is a political problem here too. It is clearly too much to expect politicians to be long-sighted and brave if they might risk seeming un-patriotic for their city or nation. Thus we have Ken Livingstone swallowing the rhetoric about Heathrow's Terminal 5 being essential for London's survival as a world city and the government giving the project the go-ahead in the name of national economic need-despite the government's ostensible commitment to regional development.[6]

International aspects of London's life affect our transport markets in other ways too. Most important, perhaps, is the distortion of investment planning in favour of radial routes linking the centre (and Canary Wharf) with the outer suburbs and Home Counties.

London depends heavily on the network of radial railways which link the centre with the suburbs and, especially, with the scattered settlements of the region where over half a million London workers live. These far-flung workers include many of the highest-paid and best-qualified staff of government and of private firms, but they also include many middle-income workers who put up with long and costly journeys because only at that distance can they afford to enter the housing market, or afford the housing standards they seek. The system is very wasteful because it is used overwhelmingly in one direction only and has massive spare capacity for reverse travel. It is also heavily congested, and that problem is aggravated by the pressure on the central area tube network which distributes these passengers to their final destinations.

Of all the pressing transport problems of London, this is the one which has received most of the campaigning energy of corporate business and its organisations, such as London First, over the last 15 years. The outcome has been detailed designs for new investments which would link railways through the centre, rather in the way that the RER serves central Paris. Crossrail would run from east to west and an improved Thameslink from north to south. A third (shorter distance) line of the same type is also proposed now, linking north-east and south-west London through the centre (Figure 4).

Peter Hall, Drummond Robson and myself proposed, a couple of years ago, that the top priority in transport planning for London should be improvements in orbital bus and rail links between suburbs, supporting the growth of sub-centres and improving the access off low-income and middle-income residents to areas where they work or might be able to work (Hall, Edwards and Robson. 1999; Edwards 2000b). These ideas do figure in the Mayor's draft plans, and one leg of the new orbital railway (Ring-rail, now re-named 'Orbirail' - Figure 5) is already under construction, but the un-glamorous challenge of improving the accessibility among suburbs seem to have a fairly low priority after the flagship schemes for radial improvements.

Just as the major transport investments of the 1980s and 90s were diverted into the valorisation of the Docklands, and especially of Canary Wharf, so we now run the risk of prioritising real estate and corporate interests in the centre, reinforcing the over-concentration of London's activity and becoming ever more dependent on inefficient tidal flows of long-distance commuting.

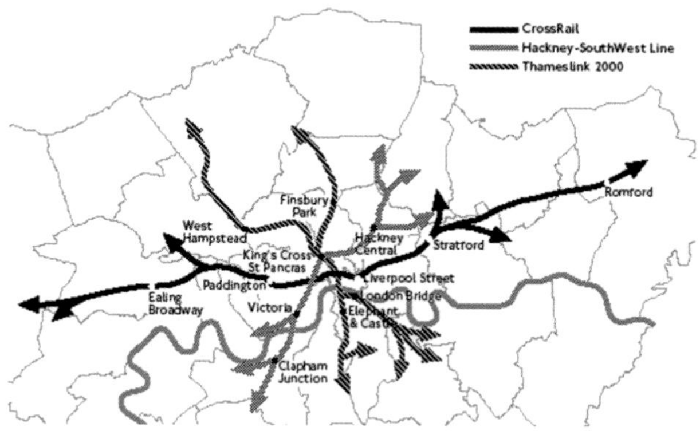

Figure 4: Radial railway proposals for London
Source: TfL (2001, Figure 4Q.1)

Figure 5: Ring-rail proposal of 1999 superimposed on plot of London's most deprived wards
Source: based on (Hall, Edwards and Robson 1999).

Markets for land and housing

It is in the land and property markets that London suffers most grievously from the way markets work. Specifically, in south east England we have an acute form of the common metropolitan problem of inadequate land supply, massively reinforced in our case by the particular history of our urban and regional planning policies.

The 'great achievement' of British planning is often claimed to be the London Green Belt, inaugurated during World War 2 and tenaciously maintained and extended ever since. This policy of 'urban containment' has results which are highly valued by many of its beneficiaries: those who live at the edge of London or in the protected landscapes of the region. Like so many other fine achievements of urban planning, this has produced (and guaranteed the scarcity of) some very fine residential settings and pushed property values up.[7]

This scarcity of supply confronts growing demand. The demand growth has many elements: the collapse of regional policy, population growth, falling average household size, real growth of incomes for perhaps half the population and a high income-elasticity of demand for housing (meaning that as people's incomes grow their demand for housing grows even faster). The effects can be characterised as a systematic structural barrier to fixed capital formation on most of the land in the region.

These pressures, sustained over decades, create a tendency towards relative housing cost inflation in our region. For those in jobs where pay is low and unions weak (such as retailing and cleaning and indeed most private-sector work) and for those whose salaries are negotiated nationally (mainly public servants, from nurses to professors) these high housing costs (along with the high cost of transport) effectively reduce real incomes. Living standards are thus depressed and this is a key part of the mechanism which makes London a poverty machine as well as a wealth machine. Low paid workers in London earn about the same as low paid workers in other regions (Figure 6) but their income buys much less.[8]

In other areas of the labour market, where employers can afford to pay to attract and retain the staff they need in shortage categories, salaries are pushed up as we can see from figure 6.

A lot of employers do badly as a result. If they fail to compensate their workers for the costs of living in London they suffer from staff recruitment and retention problems - acutely so throughout the public services. If they do compensate their workers adequately, they have to bear the cost and this reduces the competitiveness of employers in a wide belt around London, especially in the centre and west. Employers are also paying far more for their premises than they would in other regions, so it is doubly difficult for them to sell their products and services at competitive prices. High prices are a major deterrent to those who might come to London - as tourists, as students, as shoppers or as consumers of its other services.

There is a powerful distortion whereby actual investment (in new construction, repair and maintenance) is lower than it would be in conditions of easier land supply. For example:

• for households there is the familiar experience that you pay so much to service your mortgage that you can't afford to maintain or extend your dwelling;

• developers spend so much on sites that they are constrained to skimp on floor space, garden space and building quality. (Cullen 1982; Cheshire, Sheppard et al. 1985; Evans 1988). The early work of Ball (Ball 1983) was very effective in explaining the configuration of social forces which generated this characteristic form of speculative housing.

In terms of spatial structure, the property markets have been channelled in such a way as to produce regional decentralisation over long distances to towns where car-dependence for trips (within and between settlements) is strong (Ota 1995). Many parts of the region thus experience country roads saturated with traffic and severe pollution, while decentralising and growing businesses seeking locations have relatively few sites to choose among.

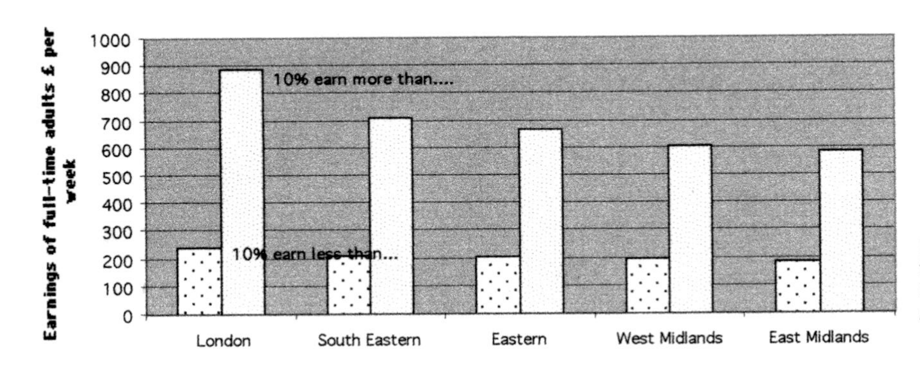

Figure 6: Earnings of top and bottom deciles of full-time Employees, 2000
Source: New Earnings Survey 2000 part E table A21

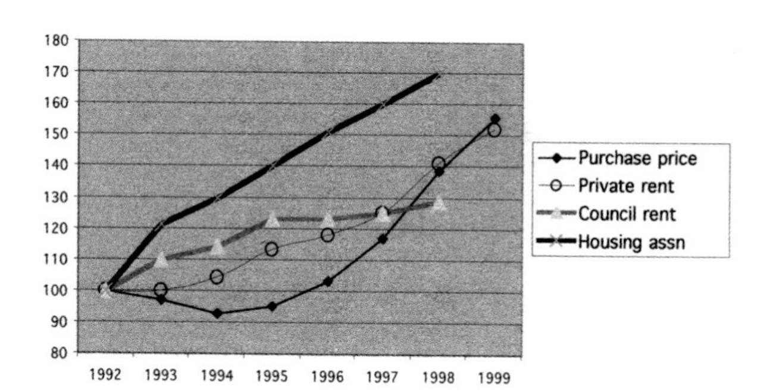

Figure 7: Index of London house prices and rents, 1992-9
Source: ONS/GoL/LRC (2000) table 4.15

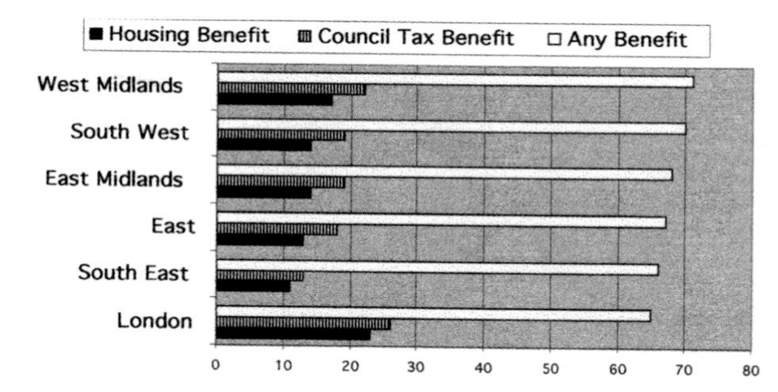

Figure 8: Proportions of households claiming benefits.
Source: Source: Regional Trends 36 (2001) table 8.8

Within the towns, especially London, this mechanism produces pressure for densification of suburbs and in-filling everywhere - often at the expense of the environmental qualities and other use-values enjoyed by established residents. This is politically very tense, and the contradictions emerge in the NIMBY (Not In My Back Yard) politics of the region very strongly.

The need for social housing becomes ever greater in these conditions because low- and middle-income people cannot afford what the market offers. In the UK a large proportion of our social housing has now been sold off through council tenants' 'right to buy' the dwellings in which they live at a discount to market value. New social housing is hardly produced any more except by non-profit-distributing, semi-autonomous, housing associations. For this housing association sector, the combination of

• high land prices,
• falling Housing Association Grant from government (HAG), and
• their consequent need for higher proportions of open market borrowing means that...
• space and quality standards are under intense pressure;
• rents have to be high and rising (Figure 07);
• their tenants can afford a housing association dwelling only if they are prosperous enough, or if they are poor enough to get state housing benefit (HB). This is a problem for those excluded, for the occupiers, for management and for the social composition of schemes.

Housing Benefit payments to tenants, 1999-2000

	London	England
% of households claiming	20%	16%
Weekly average claim	£ 68	£ 48
Annual cost	£ 2.5 bn	£ 9.6 bn
Annual cost per claiming hh	£ 4,111	£ 2.877

Figure 9 Housing Benefit payments to tenants, 1999-2000
Source: Department for Work and Pensions 2000

• only heavy government spending on Housing Benefit underwrites the market risk for lenders-a strange paradox where bankers have to defend the welfare system. Heavy HB costs arise in London as a result. While London households are, on average, less likely to be claiming benefits of other kinds, they are more likely than people in other regions to claim housing benefits (and relief from council tax) and, because of the levels of rents, their claims are much higher (Figures 7 and 8).

The cumulative effect of all these processes in the housing markets can be summarised as follows. Massive transfers of income and wealth take place, the main beneficiaries being those who own or develop land and property. Homelessness and overcrowding are acute. The inequality of living conditions is worsened, technologies we need for housing and transport are never developed or optimised and moves towards real environmental sustainability are ruled out of consideration (Edwards, 2000b).

In terms of class politics the outcome is far from clear. There is absolutely no general appreciation of the real consequences of the operation of all these markets within the straightjacket of the containment policy. The beneficiaries (institutional lenders, established owner-occupiers in the protected areas, developers and land owners) have marshalled the support of all political parties from the Tory right through to the greens in support of the sacred green belt and 'countryside'. Only a few economists (Evans and Cheshire referred to above) have noted the economic penalties and only a minority within the green movement have noticed some of the real social and environmental penalties (Fairlie and This Land is Ours 1996). Fairlie has pointed out that in much of southern England the poor and middle-earners are prevented from getting housing but required to use cars. But that is a critique from a rural standpoint: within London there is plenty of carping and protest about the symptoms of the malaise but virtually no articulate resistance and this may help to explain why in London the processes of the city are not more strongly contested.

The Mayor's approach to the housing problem in his strategies is to pin all his hopes on a new compromise (or power struggle) with the developers of new homes in London. He wants to insist, via his Spatial Development Strategy, that all new housing schemes in London should contribute a large proportion of their dwellings to the stock of 'affordable' or 'key-worker' homes: a target of 50% has been discussed. The feasibility of this approach is discussed in the conclusion of this paper.

Markets for commercial property

It is evident that the operation of real-estate markets is a key mechanism in the over-concentration of investment in commercial building in the prime areas of European cities, and in the central cities within European countries.

Ever since Hotelling's powerful modelling of the behaviour of ice cream sellers on a beach (referred to above in the context of airports), it has been clear that competitive locational behaviour by retailers can produce over-concentration which is in no-one's interests but their own. They protect themselves from competition by clustering together, although consumers would be better served by a spread distribution. When strong externalities begin to arise from co-location the effect is further reinforced (and extended to other functions) and the more so when we realise that property investors in centralised concentrations can realise and appropriate value originating in earlier rounds of investment and in the state's investment in radial transport.

On top of all this 'rational' behaviour by investors is the irrational tendency which Richard Barras has examined for central London offices where investors seem to go for the combination of low returns and high risk in their lemming-like enthusiasm. (His analysis is unpublished but the evidence is clear in the annual surveys of the Investment Property Databank.). Normally markets in investments show an inverse relationship between risk and return: high risk often comes with high return, and the safest investments are usually less profitable. But for some reason the banks and other institutions active in British property markets compete so hard with each other to obtain properties in central London that the rate of return is driven down to a low level-much lower than would be expected for such volatile and risky investments.

Of necessity, if investment tends to be too concentrated in prime locations, it tends to be under-represented in peripheral locations - partly because investors are less informed about such places, partly perhaps because they expect higher vacancy rates in such places. Certainly it appears that prospects of specially high returns are required to attract developers to provincial towns (Henneberry 1995) and the same logic applies to suburban centres in London.

The Mayor's draft strategies do correctly argue that economic growth has made business premises scarce and costly in London. The strategy so far developed in response to the scarcity, however, is just one of the available possibilities and-from the perspective advanced here-looks like a bad one. The Mayor takes it as axiomatic that growth is to be welcomed: he has clearly been advised that there is no alternative, that anything short of a pro-growth strategy (more of the kind of growth we already have) would frighten investors away and send the London economy into a downward spiral. Essentially his strategy is to encourage business space development in the East of London (excellent) but also to relax the constraints on the sideways and vertical growth of the centre: on the South Bank, in Spitalfields, King's Cross, Paddington and so on. These areas on the edges of central London are still the home to dense mixed-income populations, highly vulnerable to gentrification, and also home to small and medium enterprises of very diverse kinds: private firms in retailing, servicing of the central area and providing innovative services; public services in education, recreation and social care and many of London's non-profit and campaigning organisations (from trade unions to charities and civil-rights lawyers). There is thus a prospect of a lot of displacement of such activities by corporate occupiers in redeveloped space. This would almost certainly reduce the amount of local employment and increase the scale of long-distance commuting. And, whether or not that prediction comes true, the sheer growth of employment in the centre will further overload the rail infrastructure. The strong pressures for new investment in radial lines (referred to above) will thus be further increased although it will be at least 10 years before significant extra capacity can be built.

This permissive attitude to the growth of the centre will also make it harder to cajole developers into moving eastwards and to the suburban centres which so desperately need rejuvenation. Paris only managed to develop its sub-centres through a very restrictive approach to the centre. Berlin, which made an ambitious plan after unification to strengthen its poly-centric structure, has been utterly defeated by capitulating to a gadarene rush of investors to re-make the old centre. Alternatives do exist and should have been explored for London. It is particularly paradoxical since Ken Livingstone's top planning priority in his previous reign (the mid 1980s) was to protect the fringes of the central area through a 'Community Areas Policy' (GLC 1985).

The Main Issues Summarised

The main thrust of the argument can be summed up as follows:
1. Markets have become very much more important in determining how the London economy works, and in distributing its products, over the last two decades. Some of these markets work directly (e.g. for telecomms, water, labour) while others also operate indirectly (e.g. the effects of housing costs on employers and thus on competitiveness; their role in rationing access to the best schools).
2. International flows of investment capital, of goods and services, of customers and travellers and of labour have come to play increasing roles in the processes of the London economy and understanding of these is very limited. London's economic growth in recent decades has strengthened these influences.
3. The type of growth we have been experiencing, operating in the way it does in the framework of London's planning regime and very restricted supply of space, amplifies the housing inequalities flowing from the mounting inequality of incomes. In combination with the low salaries paid in most ordinary jobs, our form of growth intensifies poverty.
4. High costs of space increase the operating costs of all organisations needing premises in London and, through the effect on wages, those who employ labour.
5. Market tendencies to concentration of activity produce negative as well as positive effects, at international and regional scales (uneven regional development) and within the city-region (over-production of buildings in the centre, reinforced by radial transport, at the expense of sub-centres.
6. The process as a whole generates regressive transfers of wealth through the housing markets and other property markets.

What Is to Be Done?

The research agenda from all this is clear. Its purpose should be two-fold: to clarify the mechanisms linking global and local change and to demonstrate that the problems we have are of human making, not a 'natural' feature of market operations.

In the mean time London is busy with the debates on the Mayor's Strategies. Some comments on these strategies is an appropriate way to end this section.

The fact that London once again has a democratic government, rather than just an administration, is to be welcomed. The area boundary is too small, the powers few, the fiscal base negligible. But it is progress.

The first round of strategies and drafts have much to commend them and the one which has been through a cycle of consultation and revision (the Economic strategy) has been strengthened as a result. In particular, the Mayor and his agencies do acknowledge the scale of inequality.

A fundamental weakness remains, however: the largely unquestioning commitment to continued growth. The negative effects of this regressive and exploitative form of growth have been discussed by Massey (2001) and in this paper and have been the subject of intense further debate in the recent public hearings on the Draft London Plan. The opposition, however, has lacked any co-ordination, coming from a scatter of individuals and groups: greens, the Town and Country Planning Association, some community associations. It has been quite telling on many of the issues but there is neither a shared analysis nor any 'alternative' so it has been easy for the Mayor and his advisors to be totally un-yielding.

If Londoners and their Mayor decide to be a bit more choosy about the kind of growth they want, then debate should focus upon
(i) major increases in housing supply, sufficient to bring prices (and price expectations) down, with some selective use of green belt land if that turns out to be necessary and feasible;
(ii) an end to the attrition of the public housing stock through the 'right to buy';
(iii) greater emphasis on public transport improvements (and on walking and cycling) in and between inner suburbs, less on long-haul railway commuting;
(iv) protecting and expanding the supply of business premises in suburban nodes, especially where this can lead to reverse commuting, and a tougher protection of mixed-class communities and non-corporate employment in the fringes of the central area;
(v) focus resources on reducing the exclusion of under-educated young people-both ethnic minorities and poor whites.

What kind of a settlement between capital and labour would this be? The Mayor has been arguing that he's seeking reciprocity from the property sector by being tough on housing: he wants to insist that all housing schemes should include about 50% of dwellings as 'affordable' and 'key-worker' units. It seems highly unlikely that this target can be achieved, or that it could have much effect on average prices in the open market. Indeed its feasibility depends on sustained expectations of price inflation so that developers have enough profit to cross-subsidise the low-cost units at all. And since housing output remains stubbornly low even with selling prices astronomically high, this is a triumph of optimism over rationality.

The alternative sketched here would provide the prospect of stable or falling housing costs in the open market, some relief for enterprises from rocketing labour and premises costs and a more egalitarian structural evolution of London- a more even balance between rich and poor areas. This might even be more conducive to social harmony. There would thus be gainers in the business community as well as in the low- and middle-income population. The main losers would be for some real-estate interests and the speculative aspirations of established owner-occupiers. Growth of measured GDP might be slower within London but that never was a good measure of social welfare.

Appendix

Notes on the extension of markets. Sectors which are still publicly owned are in the first column, sectors which are private ar in the third. The second column, in between, comments on whatever privatisation has gone one, and further comments are at the end in column 4.

The table understates the extent of the shift to flexible private provision because of the widespread out-sourcing of many services by public authorities: cleaning, catering, security functions at the bottom of the skill ladder, but also of many professional tasks.

Public	***Transition***	***Private***	***Comments***
	no major change	**Food** and most consumer goods	
	no major change	**car** transport	Congestion charge on entry to the centre, 2003
Health remains	Private provision failed to take off but	PFI hospitals built since 1990s;	Out-sourcing extensive,
public	PFI now the dominant form for new investment		government keeps trying new attempts to gain private investment.
public until late 1990s	Privatisation failed to generate safety, investment for growth; state now heavily involved again.	**Rail** transport	Severe planning, investment, service and safety problems for London
until 2003	Partial privatisation forced through against Mayor	London **Underground**	Highly controversial
until 1980s	Privatisation by concession on routes	**Bus** transport	Works well, but at some cost to labour
until 1980s	Privatisation by sale and new entrants	**Telecomms**	Benefits from competition but failure to liberalise local loop; polarisation of access
until 1980s	Privatisation by sale; new entrants only in energy	**Energy**, water etc	? some competition benefits; adverse for environment; loss of local control
Schools	control devolved from ILEA to Boroughs, late 80s; some have private management		Access to good schools mediated through housing market
council **housing** down to 18% 2000	Council house building stopped; Hsg Assns not fully replacing it	**Owner-occupation** up to 58% **Private** rent 15% **Hsg Assoc** 8%	Rising homelessness and overcrowding; pricing out.

References

Ball, M. J. (1983), *Housing policy and economic power*. London: Methuen

Brenner, R. (1998), "Uneven Development and the long downturn: the advanced capitalist economies from boom to stagnation 1950-1988", in: *New Left Review* 229: 1-262 (whole issue)

Buck, N., I. Gordon, P. Hall, M. Harloe and M. Kleinman (2002), *Working Capital: life and labour in contemporary London*. London: Routledge

Cheshire, P. C., S. Sheppard and A. Hooper (1985), *The economic consequences of the British [land use] planning system: some empirical results*. University of Reading

Clarke, L. (forthcoming), *From Craft to Qualified Labour in Britain: a comparative approach*.

Cullen, A. (1982), "Speculative Housebuilding in Britain Some Notes on the switch to Timber-Frame Production Methods", in: *Proceedings of the Bartlett International Summer School on the Production of the Built Environment* 4: 4/12 - 4/18

Darnell, A. C. (1990), *The collected economics articles of Harold Hotelling*. New York: Springer-Verlag

Department for Work and Pensions (2000), *Housing Benefit and Council Tax Benefit: annual summary statistics*. London: the Department

Edwards, M (2000a), "Sacred Cow or Sacrificial Lamb? Will London's Green Belt have to go?", in: *City* 4(1), 105-112

Edwards, M. (2000b), "Towards a joined-up London", in: *Planning in London* 32(Jan-Mar), 41-42

Edwards, M. (2001), "Planning & Communication in London", in: *City* 5(1), 91-100

Edwards, M. and L.. Budd (1997), "Confirming conforming conventions", in: *City* 7, 171-181

Evans, A. (1988), *No Room! No Room! Costs of the British planning system*. London: Institute of Economic Affairs

Evans, A. W. (1987), *House prices & land prices in the S. E. - a review*. London: House Builders' Federation

Fairlie, S. and This Land is Ours (1996), *Low Impact Development: planning and people in a sustainable countryside*. Charlbury, Oxon: Jon Carpenter Publishing

GLC Greater London Council (1985), *Community Areas Policy: a record of achievement*. London: GLC

Gordon, I. (2001), "Unpacking 'competitiveness' as a governance issue for London", in: S. Syrett and R. Baldock (eds.), *Governing London: competitiveness and regeneration for a global city* . London: Middlesex University Press, 23-34

Gordon, I., M. Harloe and M. Kleinmann, (Eds.) (1997), *De-regulating City: London in an international perspective*. Oxford: Blackwell

Graham, S. (2001), "The city as sociotechnical process: Networked mobilities and urban social inequalities", in: *City* 5(3), 339 - 349

Graham, S. and S. Guy (1995), *Splintering networks: cities and technical networks in 1990s Britain*. Newcastle: University Dept of Town and Country Planning,

Hall, P., M. Edwards and D. Robson (1999), *London's Spatial Economy: the dynamics of change. London*: London Development Partnership (LDP) and Royal Town Planning Institute

Hardt, M. and A. Negri (2001), *Empire*. Harvard University Press

Harvey, D (1998), "Globalisation and the body", in: INURA (eds.), *Possible Urban Worlds: urban strategies at the end of the 20th century* Zürich: Birkhäuser -Verlag, 26-38

Henneberry, J. (1995), "Developers, property cycles and local economic development: the case of Sheffield", in: *Local Economy* 10(2), 23-25

Hirmis, A. (1996), *London Manufacturing*. London: Londonomics

Hirsch, F. (1977), *The Social Limits to Growth*. London: Routledge

LDA (2001), *Success through Diversity: London's Economic Development Strategy*. London: London Development Agency

Llewelyn Davies, The Bartlett School UCL and Comedia (1996), *Four world cities: a comparative study of London, Paris, New York and Tokyo*. London: Llewelyn-Davies for the Government Office for London

Massey, D (2001), "Opportunities for a World City: reflections on the draft economic development and regeneration strategy for London", in: *City* 5(1), 101-106

Mayor of London (2001), *Towards the London Plan: initial proposals for the Mayor's Spatial Development Strategy*. London: Greater London Authority

Mayor of London (2002), *Draft London Plan: the Spatial Development Strategy*. London: GLA

Mayor of London (2002), *London Divided: income inequality and poverty in the capital*. London: GLA

Mayor of London (2003), *Tackling Poverty in London: consultation paper*. London, GLA

Mogridge, M. (2000), "London just keeps on growing", in: *Planning in London*. 32 (January), 7-9

New Earnings Survey (2000), London: HMSO

ONS LRC GoL Office for National Statistics, London Research Centre and the Government Office for London (2000), *Focus on London*. London, HMSO

ONS Office for National Statistics (2001), *Regional Trends* 36

Ota, M., (1995), *Office Decentralisation: London and Tokyo*, PhD Thesis, UCL, London

Sennett, R. (1998), *The Corrosion of Character: the personal consequences of work in the new capitalism NY and London*: W. W. Norton

TfL (2001), *The Mayor's Transport Strategy*. London: Transport for London

Tomaney, J (2001), "The new governance of London: A case of post-democracy?", in: *City* 5(2), 225 - 248

UNCTaD (1997), *World Investment Report 1997: transnational corporations, market structure and competition policy.* Geneva: UN

Readers are referred to www.london.gov.uk for the Mayor's and other related publications and to www.bartlett.uck.ac.uk/planning/information/sds/ for updates on this chapter and related critical material.

Endnotes

[1] It is of course quite misleading to describe an economy of this sort as 'post-industrial': goods and services do not make themselves. People make them. We should not be fooled by the global division of labour into imagining that industry is no more.

[2] There is quite a good discussion of manufacturing in the revised Economic Development Strategy (EDS) LDA (2000); the other valuable work on this topic is by Hirmis (1996).

[3] This is a feature of all the GLA and LDA documents, but also of independent studies such as Four World Cities Llewelyn Davies, The Bartlett School UCL and Comedia (1996), discussed critically by Les Budd and myself (Edwards and Budd 1997; Edwards 2001).

[4] The changes between the draft and revised documents may reflect representations made by SERTUC (the South East Region Trades Union Congress), Doreen Massey and others (published in CITY (2001) and at http://www.bartlett.ucl.ac.uk/planning/information/sds). The first publication for the Spatial Development Strategy has a similar flavour GLA (2000).

[5] These are clear instances of what the late Fred Hirsch called the competition for 'positional goods' Hirsch (1977). There is not yet much research on the education effect on London property markets, just a lot of anecdotal evidence.

[6] Even more remarkable that this should happen just a few weeks after September 11th. The uncertainty surrounding the growth of long-haul travel, and the new awareness of what planes can do in dense cities, would have made it easy for any politician to have said no at that moment.

[7] This history is analysed from a variety of standpoints by Cheshire, et. al. (1985); Evans (1987) and Edwards, M (2000b).

[8] The situation is the same or worse for those households dependent not on current earnings but on state pensions and benefits because the benefit system goes nowhere near compensating them for the high cost of living in London.

4.5

TEXT...Michael Parkes

Community Participation and Urban Regeneration in London: King's Cross and the "Elephant and Castle."

Introduction

The following review is based upon my experience both as part time Planning Worker, for 12 years, to the King's Cross Railway Lands Group (an umbrella of local community-based organisations and individuals), and independent Community Master Planner initially to the Community Forum at Elephant and Castle and subsequently to the Development Executive Team of the Elephant Links Partnership Board (SRB). The views expressed are those of the author alone.

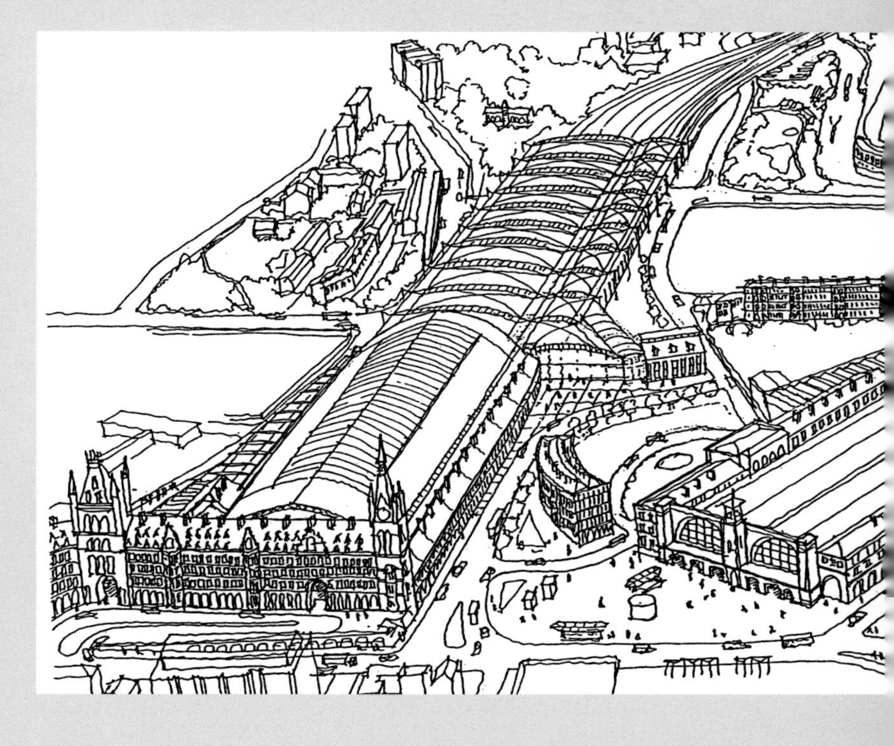

The London Context

The draft London Plan (June 2002) envisages a high level of private-sector-led economic growth as well as population growth to 2016. Population equivalent to a city the size of Leeds (700,000) is to be accommodated within the existing built up area resulting in considerably higher densities of development in certain areas. Likewise the Central Activities Zone is to be encouraged to expand principally within the Central and Eastern (Thames Gateway) sub regions of London. Two of the most important Opportunity Areas within the Central London sub region are Elephant and Castle and King's Cross. Both these sites lie within the 20% most deprived Wards in London. Development Frameworks are currently being prepared for both sites.

OPPORTUNITY AREA	SITE AREA (ha)	NEW JOBS (to 2016)	NEW HOMES (to 2016)
Elephant and Castle	23	4200	4200
King's Cross	53	11400	1250

Source: Mayor of London, draft London Plan, Table 2B

Public Participation - "High Stakes" / "Low Stakes".

Public participation (as opposed to consultation) entails at least a partnership approach to regeneration i.e. a constructive partnership between local community interests and, in the field of property development, the local planning authority and the landowner / developer, or in the field of service delivery; the local authority and the service provider (education, housing, policing etc).

Partnerships in this context, can address from the outset and in a genuine way, the planning, design, implementation, management and even delivery of certain elements of the built development or service provided. Such an approach broadly underpins the rhetoric of Neighbourhood Management and Renewal.

There are innumerable examples of successful partnerships of this kind in London where the (financial, political, strategic) stakes are low eg community policing schemes, community gardens, local management of schools, Area / Consultative Forums, social enterprises of one kind or another. These are all relatively small-scale, manageable, useful, viable, publicity-worthy schemes where there is "something in it" for all parties.

But where the financial, political, strategic stakes are high, a partnership approach of this kind, is notoriously difficult to achieve voluntarily. It can be achieved (see Spitalfields Case Study in the author's Guide to Community Planning and Development LPAC December 1995) and for a year or two, there appeared to be grounds for optimism that a similar tri-partite approach to master planning of the development at Elephant and Castle could succeed. Subsequent events have, however, proved this optimism to be ill - founded.

The Elephant and Castle

The Opportunity Area at Elephant and Castle comprises a large system-built (pre-fabricated) housing estate - the Heygate Estate - built in 1974 containing some 1200 housing units, together with the large Elephant and Castle Shopping Centre of similar vintage and the adjoining dual carriageway southern edge of the inner city ring road. In all this amounts to about 15 hectares. Both housing estate and shopping centre were considered ripe for redevelopment and tenants on the estate had largely concurred with that conclusion. In recognition of this opportunity, the Elephant Links Single Regeneration Budget (SRB) scheme was set up in Autumn 1999. Southwark Council, who are major landowners, set up the Elephant Links Community Forum to represent the local community on the SRB Partnership Board. The Forum rapidly acquired its own staff and office based in the Shopping Centre. Initially the Forum comprised a wide range of local organisations including both the Heygate Tenants and Residents Association (TRA) and similar TRA's from the surrounding estates including the 13 identified by the eventual preferred developers for refurbishment and environmental improvement works. The Forum had 6 out of the 11 representatives on the Development Executive Team (DET) set up by the SRB Partnership Board to ensure effective community input into the regeneration project.

The Forum was partly responsible for setting out the criteria for bids by competing developers and was jointly responsible, alongside the Council, for interviewing and assessing the competing developers. Fortunately both Council and Forum agreed that Southwark Land Regeneration (SLR - a consortium of developers and architects) was to be preferred and in June 2000 it was appointed by the Council to take forward the massive £1.5 billion, 15 year regeneration project.

From the outset the Forum had insisted upon an innovative tri-partite Master Planning approach. SLR accepted this, together with a commitment to setting up a Community Land Trust. This was an integral part of their ambitious Regeneration Action Plan which also included a wide range of local labour and business support initiatives, environmental improvement and other community development initiatives.

To facilitate the tri partite Master Planning approach, the Forum and then the Development Executive Team commissioned independent technical aid (legal, housing, master planning, property development, transport, community development trust) to attempt to match the range of high level consultancy services separately available to both the Council and SLR. Mediation procedures and services were also explored.

Over the period from autumn 2000 to early 2002 much good work was done by the community's consultants to prepare it for the start of the tri-partite master planning process. Sadly, however, this was never to take place because negotiations between the Council and SLR over the financial and other terms of the project finally collapsed in April 2002 and the two parted company.

It has also to be said that the umbrella of community interests that had started with such high hopes in the summer of 2000, gradually disintegrated over the next two years into total disarray. The catalyst for this arose with the identification by SLR and the Council of 26 "early housing sites" to provide replacement new housing for those on the Heygate who wished to stay in the area. Unfortunately many of these sites comprised valuable small pockets of green amenity space, kickabout and play areas within the 13 adjoining Council housing estates as well as parts of local parks, community gardens and even an area of allotments. Inevitably this, together with other matters, set up a tension between the Heygate TRA and many of the other organisations within the Community Forum. This culminated in the Heygate TRA leaving the Forum and the Forum's representation on the DET being reduced to 5 with 2 additional places allocated to the Heygate TRA ie the Forum went from being in a majority on the DET to being in the minority. The Forum also wished to ensure that the SRB Board and Development Programme was more independent of the Council. Following a four month dispute, the Council finally terminated its funding of the Forum in June 2002, workers were sacked, and legal action between the two followed.

Without a developer partner and with the community in some disarray, Southwark Council have returned to a more conventional approach to regeneration at Elephant and Castle. They are preparing a Development Framework for the area and are soon to put this out to public consultation. The Elephant Links Partnership Board is being reconstituted and the DET, if it is to continue in existence at all, is likely to see a substantial reduction in its overall remit.

KINGS CROSS GOODS DEPOT

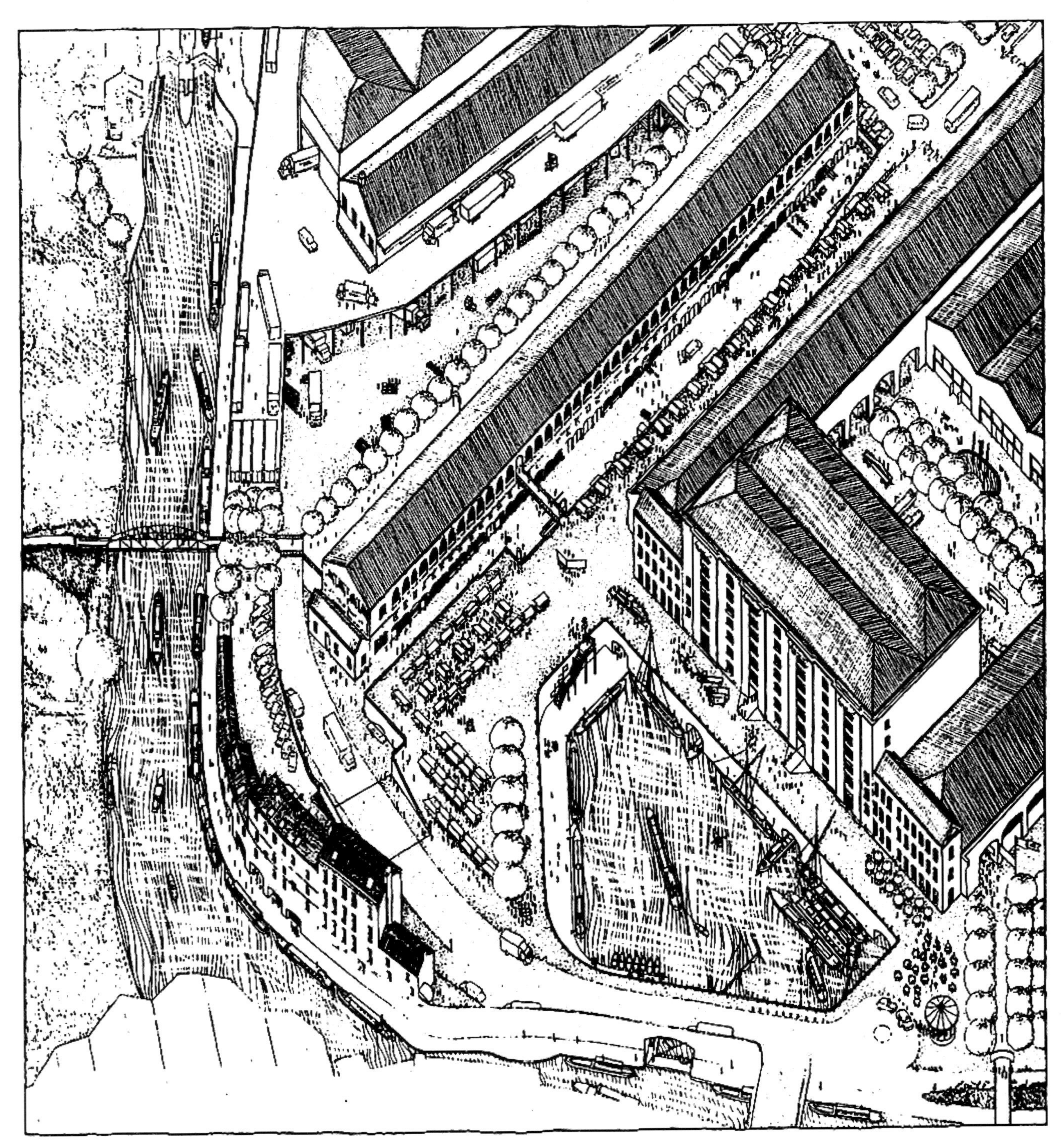

COAL OFFICES

Regeneration : Context & Potential

King's Cross

After a 16 year succession of different railway and property development proposals, London Underground and Channel Tunnel Railway engineering works have finally started at King's Cross. The latest associated property development proposals are also being taken forward by the principal landowners on the King's Cross Railway Lands (now re-imaged as "King's Cross Central"), who are London and Continental Railways and Excel, and their appointed developers Argent St George. It is hard to think of a site in London or the UK where the financial and political stakes are higher. As the table above indicates, the draft London Plan anticipates almost ten times as many new jobs as homes on this site. This has been reflected in the recent review of Chapter 13 of the Camden Unitary Development Plan (UDP) and the latest consultation document issued by Argent St George. "A Framework for regeneration" (Sept. 2002) presents consultees with a *fait accompli* ie only one possible Framework to structure nearly a million square metres of development, the bulk of which is office-orientated with "at least" 1.100 new homes, though none south of the canal. The proposals anticipate high / very high densities comparable to Bishopsgate / Canary Wharf. There are strong echoes of the original (1989) LRC / Norman Foster scheme which also started with about the same amount of square metres, albeit on a very much larger site, and was eventually abandoned.

Community participation in this process has so far been limited to an opportunity to respond to three Argent St George consultation documents and a programme of one-on-one meetings instigated by Camden Council and Argent St George, with local individuals and groups / organisations such as schools, arts projects etc, ie highly conventional and nothing like as ambitious as that funded and anticipated at Elephant and Castle 1999 - 2001.

An SRB scheme (the King's Cross Partnership) was set up in 1996 in part to facilitate community involvement in the regeneration of the Railway Lands but this proved to be 7 years too early and it effectively exited at the end of 2002. A much smaller SRB scheme (Camden Central) remains in existence and is committed to ensuring effective community involvement in the regeneration project. The Camden Central Community Umbrella will be holding a day-long Convention on the Argent St George proposals on February 1st 2003 and this will have been the first "bottom up" initiative so far organised with a chance of comprehensively considering the proposals, independently of either the Council or the developers. This is not before time as Argent St George intend to submit a planning application for the public realm framework in summer 2003.

16 years is a long time for campaigning organisations such as the King's Cross Railway Lands Group to maintain momentum and membership. Many of the Group's most active members lived on the Railway Lands and have now had to leave to make way for the current engineering works. The Group remains a priceless source of independent local knowledge and expertise. It is ironical that just when this expertise would have been of most use to ensuring effective local involvement in the regeneration process its funding was completely cut by Camden Council. Some funding may, however be secured in the near future from the Camden Central SRB.

The site is physically isolated by rail lines etc from most of the surrounding residential communities. After 16 years, these communities themselves tend to be apathetic / cynical regarding the new development, and despite considerable evidence to the contrary locally and London-wide, tend to believe there is little or nothing they can do to change the proposals. At best, there is an understandable interest only in what benefits might be obtained in the local area from the new development, and how best to minimise its environmental and other disbenefits. Any wider and longer-term appreciation of the Master Plan as a whole-its phasing, contents, balance, density, management, and the ripple effects of movement, land and rental values etc-appear largely academic.

Conclusion

London - a special case requiring special measures ? London is a World City and as such it is unique in Britain and possibly in Europe in terms of its very high land and rental values. At places next to the Central Business District like Spitalfields, King's Cross and Elephant and Castle, poor, disadvantaged and vulnerable communities, who own no land or property, are highly susceptible to the implications of say £70 per sq ft replacing £5 per sq ft. There are potential opportunities through the "Planning Gain" process but more often than not, as the economic base of an area changes, the consequential social and cultural changes lead to an inevitable and substantial "squeezing out" of such communities ie often they do not really benefit from urban regeneration.

My own conclusions after some 17 years work in this field, are that special measures are required to facilitate effective community participation in "high stakes" projects situated in a community regeneration context. Experience suggests that Local Authorities, landowners and developers in such situations prefer consultation to participation and are unlikely to voluntarily enter, from the outset, into a genuine process of partnership working with local community interests. I first advocated the setting up of "mandatory Collaborative Planning Zones which would require landowners and Councils to draw up development briefs (now development frameworks) and planning applications jointly with the local communities" in an article in Urban Environment Today (09.03.2000.). In so doing I particularly had in mind the kind of tri-partite Master Planning processes tried out at Spitalfields and anticipated at Elephant and Castle. I provided evidence along these lines to the Consultants commissioned by the Greater London Authority to advise on a strategic planning framework for community based regeneration in London. Their Report (Mayor of London, SDS Technical Report Four, May 2002) strongly endorsed these proposals but unfortunately this is virtually the only one of their recommendations which has not been taken into the draft London Plan. I remain convinced that a mandatory tri-partite Master Planning approach to urban regeneration in such situations would produce a much better balanced and more intelligent resolution to a conflict that has bedevilled London for decades. I shall try to argue this at the draft London Plan public hearings in 2003.

References

Mayor of London (2002), *Draft London Plan: the Spatial Development Strategy*. London: Greater London Authority

Parkes, M. (1995), *Good practice guide to community planning and development London Planning Advisory Committee.* (LPAC)s

Anonymous (2002), "Irreconcilable differences", in: *Regeneration and Renewal* 21.06.02. (concerning the Elephant and Castle).

Parkes, M. (2002), Briefing Paper on "A Framework for Regeneration" prepared for *Camden Central Community Umbrella*. November 2002 www.bartlett.ucl.ac.uk/planning/information/

Mayor of London, *SDS Technical Report Four*, May 2002

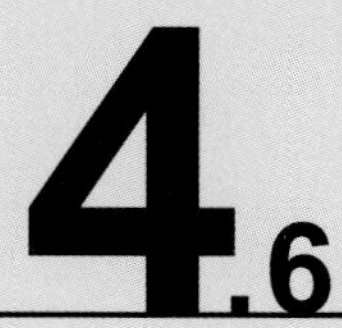

TEXT....................Esther Caplin
CARTOON....................Louis Hellman

Vision for London - a Project for a Contested Metropolis?

This article has to be cronologically related to the period preceding new Mayor's election, between the abolition of the Greater London Council and year 2000.

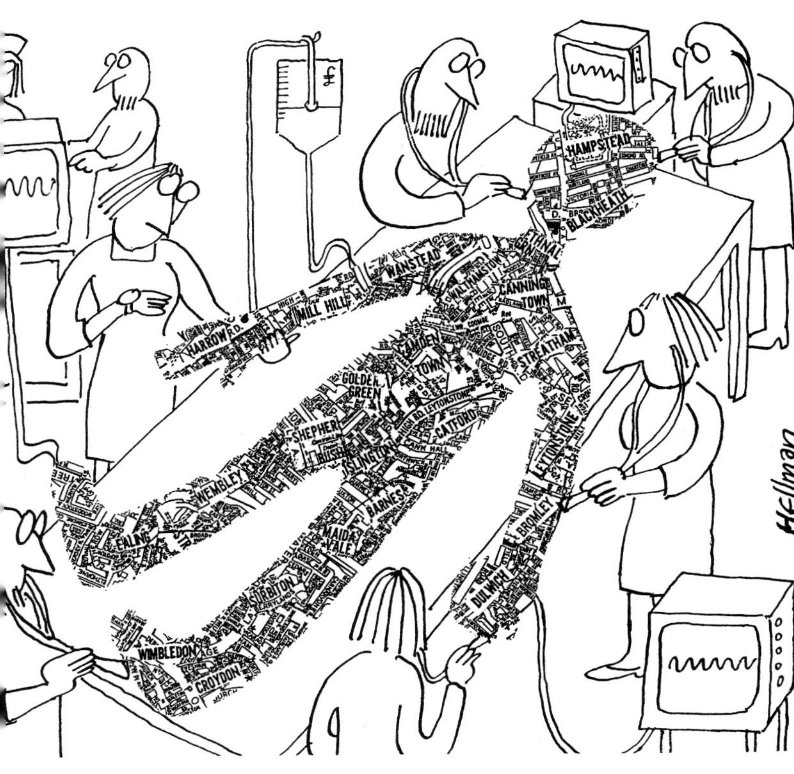

alising London's Town Centres... Louis Hellman

What Was Vision for London and Why did it Emerge?

In the dozen or so years following the abolition by Mrs Thatcher of the Greater London Council - London's Government - Vision for London established itself as the learning network for London and successfully engaged individuals and groups from the public, private and voluntary sectors including community groups and professionals in talking to each other and rethinking London and its future.

London post-GLC felt bereft, without any lead or vision, and a small group of us involved in planning and regeneration began talking about working towards a 'vision' for the capital. Nicholas Falk was a prime mover, with Rob Cowan and George Nicholson. The idea of visions was then something of a zeitgeist - 'this vision thing' - and we adopted it as our name, although really it should perhaps have been visions...

It existed for about ten years. Perhaps it could have survived longer with good management, but by then we had the prospect of the Mayor and Assembly for London, far better information dissemination about what was happening in London generally, better communication and cross sector working. So perhaps it served its - very good - purpose.

How did it Operate?

In the hiatus that existed without a government for London, a lot was going on at many different levels, but it was happening in a very disassociated way. Developing an extensive network across sectors and disciplines, and mapping all the activity were priorities, so that an 'information exchange' could exist. Bringing people together to discuss common issues at convivial meetings, seminars and exhibition, opened people's eyes and minds to other perspectives and concerns.

Its role was not to campaign, but it remained independent as a focus of common concern for London among its many stakeholders. Symposia of 50 to 100 people looked at conservation in London, the public realm, the role of town centres and the diversity of people and neighbourhoods. Local champions came from Europe and America to share their experience of initiatives that generated community involvement in Brussels, Copenhagen, Amsterdam, Berlin, Philadelphia and Washington. Events were hosted throughout London - we never had an institutional headquarters - and meant that members visited unusual venues and learnt about a range of initiatives for London, such as the London Ecology Unit and the Chelsea Physic Garden, the Tower of London, the Association of London Government, London First Centre and Bromley by Bow Centre.

Who Was Involved?

From the beginning we cast around to bring together movers and shakers in the public, private and voluntary sectors, as well as those involved in projects and initiatives locally throughout the capital. From the beginning we realised that 'people issues' were as important as physical environment issues and this was reflected in the network we built up, the information we compiled and the programme of activities we organised. Our constitution stipulated a range of people on the committee, and meetings and visits were organized to take advantage of the hospitality of a range of contenders.

What do you Think Was Pioneering?

Networking was not taken very seriously at the time Vision for London emerged, but those promoting Vision for London were pioneers in seeing its value. Not only was it cross sector networking, but it was as interactive as possible: we continually questioned members about their activities. And all this took place in the days before email, websites and even mobile phones.

Vision for London was born at a time when regeneration was seen as being more to do with the physical environment. In the later 1980s the City of London was undergoing a major redevelopment boom while Docklands was being created, and plans were afoot for other large sites. Other pioneering aspects of Vision for London that are taken for granted now - a holistic approach and joined up thinking - have become catchphrases, but were viewed sceptically then.

Vision for London embraced anything to do with London. It looked for, and found perhaps surprisingly, common ground among the many contestants in the capital. In the hiatus between GLC and GLA, it developed a new consensus building process and pioneered a partnership-type model.

In the years since its demise some of its seminal ideas have become common currency. We focused discussion on the idea of the public realm, integrated transport and conservation as well as new development. A symposium on the topic launched a series of discussions and seminars on London's Town Centres. We also raised the profile of social inclusion and introduced the concept of the positive representation of immigration and diversity. We initiated the idea of the 'Rich Mix centre' that has become a reality in the East End, although more locally than pan-London focused.

What were some Challenges and Surprises?

Dealing with London as a whole is very, very difficult - which indeed successive London governments have found. What is called London is made up of such diversity, with different parts grappling with different issues. You are constantly reminded that many of London's boundaries are administrative rather than local or historic.

The process showed how many contenders there are, how many wish to be involved and have a sense of pride and responsibility. Surprisingly, common ground exists between very different groups, and concensus, rather than conflict, is achievable if people listen to each other and understand each other's perspectives.

Vision for London highlighted the need for a new holistic approach to planning that could embrace newer contenders. The networks, the partnerships, the joined up thinking and working all theoretically exist now. If Vision for London existed now it would need to have a different remit - with a stronger local focus and quality of life as a dominant theme.

4.7

TEXT..........Bob Colenutt

Neighbourhood Regeneration; a View from the Local State

Introduction

The purpose of this chapter is to give a critical perspective on neighbourhood regeneration from inside a regeneration department in a local authority in north London. The example used here is Northumberland Park, a "target" deprived neighbourhood in the Borough of Haringey.

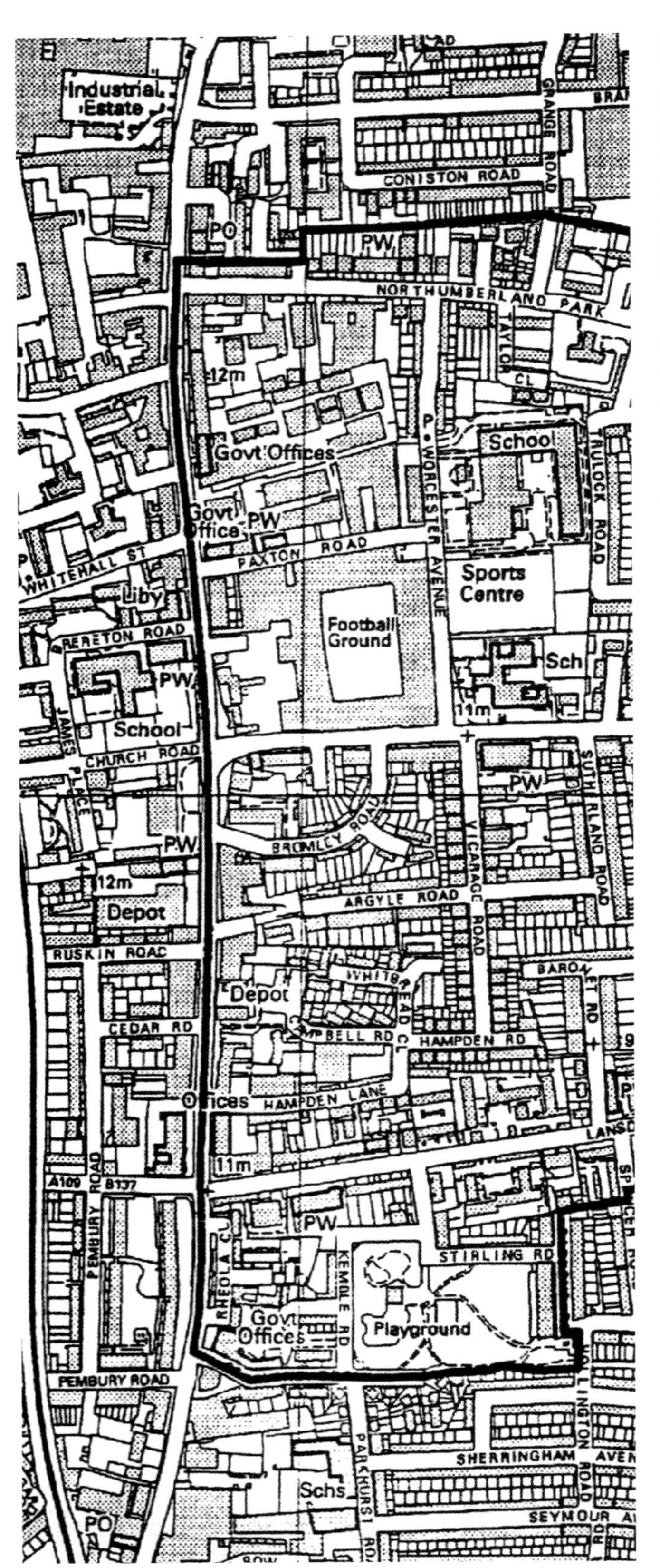

Northumberland Park

Northumberland Park is an inner suburb of North London. It houses 8000 people half living in Council flats, and half in private mainly rented accommodation. The area is one of the poorest in North London, comprising people from many different countries of origin. Many people stay only for a few months or years. There are large numbers of children in poverty, one parent families and families on very low incomes.

In the booming London economy, Northumberland Park is "marooned". Regeneration initiatives have come and gone with little impact on poverty or the environment. In I999, it was selected by the Council as a pilot for Neighbourhood Management funded from the Government's regeneration programmes.

The Council has appointed a neighbourhood officer team whose job is to deliver regeneration schemes, to engage local residents and businesses and to put pressure on agencies and the local authority to improve service delivery. Three years on, there is a new Neighbourhood Resource Centre building, a fully staffed neighbourhood regeneration and outreach team, many projects (and community events) aimed at environmental and economic improvement and public involvement in regeneration.

Why is the Local Authority Involved – what Is the Local Authority Agenda?

The local government agenda is dominated by "modernisation". This means introducing new ways of delivering services and relating to their "customers" and communities. New structures include "cabinet" decision making, scrutiny panels; public assemblies, and a wide range of partnerships with other agencies. Services (such as housing repairs, waste management; traffic management, education) are delivered through a mix of in-house and contracted out services. These changes are a response to concern about public disengagement from local government and local elections. It also reflects Government distrust of local authorities and their ability to achieve value for money.
The second reason why local authorities are engaged in neighbourhood renewal is that the Government is effectively offering additional resources to local authorities for tackling social exclusion. It is increasingly clear to local authorities that the financial and political costs of ignoring poor neighbourhoods are getting unacceptably high. Government has targeted the 800 most deprived wards in England for additional resources. As a condition, local authorities are required to set up Local Strategic Partnerships (LSPs) to deliver a range of initiatives such as allocating a special Neighbourhood Renewal Fund and piloting Neighbourhood Management.

The Government has created a Community Empowerment Fund to support community involvement in LSPs.
Thirdly, many local authorities genuinely believe that their local residents should have a say in what they do. Partnerships between local people and local authorities and other agencies are seen as the way forward. A neighbourhood approach is one way to improve and "join up" service delivery. Although funding is short term, local authorities and other agencies are expected to "mainstream" local service provision over the long term

The Strengths and Weaknesses of Neighbourhood Renewal in Northumberland Park

Strengths

- Many good local projects and events have been generated by neighbourhood programmes.
- Local authorities themselves are taking a more integrated approach to managing services in deprived neighbourhoods
- Local skills development and community work have expanded significantly as a result of neighbourhood programmes.
- There has been increased participation by residents and businesses in local initiatives and local regeneration boards.
- Neighbourhood management teams (youth, community, planners, employment services officers, regeneration project officers) with Police and other agencies are making progress in influencing service providers and getting problems sorted out.

Weaknesses

- There are too many meetings and strategies and not enough action, especially around the immediate issues that matter to people e.g. crime, youth, jobs, health, child care
- Residents who are involved are constantly reminded of the limits of their role. The agencies that provide the money also keep very strict control over what it is spent on. It is, thus, difficult to see how the new structures and funding streams will generate radical measures such as those that created Coin Street in London or Kraftwerk in Zurich.
- Local participation is limited by red tape, and exhaustion. There is sometimes a lack of belief that these programmes will make a difference. This in itself gives more control to the officers of the Councils and other bodies (whose job is to get the money in and spent to meet targets)
- Many economic and social changes e.g. transience, homelessness, high house prices, or low wages in service jobs cannot be changed by regeneration programmes.
- Short term funding for projects does not lead to long term sustainable regeneration since main programmes are not incorporating neighbourhood programmes when the regeneration money runs out

Conclusions

There is a lot to play for in neighbourhoods like Northumberland Park in terms of terms of funding, projects, meetings to go to and things to influence i.e. there is a potential political impact if residents are able to make use of the opportunities.

Although communities are effectively excluded from the strategic level of regeneration policy making, regional authorities and local government are unable to control everything. Local authorities often admit they do not have the answer to the "wicked" issues of the inner cities (crime; health, transience, rubbish, traffic, lack of respect for public realm etc) and are willing to look outside themselves for solutions.

The key challenge for local authorities is to rebuild local trust and deliver improved services. The problem for local residents is find the time and support to ensure that changes they want happen or at least get taken seriously. Local authorities quite rightly believe that they cannot expect local support without significant improvements in the services that people pay for. This challenge is greatest in the most deprived neighbourhoods.

Through neighbourhood management, local authorities have a mechanism to achieve partnerships with residents and to improve services. Both of these are difficult for local authorities. First because they do not wish to relinquish power and second because, as Borough wide authorities, they do not have the means to deliver change at a neighbourhood level.

Moreover, local authorities do not have the funds to take over regeneration funding regimes when the money from central government runs out. And they rarely have the political confidence to set up community trusts that could take over a significant part of the regeneration function of local government..

This creates a vacuum of political responsibility and initiative. In this context, there are significant opportunities for local residents to intervene – even though these changes may not be dramatic. There is funding available from a variety of sources (if communities have the energy and support to seek out these funds), and the new structures of local governance are available to those who wish to use them.

Toronto: Outside the Glamour Zones

Photo by Adrian Blackwell

5.1

TEXT......Roger Keil
PHOTOS......Roger keil

"Substitute City"

For a people which lays its whiskey and violent machines
on a land that is primal, and native which takes that land in greedy
innocence but will not live it, which is not claimed by its own
and sells that land off even before it has owned it,
traducing the immemorial pacts of men and earth, free and
beyond them, exempt by miracle from the fate of the race -
that people will botch its cities, its greatest squares
will scoff at its money and stature, and prising wide
a civil space to live in, by the grace of its own invention it will
fill that space with the artifacts of death.
(Lee, 1972: 36)

The title of this introduction was inspired by an exhibition in Toronto's Power Plant gallery. I gave a presentation of the same title as part of the Big City Forum, *The Rivoli*, organized as part of the exhibition, Toronto, April 10, 2001.

Urbanization is about substitution. From the classical cities on the Indus River and in Mesopotamia to postmodern Los Angeles, more or less rural, pre-industrial, and agricultural relationships with nature have been replaced by *urban* relationships with nature. This substitution eventually created extended 'hinterlands' around the globe for the sustenance of cities. The city did not create the countryside, but it came to dominate it. It is the most visible product of human labour - both rural and urban.

Substitution has also meant periodical replacement of one with another historical type of city. In Toronto, an aboriginal human settlement that existed in some form or another for thousands of years, was substituted by a colonial, later an industrial, and now a global city. Toronto was born a substitute city. From the beginning, it had to replace the non-city, and the subsequent human settlements that preceded it during centuries before. After substituting for a native settlement, Toronto tried hard to be English for a couple of hundred of years and was quite successful in recreating the old world in the new world. So much so that for all newcomers Toronto became 'England away from England'. This hegemony was difficult to break even when diversity trickled in during the second half of the last century.

The city of one period is substituted by the city of the next. In some instances this takes the form of entire cities disappearing from sight. Buffalo, Winnipeg, Liverpool, Detroit stand as examples for this disappearance. Their functions have been substituted by other, more efficient and modern, ways of using space economies for the accumulation of capital. Toronto was able to cushion its fall from industrial grace by playing a double role of 'capital of the rustbelt' and Canada's 'global city'.

All of these substituted types of settlement are still present in artifacts, landscapes, and cultures. They provide the layers of memory that cannot be substituted (Ross, 2002). Since early modernity, this process of substitution has coincided with a series of industrial and social revolutions. Industrial revolutions have, as David Harvey (1989) has taught us, produced the dynamics of space-time compression. This is a specific kind of substitution, in which space is compressed and the world gets effectively smaller. Cities grow and the world shrinks. Space is substituted by time. Harvey also reminds us that these industrial and economic revolutions have produced a revolving process of substitution, which he calls 'creative destruction'. As built environments get older, they lose their usefulness for the process of capital accumulation, they get torn down, altered, reconstructed. The so-called 'spatial fix' of a specific era, etched in the urban landscape, will need redesigning every so often. In some instances, this takes the form of the substitution of the entire web of meaning in a particular part of the city through another meaning. Gentrification, yuppification, lofts, Starbucks coffee shops are the harbingers of this creeping substitution of one through another spatial fix. What we have, then, is what Naomi Klein (2000) has called 'the branding of the cityscape' and Ute Lehrer (2000) terms 'the spectacularization of the city'.

Of all the kinds of substitution Toronto has performed over the years, the most incisive one has been the substitution of *nature* through *urbanity*: the replacement of first nature by the second nature of the city. This occurs in two significant ways. First, cities actually claim and change physical space. Trees are felled, forests are cleared, farmers fields are turned into subdivisions, black top goes on black soil, and so forth. This is the very core of urbanization: the spreading of human settlement in space. Today, Torontonians, like other North Americans experience this claiming of suburban land mostly as sprawl: the endless blanketing of rural landscapes with single family homes, malls and gas stations. Second, also like all cities, Toronto displaces distant land uses with its demands for food, fuel, raw materials, etc. This is what has been termed "the ecological footprint" of cities (Wackernagel and Rees, 1996). It is a curious substitution, the imperialist acquisition of other remote areas' carrying capacity for the use of a distant city. In this sense, Toronto doesn't just suck dry the rivers and moraines of its immediate hinterland but feeds off the oilfields and farmers fields of distant lands and sinks its garbage into holes in the ground in faraway places and uses the carbon sinks of remote areas in Canada and elsewhere. None of this is sustainable, of course. It is just substitution. Neither sprawl nor the extension of the foot-print are recognized as problems. They are instead fetishized in a consumer economy of unprecedented proportions, which does not reveal its destructive workings easily.

In the words of French urbanist Henri Lefebvre, "[t]he town is indeed a machine, but it is also something more, and something better: a machine appropriated to a certain use - to the use of a social group" (Lefebvre, 1991: 345). Let us turn to those social groups now. All urbanization is substitution. Yet, currently, a specific kind of substitution is occurring: In this process, Toronto becomes a substitute for the world, so poetically captured by Michael Ondaatje in this allegory of early multiculturalization:

An hour after dusk disappeared into the earth the people came in silence, in small and large families, up the slope towards the half-built waterworks. Emerging from darkness, mothlike, walking towards the thin rectangle of the building's southern doorway. The movement was quickly over, the wave of bodies had seemed a shadow of a cloud over the slope.

Inside the building they moved in noise and light. It was an illegal gathering of various nationalities and the noise of machines camouflaged their activity from whoever might have been passing along Queen Street a hundred yards away. Many languages were spoken, and Patrick followed the crowd to the seats that were set up around a temporary stage

(Ondaatje, 1987: 115).

The stage of immigration is not temporary anymore, the city's immigrants don't have to huddle in the twilight, nor do their sounds have to be hidden by machines. Toronto's multicultural character of today is tied to the city's role in the world economy. Toronto is now one of the thirty or so urban centres around the world, which scholars have come to call global cities or world cities (Brenner and Keil, forthcoming). These are the command centres of the world economy. In their downtown towers and exurban office parks the decisions on corporate policies and money flows are made. Corporations are being upsized and downsized, companies are merged and decommissioned, all to be watched in the frantic reality of the local stock exchanges. Each of the global cities articulates a regional or national economy with the world economy. Toronto's role in the global division of labour is its entrepot and financing function for the Canadian resource and branch plant economies.

Bay Street is really an extension of the mines and extraction economies of the Canadian North and West. Once the centre of agricultural financing and land machine production, Toronto is now the mill where the unrefined grains of Canada's resource industries are ground into the pastry flour of the dotcom economy. Substitution here means refinement of sorts.

In some ways, Toronto is equivalent to the City of Troy in John Berger's novel *Lilac and Flag*, a city like any other one we have seen (Berger, 1990). This kind of city is the substitution of local diversity with global sameness. Toronto has been subject to much of this kind of substituting modernization. Yet, Toronto as a global city also becomes a giant machine for the substitution of local economic activity through foreign markets, suppliers and demanders of economic goods and services. The more global Toronto becomes, the more it tends to not need itself anymore. Although the global economy creates its own needs and labour markets locally, it actually destroys the existing regional and national, even the bi-national networks of food security, social welfare, regional ecologies, etc. The urban region becomes a substitute for the entire world. This is an abstractification of urban space in the sense that local places are remade in the image of the needs of global capital. This, of course, is only one side of the story. As homogenization becomes the substitution strategy of choice in many ways - as Starbucks drives out your local coffee shop or fish and chips place - there is also a countervailing process at work simultaneously which operates from the ground up: This is the substitution of global demands for homogeneity by local diversity. To a degree, this countervailing force becomes the matter of globalization itself. Global capital markets diversity in a framework designed for homogenization. Postmodernism has helped defining the claim for diversity of product lines and consumer choice. In the end, though, making everything look alike while nurturing a culture of fake difference only goes as far as the next cultural and political revolt. Ultimately, there is always a revolution waiting to happen in those GAP jeans.

Globalization is only partly a directed, purposeful process, driven by so-called global actors. Toronto as any place of its kind is the site of a curious process of substitution wherein local and global dynamics flow into each other to create something surprisingly new. Instead of believing in the existence of two distinct spheres, one local - one global, we must understand urbanization in this current period as a process of 'glocalization'. Toronto is the ultimate city of 'glocalization' as it almost prostitutes itself to become something other than itself. Like the underachiever in the famous 20th Century ballad by that British combo The Who, Toronto outdoes itself to be the local nesting ground for all kinds of activities commonly considered global, such as the Olympic Games.

Toronto is also, of course, an extremely *political* place. The site of the largest local government in Canada, headed by a mayor, who is elected by the largest single electorate in the country, it is also the seat of the provincial government, where, since 1995, a strongly anti-urban, neo-liberal government has ruled the land. It has fundamentally transformed the political landscape of Canada's largest city. No wonder, the murmuring has grown louder in Toronto about substituting the feudal relationships with the Province by some form of self-government, chartered or not (Keil and Young, 2003). Beyond the rhetoric of autonomy, the reality is still quite different. As the city strives to become a global player on the basis of its regional economic strengths, it gets the wind knocked out of its lungs by provincial politicians who talk liberalization and global competition but have rather turned Toronto into a revanchist City of stripped services and broken infrastructures. What is offered to us is the competitive city. Closely examined, the competitive city breaks down into three components: the entrepreneurial city, the revanchist city, and the city of difference. One offers the goods, the next protects them through an increasingly aggressive, punishing (local) state; and the third turns the real liability of socio-economic difference into a display of diversity (see Kipfer and Keil as well as Kipfer and Goonewardena in this volume).

What is to be done in this situation? Let me offer a three-pronged perspective. Following Henri Lefebvre, we can distinguish three different kinds of space at work in Toronto: perceived space, conceived space and lived space or, in other words, spatial practice, representations of space and representational spaces (Lefebvre, 1991: 36-39). Briefly, these three kinds of space are defined as such: perceived space is the space of everyday practice, the ways to work, the links between individual daily routines and the changing grid of the city; conceived space denotes the conceptualizations and representations of space through intellectual or logical acts. The most typical act here is the drawing of a city plan; and finally, lived space is the space of associated images and symbols, the space of artists, resistance and reinterpretation beyond the engrained understandings of perceived and conceived space. All three notions of space are simultaneously present in each urban situation. They define the range of necessity and possibility in each urban reality. They are one in their difference.

Let us first enter the *perceived space* of Toronto. My suggestion here is to look at Toronto as one giant IKEA market. Indeed, I propose to liken the dominant spatial practice of Toronto to IKEA, the Swedish furniture company. Toronto is a substitute of the world because of its huge immigrant population. More than 40 percent of Torontonians are foreign born; 50 percent of all immigrants to Canada settle in this town. Immigrants have done so for a while, but now things have reached a certain momentum, as immigration to Toronto has visibly changed the city into something the world has not seen before. Toronto is the most diverse place on the planet, more than fifty percent of Toronto's population are 'non-white', but neither 'white' nor 'black' seem to still making much sense in this place.

Toronto's diversity, though, meets the standardized cityscape of thousands of bungalows and highrise apartment buildings which are being filled incessantly and unstoppably by the products that can be obtained at IKEA. Housed in uniformity, and furnished in Swedish wood, the diverse population of Toronto has created an everyday spatial practice, which is indeed unique: it is a landscape of accommodation of difference in likeness. The substitution of the world through the uniformity of the city. This has its most obvious expression in Toronto's inner suburbs: The ecology of *Bungalowville* (see Wirsig in this volume).

The *conceived space* of Toronto is a sad story of misguided initiative. Designed after the imperatives of the competitive city, the conceived space of Toronto is of the most trivial kind. Regenerated waterfronts, Olympic dreams, a general plan stripped of democratic input, smart growth for the hipsters of the dotcom world, condos, condos everywhere: The intellectually conceptualized landscape of Toronto has become a caricature of its own intentions: to create a good city. Behind the facades of the conceptual spaces of the downtown elites, who are entirely governed by the desires of the exurban feudal landlords at Queens Park, Toronto is developing into a sprawling monster of unbearable proportions. The conceptual space of exurban Southern Ontario is symbolized by the exurban Highway 7 that straddles the northern rim of the urban region, and captured in the lack of any serious attempt to control development. In late September 2002, as the citizens of Toronto were asked to give their input into the design of the new Official Plan, bulldozers and private police created *faits accomplis* by removing a sizable homeless population in the downtown core from a makeshift Tent City at the waterfront (see Bunce and Young as well as Blackwell and Goonewardena in this volume).

But there is hope. Caught between the regularized diversity of Bungalowville and the predictable nightmare of the elites' conceptions of Toronto's future, is the *lived space* of alternative Toronto. While usually also infused with the affirmative logic of capital accumulation, *lived space* is also an arena of possible revolt and resistance. Building throughout the 1990s as a constant reminder of unrest, Toronto's subaltern has raised its head many times. Playing the tune of utopian possibility in the face of the powers (and towers) that be, artists, rebels, and everyday resisters have given us a different Toronto, a possible urban world beyond the confines of our current reality. There are now everyday revolts against the substitutions of labour through capital, of regulation through deregulation, of the urban through the global, and so forth. The struggle against the destructive implications of globalization in Toronto has just begun.

References

Berger, John (1990), *Lilac and Flag: An Old Wives Tale of a City*. New York: Pantheon.

Brenner, Neil and Roger Keil (forthcoming), *The Global Cities Reader*. New York: Routledge.

Harvey, David (1989), *The Urban Experience*. Baltimore: The Johns Hopkins University Press.

Keil, Roger and Douglas Young (forthcoming), "A Charter for the people? A Research Note on the debate about municipal autonomy in Toronto", in: *Urban Affairs Review.* 2003

Klein, Naomi (2000), *No Logo: Taking Aim at the Brand Bullies*. Toronto: Alfred A. Knopf.

Lee, Dennis (1972), *Civil Elegies.* Concord, Ontario: Anansi Press.

Lefebvre, Henri (1991), *The Production of Space*. Oxford: Basil Blackwell.

Lehrer, Ute (2000), "Zitadelle Innenstadt: Bilderproduktion und Potsdamer Platz", in: Albert Scharenberg (Ed.) *Berlin: Global City oder Konkursmasse?*, 95-110.

Ondaatje, Michael (1987), *In the Skin of a Lion.* Toronto: McClelland and Stewart.

Ross, Andrew (2002), "The Odor of Publicity", in: Michael Sorkin and Sharon Zukin (eds.) *After the World Trade Center: Rethinking New York City.* New York: Routledge, 121-130.

Wackernagel, Mathis and William Rees (1996), *Our Ecological Footprint: Reducing Human Impact on the Earth.* Gabriola Island, BC: New Society Publisher.

TEXT....................Karen Wirsig
DRAWINGS....................Barbara Rahder

Toward a New Suburban Dream

As recently as the late 1990s, the postwar suburbs of North America were largely ignored in social policy and academic circles, and even among urban political organizers (Kipfer and Wirsig, 1999). A notable exception is Mike Davis, who suggested that "America seems to be unraveling in its traditional moral center: the urban periphery." [1] A few years later, it is indeed evident that the postwar suburbs are becoming the focus of hand-wringing, fear-mongering and, if we are lucky, a desire for a new political future.

There is no doubt that the September 2002 arrests of a so-called al-Qaeda sleeper cell in Lackawanna, barely 200 kilometres south-west of Toronto and described in a major Toronto newspaper as "a down-in-its-heels, low-income Buffalo (New York) suburb," (Toronto Star, 2002) signals a new form of racialized criminalization in urban North America.
At the same time, there is the electrifying suggestion of people (men), living in Buffalo or anywhere else in the eternal repetition of postwar suburbia, who are angry enough to consider quasi-military action against a country in which they see little future for themselves.

The existence of growing pockets of social, economic and political deprivation in otherwise wealthy contemporary urban regions finds its explanation in the latest round of uneven development in capitalist urbanization (Smith, 1984; Walker, 1981). That disillusioned working-class suburbanites are seeking ways to express their dissatisfaction should not be surprising. That there is even a possibility that a small group could fall into the clutches of a patriarchal and fundamentalist organization like al-Qaeda illustrates the tragic absence of a strong urban left opposition in North America, based precisely where the contradictions are felt most keenly.

In Toronto, the postwar suburbs are home to more than half of the city's population of 2.5 million and are exceedingly diverse demographically and variable in terms of built form. Under the metropolitan government system that existed between the early 1950s and the late 1990s, public and private rental housing, public transit and industrial jobs were all extended to them. Rows of bungalows run head-long into high-rise apartment campuses, cul-de sacs careen into six-lane arterial roads. Immigrants who arrived in the last five years live next to second, third, fourth generation Canadians. Young families share hallways and crescents with seniors.

Beyond the affluent enclaves of single-family housing tracts still found there, is a cornucopia of workers, recent immigrants, people of colour, single mothers, unemployed young people and seniors. The latter have not been unified under a progressive citywide political force and are basically absent from the formal political processes in the city.

A variety of sources, from newspaper articles to city reports, indicate the living conditions of these groups got worse, in the aggregate, over the last decade, a trend experienced in most urban regions considered successful in the global economy. Of those who can gain access to the labour market, many are tenuously employed in low-wage jobs. The rest are living on a fixed and inadequate pension or welfare cheque, or are completely dependent on relatives. A growing number of people across the city are a paycheque away from losing their housing, living in cramped quarters to share on rent, or already homeless and staying in emergency shelters or sleeping rough in the city's celebrated ravine system.[2] In 1998, it was estimated that more than 80,000 people were at risk of becoming homeless and another 25,000 were effectively homeless (Mayor's Task Force, 1998).

The persistent lack of political power of the groups of people being ghettoized in pockets of the postwar suburbs means that their day-to-day living conditions have, at best, not improved and, at worst, bottomed out. Racism limits people's job and housing choices and makes them bigger targets for police. Low incomes limit people's options, and particularly those of women and seniors living in abusive situations who have nowhere else to go. The ever-higher cost of transportation and inefficiency of local transit routes in the suburbs, as well as sparse or over-policed public spaces, reinforces isolation and alienation.
In 1998, an amalgamation forced by the Conservative (neo-liberal) provincial government brought together the six local municipalities that had been under the Metropolitan Toronto regional government into a single new city. In all the years under the Metro government and then in the new city, Toronto's postwar suburbs - already overtaken by more glamorous or affordable exurban settlements further from the core whose collective population is now greater than that of the city - did not shed their uncomplicated suburban veneer.

Only recently have there been real signs of acknowledge-ment that these inner suburbs are not homogeneous com-munities of middle-class (mainly white) homeowners pre-occupied with protecting their property values and property-based local services such as policing, waste collection and street maintenance, while keeping taxes down. Maps crea-ted by city staff in the late 1990s began showing the pattern of poverty in the city, which follows a U-shape up from several public housing neighbourhoods in the core, out along the main railway tracks, and into the postwar sub-urbs.

City-wide charities, social policy analysts, downtown social democrats, and the police have begun to place emphasis on the social and political conditions in the suburbs. They have suggested or enacted everything from limited social welfare provisions to soft crime control to active criminaliza-tion.

For example, the United Way, one of the biggest charitable funders in the city, which raised more than CDN $75 million in 2001, is dedicating a token CDN $1.6 million over three years to “underserved neighbourhoods and populations in suburban communities.” [3] Social democratic councillors representing downtown wards have begun strategizing to get more of their brethren elected in the postwar suburbs, while supporting expansion of community services and soft crime control initiatives, such as publicly funded basketball programs in which young men play with police officers.

The federal government jumped on the bandwagon with funding to several suburban crime-prevention projects under its National Crime Prevention Strategy. This parallels a recent focus by U.S. progressives on “at-risk suburbs” as locations in which to form a new political coalition (Orfield, 2002). By and large, the collected efforts of politicos and policy wonks have contributed as much to the pathologization of the low-income neighbourhoods they target as to any serious relief of everyday struggle experienced there.

A recent acknowledgement of this fact came from an unlikely source. A right-of-centre, fiscally conservative city councillor from the most racially diverse inner suburb of Scarborough resigned from his coveted position on Toronto’s police services board (the less-than-adequate civilian oversight body) citing, in part, concerns about the policing of young people (Di Matteo, 2002). Himself an immigrant of colour who had always understood his constituency as tax-conscious, middle-class homeowners, suddenly found himself approached by people with stories about ill treatment by the police and discovered there wasn’t much he could do about it.

Meanwhile, research on income, race and gender in Toronto has shown it is particularly non-White people who are being left out of the formal labour market and have the lowest incomes in the city (Ornstein, 2000). Statistics suggest that around three-quarters of women of colour are stuck in de-skilled, low-paying jobs.[4] Their communities - both geographic and identity-based - are in the direst need, while their children are most likely to be targeted by police and least likely to be well-served by the public education system.

Criminalization, and responses to it, tend to put the focus on men. But if a few boys are able to get into recreational programs explicitly designed to keep them off the streets, what is going on with their sisters?

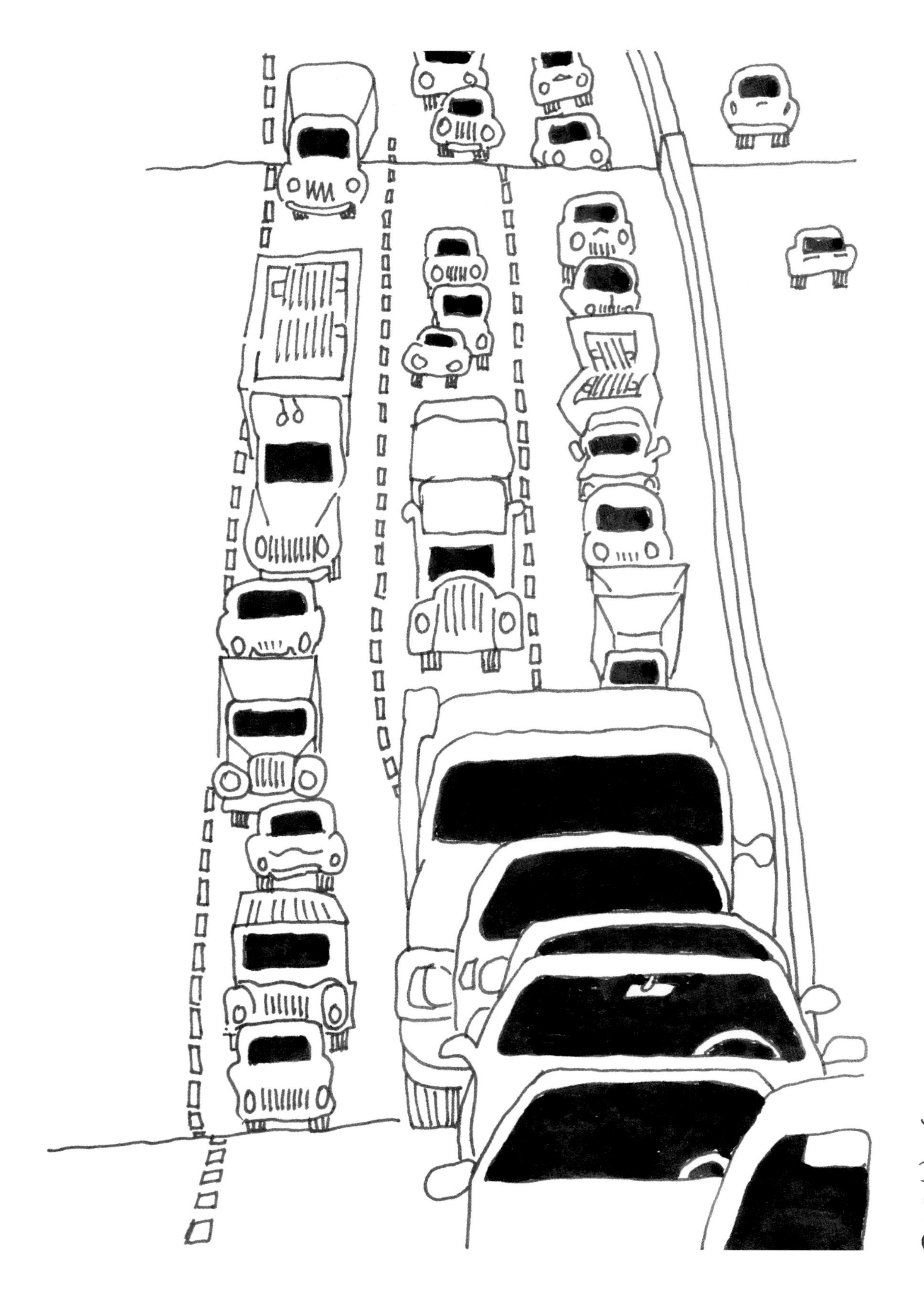
©B.Rahder '02

As feminist activist and researcher Punam Khosla has explained, the crime prevention approach emphasises programs to keep boys and young 'out of trouble.' [5] Meanwhile, girls and women are left to fend for themselves as they struggle to hold together the threads of their low-income neighbourhoods [6]. Cutbacks to social programs and welfare benefits, the lack of affordable rental housing, childcare and recreational space and programming, and a gradual deconstruction of women's anti-violence programs, such as rape crisis centres and battered women's shelters, have made their lives extremely difficult. Political action and organizing under these conditions often has the status of luxury as these women struggle to counter their own person isolation and meet their everyday needs.

Creating public spaces where everyday solidarities can be strengthened while collective needs are being met remains a significant challenge in a city where public infrastructure is receding because of budget cuts. Meanwhile the city discusses facilitating the development of new bourgeois, commodified spaces through byzantine public-private partnership deals in places chosen ostensibly by the market, committing to massive infrastructure projects such as new roads and pipes, under some fantasy of attracting the 'desirable' high-tech and office workers and their employers. The rest of the people in the city eke out each day and many dream about other possible urban worlds.

And there is still the hope that those who don't take flight to the exurbs at the earliest possible opportunity will stick around to carve out a humanized urban future. Thus-far ephemeral citywide political movements call for access to public recreation facilities and programs, emergency homeless shelters, affordable housing, better transit service, and better-funded community services and programs to combat violence against women. Groups have also come together to oppose racist comments by the mayor, and policing targeting people of colour, youth, and the poor. These movements involve mainly women, tenants, workers, young people, seniors, new immigrants, along with a number of community agency workers straining against the constraints of charity and service hegemony.

The political challenge is for these often-isolated demands - and isolated groups - to be turned into a force of people who can claim their rights to the city, and thus avoid being taken up as charitable causes or urban problems to be solved.

References

Davis, Mike (1998), *Ecology of Fear.* New York: Metropolitan.

Di Matteo, Enzo (2002), "Another bites the dust", in: *Now Magazine*, April 18-24.

Dunning, Will, Morris, Bill and the Planning Alliance Inc. (2002), *Housing Needs Study*. Toronto: South Etobicoke Regeneration Project.

Edwards, Peter (2002), *Toronto Star*, September 20.

Khosla, Punam (2002), "The Situation of Women in Low-income Neighbourhoods", in: *Toronto.* Toronto: Toronto Women's Network, forthcoming.

Kipfer, Stefan and Wirsig, Karen (1999), "Politics and Possibilities: reliving the suburban paradox in the new Toronto", in: *Inura Bulletin* 17, pp. 13-16.

Mayor's Homelessness Action Task Force (1998), *Taking Responsibility for Homelessness: an action plan for Toronto*, City of Toronto.

Orfield, Myron (2002), *American Metropolitics: the new suburban reality.* Washington D.C.: Brookings Institution Press.

Ornstein, Michael (2000), *Ethno-Racial Inequality in the City of Toronto: an analysis of the 1996 census.* Toronto: Access and Equity Unit, City of Toronto.

Smith, Neil (1984), *Uneven Developments: nature, capital and the production of space.* Oxford: Basil Blackwell.

United Way of Greater Toronto and Canadian Council for Social Development (2002), *A Decade of Decline: poverty and income inequality in the City of Toronto in the 1990s.* Toronto: United Way of Greater Toronto.

Walker, Richard A. (1981), "A Theory of Suburbanization: capitalism and the construction of urban space in the U.S.", in: M. Dear and A.J. Scott (eds), *Urbanization and Urban Planning in Capitalist Society.* London: Methuen.

Wirsig, Karen (2000), "Inequality in Mel's fat city", in: *Novae Res Urbis.* October 6, p. 2.

Wirsig, Karen (2001), "Inequality in Toronto", in: *Novae Res Urbis.* February 15, p.3.

Wirsig, Karen (2002), "Mayoral Race 2003: will the campaign open up a public debate on the city?", in: *Novae Res Urbis.* August 23, p. 1.

Endnotes

[1] Davis, 1998, p. 400.

[2] On living conditions in the city, see, for example, United Way and Canadian Council on Social Development (2002), Dunning, Morris and Planning Alliance (2002), Khosla (2002), Wirsig (2001).

[3]United Way and Canadian Council on Social Development, 2002. The charity also funds some agencies in suburban areas through its core grants program.

[4] Ornstein's report, commissioned by the City of Toronto, includes detailed data runs on the 1996 Census returns for the city, providing a breakdown of income and employment by "ethno-racial" group. The poverty and employment statistics for people identifying themselves as Polish, Russian and Serbian are also not rosy

[5] Based on personal conversations and organizing work with Punam Khosla.

[6] One must consider, for example, the women of Lackawanna, who have been all but ignored in the rush to put their brothers, husbands, sons or friends into jail on suspicion of participation in an al-Qaeda sleeper cell.

TEXT..........Susannah Bunce and Douglas Young
PHOTOS..........Roger Keil

Image - Making by the Water: Global City Dreams and the Ecology of Exclusion

In late September , 2002 dozens of security guards backed up by dozens more police officers removed the residents of what had come to be known in Toronto as Tent City. About one hundred of the city's several thousand homeless had created Tent City on a vacant piece of waterfront land situated two kilometres east of the Financial District's office towers. Tent City became an international embarrassment for Toronto boosters after the New York Times featured it in a story about the demise of Toronto's livability (Krauss, 2002). Home Depot, the owner of the Tent City lands (and ironically a chain of stores that provide supplies for people building or renovating homes), has now secured the site with a three metre high chain link and barbed wire fence, high intensity lighting and a crew of around-the-clock guards. The Tent City site could now be mistaken for a maximum security prison; a prison designed to keep people out rather than in.

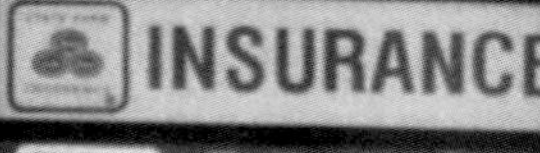
PROGRESS
PARK
Centre
DR. S. STARKMAN
FAMILY DENTISTRY
INSURANCE
VP
289-3747
Music
School
LEASING INFO
(905) 764-8116

Toronto's dream of achieving Global City status is pinned on the redevelopment of its waterfront, and a community of squatters living in self-built homes has no place in that dream. The shape of Toronto's global dream is clearly spelled out in a recent planning document, *Making Waves: Principles for Building Toronto's Waterfront* (City of Toronto, 2001). It states that "[a] renewed Central Waterfront will become Toronto's international postcard image and reaffirm our reputation as one of the most livable cities in the world." (Ibid.: 8) *Making Waves* makes absolutely clear that public sector planning in Toronto has thrown in its lot with the image makers and civic boosters. It now sees its role as one of facilitating the creation of a "postcard image" of a city that will be attractive to "to the legion of knowledge workers who can locate themselves and their businesses anywhere in the world." (Ibid.: 13) Planners themselves propose the dismantling of the current regulatory framework within which property capital operates to make the city attractive to 'footloose capital'. In this sense planning in Toronto has become an important and co-operative participant in a general and global restructuring of the local state in post-Fordist urban regions. The social democratic municipal governments of the late Fordist era have been replaced by lean and mean, entrepreneurial governments, in Toronto and in cities around the world. Their goal is no longer the regulation of development but rather its opposite - de-regulation. The social democratic 'city that works' is refashioning itself as the Schumpeterian 'city that competes' (and wins). Toronto's citizens are told that there is no choice but to engage in what is perceived as a zero sum game of globalization. 'Winning', they are told by the authors of *Making Waves* in purple prose thick with water metaphors, will be good for everyone: "[t]he benefits that will ripple out from a revitalized Central Waterfront will extend beyond its boundaries and will wash across the whole of the city." (Ibid.: 13) Just how important the waterfront is to Toronto's global dream can be seen in the rare co-operation of federal, provincial and municipal governments, each of which has committed substantial monies to kickstart redevelopment. Other items on the 'urban agenda' in Canada, like social housing and public transit, have not fared so well.
Creating Global Toronto's "postcard image"on the waterfront also reflects conflicting and contradictory ideas about nature and ecology. One of the justifications for the evictions of the Tent City residents was concern for their health as the soil on which they had built their homes is highly contaminated; a victim of Fordist disregard for 'the environment'. Indeed, workers brought in to 'clean up' the site wore protective clothing and face masks as they set to the task of weed-whacking. Yet the concern Home Depot had for the squatters' health evaporated as soon as the formerly homeless were made homeless once again. The Tent City site and other brownfield properties on the edge of the lake are considered degraded and contaminated - material evidence of the unnaturalness of the city - yet at the same time their bright future as part of the global-city-in-the-making is guaranteed by their connection to nature in the form of a 'rediscovered' Lake Ontario. Plans for the new communities to be created along the waterfront also naturalize existing social inequalities in the city. It is deemed natural that the waterfront will become home to the much sought after and glamourized New Economy knowledge worker, and natural that the homeless should remain homeless somewhere else. There is a parallel to the cleanup of the soil in the waterfront and the eviction of Tent City. In both cases the unnatural is being removed; toxic soil removed to make room for the 'better' nature of the lake, Tent City removed to make room for those who have a 'natural' claim on the city's 'better' or most prestigious natures.

The Central Waterfront, including the former industrial area of the Port Lands, has been targeted as an "Area for Reinvestment", by the City of Toronto. The City's notion of reinvestment seems to be a two-pronged approach to stimulating economic investment and fostering physical rehabilitation through careful land-use changes that make a more 'friendly' environment for private investment. The *Making Waves* plan strengthens the municipal planning department's ability to facilitate the approval of proposed residential and commercial developments along the water-front. At the level of the planning department, this will entail a major alteration to the current planning approval process. With the new approval system, development applications will be assessed by one administrative body instead of a two-tiered minor variance and zoning amendment approval process (City of Toronto: 2000). The proposed system is argued to provide a "more flexible approach to zoning by allowing for a broader range of uses, incentives or alternative requirements" (City of Toronto: 2001, 49). Such a simplified approval process, intended for large-scale use in so-called Reinvestment Areas, is reflective of a larger trend towards de-regulating development approval processes. For example, simplified planning approval processes, based upon the devolution of bureaucratic levels of planning approval, have been common in Britain since the 1980s. De-regulated development approval processes were
considered central to the implementation of Thatcher's urban strategy to foster private investment in infrastructure development (Allmendinger: 1997, Allmendinger: 2002). In practice in Toronto, this simplified planning approval system will play a similar role by massaging the interests of the elusive 'footloose capital' that is being catered to in the *Making Waves* document.

CANADIAN TIRE

Simplified planning approval for the Waterfront will occur alongside the flexibilization of land-use designations and the removal of density limits (City of Toronto: 2001).Working concurrently with a larger municipal planning emphasis on densification in Toronto's downtown core, such a 'one-stop' planning approval process has the potential to strongly affect the type and appearance of new developments. Most alarmingly, the development approval process is not defined at all in the *Making Waves* plan. It seems that the process will rest entirely on the administrative discretion of municipal officials who support the intentions of the *Making Waves* plan. Through new development permit by-laws, considered for most of the Central Waterfront, aspects such as the density and height of proposed developments will be considered on an individual basis by the one development approval body. In terms of the physical appearance and housing tenure of residential developments along the waterfront, there is strong evidence that future development will follow current trends toward high- rise condominium buildings marketed towards the stereotypical young urban professional. As a result, this space-efficient and profit-maximizing form of development is an inevitable prototype for market-driven housing. In the absence of governmental regulation that would ensure the availability and affordability of rental housing and other income accessible housing types, there are strong grounds for concern about the real affordability of future developments.

The current CityPlace re-development on the once municipally owned 'Railway Lands', located near the city's financial district and just north of the waterfront, is a good example of the recent trend towards the construction of high-rise condominium buildings. The approved plans for CityPlace centre on twenty high-rise condominium buildings as the development's focal point, surrounded by 'walk-up' low-rise residences. In total there will be 6,000 dwelling units in buildings as tall as 49 storeys.Concord Adex, the CityPlace developer,has no plans to supply rental housing; all of the units will be available for purchase either by owner-occupiers or investors (CityPlace promotional presentation: 2001). Such investors will stand to gain high returns in leasing out units in Toronto's tight and unaffordable rental market, particularly exacerbated by recent governmental de-regulation of rent controls and legal amendments that favour the profit interests of landlords. Thus, the rental units that will be available in CityPlace will no doubt rent at or above current average market rents. Concord Adex's plans have been considered to be a successful scheme for residential redevelopment by municipal planners and recently earned a national planning award from the Canadian Institute of Planners on the basis of their so-called "progressiveness". Of utmost concern here is that professional planners are praising profit-centred re- development as an example of progressive planning, and that a residential plan with no affordable, publicly subsidized rental housing is considered successful.

This prototype of re-development has serious implications for the future of waterfront redevelopment and issues of 'affordability' highlighted in the Central Waterfront plan.

Making Waves establishes as a goal (but not a requirement) that 25% of all housing built in the Central Waterfront be 'affordable".It defines affordable housing as housing that is affordable to households in the lowest 60% of Toronto's tenant income demographic. Total annual housing costs should not exceed 30% of gross annual household income (City of Toronto, 2001, 57). With this calculation, a person earning a gross income of $2000 per month (while a modest salary, still far above the gross minimum wage of $1160 per month) would only be able to spend $600 on per month rental housing. With these numbers in mind, the planning department's inclusion of an affordable housing rubric provides only lip service to concerns about residential affordability. In Toronto's rental market, where one-bedroom apartments in the downtown core can rent for over one thousand dollars per month, spending less than 30% of gross annual income on rental housing is an impossible option for tenants earning minimum wage, or indeed anyone with income of less than $3,000 per month. This becomes less tangible for tenants who rely on provincial government social assistance or federal government disability incomes, or low-income families with children who require more space than one-bedroom rental accommodation. When such an affordable housing formula is paired with planning emphasis on the facilitation of approvals for market-driven residential development, it becomes clear that the prospects for real affordable housing are bleak. *Making Waves* places total faith in private real estate development as the chief planner and designer of future residential communities along the Waterfront. By doing so, municipal planners have ignored the fact that historically, private developers have been largely uninterested in building affordable rental housing in Toronto and will continue to be so.

The eradication of Tent City from Toronto's waterfront can perhaps be seen as the first step in the implementation of the *Making Waves* plan. With homeless people in makeshift housing out of the way, the City can now embark on creating the 'post-card' image of Toronto. This image, which is already so clear, is one of tall, glistening buildings filled with youthful professional 'new economy' workers, enjoying their proximity to the downtown core and leisure trails along the waterfront.

References

Allmendinger, Philip. (1997), *Thatcherism and Planning: The Case of Simplified Planning Zones.* Aldershot: Ashgate Publishing Ltd.

Allmendinger, Philip. (2002), *Planning Theory*: Houndmills: Basingstoke

City of Toronto (2001), *Making Waves: Principles for Building Toronto's Waterfront (Central Waterfront Part II Plan)*, Toronto: City of Toronto.

CityPlace Promotional Presentation: Concord Adex, Toronto. August 8, 2001.

Krauss, C. (2002), "Amid Prosperity, Toronto Shows Signs of Fraying", in: *New York Times.* June 16, 2002.

5.4

TEXT......Adrian Blackwell and Kanishka Goonewardena - for Panning Action
PHOTOS......Adrian Blackwell

Poverty of Planning: Tent City and the New Official Plan

Tent City and the Official Plan

On September 24, 2002, the Toronto media reported two events under two headlines.

The smaller headline was about the unveiling of the new Official Plan of the City of Toronto. This began with news of presentations by Mayor Lastman and the Director of the Planning Department as to how they were going to make Toronto the greatest and most beautiful city. It was followed by public testimony, almost all from well-groomed supporters of the Plan, including the usual suspects like developers and taxpayers, as well as world famous experts like Jane Jacobs.

While that show was dragging on in City Hall, security guards hired by Home Depot, under the “supervision” of the police, were on a rampage - kicking people out of Tent City, the post-industrial no-man’s land on Toronto’s Waterfront that has been home for a few years to the city’s largest concentration of homeless people. The site was legally taken over on this day by Home Depot, confiscating the improvised homes and modest possessions of the homeless people. That sorry spectacle made the bigger headline, under which appeared even more infuriating stories that blamed the victims while justifying the brutal manner of their eviction, even as relocation plans were being explored.

City Hall and Tent City

But why two headlines when both news items were really part of the same story? No one in the mainstream media bothered to note how the people evicted from Tent City stormed into City Hall that afternoon, looking for the real perpetrators of their eviction-those politicians and planners who were shameless in their enthusiasm for a Plan catering so earnestly to the interests of developers, taxpayers and multinational corporations, at the expense of those who don't own and can't afford properties in the city. Most Torontonians don't need rocket science to see the link between what happened in City Hall and in Tent City on that day.

The very logic of urban development endorsed by the Plan - the kind of city planning that is just a code-name for selling the city to the highest bidder - created Tent City in the first place. It also forced its (former) residents into a bizarre confrontation with ecstatic fans of the Plan inside City Hall. According to one eye witness, "all of a sudden a bunch of people who looked like they weren't supposed to be there seemed to take over the Council Chambers." These were not the folks you often see rubbing shoulders with the power brokers of City Hall. Rather, they were the representatives of a large population that just didn't appear anywhere in the hyperbolic "vision" of the Plan.

City planning and urban design, which are meant to create spaces for a better life for everyone, have been hijacked from the start by the powers that be. Over 150 years ago, Friedrich Engels quite correctly called planning in capitalist cities "hypocritical," explaining in his famous study of Manchester how "town planning" was really about "hiding from the eyes of wealthy ladies and gentlemen with strong stomachs and weak nerves the misery and squalor which are part and parcel of their own riches and luxury."

Not much has changed since Engels' time. The former Tent City and its vast, underutilized surroundings are imagined today by developers and planners alike not as the ideal location for social housing and other public amenities, but as a gigantic bourgeois playground and high-tech entertainment complex generously sprinkled with high-end condos-a bright, guilty place where dot-coms and related yuppies of all countries can unite!

Who is this Plan Talking to?

What does the Plan say? Whose Toronto are we talking about?

The Plan takes up the task of guiding the development of Toronto over the next thirty years with a great vision for the city - one that claims to improve transit, create a more compact urban form, encourage economic growth, and beautify the city. The language and the pictures of the Plan are most seductive and make you want to believe. But when you look through the glossy pictures and read between the lines, you begin to see what's really going on.

The Plan rests on a number of cozy assumptions. It assumes that planners will be reasonable, developers will be benevolent, architects will be brilliant, and citizens will be quiet. City planning is presented here as a conflict-free process in which everyone, by the grace of the "free market," is a winner.

But as Tent City folks and many others who rarely make news will tell you, planning is no win-win game. In the social struggles over space in the city, there are, sure enough, losers. They are the people altogether missing from the Plan. That's why their abrupt appearance in City Hall on September 24 was both odd and apt. To deflect attention away from what the Plan can't see (or, rather, what it does not want you to see), it speaks in animated tones about not only what it chooses to see but also how it sees. And it urges everyone else to see the city the same way. So the Plan looks down upon the city through what it calls the three lenses.

The Vision of the Three Lenses

If we adopt the visionary language of the Plan for a moment, what do we see through its first lens? We see downtown spaces and former industrial areas-large areas cleared for intensive development by the removal of existing planning controls (such as zoning), There is hardly a thought for existing uses or users. In other words, open season for developers to move in, build and make the best bang for their buck.

The second lens zooms in on the "Avenues." Large suburban east-west roads like Eglington, Lawrence, and Finch are strategically primed for gentrification, but without offending "Not In My Back Yard" (NIMBY) taxpayers. With no investment in social housing (about which the Plan is mute), the intensification of development on these avenues can only displace existing businesses and residents. Small-scale, start-up business people and renters unable to afford the new luxuries promised in these hot spots will have to pack up and leave.

In the third lens we see what the Plan quaintly calls "Neighborhoods," which account for 75% of the land area of the City. Here change is forbidden. This obviously caters to NIMBYism, which official planners hold in the same high regard with which they consider the economic wisdom of laissez-faire development. In the context of a city otherwise ruled by developers, this 'Neighborhood" designation (distinct from the already dense "apartment neighborhoods" where further densification is encouraged!) promises to send property values skywards.

In fact, the Plan's language of lenses is deeply misleading. They do not represent different ways of seeing, or distinct perspectives. They simply refer to three levels (densities) of development-high, medium and negligible. These designations serve the interests of people who own property and people who develop land. The deregulation of land use in former industrial zones, now called "employment areas," caters to powerful players in the global economy, creating "flexible-enterprise zones" with publicly subsidized streets, services and spaces.

When you really look at it, then, the function of the three lenses becomes obviou - to partition the City into three distinct zones, one for each of the three dominant interest groups served by the Plan: developers, taxpayers and global capitalists. It has nothing to say to anyone else. What the language of lenses obscures is therefore clear: the questionable reasons and mechanisms for favoring the interests of these powerful groups.

What Will be the Effects of the Plan?

While the Plan represents a victory for the ruling classes of Toronto and the world, some of the background documents prepared for the Plan reveal traces of a social struggle, even within City Hall. Toronto at the Crossroads, for example, includes a crystal clear map of the concentrations of "socially vulnerable areas" in the city. It illustrates the growing economic polarization and pockets of poverty that form a ring running through the outer suburbs and around the inner city. Any reasonable official plan aiming to build a sustainable and equitable urban life here would have started with these realities - the majority of actually existing people in the city-rather than banking on an exodus of dot.com millionaires and other inflated dreams of the "knowledge economy."

The urgent question, then, is this: what will happen to the various socially vulnerable groups in the city whose neighborhoods are either ignored in this plan or earmarked for gentrification?

The Plan actually paves the way to remove people from strategic downtown neighborhoods, concentrating poverty in high-density suburban spaces whose reality is deliberately hidden in its three-lens vision. Complementing this violence of eviction is the alienating physical and symbolic violence constantly inflicted on individuals forced to live in these suburban spaces. These have a number of real effects.

The physical distance between social classes protects affluent people from the violent power and frustration that economic exploitation creates.
The physical separation prevents middle and upper class Torontonians from having to experience poverty first hand, allowing them to indulge a fantasy of equality, while breeding stereotypes about people they don't have to interact with every day.

Separation organizes the city so that affluent people have much better access, not only to luxury goods, but also to essential services like healthy food, a clean environment, health care, public transportation, parks, public spaces and jobs.

Isolation atomizes the very communities that could otherwise create unified resistance to this alienating condition. One of the lasting legacies of Toronto's high-density modernist housing is a situation where people are concentrated and isolated from one another at the same time.

Real separation and isolation are symbolically overcome in the image of the beautiful city. The objective of urban design here is to mask beneath the spectacle of dazzling urban space the potentially explosive realities of the new amalgamated city of developers, taxpayers and global capital.

The relegation of poor populations to badly maintained suburban spaces and the constant move towards the gentrification of downtown neighborhoods is just the current manifestation of a long legacy of "progressive planning" in Toronto that was born in the early 1970s with the movement to stop the Spadina Expressway and save historic downtown neighborhoods. In the early days lip service was paid to the construction of affordable housing, the protection of downtown industries and the maintenance of diverse populations, but by the early 1980s these explicit goals had all but disappeared. What has remained a constant since 1970 is the project of recuperating Toronto's "livable downtown" for middle and affluent classes. The result of this planning legacy - which the new Official Plan continues - has been the increasing concentration of poverty in dense suburban neighborhoods.

Communities of Resistance

The new Official Plan packs a lot of power: the financial power of business elites; the ideological power of mainstream planning intellectuals and professionals; and the coercive power of a questionably politicized police force. But the political-economic-bureaucratic logic of the Plan also has its Achilles heel - the people it dispossesses.

What Toronto really has going for it is neither the "free market" nor its global city status, but its diverse community of committed people not willing to put up with the violence of city planning-no matter how rational it seems to the "common sense" of corporate greed, professional planners and academic consultants. It has not gone unnoticed to these activists how the removal and dilution of various planning controls in the new plan (lax zoning, streamlined approval process, restricted public consultation, behind the scenes maneuvering, etc.) amounts to an erosion of democracy in the planning process and a submission of urban life to the merciless logic of the "free market."

In recent years direct actions led by the Ontario Coalition Against Poverty (OCAP) and others have applied pressure on downtown neighborhoods, rudely awakening Toronto's elite from their gentrified dreams. What is required as a complement to the fight against gentrification, however, are effective strategies and tactics of resistance emanating from Toronto's suburban spaces-initiatives designed to overcome the very real isolation found in the peripheral areas of the city. An example was set by the Los Angeles Bus Riders Union, founded by dispersed riders spread throughout the Los Angeles area.

Toronto doesn't need a plan driven by corporate interests, developers and taxpayers, but a set of planning strategies produced by diverse communities already struggling against economic, cultural and ecological injustice-to open up spaces for people to imagine, transform and enjoy their city. This struggle for justice in the city is also one to reclaim the promise of planning for the very people whose fundamental right to the city is violated in the new Official Plan.

TEXT..........Kanishka Goonewardena and Stefan Kipfer
PHOTOS..........Roger Keil

Creole City: Culture, Class and Capital in Toronto

'The only minority is the bourgeoisie'.
-Krisantha Sri Bhaggiyadatta

"I can be anything you want me to be", says sultry escort girl Sue to young, Indo-Canadian dot-com millionaire Rahul at a fancy Toronto night club in Deepa Mehta's new movie *Bollywood/Hollywood*. 'Anything' can of course mean anything, especially when the tantalizing word is softly spoken by a seductive young woman to a single guy who's not so bad looking himself. But Sue is being rather specific here, saying that she could agree to masquerade, in spite of her Spanish good looks and dance moves that intrigue Rahul's Indian Diasporic taste, as this very eligible Non Resident Indian's fiancée through the festivities culminating in his sister's wedding-for a sumptuous fee that would not include sex.[1]

This - the lack of sex - may be one weakness of *Bollywood/Hollywood*; but the alluring prospect of a gorgeous 'Spanish' woman passing for 'Indian' in Toronto is not only the selling point of the movie's otherwise bland plot, but also what excites contemporary urban cultural theory in this city even more than sex. At stake here is nothing less than the seemingly limitless potential of socio-cultural identities somehow liberated from their traditional ethno-cultural moorings - a hope celebrated as reality in paperback best-sellers like Pico Iyer's *Global Soul: Jet Lag, Shopping Malls and the Search for Home* and even grafted onto such pioneering post-structuralist and post-colonial theoretical concepts as 'performativity' (Judith Butler) and 'hybridity' (Homi K. Bhabha) - that is discerned by some observers to be the very substance of everyday life in Toronto (and other ethno-culturally diverse 'global cities'): *creolization*.

Creolization - which is obtained in theory by deconstructing all those essentialist identities adding up to the liberal pluralist formation of multiculturalism, and then freely mixing up the resultant shreds of former identities in a myriad of new fusions - is both delightfully *descriptive* (look at all the 'fusion' restaurants in Toronto!) and *prescriptive* (now, instead of having to be this, that or the other, wouldn't you like to be anything you want to be?). That's why *Bollywood/Hollywood* disappoints, in fact, precisely when the Spanish Sue anti-climactically turns out to be Sunita Singh, just another Indian Diaspora girl - the identity she was *not* supposed to first conceal and then reveal, as it happens in the movie, but to *perform* and *deconstruct*, with an original Spanish touch to make it ever so special. For after that post-multicultural expectation fails to pan out, it becomes just a another Toronto-based 'Indian movie' about the diaspora made for Toronto's multicultural eyes cinematically seasoned by Hollywood as much as Bollywood. *Bollywood/Hollywood* remains true to its name, nonetheless, by combining the worst-or the best-of both celluloid worlds into yet another predictably entertaining product from the now global 'machine for producing the heterosexual couple'. More intriguingly, it calls into question this city's latest discursive utopia of plastic identity - which, as a symbolic resolution of the real anxiety of discriminatory racialization still rampant, invests itself libidinally in the colourful rhetoric of creolization.

Sunita Singh is the daughter of a poor auto-mechanic and a factory worker living next to the city's international airport - along with thousands of other new immigrants packed into Toronto's ring of inner suburbs, through which the city's growing underclass has etched a U-shaped curve around downtown in recent maps surveying increasing social polarization and spatial segregation. As detailed in Karen Wirsig's contribution to this volume, the suburban, working class existence of Sunita's family is literally worlds apart from the new economy's dot.com fortunes adorning this 'competitive city' with increasingly exclusive neighbourhoods and a new wave of luxurious downtown condos - the habitat of Rahul. His condo in the King-Spadina district of downtown - one of the first areas to be 'liberated' from planning controls in order to court global capital under the popular guise of 'mixed-use' and 'innovative' urban redevelopment-is, in Rahul's grandma's queen's English, his 'love nest'. Quite a contrast from Sunita's humble abode. But 'can love cross the boundaries of class and prejudice?' - bridge King - Spadina's yuppie condos with Etobicoke's suburban Third World? - asks the film's promotional website.[2] *Bollywood/Hollywood* being a movie, the question is rhetorical: the answer is yes. Yet its audience, having had the light entertainment they deserved after a long day at work, step back into the streets of Toronto knowing well that the Rahuls and the Sunitas of this world don't get together like that for real-unless, of course, they have been seduced by the latest theory of creolization coming out of York University-based Culture of Cities project.[3]

In order to make sense of the utopian desires coded into the notion of creolization - including the honourable *wish* for a political community not divided by race or ethnicity - it will be useful first to note what this 'new' term seeks to substitute in Toronto (and elsewhere): the multicultural city. Multicultural*ism* in the Canadian context refers not only to a way of reading demographic reality, but also to an official state policy dating back to the early 1970s. Even though multiculturalism exists in a tense relationship to the super-ordinate doctrine bilingualism (and the two-nation theory of citizenship it implies) and the colonial First Nations policies of the Canadian state, it has become constitutive of Canadian national identity since 1971. Now enshrined in the Canadian Multiculturalism Act of 1988 and connected to a myriad of national, provincial and local policies (of immigration, settlement, public education, cultural production, etc.), multiculturalism enthusiastically admits and promotes the preservation of 'ethnic' (i.e., non-English, non-French) immigrant cultures. As a result of social struggles that have attempted to contest and deepen what was essentially a folklorist notion of heritage in the 1970s, the 1988 Act now includes a sprinkling of recommendations to promote the equality and participation of all Canadians in all aspects of life,[4] even as its scope remains restricted to a cultural realm defined in ethnicized and racialized terms.[5]

What, then, is the matter with multiculturalism? The complaint lodged against multiculturalism by the Culture of Cities project and other deconstructionists of cultural identity consists in the rejection of a central axiom of the 1988 Act that is also taken for granted in the popular discourse on multiculturalism, namely, the existence of a plurality of 'communities whose members share a common origin' and therefore a *common culture*. Exponents of the Culture of Cities project such as Jenny Berman dismiss this notion as both 'repressive' and 'obsolete', questioning the multiculturalist assumption that 'people wish to keep living in their ancestral culture'[6]

According to them, city regions like Toronto, where almost half of all immigrants to Canada settle, should no longer be seen as an array of shared cultures that coexist uneasily with a Canadian mainstream. Their claim, rather, is that actually existing 'ghetto cultures' have been attenuated and, in the words of project leader Alan Blum, that 'there just isn't a shared [mainstream Canadian] culture anymore'.[7] Instead, we now live in the Creole City-the Diasporic City of Toronto. To speak with pop-writer Pico Iyer, in this 'global' city of mongrel identities and miscegenated mindsets, nothing sits still; everything, including all manner of collective identity, is in postmodern 'flux'. Here is a city 'speeding into a post-national future willy-nilly'.[8] Fortunately, it is full of fusion restaurants (the 'Little China Restaurant which advertises Pakistani-style Chinese food' is Iyer's favourite) and home to the Caribana Festival, the 'quintessential diasporic event' of our time.[9] 'That's why', announces Jenny Burman, 'I love Toronto'.

What such teary - eyed celebrations of the *culture* of creolization fail to see, however, is the *socio-economic* reality of Toronto that is integral to the relentless commodification of 'ethnic' foods and festivals - among other 'differences' relished by postmodern consumers of 'cultural studies' - in our putatively post-multicultural era. Take, with the delicacies of diaspora, a tiny taste of the seemingly invisible statistics concerning our 'visible minorities'. Whereas the adult unemployment rate for Torontonians of European origin is under 7%, for non-Europeans it is 12.5%; while 14% percent of European-origin families live below the LICO (Low Income Cut Off), the poverty rate ranges from 32% for Aboriginals, 35% for South Asians, 41.4% for Latin Americans, 45% for Africans, Blacks and Caribbeans to 45% for those of Arab and West Asian origin; Sri Lankans (51%), Somalians (62.7%), Ethiopians (69.7%) and Ghanaians (87.3%) suffer most from poverty as well as police harassment; although non-European families make up less than 40% of all families in Toronto, they account for nearly 60% of all poor families; and their family poverty rate is 34.3%, which is more than twice the figure for the Europeans and Canadians.[10]. All this (and more) in a city that delights so many with the cultures of ethnic and national minority groups! And in a country so proud of multiculturalism!

None of this appears to overly bother Pico Iyer or the Culture of Cities project. The latter's 'mandate', rather, 'is to get away from the jargon and number-crunching of the social sciences and discover, in the words of . . . Blum, "the specificity of cities"', which is to be found in such objects of research as 'the proliferation of cocktail bars in beer-drinking Berlin' and 'movie-house architecture' in Toronto, with special attention to the question of 'what kind of people go to matinees'.[11] The 'specificity' of Toronto resides, for boosters of deconstructed difference, in the shibboleths and platitudes of what often passes nowadays for 'cultural studies': fluctuating identities, global-local flows of all kinds and the Disney-inspired discovery that 'It's a Mall World After All'. Symptomatically absent from their 'specificities' are the all too evident - in everyday life as much as in statistics - social and spatial polarizations in the city and systematic discriminations against its minorities (save the bourgeoisie and a few 'global souls'), not to speak of the political-economic forces and neoliberal planning practices primarily responsible for these increasingly dubious trends. Such patently ideological omissions and biases are of course not uncharacteristic of the kinds of 'cultural studies' shackled by the post-structuralist intolerance of 'totalizing' thought and oblivious to the link (influentially demonstrated by Fredric Jameson) between 'postmodernism' and 'the cultural-logic of late capitalism'.[12] Lacking a concept of mediation to theorize the relations between the relatively autonomous yet dialectically linked levels of the cultural, the economic and the political within the social totality of global capitalism (at the urban scale), the entire discussion of culture and difference in this creolization discourse, notwithstanding its avowed commitment to the 'specificity of the city', remains predictably symptomatic rather than critical of commodification.

A *radical* response to socio-cultural diversity in Canada and Toronto could be more usefully and forcefully articulated as an *immanent critique* of the 1988 Act, by pointing to the glaring gap between the hopes provoked by multiculturalism-citizenship beyond ethnocentrism, broader equality - and creolization - a future beyond cultural nationalism - *and* their limited actualization in reality. Such a critique should of course also highlight the perils of *culturalism* in not only 'official multiculturalism' but also its 'critics'. The best example of *this* kind of critique in fact comes from Ambalavanar Sivanandan, long-time editor of *Race and Class* and London-based veteran of anti-racist struggle, in his sharp exposé of the philosophy and practice of the British equivalents of Canada's Multiculturalism Program - especially the Racism Awareness Training (RAT) program and the Race Relations Act of 1976.[13] Sivanandan tells the story of how the British state co-opted and neutralized into harmless 'cultural politics' a radical urban-based struggle against racism and imperialism that was also one with the struggle to liberate the working class.[14]

By emphasizing 'cultural diversity' and 'cultural integration' as the main issues, the British state orchestrated the attenuation and disintegration of the 'black community', the *political-cultural* community, not of ethnicity and nationality, but of class-based resistance against racism (in Britain) and imperialism (in Africa, Asia and the Caribbean). The state's "strategy of promoting individual cultures, funding self-help groups and setting down anti-discriminatory and equal opportunity guidelines (*à la* RAT) [...] deflected the political concerns of the black community into the cultural concerns of different communities, the struggle against racism into the struggle for culture". The result was a "divisive culturalism that turned the living, dynamic, progressive aspects of black people's culture into artifact and habit and custom - and began to break up [the] community [of resistance]".

The kind of radical black politics encountered by Sivandanan in Britain, made possible in part by a consolidated political culture of class consciousness and traditions of local socialism, never came to pass in Canada. In this vast white settler colony and country of immigrants marked by weak national cohesion and deep territorial and linguistic divisions, class politics has often been refracted through regional or 'ethnic' divides long before multiculturalism became national policy. As such, Canada was predisposed, much more than the imperial metropole Britain, to develop a comparatively early form of multicultural diversity management.[15] Indeed, the latter emerged not as a response to a challenge of black politics but as a reaction to the aspirations of Quebec nationalism and European immigrant groups.

This much said, Canada has developed important socialist feminist and anti-racist currents, whose critiques of multiculturalism in the 1970s and 1980s are much richer and deeper than those of the more recent 'creole' critics. The sharpest exponent of those currents is Himani Bannerji. Bannerji's marxism has much in common with that of Sivanandan, but her feminist orientation has brought vital critical dimensions to an analysis of multiculturalism that are secondary in Sivanandan's perspective on 'race and class'. But just as Sivanandan does, Bannerji levels a double critique against, on the one hand, reductive and objectivist versions of marxism in the 'white' Canadian left (which for her includes colour-blind socialist feminists), and, on the other hand, the conservative culturalist nationalisms that have thrived within the 'ethnicized', state-sponsored institutions of Canadian multiculturalism. What disturbs her in particular about the latter form of 'ethnic' communitarianism is its persistent-yet rarely noted-anti-feminist tendency. Her critique of the "cultural reductionism [...] of 'identity politicians'",[16] moreover, can be said to apply not only to state-sponsored cultural nationalism but also to the cosmopolitanism of its 'creole' critics.

For if the latter have appropriately targeted rigid notions of multi-culture for critique, they nonetheless limit themselves to - in Bhabha's words - merely 'shifting the boundaries' of categories of identity/difference which otherwise remain explicitly culturalist and implicitly racialized.[17]

If neither multiculturalism nor its culturalist critique will do, what, then, are the prospects for a *radical* politics of difference in the city? Or, to put the emphasis firmly on our fascinating urban situation, how could the space of the city as we know it today provide the conditions of possibility for a politics of emancipation from class, race, gender and other social determinants of our problematic identities? In short, what kinds of spaces and politics might produce *true* difference? We can end by pointing to the *beginning* of a response to these questions in Henri Lefebvre's distinction between maximal, or produced, and minimal, or induced, difference - which represents a radical departure from the dominant discourse on difference.[18] With minimal difference, Lefebvre describes the lived experience of the spatialized clock-time of capitalism, where difference appears as a purely quantitative distinction between serialized, homogeneous and entirely interchangeable fragments. In our context, minimal difference appears in fragments of cultural hybridity or multi-culture that are captured by the commodity form or bureaucratic logics: fashion items, cosmopolitan cultural festivals, 'ethnically' re-decorated properties in endless bungalow tracts and condominium projects. With maximal difference, Lefebvre refers to those rare affective and liberating urban moments of rupture in everyday life or political mobilization - the Paris Commune, May 1968, or perhaps more recent events in Quebec City (2001), Genoa (2001) or Mexico City (2001) - which anticipate, even if imperfectly, the possibility of a qualitatively *different*, post-capitalist society. For maximal difference refers to actively produced, qualitatively new forms of plurality and individuality that are defined by use-value purposes, self-management processes, and the actualization of unalienated human relationships.

The distinction between maximal and minimal difference develops an essentially marxist critique of commodity fetishism through Lefebvre's critique of everyday life, his arguments about the right to the city, and his notion of the production of space. In no small measure, these definitions stem from his conception of urbanity as *centrality* - the urban as an 'ensemble of difference' that renders the lived experience of the city fundamentally 'contradictory' and fraught with the tensions between use value (sensuous and qualitative space: concrete and 'subjective') and exchange value (quantitative and universal space: abstract and 'objective') running through all modalities of space ('lived', 'conceived', 'perceived'). Herein lies, for Lefebvre, the possibility of difference understood as the claim for a *different* city - marked by the *right to the city* of different social groups - that also entails a different social order released from the alienating forms of difference offered to us by this one. Indeed, writing just after 1968, Lefebvre recognized that in political struggle, the possibility of *maximal* difference emerges out of the contradictions of everyday life as they are articulated by claims rooted in the specific experiences of social difference of by diverse groups (workers, students, immigrants) that are reified not least by the separations and segregations characteristic of contemporary urban life.

If struggles for the right to the city can be understood as a prism through which multiple, disconnected claims to the right to maximal difference are at once connected and mutually transformed, then one may plausibly link Lefebvre's ruminations to critics like Sivanandan and Bannerji, whose perspectives on the everyday have captured the concrete processes through which alienation based on class exploitation, racialization and patriarchy become enshrined in minimal forms of difference such as aestheticized ethnicity or bureaucratic multiculturalism. Of course, a politics of 'produced' and 'maximal' difference today 'must take place, at least in part, through alienated forms'.[19] Here the promise of the city consists *not* in the plurality of *actually existing differences* given to us for celebration under the signs of 'cultural diversity' - multiculturalism, diaspora or creolization. It lies, on the contrary, in actually existing attempts to extract promising desires - for un-coerced human relations of solidarity and freedom, labour and love - out of these minimal differences *induced* by the postmodern culture industry - Hollywood or Bollywood - and ideological state apparatuses in the name of a plethora of differences *produced* in everyday life and aimed at a genuinely socialist 'diversity founded on a far greater plurality and complexity of possible ways of living that any free community of equals, no longer divided by class, race or gender, would create'.[20] For only in a disalienated city that is wholly *produced* by citizens in their everyday life can we find our true identity amidst real difference.

Endnotes

[1] For an account of the Non Resident Indians (NRIs) in particular and a penetrating cultural-political analysis of the Indian Diaspora in North America, see Vijay Prashad, *The Karma of Brown Folk* (Minneapolis: University of Minnesota Press, 2000).

[2] See http://bollywoodhollywoodmovie.com.

[3] For details of this project, which also involves the cities of Berlin, Dublin and Montreal, see its website: http://www.yorku.ca/culture_of_cities/

[4] *The Canadian Multiculturalism Act*, according to which 'multiculturalism is a fundamental characteristic of Canadian heritage and identity', can be accessed at: http://laws.justice.gc.ca/en/C-18.7/29493.html#rid-29500. On the contested history of multiculturalism policy, see Yasmeen Abu-Laban, 'The Politics of Race and Ethnicity: Multiculturalism as a Contested Arena' in James Bickerton and Alain Gagnon, ed. *Canadian Politics*, 2nd edition (Peterborough: Broadview, 1995); Vic Satzewitch, 'Race Relations or Racism: Unravelling the New 'Race' Discourse in Canada' in Les Samuelson, ed. *Power and Resistance* (Halifax: Fernwood, 1999).

[5] *Annual Report on the Operation of the Canadian Multiculturalism Act* (1999-2000): 10.

[6] Quoted in *The Globe and Mail*, by John Barber ('Out with multicultural, in with diaspora', 8 June 2002) and Ray Conlogue ('Melting pot gets a Creole flavour', 4 September 2002).

[7] Conlogue, op. cit.

[8] Pico Iyer, 'Imagining Canada: An Outsider's Hope for Global Future', Hart House Lecture, University of Toronto, 5 April 2001. The text of this aggressively-advertised talk can be found at: http://www.utoronto.ca/harthouse/lectures/images/HHL2001,%20Digital%20Edition.pdf (here: 34).

[9] Barber, op. cit.

[10] Michael Ornstein, *Ethno-Racial Inequality in Toronto - An Analysis of the 1996 Census* (Toronto: City of Toronto and Centre of Excellence for Research on Immigration and Settlement, May 2000) ; this indispensable study is available at: http://www.city.toronto.on.ca/diversity/pdf/ornstein_fullreport.pdf.

[11] Conlogue, op. cit. For a longer list of research topics, methodologies and theoretical perspectives informing them, see the Culture of Cities project's website: http://www.yorku.ca/culture_of_cities/

[12] See his *Postmodernism, or, The Cultural Logic of Late Capitalism* (Durham: Duke University Press, 1992).

[13] A. Sivanandan, 'RAT and the Degradation of Black Struggle' in *Communities of Resistance: Writings on Black Struggles for Socialism* (London and New York: Verso, 1990): 77-122.

[14] All quotations which follow, unless footnoted, are from Sivanandan, op. cit.

[15] On the distinction between imperial and republican citizenship regime of Britain and the multicultural model in Canada, see Stephen Castles and Mark Miller, *The Age of Migration* (New York: Guildford, 1993).

[16] Himani Bannerji, *Thinking Through: Essays on Feminism, Marxism and Anti-Racism* (Toronto: Women's Press, 1995),: 35; see also her *The Dark Side of the Nation: Essays on Multiculturalism, Nationalism, and Gender* (Toronto: Canadian Scholar's Press, 2000), and, with Shahrzad Mojab and Judith Whitehead, *Of Property and Propriety: The role of Gender and Class in Imperialism and Nationalism* (Toronto: University of Toronto Press, 2001); cf. Eva Mackey, *The House of Difference* (London: Routledge, 1999).

[17] See Bhabha's revealingly dismissive comments about Fanon's new humanist quest beyond 'race' ('Remembering Fanon: Self, Psyche, and the Colonial Condition' in Nigel Gibson, ed. Rethinking Fanon [Amherst: Humanity Books, 1999], pp.179-96).

[18] Essential to the study of difference we propose, which can barely be outlined here, are Lefebvre's *Le manifeste différentialiste, The Right to the City* (in *Writings on Cities*), *The Production of Space*, *Introduction to Modernity* and the three volumes of the *Critique of Everyday Life*, particularly volume III. For a first sketch, see Stefan Kipfer, 'Urbanization, Everyday Life, and the Survival of Capitalism: Lefebvre, Gramsci, and the Problematic of Hegemony', *Capitalism, Nature, Socialism* 13/2 (2002): 117-149.

[19] Peter Osborne, *The Politics of Time* (London and New York: Verso, 1995):. 193-194.

[20] Perry Anderson, 'Marshall Berman: Modernity and Revolution' in *A Zone of Engagement* (London and New York: Verso, 1992):. 45.

5.6

TEXT..Stefan Kipfer and Roger Keil
PHOTOS ....Roger Keil

In Lieu of a Conclusion: Beyond the Competitive City?

Writing about Toronto in "Possible Urban Worlds" was full of impressions about the wave of mass mobilization that had swept the city between 1995 and 1997 to protest the newly elected authoritarian populist provincial government. At the time, it was unclear whether these forms of resistance were rearguard actions to safeguard 'the status quo' (what remained of to the social democratic postwar compromise or the subsequent era of local urban reform) or preludes for novel, more explicitly urban and less compromising forms of politics (that are now commonly linked to the movement(s) against capitalist globalization) (Kipfer, 1998). In any event, by the end of 1997, this wave of mass mobilization had subsided with few immediate results, exhausted and demobilized, leaving the door open for an entirely different claim to the city: the project to entrench the 'competitive city' in the now amalgamated City of Toronto, the municipality representing the inner half of the urban region.

As we have argued elsewhere (Kipfer and Keil, 2002), the project for a competitive city represents a new modality of city politics, a set of policies, ideologies and state forms linked to broader accumulation strategies, patterns of class formation, and forms of social control. Competitive city projects pursue an overarching imperative of inter-city competition that treats cities as homogeneous that compete with each other for investment and mobile segments of new urban middle classes. At a deeper level, the competitive city is not only a neoliberal doctrine but rests on claims to urbanity that attempt to reorder the moral landscapes of cities and re-establish bourgeois hegemony over urban life as embodied in the tastes and sensibilities of gentrified and exurban milieus.

Competitive city projects represent a shift not only from the Keynesian/Fordist era of managerial city politics (Harvey, 1989). It also signals a move away from the interlude of urban revolt, social movement politics, and urban reform that challenged the postwar city in the 1960s and 1970s and then coexisted in a number of cities with the shift to entrepreneurial city politics during the 1980s and 1990s (Mayer, 1987). Competitive city projects consolidate, formalize and magnify entrepreneurial trends in urban politics that have been operating in different forms over the last two decades. While varying from city to city, the competitive city experience is no longer restricted to those British and U.S.-American cities with the longest experience with neoliberal and authoritarian populism. Competitive city projects are also promoted in Canadian and continental European cities. Indeed, promoted through transnational policy experiments such as 'workfare' and the 'Giuliani model' of urban policing, competitive city projects run parallel to projects for a 'transnational constitutionalism' aimed at consolidating the new world order (Gill, 1992).

In Toronto, the competitive city project in the newly amalgamated City is a new modality of regulating longer-term *structural* processes of urban change and global-city formation.This modality emerged out of the political *conjuncture* of the 1990s, which was characterized not only by the aforementioned political implosion of left and progressive movements but also the effects of the deep slump of the early 1990s, the fall-out of continental 'free trade', and the accelerated rescaling of Canada's already porous federal state. The latter process of rescaling was propelled by a vicious cycle of aggressive monetarism and fiscal decentralization at federal level and one of the most far-reaching transformations of the local state undertaken by Ontario's newly elected Tory regime. The latter entrenched inter-jurisdictional competition between Toronto and exurban municipalities, imposed severe fiscal constraints on local governments, and strengthened the power of landed capital across the urban region.
After amalgamation in 1998, these structural and conjunctural forces helped forge a ruling alliance in the City of Toronto made up of Bay Street finance and real estate interests, property owners in postwar suburbs, and the expanding downtown gentry. Tied together by a populist mayor, power brokers and lobbyists, this alliance was bolstered in no small measure by the successful, if circumscribed and often symbolic incorporation of politicians, planners, consultants, and architects with ties to the urban reform regimes of the 1970s and 1980s.

Based on this loose socio-political alliance, the competitive city has been pursued in three ways. First, **entrepreneurial** economic and planning policies have advanced supply-side economics primarily through cost competition (fiscal austerity, deregulation, and marketization) (Albo, 1997). In the new City, economic development is understood as a way to promote Toronto as an investment platform, pursue mega-projects such as the (failed) bid for the 2008 Olympics, and reinforce the dominant global city industries: finance, producer services, media, information technology, tourism and entertainment. Land-use planning is about deregulating planning controls, striking permissive deals with developers, facilitating real estate 'reinvestment' in strategic areas, and promoting regressive (if 'beautiful') bourgeois utopias of waterfront revitalization. (see Kipfer and Keil, 2002; Bunce and Young, Blackwell and Goonewardena, this volume for more details). Selective fiscal austerity and a centralized budget process, which has been used to force most City departments (but not the Toronto police) to rationalize their operations, has had disproportionately negative effects on departments with redistributive functions (public transit, recreation, public health, public housing, child care). Amalgamation has been used as an opportunity to reconstruct the City administration along the latest corporate management principles. "New public management" is being promoted by discourses of "alternative service delivery" and "public-private partnerships" and strategies to centralize financial 'controls', benchmark departmental operations to private-sector 'competitors', extend market pricing for services, and 'flexibilize' public sector work.

Second, the City has been pursuing **differentialist** policies that promote the integration an aesthetic of diversity into urban development, economic competitiveness and the commodfication process (Zukin, 1995; Welz, 1996). Consistent with the long-standing myth of Toronto as a multicultural place of 'ethnic harmony' (Croucher, 1997), numerous mayoral speeches, policy documents and publicity stunts have promoted Toronto's multiculturalism and vibrant gay subculture to attract tourism and knowledge workers, brand glitzy new condominium towers and waterfront revitalization efforts as hallmarks of cosmopolitan 'beauty' and market the City's (failed) bid for the 2008 Summer Olympics. The City's equity policy now goes under the rubric of 'diversity management and community engagement' and is relegated in practice to powerless citizen advisory committees that foster competition among oppressed groups, whose aspirations are reified within narrow, bureaucratically policed categories. Meanwhile, entrepreneurial and revanchist policies reinforce the processes of polarization and exclusion that affect women, first nations, new immigrants and people of colour disproportionately. In this context, policies of "diversity management" and discourses of diversity are best understood as articulations of 'minimal difference' that have populist appeal in a city of immigrants but help aestheticize social relations in ways that subvert the possibility for 'maximal' claims to difference and the city (Goonewardena and Kipfer, this volume).

Third, the new City has pursued a number of law and order campaigns that appear to foster **revanchist** consent about the need to combat crime by fighting 'pathologies' of urban disorder and promote competitiveness by making urban space safe, clean, and secure for investors, real-estate capital, property owners and the new urban middle classes (Smith, 1996, Grell et al., 1998; Ronneberger et al., 2000). In Toronto, urban revanchism is driven by the city's eagerness to exceed provincial workfare/welfare reduction targets and 'zero-tolerance' and 'broken-windows' policies of crime control. Pushed by the mayor's office, the police chief, and the police union, the new City has dramatically increased police budgets over the last five years and initiated provincial legislation to criminalize squeegeeing and 'aggressive' panhandling. Supported by the overwhelming majority of City Council, including most 'progressive' Councillors, the Toronto police have implemented a 'target policing' initiative to weed out criminal 'hot spots' and 'clean up' Toronto's rapidly gentrifying downtown. Media and police campaigns against "youth gangs" and "black-on-black crime" have made a virtue out of long-standing practices (by police, school boards, and private security forces) to racially profile people of colour, harass street people, raid gay bars and criminalize youth of colour as gang members and drug dealers. Sustained law-and-order campaigns have already reframed social policy and urban planning as instruments to do city dwellers by policing the public order.

Five years after amalgamation, fissures have appeared within the competitive city project. The entrepreneurial, differentialist and revanchist dimensions of competitive city politics continue to shape political realities in Toronto. And the conditions for competitive city projects - capitalist urban restructuring, inter-territorial competition, state rescaling and the expansion of bourgeois urbanities downtown and in the exurbs - still exist. But the leadership capacity of the ruling bloc at City Hall has suffered after the second municipal election (which narrowed the right-wing majority on council) and a number of widely publicized scandals and racist ruminations by Toronto's populist mayor. At the time of writing, Toronto's own Enron affair - a public inquiry into dubious computer leasing contracts between the City and a financing company - has laid bare tight relationships between senior bureaucrats, the mayor's office, key politicians, corporate lobbyists and downtown powerbrokers and may yet question the viability of further new public management initiatives. The law and order agenda - although substantially bolstered after September 11, 2001 - has experienced temporary setbacks after the proto-fascist police union's attempt to intimidate politicians caused a (short-lived) backlash on City Council, media reports confirmed widespread racial profiling in the justice system, and investigations were launched into corruption within the police force. The once glorious claims to waterfront revitalization have become strained after Toronto lost its Olympic bid and contradictions between among corporate interests and state agencies with stakes on the waterfront have resurfaced. Waterfront redevelopment projects are still being pursued (see Bunce and Young, this volume), but now in the piecemeal and narrow-minded fashion typical of Canada's fragmented bureaucracy and Toronto's landed bourgeoisie.

As a result of these contradictions within state and capital, cracks in the 'beautiful' and slick veneer of the competitive city are evident. The solidity of the power bloc at City Hall has become more tenuous and in some cases, competitive city projects now appear less an inevitable product of 'common sense' than hobby-horses of particularistic, even corrupt ("economic-corporate") interests (contractors, developers, state agencies etc). Progressive and left activism has contributed to the (still partial) erosion of the hegemonic integrity of competitive city strategies. A number of preexisting activist networks within people of colour, anti-poverty and gay and lesbian circles have resurfaced to highlight the gap between the City's incantations of diversity and the realities of gendered and racialized polarization, racial profiling and target policing. A labour-community alliance of public sector workers and environmentalists has stalled the creeping privatization of Toronto's water system. Promising new forms of activism have also emerged. An initiative to counter the privatization of Toronto's public recreation system organized residents (many of whom low-income tenants and working-class women of colour) to underline the death of public space in the postwar suburbs (see Wirsig, this volume). And local anti-poverty activists staged political squats that brought a new dimension to housing struggles in Toronto. Together with attempts to stop deportations of refugees and a successful campaign to drive a NIKE outlet from a central city neighbourhood, these squatting actions (which were linked to occupations in Montreal, Vancouver and Ottawa), were buoyed by the energies of the anti-capitalist globalization and anti-war movements that since 1999 have produced new generations of activists.

The selective resurgence of activism and the emergence of new forms of mobilization have helped shrink the hegemonic integrity of the competitive city by *beginning* to repoliticize urban politics and question the legitimacy of once sacrosanct principles such as privatization and diversity management. At the same time, contemporary movement activism has polarized between marginal or oppositional networks and established pragmatic sectors with close ties to the local state. Promising organizing is often isolated in socio-spatial milieus (such as downtown student and activist circles, the rarefied halls of City Hall, or the self-referential worlds of the non-profit sector) that are only weakly linked to other parts of Toronto's segmented urban region, notably vast stretches of postwar suburbia. Segmentation within the Toronto left facilitates a realignment of 'progressive' forces into neo-corporatist arrangements.

Swing by the office.
CITYPLACE
DOWNTOWN GOLF
9-Hole Golf Course. Opening here soon.
Construction Area
NO TRESPASSING
AUTO TINTING
$99.00

The possibility of such a realignment has been shown in a campaign for a new City Charter for Toronto, a business-backed "City Summit Alliance", and the push by the Canadian Federation of Canadian Municipalities for a federal urban policy. Growing out of contradictions of competitive city politics that manifest themselves as traffic congestion, housing crises, and ecological degradation, these initiatives brought together the Board of Trade, left-liberal urbanists, journalists and politicians as well as selected leaders from charities, non-profits and labour to demand more municipal fiscal autonomy or federal financial support for cities. These initiatives signal a divergence between oppositional, anti-authoritarian, anti-racist, and feminist circles (some of whom connected to the anti-capitalist globalization milieus) and those willing to close ranks in order to make the supposedly united interests of "Toronto" bring to bear on attempts to re-scale Canada's federal state and reframe the competitive city project in Third Way terms.

The prospect for a new corporatist realignment to reframe competitive city politics indicates that resurgent and new forms of mobilization have to yet to move beyond issue-specific achievements and ideological victories. Recent experiences point to a few important considerations for the future of urban left politics, however. First, aspects of the urban - housing, urban planning, architecture, spatial relations of segmentation - must be seen as strategic, not secondary areas for organizing. Otherwise, urban questions will continue to be monopolized by Toronto's 'urban reform' establishment that has played an important role in buttressing the competitive city. Second, taking the urban dimension of left organizing seriously is essential if more than lip service is to be paid to the everyday realities of city life. This certainly means addressing the territorial and organizational walls that entrap the daily life (of activists and intellectuals) in racialized, commodifed and bureaucratized forms of 'minimal difference' (Goonewardena and Kipfer, this volume). The postwar suburbs - now stylized as Toronto's new 'inner city' - are of strategic importance in this regard (Wirsig, this volume). Third, an opportunistic politics of compromise in the current conjuncture is likely to facilitate the kinds of neo-corporatist, "pro-urban" alignments already underway. Two years after Quebec City and Genoa, further discussions are needed about the prospects for a countervailing project that can engage neo-conservative and competitive urbanisms *on their own terrain*, with sustained radicalism, links to transnational anticapitalism, and open-ended dynamics of mobilization.

References

Albo, Greg (1997), "A World Market of Opportunities?", in: *Socialist Register* . 1997, 5-47.

Croucher, Sheila (1997), "Constructing the Image of Ethnic Harmony in Toronto", in: *Urban Affairs Review* 32 (3), 319-52.

Gill, Stephen (1992), "The emerging world order and European change", in: *Socialist Register* 1992, 157-69.

Grell, Britta, Sambale Jens, and Dominik Veith (1998), "Inner!City!Action!", in: INURA *Possible Urban Worlds*. Basel: Birkhäuser, 208-15.

Harvey, David (1989), "From Managerialism to Entrepreneurialism", in: *Geographiska Annaler.* Series B 71B (1), 3-18.

Kipfer, Stefan (1998), "Urban Politics in the 1990s: Notes on Toronto", in: INURA *Possible Urban Worlds*. Basel: Birkhäuser, 172-9.

Kipfer, Stefan, and Roger Keil (2002), "Toronto Inc? Planning the Competitive City in the new Toronto", in: *Antipode* 34.2, 227-64

Mayer, Margit (1987), "Restructuring and Popular Opposition in West German cities", in: Michael Smith and Joe Feagin (eds.), *The Capitalist City*. Oxford: Blackwell, 343-63.

Ronneberger, Klaus, Stephan Lanz, and Walther Jahn (2000), *Die Stadt als Beute*. Bonn: J H W Dietz Nachfolger.

Smith, Neil (1996), *The New Urban Frontier*. London: Routledge.

Welz, Gisela (1996), *Inszenierungen kultureller Vielfalt*. Berlin: Akademie.

Zukin, Sharon (1995), *The Cultures of Cities*. Oxford: Blackwell.

Zürich: from Paranoia City to Ego City

Photo sequence in front pages of this chapter by Andreas Hofer

TEXT........ Christian Schmid
TRANSLATION........ Barbara Stiner
MAPS [1]........ ETH Studio Basel

A New Paradigm of Urban Development for Zurich

Zurich today is a global city, one of a group of global control centers of the world economy. In international comparisons, Zurich has for many years been routinely placed in second or third position in the global city hierarchy, together with cities like San Francisco, Sydney, or Toronto (cf. e.g. Thrift 1987, Friedman 1995, Taylor and Walker 2001). But from an international point of view, Zurich is a small city. In 2000 the municipality of Zurich (Zurich City) had a population of 360,000, the agglomeration of Zurich 1.1 million, and the urban region ca. 2 million inhabitants.

Fifty years ago, Zurich was an industrial town with a strong position in the machine-building and armament industries. In 1950, more than half of the total workforce was employed in the manufacturing sector. In the period after World War II, Zurich grew to be the center of the Swiss economy, and in the seventies, with the increasing deregulation and globalization of financial markets, the transformation into a 'global city' began (Sassen 1991). Zurich became the undisputed center of Switzerland as a location for finance, and a headquarter economy established itself, specializing in the organization and control of global financial flows. In 2001 only around 7% of all persons working were still employed in manufacturing (not counting construction), while 36% of employment was concentrated in the core sectors of the global city economy (financial industries, insurance, and business services).[2]

This radical economic transformation has caused a fundamental change in the urban development of Zurich in the last three decades. Yet, even if it directly depended on global lines of development, the rise of Zurich to a global city was still a contradictory and crisis-prone process, which was also strongly marked by local relations of forces and fields of conflict. In this development, two historic phases characterized by differing models of urbanization can be distinguished. Each of these models was identified by specific paradigms of urban development and concepts of what is 'urban'. In this context, there were radical changes and ruptures, along with elements of continuity.

The 1970s and 1980s were marked by the process of formation of Zurich as a global city. In this context, two local lines of conflict proved to be crucial: the controversy concerning the modernization of the city, and the question of 'urban culture.' Zurich's model of urbanization was growth oriented, but it was also characterized by a strong regulation of urban development and the conservation of inner-city areas. In the nineties, a change of paradigm began to appear. With the process of metropolitanization and the expansion of the global city into the region, a new model of urbanization established itself characterized by a neoliberal policy of urban development, the emergence of new urban configurations, and a new definition of the urban.

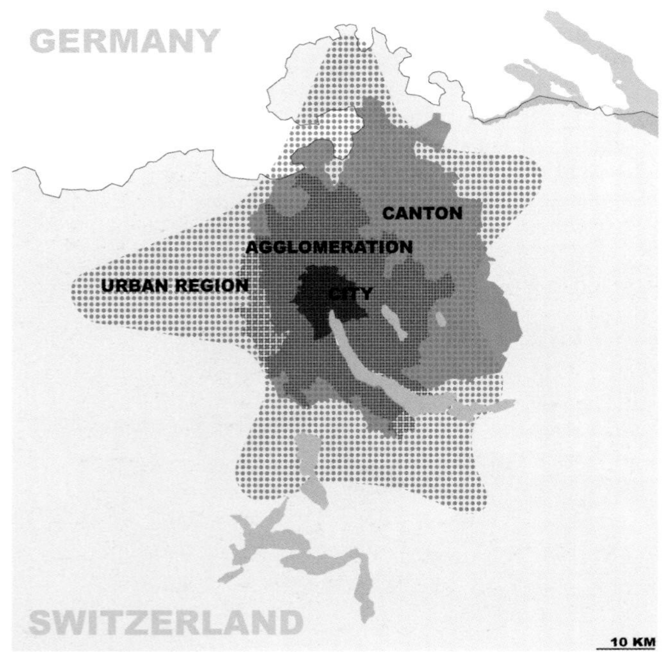

The Zurich Region.
© ETH Studio Basel 2003

Global City Formation: Territorial Compromise and Urban Revolt

In the decades after World War II, urban development in Zurich was defined by an encompassing growth coalition consisting of right-wing and social-democratic forces, following a relatively moderate course of modernization (Schmid 1997). These conditions changed at the beginning of the 1970s: the protest movement of the late 1960s opened the path for a radical questioning of a functionalistic urban development, and the economic crisis ended the "golden age" of Fordism. In the mid-1970s, the development of Zurich towards a global city began.

This changed the situation in very basic ways. With global city formation, globally defined claims of "headquarter economy" collided with the locally defined everyday concerns of a large proportion of the residents. The growth coalition fell apart, and the city was divided into two camps quarrelling about the urban development of Zurich. On the one hand, a new modernizing coalition was taking shape, consisting of right-wing parties and the growth-oriented sections of the trade unions, which promoted the development of Zurich as a financial center, the extension of the CBD, and the extension of traffic infrastructure. On the other hand, in the wake of the movement of 1968, a position was forming which was critical of urban growth; left-wing parties and various action groups and neighbourhood organizations united in a heterogeneous and fragile "stabilization alliance", fighting for a livable city, low rents and the preservation of residential neighbourhoods in the inner-city. On occasion, this alliance was also supported by conservative forces (see also Kipfer 1995). Through the Swiss system of direct democracy, in which many questions and projects have to be decided by referendum, these opposing positions were transferred directly to the level of practical politics. In this conflict, both parties had their victories and defeats, but in the end neither side was able to win decisively (a vivid illustration of this conflict is shown in the example of the history of Eurogate, cf. Wolff in this chapter). Thus for two decades, from the mid-seventies to the mid-nineties, the urban development of Zurich was in fact determined by a precarious political stalemate resulting in a specific type of a "territorial compromise", which included a rejection of large-scale modernizing strategies and which considerably slowed down the transformation of inner-city residential neigbourhoods. Yet, global city formation and the dynamics of urbanization were not fundamentally challenged (see Hitz, Schmid and Wolff 1995).

This territorial compromise, however, covered a second line of conflict, which for a long time did not come into the open. At the level of everyday life, the small-town, provincial forms of social regulation originating in Fordism and which aimed at social control and conformism clashed with the demands of cosmopolitan open-mindedness and urban culture created by global city formation. In the seventies, public life in Zurich was still characterized by a crushing parochialness which left hardly any margin for new lifestyles or alternative forms of cultural expression. This situation eventually caused a social explosion: on May 30, 1980 an urban revolt began (Nigg 2001). With riots, happenings and actions of all kinds, a new cosmopolitan urban generation demanded what Henri Lefebvre (1968) once called "the right to the city". Although the urban revolt collapsed after two years, its consequences became evident in later years; the movement had changed Zurich's everyday life, its cultural sphere and its public spaces. A cosmopolitan ambience evolved. The city government started to promote all kinds of cultural projects, and a cultural and artistic scene established itself, radiating far beyond Zurich. This created the basis for a successful economic sector of "cultural production", including design, image production, events, etc. (cf. Klaus in this chapter). This economic sector today plays a key role in the international competition between global cities. The urban revolt thus became in itself a constituting factor of the global city formation of Zurich (Schmid 1998).

As a result of these two lines of conflict, a model of urbanization was established based on this specific blend of modernization, stabilization and economic as well as cultural globalization. This model contained a concept of the city, which was at the same time metropolitan and exclusive, based on the classical western image of the city as a coherent, dense and innovative whole. This concept ultimately reduced the focus of urbanity to a narrow fraction of urban reality, to downtown Zurich. Seen from the urban center, all areas outside this restricted district were considered boring urban periphery.

Metropolitanization: the Regional Scale

As a consequence of this concept of the city, urbanization underwent a fundamental change in orientation. While the inner-city evolved into a culturally and socially pulsating urban center, opportunities for the construction of new offices and the expansion of the central business district were massively restricted, and service and financial enterprises were compelled to establish their additional offices at other locations. First, they moved into the vacated industrial zones inside the municipality of Zurich, and in the course of the eighties increasingly to the city's outskirts. In various places outside Zurich, new strategic centers of Zurich's headquarter economy were developing. This process can be seen as an "explosion of the center": The global city functions were spread over an extended region, which in itself was structured as a "center" (Sassen 1995). Thus, a new urban configuration evolved, characterized by the regionalization of the economy and society. The city expanded to regional dimension, the region became the unit of everyday life. This could be described by the metaphor of the supermarket, including many very different places interconnected by a dense tissue of overlapping networks of interaction. In a general sense this process can be understood as metropolitanization (Ascher 1995).

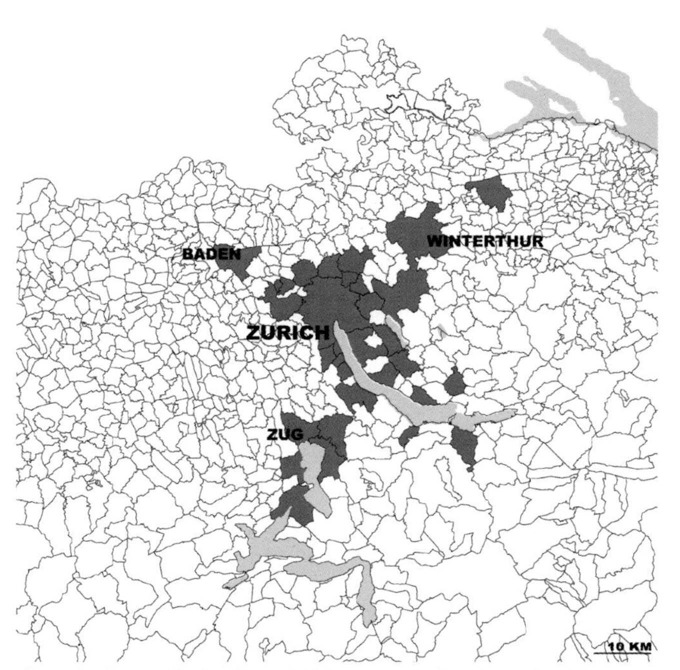

Global City Region: Municipalities with high percentage of jobs in the global city sector.
Source: Rüfenacht 2002: 146.

As in many other cases, the precise demarcation of this new regional city is quite difficult, since it is not formed as a coherent unit. More and more towns and villages in the densely populated lowlands of Switzerland are coming under the influence of Zurich's headquarter economy and becoming metropolitan in character. Therefore, depending on the criteria selected, greatly varying "regions" can be delineated.[3] Contrary to many other comparable examples, Zurich has so far not developed as an institutional unit in regional terms.[4] Today the metropolitan area of Zurich covers hundreds of municipalities in seven cantons, each of which - this being federalistic Switzerland - jealously guards its autonomy. In large parts of this region, an anti-urban, or rather anti-metropolitan attitude prevails: the urban reality is denied and concealed by a rural ideology.

The same heterogeneous aspect as we find on the political level is also apparent in the interior structure of this amoebae-like space, which is characterized by floating centralities with ever new and surprising urban configurations popping up. Analysis and deconstruction of this urban universe has only just begun.

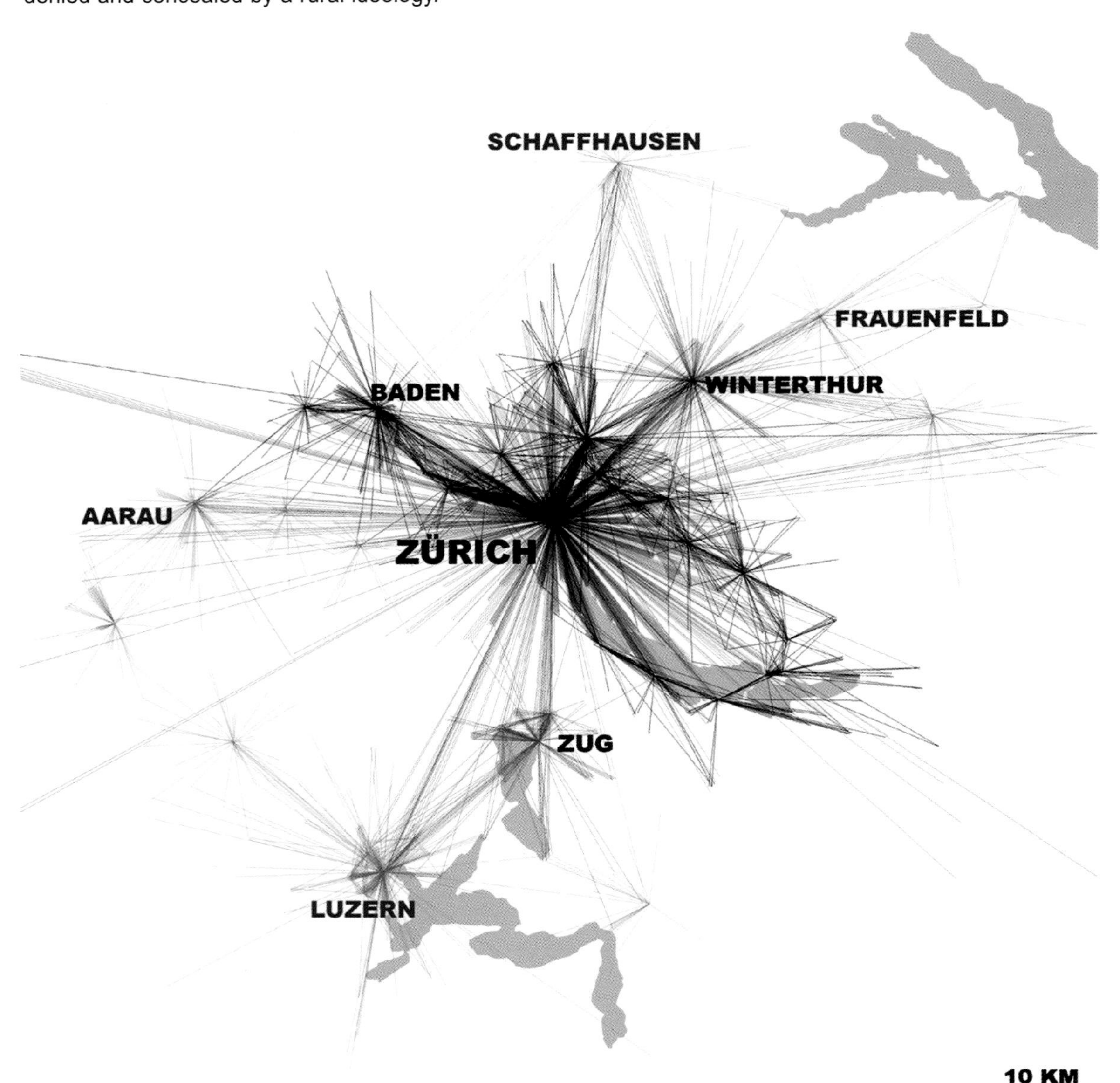

Commuters in the Zurich Region (1990). Each line represents 100 commuters.
(source: Swiss Federal Statistical Office)
© ETH Studio Basel 2003

The map of commuter flows clearly indicates the polycentric structure which has evolved in Zurich. Besides the main center of Zurich, there are a number of new centralities of quite different character. There are the old industrial towns of Winterthur, Baden and Zug, which have been drawn into the sphere of influence of Zurich's headquarter economy and are undergoing a process of restructuring. This is particularly evident in the tax haven of Zug, which has become a center for globally operating holding and trading companies. Then there are the two main axes with smaller centers, developed along two valleys. The valley of the Limmat to the west of Zurich still has a strongly industrial identity. The Glatt valley, on the other hand, north of Zurich, where the airport is also located, has become the largest and most dynamic development area in the whole of Switzerland. A series of "edge cities" (Garreau 1991) have developed here, growing into a ring that forms a kind of post-modern twin city of Zurich. This "new" city is called simply "Zürich Nord" (Zurich North) in public discussion.

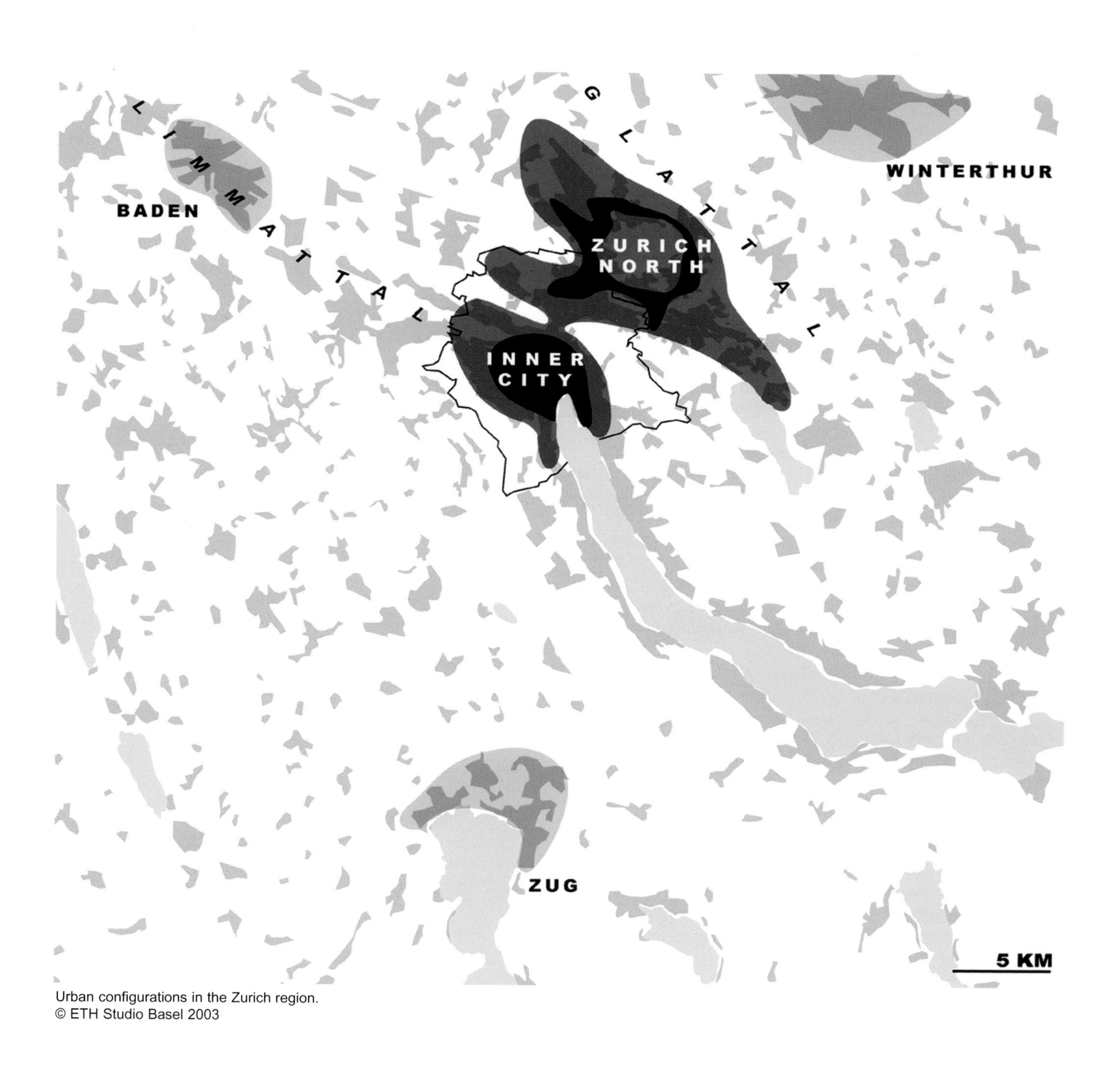

Urban configurations in the Zurich region.
© ETH Studio Basel 2003

Exopolis: the Case of Zurich North

Zurich North is a showcase example for these new urban configurations as they have developed in many places around of the world. Edward J. Soja named these amorphous implosions of archaic suburbia "*Exopolis* - 'the city without' - to stress their oxymoronic ambiguity, their city-full non-cityness. These are not only exo-cities, orbiting outside; they are ex-cities as well, no longer what the city used to be" (1996:238f).

In a narrow sense, Zurich North includes 8 municipalities and two districts of the city of Zurich. With 147,000 inhabitants and 117,000 jobs (in 2001), this area is today the fourth largest city in Switzerland – it is even bigger than Berne, the capital (Loderer 2001). The emphasis is on activities of the headquarter economy, predominantly producer services, banking, and IT industries. The concentration of these activities in this area is based less on the effect of the immediate (physical) vicinity than on the opportunities for flexible interconnections in some higher "logistic space" (Veltz 1996), that stretches from the airport to the national highway system and electronic networks.

Some twenty years ago, Zurich North was all classical middle-class suburbs. Planning was in the hands of the individual municipalities, which as a rule followed a simple planning concept: they tried to safeguard the historic core of the settlement, expanding the inhabited area concentrically around the core and placing any operations causing waste emissions, i.e. the industrial zones, at the outskirts of the municipal territory. But following de-industrialization and global city formation, it was not the industrial operations but the headquarter functions of global corporations that came to these industrial zones. Consequently, satellites of the headquarter economy developed, consolidating in an odd kind of belt located at the periphery of the old core of the settlement, where high-quality business intermingles with highways or even waste incineration plants. The geographic center of this belt is a forest, and so a kind of circular town emerged with an "empty" center. This shape corresponds exactly to the "doughnut model" Soja described for Orange County (cf. Soja 1996).

Fascinating as this urban patchwork may appear to the observer (cf. Campi, Bucher and Zardini 2001,) it nevertheless produces severe problems: since the new centralities are dispersed over a wide area, this fragmented non-city is largely dependant on private cars, which produces traffic jams and air pollution. In addition, the environment is often a not at all attractive. In most of the new centers there is a lack of urban infrastructure, restaurants, meeting places and cultural establishments, but also of elements creating a sense of identification and a truly urban atmosphere. Accordingly, many residents and employees are not at all happy with the quality of everyday life in this urban patch-work, which to this day has not been able to overcome its peripheral status (Gisler 2001).

As opposed to many other places like this, in Zurich North this lack of urban character has increasingly been perceived as a deficiency. The attitude has gradually been changing, and the declared intention, that of creating an urban region from this patchwork by achieving a certain architectural and social coherence, become manifest. The first initiatives of cooperation and coordinated planning among municipalities already appeared at the beginning of the nineties, and in 2001 the association "glow.das Glattal" , consisting of eight municipalities (cf. Thierstein,Held and Gabi 2003) was created. The new label for Zurich North was "Glattstadt" (City of the Glatt Valley). This name is meant to stand for a new region with its own identity and ideas (www.glow.ch), at the same time as it indicates its separation from the city of Zurich. Therefore, the city of Zurich is not included in this new organization, even if its northern neighbourhoods belong to Zurich North.

By far the most important project in this new cooperation is the construction of a tram line, which was approved in a cantonal referendum in spring 2003. This line is not only meant to open up and connect the various new centers of Zurich North, but is also the symbol of the newly discovered self-confidence of this new "city of the future". This is why it is officially called "Stadtbahn" (city train) instead of tram, the traditional term for streetcars in Zurich.

While a certain coherence can be perceived at the level of planning, the Glattalstadt is also faced with new problems. The airport, located in the middle of this region and its central economic motor, is in serious trouble. Shortly after September 11, 2001, the grounding of Swissair heralded not just the end of Swiss "exceptionalism", but also very uncertain perspectives for the future of Zurich North as well as for Zurich as a whole. Today, the airport itself is being called into question: in Spring 2003, Germany, whose territory is affected by many of the landings, proclaimed a strict limitation of overflights. As Switzerland is not a member of the EU, its negotiating position is precarious. There is a very real threat that even the quieter parts of Zurich North will be disturbed with noise from air-traffic, which might lead to even more fragmentation and insecurity.

Thus the "model of exopolis" remains delicately balanced: on the one hand there are the attempts to make Zurich North into a true city. At the same time, however, the underlying historically developed patchwork structure of the area is continually creating new difficulties and surprises.

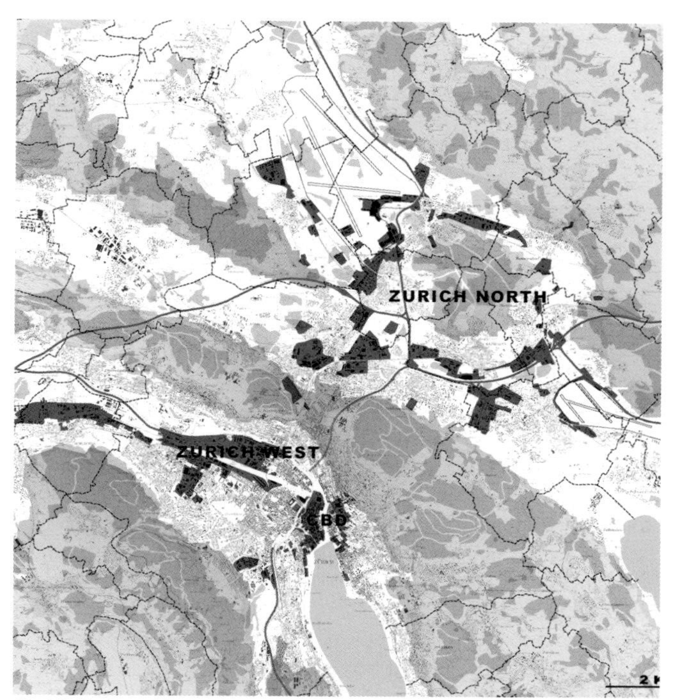

Zurich North and Zurich West.
© ETH Studio Basel 2003

The Metropolis Alliance: Paradigm Change in Urban Development

While the global city has been expanding into the region, the situation in the central city of Zurich has undergone fundamental changes. In the course of the nineties, a real change of paradigm in urban development has become apparent.

This change of paradigm originated in a double crisis. On the one hand, in the beginning of the 1990s, Switzerland - like most west European countries - was in the grip of a long term economic crisis, and growing deficits forced public authorities to carry out rigorous measures to economize. On the other hand, the social consequences of globalization became visible: similarly to many global cities, marked economic and social polarization and fragmentation become apparent. These developments were accompanied by fundamental shifts in the political landscape. In reaction to globalization and urbanization, an aggressive right-wing populism started to take shape, something new for Switzerland. It grew first at the margins of the unravelling metropolis, in the suburban and "periurban" areas, but soon it started to take hold in the center as well. It is true that in 1990 for the first time since the 1930s, a left (red-green) majority was elected to the city government. But at the same time, right-wing populist forces went organizing themselves against the red-green majority and against the social and cultural open-mindedness of the eighties. Through an aggressive campaign, these forces succeeded in making drug policies and the asylum question the main political issues. In the following years, the political and social climate clearly deteriorated (cf. Schmid and Weiss in this volume).

Against these right-wing populist political activities, the positions of liberal and social-democratic forces drew closer. The positions of confrontation between the modernizing coalition and the stabilisation alliance softened, and the moderate forces began to look for pragmatic solutions across ideological and partisan boundaries (Eberle 2003). For a number of the main issues, trailblazing compromises were reached, first over the drug question (the drug policy compromise 1995, see Schmid and Weiss in this volume), and then over traffic policy.

This political shift is perfectly expressed in urban development policy, which at the beginning of the 1990's was dominated by a central question - the revision of the land use plan. Initially, habitually opposed positions once again clashed with all their usual vehemence. The modernizing coalition demanded the opening of the city for office buildings while the red-green majority wanted to continue a policy of stabilization into the next century. In 1992, the stabilization alliance achieved its greatest success so far, when a rather restrictive land-use plan was accepted by referendum. However, this success did not last long. After the enactment of the plan had been delayed for years by legal action, the predominantly right-wing cantonal government intervened: in 1995, in a surprise move that contravened all conventions of federalism and direct democracy, it cancelled the existing plan and decreed new regulations. In the end, the liberal and left forces of the city converged and issued a new plan, by which they themselves initiated a shift towards a neoliberal urban development policy (cf. Hofer in this volume and Eberle 2003).

Thus the territorial compromise, which had existed for two decades, was broken and a new hegemonic political alliance emerged - the metropolis alliance. While urban development policy in the city of Zurich up to the nineties had been striving to conserve the historically developed structures with their quality of everyday life and to defend the "city of residents" against the headquarter economy, now the focus was on competition: international investors, global capital and groups of affluent residents were to be attracted to Zurich. From an historic perspective, this indicated a disavowal of the basic principles of urban planning that had dominated the development of the city of Zurich for about a hundred years, which had aimed to determine a clearly defined, coherent urban structure for the entire city (Schmid 1997). At the level of urban planning, the city started to be assimilated to the region.

The Reconstitution of the City: the Case of Zurich West

While in the course of the 1990s the processes of urbanization in the city and the region were coming closer and the disintegration of the city into the region was advancing, a remarkable reversal occurred: the reconstitution of the city and the reproduction of the old center/periphery dichotomy.

Based on the analysis of national referenda in the last 20 years, this tendency can be illustrated in detail at the political level (Hermann and Leuthold 2002): while in the region there was a strong tendency towards right-wing populist positions, the city of Zurich, and in particular the inner-city neighbourhoods, showed an increasingly left-liberal orientation. This tendency was registered for the entire German speaking part of Switzerland, but most distinctly in Zurich. The political polarization does not run along socio-economic disparities, rather it reflects different preferences in every-day life and cultural activities. Obviously, within the Zurich region differing lifestyles have evolved which are segregated physically. While suburban life still has a great attraction for many, others seek a distinctly urban lifestyle. The vicinity of cultural facilities, a cosmopolitan *milieu* and, last but not least, a trendy image have become important location factors, not just for lifestyle-conscious “urban professionals”, but increasingly for companies as well. These factors are still to a large extent concentrated in the center.

The "new" urban feeling manifests itself most visibly in "Zurich West", the trendy new neighbourhood in Zurich. As late as in the eighties, this inner-city area was still one of the main centers of the Swiss engineering industry. Consequently, it was *terra incognita*, "forbidden territory" guarded by factory squads. Due to dislocation of production and de-industrialization, more and more industrial activities moved out. At that time, the area was earmarked for the expansion of the financial sector. Because of the stalemate in urban development policy, and the conseguences of the economic and real estate crisis, development projects remained frozen for years. Eventually, the impressive industrial landscape, with its imposing halls and austere charm became a utopian place, a projection area for fantasies, a promise of opportunity. A take-over for different utilization began, sometimes in secret, sometimes in the open. Small, financially weak businesses, illegal or semi-legal bars and discos, theaters, hang-outs, workshops, artist's studios, projects of all sorts came into existence.

From the very beginning, this take-over process also included a component of the market economy: one of the first projects was a condominium with luxury lofts and a multiplex movie theater. The result was a highly urban blend of both the commercial and the ephemeral, something extraordinary, and not only for Switzerland. The new combination of working, living and entertainment as well as the unconventional atmosphere of the new neighbourhood of "Zurich West" attracted a wide range of other utilizations, from hotels to international consulting firms (Eisinger and Schmid 1999). A veritable cultural zone developed housing several renowned institutions of arts and culture. The “brownfield” was thus transmuted into an elegant urban neighbourhood, which was presented to astonished visitors as the "Swiss Greenwich Village". Many pioneer projects from the early days have been displaced in the meantime, but a number of remarkable alternative projects succeeded in securing a lot while real estate prices were still low (Wirz in this volume).

So Zurich West today stands for the new model of inner-city development. Nevertheless, the new neighbourhood differs radically from the existing downtown area. It presents an amazingly high density and diversity of varying utilizations and different social groups. These are, however, hardly interrelated, but rather live side by side in an overlay of social and economic networks extending over the entire metropolitan region. The area basically consists of individual islands belonging together less on the basis of interactive processes than on the basis of the urban *milieu* and the metropolitan image. This is not only an effect of the large scale structure of the built environment, originating in the previous industrial utilization, but also the result of the changed everyday routines of the metropolitan population.

The New Model of Urban Development

More than ten years ago, urban researchers discovered fundamental transformations and postulated a paradigm change in urban development. They postulated a new urban era and stated that the present cities did not resemble in anyway the traditional cities of the past (cf. e.g. Garreau 1991, Soja 1996). Los Angeles, with its polycentric and excentric development, was declared the "paradigmatic industrial metropolis of the modern world" (Soja and Scott 1986). In the meantime, things have settled at Exopolis. What is it that's new? What does the paradigm change consist of? The example of Zurich reveals some points of reference.

First: The polycentric development of cities and the formation of urban regions have become a general phenomenon. Even smaller towns follow this development trend. At the same time, the example of Zurich also illustrates that specific local traditions and constellations may have a decisive influence on the development: the concept of what a city is, traditional values, but also present controversies about the city, debates and compromises define the specific form the urbanization process takes.

Second: The process of metropolitanization breaks up the unity of the city. It is no longer possible to define the urban clearly: it is made up of overlaying configurations and unexpected constellations. In Zurich, two ideal typical configurations can be distinguished, giving an impressive illustration of the change: on the one hand the "exopolis model", as exemplified in Zurich North, on the other hand the "inner-city model", as manifested in Zurich West. Both areas stand for differing urban forms developing at the same time. Yet the two models do not differ as much as may seem at first sight. In Zurich North there is an attempt to reintroduce a classical conception of urbanity into the excentric urban chaos and to create new, coherent urban structures. On the other hand, the new "inner-city" model does not correspond to the traditional image of a downtown neighbourhood, with its dense network of social interaction. Indeed, it represents a junction of regional networks which are hardly interrelated in everyday life at all.

Third: in spite of the trend towards polycentrality, the relationship between center and periphery remains highly contradictory. In the case of Zurich, the dichotomy between center and periphery has not weakened in this process, but rather strengthened. Politically and culturally, center and periphery have drifted further apart. While the center exploded and disintegrated into the region, the city was reproducing itself at the level of everyday life.

The new model of urban development has proved to be contradictory and indeterminate. The contributions that follow in this chapter illustrate individual aspects of a paradigm change in urban development, due to which general living conditions as a whole have changed fundamentally.

References

Ascher, François (1995), *Métapolis ou l'avenir des villes.* Paris: Jacob

Blotevogel, Hans Heinrich (2001), "Die Metropolregionen in der Raumordnungspolitik Deutschlands – ein neues strategisches Raumbild?", in: *Geographica Helvetica* 3/56, 157–168.

Campi, Mario / Bucher, Franz / Zardini, Mirko (2001), *Annähernd perfekte Peripherie: Glattalstadt/Greater Zurich Area.* Basel/Boston/Berlin: Birkhäuser

Eisinger, Angelus / Schmid, Christian (1999), "Stadtumbau", in: *Werk, Bauen + Wohnen* 11, p.27 - 29.

Eberle, Orlando (2003), *Konflikte, Allianzen und territoriale Kompromisse in der Stadtentwicklung. Eine Analyse aus regulationstheoretischer Perspektive am Beispiel Zürich West.* Diplomarbeit, Geographisches Institut, Universität Bern.

Friedmann, John (1995), "Ein Jahrzehnt der World City-Forschung", in: H. Hitz et al.: *Capitales Fatales: Urbanisierung und Politik in den Finanzmetropolen Frankfurt und Zürich.* Zürich: Rotpunkt, 22-44.

Garreau, Joel (1991), *Edge City. Life on the New Frontier.* New York: Doubleday.

Gisler, Bettina (2001), *"und dann hat es geheissen...": Standortverlagerungen aus der Sicht von Angestellten.* Diplomarbeit, Geographisches Institut, Universität Bern.

Harvey, David (1985), *The Urbanization of Capital.* Baltimore, Md.: John Hopkins University Press.

Hermann, Michael / Leuthold, Heinrich (2002), *Stadt-Land-Cleavages einer urbanisierten Gesellschaft.* Arbeitspapier zum Jahreskongress der Schweizerischen Vereinigung für Politikwissenschaft, Fribourg. Draft.

Hitz, Hansruedi / Schmid, Christian / Wolff, Richard (1995)," Boom, Konflikt und Krise - Zürichs Entwicklung zur Weltmetropole", in: H. Hitz et al., *Capitales Fatales: Urbanisierung und Politik in den Finanzmetropolen Frankfurt und Zürich.* Zürich: Rotpunkt, 208-282.

Kipfer, Stefan (1995), *Transnationalization, Hegemony, and Local Politics - The Case of Zurich.* Master Thesis for the Faculty of Environmental Studies, York University, Toronto .

Lefebvre Henri (1968), *Le droit à la ville.* Paris: Anthropos.

Loderer, Benedikt (2001), "Glattalstadt – Die heimliche Hauptstadt", in: *Hochparterre* 10, 14-21.

Nigg, Heinz (ed.) (2001), *Wir wollen alles und zwar subito! Die Achtziger Jugendunruhen in der Schweiz und ihre Folgen.* Zürich: Limmat Verlag.

Rüfenacht, Sandra (2002), *Global City Zürich. Regionalökonomische Untersuchung der strukturellen und räumlichen Entwicklung einer urbanen Grossregion.* Diplomarbeit, Geographisches Institut, Universität Bern.

Sassen, Saskia (1995), "Global City - Hierarchie, Massstab, Zentrum", in: H. Hitz et al., *Capitales Fatales: Urbanisierung und Politik in den Finanzmetropolen Frankfurt und Zürich.* Zürich: Rotpunkt, 45-60.

Sassen, Saskia (1991), *The Global City: New York, London, Tokyo.* Princeton: Princeton University Press.

Schmid, Christian (1998), "The Dialectics of Urbanisation in Zurich" In: INURA (ed.), *Possible Urban Worlds.* Basel/Boston/Berlin: Birkhäuser, 216-225.

Schmid, Christian (1997), "Zürich als Global City", in: Marco, Daniel et al., *La ville: villes de crise ou crise des villes.* Rapport scientifique final pour le 'Fonds national suisse de la recherche scientifique'. Institut d'Architecture de l'Université de Genève.

Scott, Allen J. (ed.) (2001), *Global City-Regions: Trends, Theory, Policy.* Oxford: Oxford University Press.

Soja, Edward W. (1996), *Thirdspace.* Cambridge, Ma./ Oxford, UK: Blackwell.

Soja, Edward W. / Scott, Allen J. (1986), "Los Angeles: Capital of the Late Twentieth Centur", in: *Environment and Planning D: Society and Space*, 4, S., 249-254.

Taylor, Peter J. / Walker D.R.F. (2001)," World Cities: A First Multivariate Analysis of their Service Complexes" In: *Urban Studies* 38.1, 23-47.

Thierstein, Alain / Held, Thomas / Gabi, Simone (2003), "Stadt der Regionen. Die Glattal-Stadt als Raum vielschichtiger Handlungsebenen braucht institutionelle Reformen", in: A. Eisinger / M. Schneider (eds.): *Stadtland Schweiz.* Basel/Boston/Berlin: Birkhäuser, 273-307.

Thrift, Nigel (1987), "The Fixers: The Urban Geography of International Commercial Capital" In: J.Henderson / M.Castells (Hg.): *Global Restructuring and Territorial Development.* London: Sage, 203-233.

Veltz, Pierre (1996), *Mondialisation, villes et territoires: l'économie d'archipel.* Paris: PUF.

Endnotes

[1] The maps published in this article are produced as part of the research project "Die Schweiz – ein städtebauliches Portrait" by the ETH Studio Basel (Faculty of Architecture, Swiss Federal Institute of Technology Zurich).

[2] Source: Swiss Federal Statistical Office.

[3] The technical terms used to designate the new regional city differ correspondingly: "urban region" (Harvey 1985), "global city region" (Scott 2001), or "metropolitan region" (Blotevogel 2001).

[4] The only unit existing so far is the organization for economic development, "Greater Zurich Area" organized under private law, which, however, is of little political significance.

TEXT..........Andreas Hofer
PHOTOS..........Andreas Hofer

Postindustrial Zurich 15 Years in Search of a New Paradigm of Public Planning

Local Politics and Global Trends

After the fall of the Berlin wall, the end of bipolarism, a certain pressure on public mechanisms of regulation can be observed. Authorities are now obliged to prove that legal frameworks are not obstacles to economic development. The state is supposed to become leaner, more efficient, more helpful to private economic enterprise. In this process public planning is faced with a systematic problem of legitimation. Why should self-regulating processes be interfered with, how can plus-value be generated by planning rules enforced by public planning? During the last 15 years this pressure has led to a fundamental change of the planning culture in Zurich. New instruments have been created, the political dialogue has been transformed, the public planning authorities have become partners and co-promoters in the process of urban development. This change is still ongoing. Planning laws, which cannot be adapted quickly enough, are being combined with new instruments.

The second most important factor after the pressure towards deregulation has been the economic development of the city. In the nineties the economically pampered city of Zurich suffered a long period of recession, which hit the real estate market particularly hard. Job losses in manufacturing that began in the sixties could be compensated by the growing sector of general and financial services. Now even this sector was characterized by mergers, bankruptcies and cut backs; unemployment rose to unprecedented heights and the demand for office space declined. The desire to revise and make more business-friendly instruments to boost the economy increased the pressure to revise laws aiming primarily at protecting the resident population against the expansion of the financial service sector.

Two charismatic personalities of clearly different political orientation were of the city planning department in these years. Between 1986 and 1998 Ursula Koch, was director of the department; in 1998 Elmar Ledergerber became her successor. Both are members of the Social Democratic Party, which has governed the city with a majority supported by the Green Party and by a dissident Christian-Democratic councillor.

Ursula Koch's policy consisted in social-democratic regulation of urban development, assuming a critical distance from real estate owners, in defense of the underprivileged and the environment. Elmar Ledergerber is advertising a more business-friendly attitude, facilitating pragmatic solutions through cooperative processes and trying to stimulate urban development actively with large-scale projects. In spite of the media's predilection for this kind of characterisation and the fact that even politicians of the Social-Democratic Party are overemphasizing the gap between the two personalities to give their party a modern, dynamic image, there is in fact great continuity in the urban development process of the last fifteen years, which has remained unaffected by these personal differences. Both Ursula Koch and Elmar Ledergerber have been working for the new paradigm of urban development that was enforced by the econonomic development of the nineties.

Murder in the City Building Department

A few weeks before Ursula Koch took office, Günther Tschanun, a longtime senior officer in the department, killed four colleagues in their workplace. The unbearable atmosphere in the office had driven him to this act. Terrible working conditions had been the result of a rotten record of office procedures, including favoritism and corruption leading to a series of scandals. It is no surprise, that faced with this situation, Ursula Koch set out to cleanse the Augean stables with an iron broom and high moral standards. Planning laws were to become dependable, fair and binding. Office policy was to be based on clear rules and mutual human respect. The revision of the building and zoning law was to be the first test of these principles. This set of planning rules, which regulates the utilization, the density and the construction of buildings for the whole city, was to be adapted every few decades. Such a revision was due. The economy was booming, the need for office space for financial services seemed without limits, Zurich had become the undisputed economic centre of Switzerland. Housing underwent pressure and there was a shortage of flats even though the city was losing inhabitants.

Flats or Offices? A City to Work in or to Live in?

The conflict between the resident population, suffering from housing shortages and increasing rents, and the service industry, which demanded liberalized access to limited land resources for its expansion, determined the approach to the new building and zoning law. The discussion focussed instantly on the emptying industrial areas near the city-centre. Here space that would be sufficient for the demands of the growing financial service industry seemed likely to become available in the following years. But the unrestricted opening of these industrial zones for office buildings carrying some risks. The population feared that rising real estate prices could increase the pressure towards gentrification on the adjacent traditional working class neighbourhoods. Industry and small businesses saw their existence threatened by the competition of the financially strong service industry.

In 1992 a compromise proposal, worked out after long years of media debates and largescale neighbourhood consultations was accepted by a narrow majority of voters. The protection of housing space in the residential neighbourhoods was maintained (the land use plan prescribed a certain percentage of space reserved for housing for every area of the city). It was supposed that slightly higher density in selected areas, subsequent legalisation of office buildings erected on industrial areas and the offer of area development plans to make industrial areas accessible to service utilisation, would satisfy the space demands of the economy and simultaneously protect existing social structures. In hindsight this plan can be considered as the last attempt to create a valid order for all the interest groups involved and for the whole city area based on a democratic bargaining process. The area development plans were the flexible element that allowed the opening of additional land through negotiations between authorities and private owners, under the condition that private land owners were ready to make concessions in the higher interest of the city.

Negotiation and Backstabbing

In 1991 the real estate market collapsed. In the Greater Zurich area 1,000,000 square meters of unused office space suddenly became available. This weak demand facilitated negotiations between real estate owners, who expected to prepare their properties for the next boom, and the city. Large industrial areas in the west and the north of the city underwent area development planning in the first half of the nineties.

Parallel to this large scale planning, the legal dispute on the lawfulness of the new land use plan continued. The law accepted by the people could not come into force in all the city territory. Several hundred objections (mainly by land owners) had to be judged by the courts. From the point of view of the planning law, the situation was extremely confusing. On a specific lot, the old laws of 1962 could be valid in part together with regulations of the new law because an appeal was under way, while land owners were working with the city on completely new rules in the framework of new area development plans. The building lobby complained in the media about legal insecurity. Even the land owners cooperating with the city took part in these campaigns. They bemoaned the lengthiness of the procedures and the toughness of the negotiations with the city authorities. Criticisms of the person at the head of the building department became sharper and sharper. She was accused of not being flexible enough and open for compromise. The call for clear solutions grew louder and louder.

In 1995 the building department of the canton of Zurich (in the Swiss federalist system, the next higher authority) *suspended the building and zoning law of 1992 and replac*ed it with its own bill. The right-wing governed canton practically declared the Social-Democratic city a "Free Enterprise Zone". With the exception of the residential neighbourhoods of the rich, massive densification was made possible everywhere, the protection of housing was weakened and in the so-called developing areas (the industrial areas), any land use and density an investor could dream of was made legal. The consequences of this political *coup de main* remained bearable only because the largest areas had already been secured by area development plans that even the land owners were not willing to question, and because - counter to the assumptions of the cantonal government - the crisis was not in fact a consequence of over-regulation and persisted even after the liberalisation coup.

Ursula Koch persevered for another three years. She completed the plans already initiated, but didn't attempt to replace the three parallel valid building and zoning laws (the law of 1962 she had wanted to revise, her new law of 1992 and the decree of 1995) by a single new valid one. She left this job to her successor Elmar Ledergerber who took office in 1998. In the last year of her time in office, from 1996 to 1997, a "City Forum" was organized, which provided some of the foundations for the work of her successor in office.

The "City Forum" : an Attempt to Provide a Comprehensive Framework for Cooperative Processes

Weakened by legal conflicts, the city building department found it more and more difficult to organize a discussion on the future of the city. And what is more, it became more and more evident that in the areas developed by area development plans the city was faced with infrastructural tasks. Appropriate instruments to tackle these problems were lacking. These questions were discussed in the City Forum using the example of the industrial areas in the west of the city. It was the city mayor who had initiated the City Forum, in order to show that for the city of Zurich planning should not be a merely technical task.

The city mayor appointed a committee of scientists, representatives of the business community, of the population, of the land-owners and of the city administration to discuss the future of the industrial areas in the west of Zurich for one year. Although this committee had neither political legitimation nor a budget, it succeeded in developing a common vision for the future in a consensus-oriented process. The City Forum departed from plans to transform industrial areas into monofunctional secondary city centres devoted to services. The new vision was a mixed, attractive neighbourhood with room for innovative projects. A gardening exhibition was included to emphasize the importance of public spaces and parks.

Subsequently this consensus regarding the future of the area could not be put into action. The next committee of the City Forum met for two more years, but was not able to realise a single project - the gardening exhibition was buried for lack of investors. Whereas the city building department transformed the recommendations of the City Forum into a non-binding development concept, investors optimized their profit on their individual allotments and refused to help finance public infrastructures. The authorities lacked legal instruments to enforce obligations beyond those concerning property limits.

The results are of an astounding quality. Along streets and rail tracks that originally connected warehouses and factories, a dense urban patchwork was created. Projects of the early nineties, experimental projects like KraftWerk1 (see article of Andreas Wirz in this chapter) and spectacular conversions of industrial and office buildings were now realized.
The area now projects an image of cultural innovations and of an economic prosperity.

Although the results of the City Forum have been extremely modest, the city politicians claim this positive development for themselves. Although coordination of the various planning procedures and the provision of adequate infrastructures have been the weaknesses of the development process up to now, the positive image of the neighbourhood legitimizes a policy that is veering away from its original objective of creating a dependable framework for investors. The city is assuming a role as partner of developers, and is trying to initiate projects of its own as points of cristallization of urban development. It does not authorize buildings anymore, it makes them possible. A lean, efficiency-oriented authority does not want to limit itself to restrictive action, but is prepared to be pro-active. In the best case the authority will become the cleverest investor: through its strategic efforts it can give economic impetus to a wide field and is able to increase its stake with the returns.

A Stadium as a Motor of Development

The planning for a new stadium in Zurich West can be seen as the provisional climax of this strategy. Shortly after he took office, looking for a project of high prestige that could serve as an example for the reconciliation of public interest and private profit-maximation, Elmar Ledergerber chose sports. Football is proletarian, main-stream and anti-elitarian. To muster enough support for the project, he proposed to combine the two local national league teams and athletics in one multifunctional stadium in Zurich West. The project was meant to be a motor for urban development in the area. The project perimeter comprised a large area in the proximity of the to-be stadium. Here, the plus-value that would be generated would make the stadium possible at no cost to the city. With great haste international competitions were organized, areas re-zoned, free city land promised to investors, and recently developed urban development concepts abandoned to make possible the opening of the stadium for the European Championship in 2008.

A Deregulated City

When Ursula Koch decided to shape the conversion of industrial areas in a negotiating process between private investors and the city authorities, she divided the city into a largely completed, slowly evolving city core and dynamic areas where the future of the city could be determined strategically. This separation is purely architectural and technocratic. It ignores social problems, the demands for different uses and rampant structural deficits in existing neighbourhoods. This kind of city planning focusses on the spectacular areas of high creative potential. Elmar Ledergerber went one step further by giving up the traditional regulatory role of the city administration and becoming a co-investor and developer of leading projects.

The image of a polis shaped by a democratic process was lost. At the moment, nobody cares about strategic questions of a sensible mix of housing and workplaces, the changes in the workplace caused by technological innovation, the embedding of the city in an urbanizing region, the transformation of socially troubled existing neighbourhoods. Local politics - and is all the more surprising as Zurich has been governed in all these years by a Green/Social-Democratic majority - puts all its resources at the disposal of the growth interests of the real estate sector. This development can only be understood by taking into account the second strong influence on urban development - the business cycle. The long-lasting crisis, which had caused unemployment, zero-growth and empty office buildings, all things that had been unknown in Switzerland for decades, dissolved the old conflict between a growth-prone economy and a growth-critical resident population. The permanent housing shortage, a side-effect of the expansion of the service industry, lost its urgency. So as not to put any state-regulatory obstacles in the way of the ailing economy, the Fordist compromise of functional separation between residential and industrial city areas was suspended. This development only went relatively smoothly, because the potential opposition, the creative, (sub-)cultural milieu, was allowed to use all kinds of niches. A lively mix of provisional utilizations took root in the industrial areas, and some projects, like KraftWerk1, even managed to occupy niches permanently. Zurich's cultural life, gastronomy and housing blossomed beyond the projects that had formerly been fought for with state help.

As city politics are not likely to win back their regulatory power, the shape of the city will be the result of local bargaining among agents in the future. Taking into account the current power balance, a certain fragmentation is bound to happen. No participant has the power to develop larger areas alone. Depending on business cycles, niches will open up. Speculative, monofunctional service buildings, investments of the locally strong and socially committed cooperative movement and guerilla-style transformations of failed investments will form a patchwork full of conflicts. The quality of life in the city will depend entirely on the capability of socially responsible investors to compensate their relative financial weakness by the cleverness and speed with wich they operate in future confrontations with speculative developers.

TEXT....................Christian Schmid and Daniel Weiss
TRANSLATION....................Connie Carr, Barbara Stiner and Stefan Kipfer
PHOTOS....................Katharina Rippstein

The New Metropolitan Mainstream

Secondo Pride and Swiss Image

"Secondo". Printed in black Gothic font on pastel-blue T-shirts, this word could not be overlooked on the streets of Zurich 2002 summer. What at first sight could be taken as a trendy logo, in reality is a self-confident statement of a marginalised identity and refers to the recent debate on migration problems, for it is the Swiss-German term of Italian origin for second generation immigrants. The T-shirts were designed in the trendy formerly working-class neighbourhood "district 5" by the label "Atelier Shirts", which specialises in witty lifestyle T-shirts and merchandising products for alternative small businesses.

In the previous season the fashionable streetwear boutiques were full of red T-shirts with a white Swiss cross. Are those the signs of a culture war on the streets? In the same way that the Secondo T-shirt was not necessarily worn by a person of that description and did not express a specific political commitment, the exploitation of the Swiss national flag as a fashion statement did not imply patriotism. Only ten years after artists and intellectuals had boycotted the 700-year-celebrations of the mythical founding date (1291) of the Swiss Confederation, neither Swiss nor foreign citizens seemed to have any problems.

The export hit Swatch, the corporate image of the new Swiss International Airlines ("Swiss"), designed by the Canadian star designer Tyler Brûlé, and the decidedly innovative national exhibition "Expo 02" all emphasize the same message: Switzerland is cool. Swiss elites manifest an open, metropolitan cosmopolitan attitude and make playful use of symbols which expresses a cultural sublimation of social conflicts and contradictions. This self-image is laying claim to a new Swiss identity, but is in fact mainly produced in Zurich, strongly influenced by the lifestyle of the booming art, advertising and graphic-design *milieux*, as well as by the new metropolitan consciousness that is taking hold in Zurich.

The New City Limits

Zurich seems to have evolved into a metropolis not just in the economic, but also in the everyday sense of the word. But how deep is this "metropolitan" attitude? A national referendum held in the fall of 2002 allows some conclusions regarding this question. The referendum was launched by the SVP (Schweizerische Volkspartei, Swiss Popular Party) and targetted "abuses of the right to asylum". In fact it aimed at a further massive dismantling of the Swiss refugee laws.[1] After heated debates before the referendum, and in spite of a clear rejection by almost all large parties as well as the national Parliament, the referendum was rejected only by a very small margin. In the canton of Zurich, a majority of voters accepted the referendum. A geographical break-down of votes showed that the referendum was accepted in a majority of municipalities in the canton of Zurich, in some with strong majorities. It was rejected with relatively narrow margins in the city of Winterthur and a number of affluent municipalities south of the city of Zurich. On the other hand, the initiative was clearly rejected in all inner-city districts of the city of Zurich. Surprisingly, both traditional upper-class neighborhoods and the classical strongholds of the political left voted against the proposal. At distance increased from the city center, however, public opinion was reversed. In the peripheral neighbourhoods of the city in the north and west, the referendum got clear majorities. If this referendum is taken as a gauge for a basically tolerant and therefore metropolitan attitude, urban Zurich today appears as a liberal, cosmopolitan island in the middle of a mainly xenophobic, right-wing conservative region. The boundaries of this island pass right through the municipality of Zurich.

The "original" Secondo-T-Shirt.

Invitation to an event in "Tonimolkerei", one of the most trendy entertainment places of Zurich.

From these results, the conclusion might be drawn that in the center of Zurich a kind of detached liberal consensus has been formed with respect to the handling of social questions. This would confirm the familiar thesis that the city is the cradle and the hearth of civilization (cf e.g. Häussermann/Siebel 1987). A more precise analysis of the reasons for rejection indicates, however, a different picture (NZZ 2002): Many of those who rejected the asylum referendum agreed with its intention to cut down the number of refugees allowed into the country, but thought that the referendum only served to stir up emotions, thus accentuating the problems instead of solving them. For these people, there is no need to engage in debates of principle and ideological trench warfare. They want efficient, pragmatic solutions.

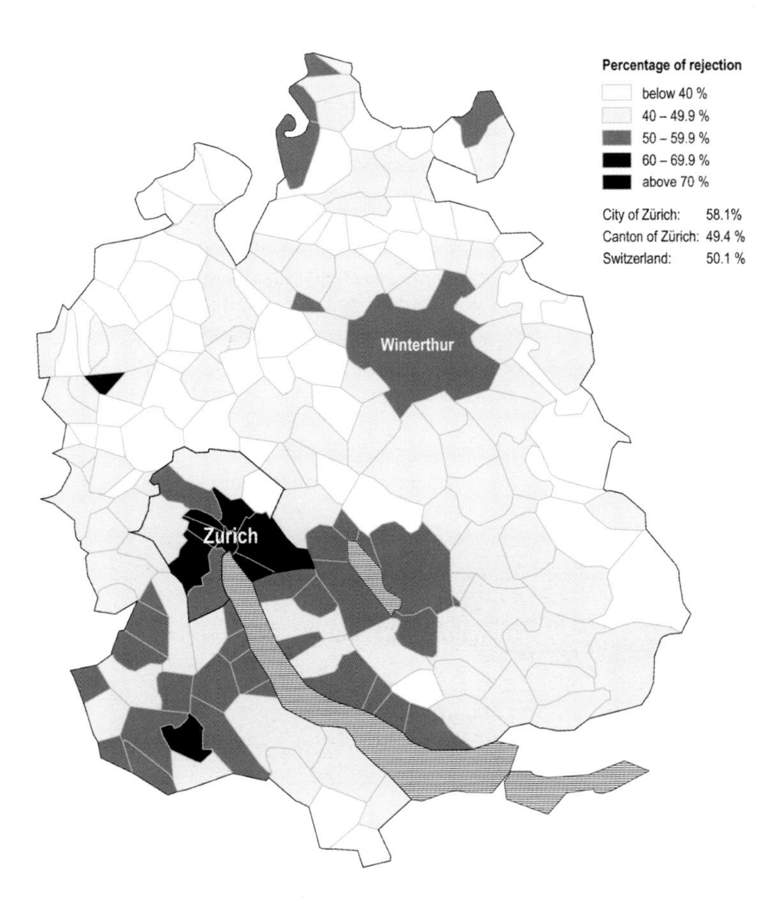

Ballot results of the referendum "against abuses of the right to asylum" from November 24, 2002 in the municipalities of the canton of Zurich and in the districts of the city of Zurich.
Source: Statistisches Amt des Kantons Zürich. © sotomo, Department of Geography, University of Zurich, 2003

Between Openness and Repression

The Zurich region is clearly divided. While a large part of the population in the metropolitan center prefer pragmatic, integrative and productive approaches, the majority of voters in the metropolitan hinterland take non-compromising, right-wing conservative and xenophobic positions. Many other referenda could be shown to present a similar picture (cf. Hermann/Leuthold 2002a).

This rupture has manifested itself for some time. Beginning from the suburban and peri-urban regions, which have been characterized by solid right-wing majorities, and specifically by an anti-urban attitude for decades, a new type of right-wing populism has begun to take hold in the Zurich region. A prelude to this shift was the unexpected electoral success of the "automobile party" (*Autopartei*) in the 1980s. This small splinter group made the vested interest of car owners the focus of its politics, and stirred up emotions against asylum seekers and immigrants. Increasingly drawn into the maelstrom of right-wing populism was also the SVP, a traditional conservative party which had represented small business and rural regions in the cantonal government for decades. In the 1990s, under the leadership of the entrepreneur and billionaire Christoph Blocher, the party metamorphosed into an efficient, nationalist-conservative melting pot fusing a patriotic, xenophobic, isolationist and anti-metropolitan mission with a neoliberal economic policy.[2]

Opposed to these repressive currents, the city of Zurich experienced a remarkable cultural and social opening, essentially initiated with the urban revolt of 1980/81 (cf. Schmid 1998). At that time, a broad heterogeneous movement with both political and cultural objectives protested against the repressive, narrow-minded and provincialism which marked everyday life in Zurich. Through street fighting, but also through cheerful happenings and creative action, they demanded a different, vibrant and open city. This urban movement fell apart after two years, but it changed public life in Zurich fundamentally, stimulating, among other things, the development of a milieu of cultural producers, which now embodies "cool" Switzerland.

With the onset of an extended period of economic recession and the unexpected victory of a left-green coalition in municipal elections, the political climate changed again in the early 1990s. Supported by other conservative forces, the SVP launched an aggressive campaign against the cultural and social opening of the 1980s. Their first target was the highly visible community of heroin users, which had achieved international publicity.[3] Under massive political and judicial pressure, in February 1992 the city government decreed the precipitous eviction and dispersion of the heroin milieu, with disastrous consequences.

Heroin users and dealers were pushed into the neighboring districts 5 and 4, traditional working class and immigrant neighbourhoods, which since the seventies had also become strongholds of the left-wing-alternative milieu. These neighbourhoods were now at the core of a sort of "war against drugs". Many residents and local businesspeople began to barricade passages and courtyards with grids. Blue lighting in frontyards, in house entrances and toilets was used to stop people from injecting. A massive police presence, with chases, arbitrary arrests and humiliating public body searches produced a feeling of a permanent state of emergency. In spite of this, the heroin milieu persisted. After only four months, on the outskirts of the same neighborhood, a new open heroin milieu, larger and more wretched than ever before, installed itself on abandoned railway tracks (see Heller/Lichtenstein/Nigg 1995).

The controversy around the heroin problem changed the social climate in the entire city, particularly in the neighbourhoods concerned. Many existing social networks, which had created some degree of cohesion or at least mutual respect among the different social groups, dissolved and a discourse of exclusion started to take place, increasingly involving even left-wing-alternative and urban cultural groups. At the height of the crisis even the Social-Democratic head of the police was making "foreign drug dealers" and "criminal asylum seekers" responsible for the drug problem. In addition, there was a unrivaled campaign going on, encouraged by the media, which exaggerated the reputation of the neighbourhood concerned as a drug inferno, comparing it to the Chicago of the thirties. In the name of "national security" and under pressure from Zurich's city government, which asked for "emergency measures", the federal parliament passed a new law in 1995 that consirably tightened regulations for foreigners while extending police powers (cf. Stern 1994, 1995).

The lack of success of this purely repressive policy eventually caused a change in doctrine. Confronting the right-wing populist opposition, left and conservative forces agreed on a "drug compromise". In February 1995, the open heroin milieu was once again cleared, but this time the city government implemented a whole range of preventive and supporting measures, including controlled heroin distribution, but also new jails, intervention task forces and special regulations. With this mix of repression and support, it was eventually possible to get the heroin milieu under control.

Cascade of Exclusion

Despite the compromise over the heroin question, the hardened social climate remained. During the early 1990s, the social image of the city had changed profoundly. The city was increasingly seen as a "garbage can", with all the problems characteristic of a global society. A social scientific model of this view was the "A-City" (A-Stadt) (c.f. Frey 1996: 15). In German, this term refers to a whole range of words which all begin with the letter "A": old, poor, single parents, dependent, trainees, unemployed, immigrant, asylum seeker, social drop-outs.[4] An "A"-City is therefore a city where one finds these groups concentrated in high numbers. This is said to result in a vicious cycle of deepening urban social problems, and increasing costs for social services. This (negative) conception of the city allowed numerous political initiatives to increase financial support for the city and launch a new urban policy.

In the mid 1990s, the city of Zurich implemented a series of measures. First on the agenda was a strategy to increase control over public space, which was supported not only by the center and the right but also by many on the left. The social construction of dangerous groups - including the racist stereotype of "drug-dealing foreigners" - found broad acceptance. This resulted in a "cascade of exclusion" of more and more social groups (see Innen!Stadt!Aktion! 1997). After the junkies, dealers, and immigrants, this policy focussed on criminalized women sexworkers. The slogan, "No sex or drugs in neighbourhoods that have started to breathe again" (advertisement in several newspapers by various housing co-operatives in November of 1996), challenged the street as the basis of their livelihood. Corresponding public actions were not taken against clients of prostitution or owners of sex-trade enterprises. By strict regulations, the city government tried to ban street prostitution and force it away from the city center and hence from public view. Following the same logic, meeting places for alcoholics and homeless were cleared, and punks were prohibited from certain areas. Another example of this strategy was the campaign "Welcome to Zurich." Yellow banners and posters in public parks and green spaces declared new codes of conduct.

These measures stand for a policy that attempts to reserve public spaces for "desirables"and expel the "others". For the latter, this means exclusion from various public spheres. In the end, these processes create a particular image of the city - one that neither affirms nor acknowledges marginalized social groups. Instead these groups vanish from public view, they are denied the material resources and the opportunities to build social relationships, and their representation within the urban sphere is cancelled. Public space thus becomes a contested terrain, where struggles over ways of life are fought out.

The Bus stop at Militär-/Langstrasse shortly after the removal of the shelter.

Placard posted by the Zurich Transport Service (Verkehrsbetriebe Zürich, VBZ). The placard reads, "Demolition of Bus Shelter at Militär-/Langstrasse. Dear Passengers, this bus shelter will be closed for an indefinite length of time. It was, unfortunately, misused by various groups as a meeting place and could therefore not be used as a waiting space. We are making efforts to find a solution quickly. We thank you for your understanding. Your VBZ Züri-Line".

WILLKOMMEN IN ZÜRICH

Die Regeln bei uns:

Abfall und Gratiszeitungen in die Kübel

Keinen Lärm nach 22 Uhr

Keinen Hundedreck liegen lassen

Nicht im Freien pinkeln

No drugs, no deal

 Erlaubt ist, was nicht stört. 

Campaign Flyer of the City of Zurich 2000/2001. It reads, "Welcome to Zurich! Our Rules: Garbage and Newspapers are to be deposited in containers provided. No noise after 10 p.m. Leave behind no dog excrement. No urinating in public. No drugs, no dealing. only what creates no disturbance is permitted."

Upgrading and Gentrification

In 1998, the city government developed this policy of social control further still through a program of "upgrading distressed neighbourhoods" - a program that ran parallel to measures aimed at "integration" and "security" (Wehrli-Schindler 2002). The program attempted to strengthen the social fabric of so-called problem neighbourhoods by luring "stable" and affluent residents into the area. Defined as areas with a high concentration of migrants and a high level of fluctuation and transience, "problem neighbourhoods" were to be revitalized by improved physical design, social work and public relations. Soon, every run-down area of Zurich was named a "slum" - in comparative terms, a ridiculous exaggeration.

Upgrading also affected the housing co-operatives and the city's public housing projects, which together account for approximately 25% of Zurich's total housing stock (Koch/Sommadin/Süsstrunk 1998). In the city's view, the main problem is that most public housing units are too small for the well-to-do. To reverse this situation, the city launched an ambitious renewal program in 1998. In 10 years, new construction and renovation was to create 10,000 large, attractive appartments. This was intended to have the added benefit of altering the social composition of inner city neighbourhoods by settling more affluent taxpayers (Stadtrat 1998). A clear example of this strategy is a plan to demolish a large public housing development in the neighbourhood of "Grünau", built in the 1950s. The city argues that the 267 apartments, small but cheap, should be redeveloped because they don't meet contemporary standards, and because the neighbourhood should become more socially mixed (Seitenblicke 2002).

Given Zurich's wealth, it is astonishing to see such an upgrading and regeneration program. This program neither signals the end of the city's social policy nor entails the large-scale displacement of economically marginal social groups. It focusses on specific targeted interventions, which do however have severe consequences. Alongside the demolition of physical structures, existing social networks, personal relationships, and spaces for social interaction are being torn down and lost. Furthermore, if placed within the context of increased control over public space, these measures take on the character of an effective strategy of neigborhood cleansing. Instead of encouraging the potential and the creativity of social processes, this strategy attempts to domesticate urban life by subjugating it under a new, repressive normality.

Accordingly, these measures also support the market-oriented trend of gentrification - a process that has accelerated in the last ten years. To date, there are no studies that provide a quantitative analysis of the gentrification process (for qualitative studies see Berger/Hildenbrand/Somm 2002 and Hermann/Leuthold 2002b). However, one indicator might be the proportion of non-Swiss residents in a given neighbourhood. During the 1990s, several trends could be observed. The number of non-Swiss residents remained constant in middle or upper class neighbourhoods, while it increased in neighbourhoods in the outskirts. In contrast, it decreased in the traditional working class and immigrant neighbourhoods of the inner-city (districts 4 and 5). In district 5, the percentage of residents without a Swiss passport gradually increased after World War II and peaked at 50% in 1994. After 1994 this percentage decreased every year. In 2001, the percentage of non-Swiss residents was 40%. In only seven years, the absolute number of newly-arrived immigrants in the neighbourhood decreased by 13.5%. In district 4, a similar development could also be observed (source: Statistisches Jahrbuch der Stadt Zürich, different volumes).

This process shows a paradoxical, and yet logical, development. In places where metropolitan Zurich pulsates today, there is little space for underprivileged social groups. They are pushed into neighbourhoods on the outskirts, where predominantly petty bourgeois and proletarian residents who have been further demoted by Zurich's global city economy demonstrate a strong tendency towards xenophobia and a low level of tolerance. Even in these peripheral areas, upgrading is planned [5], and the socially weak have been pushed out. Along highways and under flight paths, the formation of pockets of deprivation, emerging territorial traps can be seen.

One thus observes a basic contradiction, which is visible not only in Zurich but in other metropolises as well. Although urban centres celebrate diversity and portray themselves as open-minded, and although these urban centres indeed demonstrate integrative potential, the demands for vibrant urban spaces often results in the exclusion of the very groups that created the spaces in the first place. As the city becomes a privileged space for a well-to-do urban middle class, a loss of urbanity and creativity inevitably follows. In his discussions of Paris, over 30 years ago, the French philosopher Henri Lefebvre had already described this paradox: "It is not in the interests of the political establishment and the hegemonic class to extinguish this spark, for to do so would effectively destroy the city's worldwide reputation - based, precisely, on its daring, its willingness to expose the possible and the impossible, its so-called cultural development, and its panoply of actions and actors [...]. Yet at the same time the political powers and the bourgeoisie controlling the economy are afraid of all such ferment, and have a strong urge to crush it under suffocating central decision-making." (Lefebvre 1991, p. 386)

Langstrasse Zurich, the main axis of districts 4 and 5.

From Paranoia City to Ego City

Strategies of increasing control over public space and processes of upgrading and gentrification have faced next to no resistance in the last few years. This is somewhat puzzling when one considers Zurich's history as a hot bed of squats and struggles against speculation and the destruction of inner-city neigborhoods (see Stahel 2001 and Infoladen 1988). Buildings are still squatted in Zurich, but they are usually located in peripheral neighbourhoods. Very few abandoned buildings remain in the city centre. The few squats that have happened recently are strongly culturalist in orientation.

One spectacular action was the squatting of the legendary Cabaret Voltaire - one of the original and most important centres of the Dada movement during the First World War. For decades, this historic site received no attention, as it managed a meagre existence as a club that reminded no one of its background. In 2001 however, the building changed hands and was targeted for renovation. A group of young artists squatted the premises, staging dadaist performances and demanding the establishment of a new Dada center.

This new mix of culture and politics could also be seen in another centrally located squat, "Ego-City." This relatively small building serves as a meeting point where parties, concerts, and political debate shade into each other. There, squatters no longer simply argue against the global city of financial Zurich and against the expansion of the CBD. They consider subculture as a productive component of late capitalist society. Although this cultural squat does see itself as a countercultural project and a form of political resistance, it also problematizes its participation in the yuppification of adjacent neighbourhoods, and the reproduction of an achievement oriented society (*Leistungsgesellschaft*).

In the words of one squatter: "Perhaps our response to this system lacks perspective, since we are, in fact, the offspring of a privileged middle class in one of the richest cities in the world. Hence the character of our response to this system" (megafon 2001).

The name "Ego-City" reminds one of another name from another time, which signaled a similar critique: "Paranoia-City". This name, coined by an anarchist bookstore in the 1970s, crystalized the atmosphere of the era. It stood for a city that was paranoid and fostered paranoia, a city that prohibited everything that was fun, a city that saw alternative life styles as attacks on society as a whole. In the end, this situation provoked the urban revolt of the 1980s.

Comparing Paranoia-City with Ego-City pointedly reveals the shifts in everyday life occurred from the 1970s to now. The narrow-minded, provincial anxiety which suffocated all creative initiative has yielded to a smug productivism. Today, Zurich is a city of creative individualists, a city where everybody produces their own ego. In 1980, demonstrators chanted "Produce! Produce!" (*"Schaffe! Schaffe!"*) to express an ironic critique of the oppressive work ethic in what was then puritanical Zurich. Today, many of those demonstrators are themselves workaholics, thus indicating the success as well as the failure of the revolt that fought for an open, metropolitan city and, at the same time, a different way of life.

Zurich is no longer the cosmopolitan, yet introverted city of the 1980s. Under today's changed conditions, the city portrays itself as open-minded, neoliberal, productivist, culturalistic, consumerist, and growth-oriented. Summer months thrive with events of all sorts from the "Iron Man" competition to the Street Parade, and one reads regularly that Zurich ranks as one of the trendiest cities in Europe. In this new metropolitan mainstream, the social has become ambivalent.

Ego-City (Photo by Daniel Weiss)

References

Berger, Christa / Hildenbrand, Bruno / Somm, Irene (2002), *Die Stadt der Zukunft. Leben im prekären Wohnquartier*. Opladen: Leske + Budrich.

Eberle, Orlando (2003), *Konflikte, Allianzen und territoriale Kompromisse in der Stadtentwicklung. Eine Analyse aus regulationstheoretischer Perspektive am Beispiel Zürich West*. Diplomarbeit, Geographisches Institut, Universität Bern.

Frey, René L. (1996), *Stadt: Lebens- und Wirtschaftsraum. Eine ökonomische Analyse*. ETH Zürich: vdf.

Häussermann, Hartmut / Siebel, Walter (1987), *Neue Urbanität*. Frankfurt/M: Suhrkamp.

Heller Martin, Lichtenstein Claude, Nigg Heinz (eds.) (1995), *Letten it be. Eine Stadt und ihr Problem*. Zürich: Museum für Gestaltung.

Hermann Michael / Leuthold Heinrich (2002a), *Stadt-Land-Cleavages einer urbanisierten Gesellschaft*. Arbeitspapier zum Jahreskongress der Schweizerischen Vereinigung für Politikwissenschaft, Fribourg. Draft.

Hermann Michael / Leuthold Heinrich (2002b), "Die gute Adresse. Divergierende Lebensstile und Weltanschauungen als Determinanten der innerstädtischen Segregation", in: A. Mayr, M. Meurer, J. Vogt (eds.), *Stadt und Region. Dynamik von Lebenswelten. Tagungsbericht und wissenschaftliche Abhandlungen zum 53.* Deutschen Geographentag in Leipzig. Deutsche Gesellschaft für Geographie, Karlsruhe, Leipzig.

Infoladen (1988), *Zonen*. Zürich: Infoladen für Häuserkampf.

Innen!Stadt!Aktion! (1997), *Gegen Privatisierung, Sicherheitswahn, Ausgrenzung. Eine Beilage der Innen!Stadt!Aktion! in Berner Tagwacht, scheinschlag, die tageszeitung, die WochenZeitung*. Berlin.

Koch, Michael / Somandin, Mathias / Süsstrunk, Christian (1998), *Kommunaler und genossenschaftlicher Wohnungsbau in Zürich 1907 - 1997*. Zürich: Stadt Zürich.

Lefebvre, Henri (1991), *The Production of Space*. Oxford: Blackwell.

megafon (2001), "Gegen jede Form der Institutionalisierung. EgoCity in Zureich", in: *megafon - Zeitung aus der Reithalle Bern*, 239, 12-13.

NZZ (2002), "Analyse der Abstimmungsresultate vom 24 November", in: *Neue Zürcher Zeitung*, 11/26/02, 26.

Schmid, Christian (1998), "The Dialectics of Urbanisation in Zurich", in: INURA (ed.), *Possible Urban Worlds*. Basel/Boston/Berlin: Birkhäuser 1998, 216-225.

Seitenblicke (2002), *Seitenblicke - Quartierentwicklung in der Grünau, 1*. Zürich: Stadt Zürich.

Stadtrat (1998), *Programmschwerpunkte des Stadtrates von Zürich für die Legislaturperiode 1998 bis 2002*. Zürich: Stadt Zürich.

Stahel, Thomas (2001), "Wo Wo Wonige! Die Bedeutung des Wohnens für die Zürcher Jugendbewegung", in: H. Nigg (ed.), *Wir wollen alles und zwar subito! Die Achtziger Jugendunruhen in der Schweiz und ihre Folgen*. Zürich: Limmat Verlag, 392-399.

Stern, Daniel (1995), "Aktion Paukenschlag. Zwangsmassnahmen in Zürich", in: *Die Beute* 2, 113-117.

Stern, Daniel (1994), "Langzeitschäden im Kreis 5", in: *Die Beute* 3, 27-38.

Vogler, Gertrud / Bänziger Chris (1990), *Nur sauber gekämmt sind wir frei. Drogen und Politik in Zürich*. Zürich: Eco-Verlag

Wehrli-Schindler (2002), "Ansätze und Folgen integrierter Stadtteilentwicklung". In: Fachstelle für Stadtentwicklung (ed.), *Aufwertung als Programm?* Zürich: Stadt Zürich, 7-14.

Endnotes

[1] The referendum proposed that persons who had entered the country through a "safe third country" (which today would include more than 90% of all petitioners) should not be allowed to ask for refugee status. All other asylum seekers would have faced more restrictions on their right to work and a reduction in their social welfare benefits.

[2] The party took its profile in part from sensationalistic campaigns against Swiss membership in the European Union and the UN, or as regard the referendum mentioned above, with propositions for tightening refugee and immigrant policies. In its aggressive, black-and-white propaganda it successfully took advantage of existing resentments. Today, SVP with 30% of the votes, is the strongest party in the canton of Zurich, while in the Swiss average it reaches approx. 20%.

[3] After the heroin milieu had been chased across town from one place to the other for years (Vogler/Bänziger 1990), it had eventually, towards the end of the 1980s, established itself in a public park behind the main station. This park made international headlines as "needle park" and became a symbol of the unsolved drug problem in the whole of Europe. Politically, however, a remarkably liberal position gained ground, characterized by the principle that the use of drugs had to be accepted as a societal phenomenon. On site, a number of proposals for assistance and a survival infrastructure were established, including medical and social care, AIDS assistance, and the distribution of syringes.

[4] In German: Alte, Arme, Alleinstehende, Alleinerziehende, Abhängige, Auszubildende, Arbeitslose, Ausländer, Asylbewerber, Aussteiger.

[5] E.g. in the neigbourhood of Aubrugg (City of Zurich) or the municipality of Opfikon.

TEXT.......Philipp Klaus
TRANSLATION....... Constance Carr
PHOTOS.......Philipp Klaus

Creative and Innovative Microenterprises Between Subculture and World Economy

Zurich is one of the "coolest" cities in Europe. Offering a wide spectrum of cultural and leisure activities and a finance sector with a worldwide influence, the city positions itself as a world-ranking metropolis. This was, however, not always the case. Various economic changes, in combination with an urban revolt, enabled Zurich to transform itself into a city with an attractive urban setting, and this is the thesis of this paper.

Microenterprises in Flexible Production Systems

There were three processes of urban economic transformation during the 1990s: flexibilization of production, culturalization of the economy, and commodification of culture. The first, flexibilization of production is characterized by processes like downsizing, outsourcing, and merging. Companies pushed restructuring through, while concurrently they concentrated on preserving their own central business concerns. Production was moved to low wage countries, and services and products were bought from subcontractors. Also, synergies and partnerships with similar enterprises were sought, thereby maximizing economic performance in international markets and reducing costs (usually in the form of reduced labour expenditure).

These processes resulted in a major shift in the business landscape. Large enterprises merged, while small and flexible enterprises emerged, ready and waiting to act and transact. More and more individuals were employed in small or very small business operations. In Switzerland, the number of persons working in microenterprises (businesses that employ 9 employees or less) increased by about 4% (equal to approximately 40,000 individuals), while overall employment between 1991 and 1998 decreased by about 8%. The rise in the number of new businesses was a warmly welcomed statistic among politicians and economic leaders, although it overshadowed (if not hid) growing unemployment. Flexibility was imposed on and demanded by the population (Sennett 1998), although it was clear that microenterprises alone would not solve for the unemployment problem. At the highest risk of poverty under these economic conditions were the "Working Poor," who, in Switzerland, made up 7.5% of the employed population, and were primarily single parents, large families, low qualified workers, and free lancers (Bundesamt für Statistik, 2001).

Culturalization of the Economy

In addition to the flexibilization of production, another process of economic transformation occurred: the culturalization of the economy, in which culture grew into a vehicle of and for economic interests. The product design, for example, became an essential carrier not only of content, but also of identity. "Goods for consumption have become equally valuable to their owners - either as status symbols, cultural objects or defining symbols - as symbolic capital in the competition towards societal recognition," (Helbrecht 2001). The kind and condition of the product itself became secondary - a characteristic of a process that Lash and Urry (1994) called the "economy of signs".
Among the most important signs in the culturalized economy were logos or brand names. Klein (2000) described the emerging entrepreneurial tactic that emphasized the priority given to the production of brands and not the product itself. Enterprises concentrated on the development of brands and a corresponding feeling and identity, which, during the 1990s, also brought about an increase in advertising expenses. Walt Disney´s advertising budget, for example, increased from 150 million US dollars in 1985 to 1.3 billion US dollars in 1995 (Klein 2000). Other superbrands, such as Coca-Cola, McDonalds, and Nike, exhibited similar developments.

Culture became a vector in the distribution of brand names. Through the sponsoring of cultural events such as concerts, exhibits, techno-parties, and cinema, many transnational enterprises discovered that they were able to reach mass numbers of individuals. Spaces that originally held the status of underground or subcultural became home to advertisements for cigarettes, beverages, telecommunications (Klaus 1998). In addition, subcultural codes and signs began to be appropriated by professional "coolness hunters" who actively scanned poorer neighbourhoods for signs to transport back to transnational enterprises (Klein 2000).

The Commodification of Culture

The last process of economic transformation was the commodification of culture, whereby some parts of cultural production grew into an important component of the economy. This was welcomed by local, regional and national elites as it signified a possible boost in employment. "With the disappearance of local manufacturing industries and periodic crises in government and finance, culture is more and more the business of cities." (Zukin, 1995).

It is not easy to define the cultural sector and differentiate it from other sectors of economic activity. There is also significant lack of systematic research in this field (Power, 2002). In the 1950s, the industry of cultural production was distanced from Fordist mass production systems. The music industry, for example, was an almost completely irrelevant economic sector. It was not until the 1960s with the emergence of giant pop and rock bands (especially the Beatles), that a boom in the record industry took hold. It was only the film industry that had a foothold in the economic mass production systems of the 1950s (cf. Lash & Urry 1994, 123). Scott studied the industry of cultural production in Los Angeles and concluded that this industry may not have been the largest but, indeed, the fastest growing. Scott also showed that the cultural production industry had the potential to become the, "most vibrant industrial complex of the twenty-first century," and, therefore, advised politicians to protect this sector (1996, 319). Furthermore, it could also be observed that employment rates in this sector had grown - not just in Los Angeles, but also worldwide.
Although it remained a growing industry, the cultural sector was not spared from processes like flexibilisation (cf. also McRobbie 1999). In fact, the production of culture is, "an example of the flexibilized and highly networked form of societal production," (Krätke 2002, 73), comparable to the sectors of research and technology in its organizational structure.

Culture and Urban Setting in the Competition among Cities

During the 1990s, many cities invested in the production of culture in attempts to entice national capital and international investment (Zukin 1995 / 268, Harvey 1989, Griffiths 1999, Le Galès 1999). Many cities followed such strategies of urban marketing by producing festivals, media events, and unveiling flagship projects - for which internationally renowned architects were often solicited - such as operas, theatres, museums, or congress centres. Topped with an active nightlife, trendy bars, life-style shopping, and a multicultural gastronomy, an urban setting is created that boosts a city's competitive ability.

Cultural life became a defining factor in the quality of life of cities in the world economy (Zukin 1995, Sassen 1996, Hoggett 1999), and "urban life", as a contributing factor towards a city's attractiveness, became an increasingly popular object of study. The urban setting, as a basis of "urban life", became very important to enterprises and especially to transnational enterprises because highly qualified labour forces required an attractive city environment. Big businesses wanted to position themselves where it was "cool," where there was the greatest cultural selection, where the best meeting places could be found, and where nightlife thrived. Cultural life became one of the most important quality of life indicators for global cities. Florida (2002) examined the relationship between the presence of urban artists and the presence of high-tech businesses in US cities and found a significant correlation between them. Above-average clusters of high-tech enterprises were found in metropolitan areas where artists and bohemians also concentrated. This was especially noticeable in San Francisco.

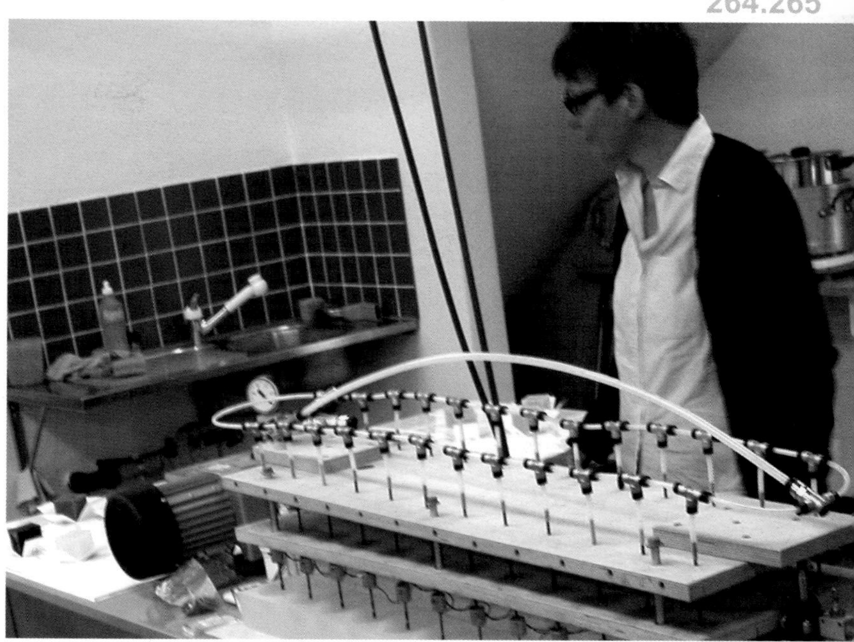

Zurich's Urban Setting

Zurich is not only an important city in the global economy, thanks to its finance sector, ranking as a "Beta-World City" (Beaverstock, Smith, Taylor 1999), but it is also featured in the Mercer Human Resources Report (www.mercerhc.com) as having the highest standard of living out of 215 other cities in 2001 and 2002 - above Vienna and Vancouver. Indeed, Zurich does offer an extraordinary urban setting. Firstly, it is located next to an international airport that connects it to the world at large. Secondly, the city is situated within a remarkable natural environment with a scenic lake and surrounding hills and forests. Thirdly, the city offers a broad range of cultural activities, despite its small size [1]. This combination of factors enables Zurich to compete with other global cities. In addition to an opera house, numerous theatres and museums (directed by big names), there are also techno-parties in old industrial halls, hip and chic bars, trendy and/or multicultural restaurants, as well as the alternative cultural centre, the Rote Fabrik (s. Wolff 1999). Zurich is also often host to debut films after London or Paris. Lastly, (but not least) there is the annual "Street Parade" - a carnival of techno-music that draws up to one million visitors each year during the second weekend in August.

The Urban Revolt and Resulting Cultural Development

Zurich, however, was not always the exciting and enticing city that it is now. In the 1970s, Zurich was a boring city with little happening. At that time, such venues as dance clubs, jazz bars, and theatre spaces were rare. One might say that Zurich exhibited a sort of "cultural poverty," and this fostered much dissatisfaction among youth. In 1980, the fight for space for alternative culture began in front of Zurich's opera house (see Schmid 1999). The urban revolt, which began with a night-long street fight, grew into a social movement that, in the end, achieved several successes - including Rote Fabrik (Klaus 1999). Between 1982 and 1990 the municipal budget for alternative culture was increased from 1 to 11 million SFr.[2] Political events, concerts, and parties were organized in squatted houses and abandoned industrial sites. Together with the bars and clubs that sprouted up everywhere, the foundations of a vibrant party scene were laid.

It was not only the revolt that helped create an attractive urban setting. In 1991, an economic crisis prevented the growth of the service sector in abandoned industrial areas. This freed up even more temporary space at low cost rents. Warehouse and office spaces were vacant and artists were able to use these spaces cheaply. As a result, their presence in the city multiplied. Free theatres and theatre companies experienced an upturn. Illegal parties were held everywhere. Later in 1998, the liberalization of food catering legislation made it relatively easy to open and manage restaurants and bars.

The urban setting that had slowly grown since 1980 - after the fight for space for alternative culture - was, by and large, built from the bottom up, estabilishing a club, bar, and restaurant scene that would set life style and shopping trends for the 1990s. The subcultural language of signs created itself in Zurich´s urban setting and became an important factor in defining the city's "urban life." The Street Parade (a carnival of techo music) also played an important role in this development, despite the fact that in the beginning it was very controversial and, in 1994, nearly forbidden. It is in this example, too, that one can observe Zurich´s fundamental changes. It is recognised, in general, that the Street Parade has become an important economic factor in Zurich, creating a turnover of about 150 million SFr. each year. Sometimes, in the front pages of Zurich's tourist guide books one can see photos of the masses at the Street Parade, and this is meant to illustrate how colourful and cheerful the city has become. Trend magazines all over the world have begun reporting on Zurich as a hip and trendy city. Nine hundred media items about Zurich as a party city were registered world wide in 1999 alone.[3]

On shopping pages of tourism magazines one can now find, next to the designer shops and high price sectors, the witty and creative shops originated in Zurich's subculture and are today emblematic of the city's cool and trendy image. In an economy of signs these crazy and creative enterprises complement an urban setting that can be marketed and sold. Klein (2000) has described the adaptation of subcultural signs. In the poorer neighbourhoods of New York and other metropoles, "coolness-hunters" track down new fashions and trends in music. These signs are, then, integrated into the marketing strategies of transnational enterprises - which use them in advertising and product labels.

Creative and Innovative Microenterprises

The culturalization of the economy, in combination with the emergence of accessible space, has encouraged many artists to start a business. "I am a product of temporary use!" declared a research interviewee, who was able to establish herself in the design sector - in one of many creative and innovative microenterprises that were founded. Zurich´s graphic art, design and media sectors have experienced a boom that has attracted skilled young workers from all over Switzerland and beyond. A new, upcoming labour force has begun to feed the ever emerging urban setting. Bars and clubs are filled with exotic, exciting people. As a result of this momentum, many successful operations have been launched - many of which have come directly out of the subculture.

Still, as ever, innovative and creative microenterprises lived and produced both in and for the subculture. They turned out products and services that could be demanded by individuals as well as large companies. They designed annual reports for large banks like the Union Bank of Switzerland, produced web sites for industrial companies like Siemens, and polished the fine touches of logos for industries like Rolls Royce. Other microenterprises created extraordinarily styled clothing accessories and furniture that could hardly be afforded by low-income earners. Still other enterprises designed the interiors of trendy bars, managed cool shops, or produced art and entertainment in the form of theatre, film or exhibitions.

The flexibilization of Zurich´s production systems, the culturalization of the economy, and the commodification of culture are shown in the statistics. Between 1995 and 2001, employment in the industry of cultural production increased about 12% - equivalent to about 8% of the entire workforce of 340,000. The employment rate in graphic arts and design as well as film and video production has more than doubled, and the business activity of bars and dance clubs has almost tripled. The sectors of advertising, consultation, and television have grown approximately 25%. The flexibilization of production has manifested itself especially clearly in the culture sector: 36% of all employees in Zurich's cultural industries work in microenterprises that employ 1 to 9 persons, while only 20% of the total workforce are employed by such small businesses.

Cultural Enterprises in Cool City Neighbourhoods

The avant-gardes of these creative and innovative microenterprises have kept their operations in neighbourhoods with a high percentage of low-income earners, more than 40% of whom are immigrants. These specific locations play an important role in an economy of signs, in which the microenterprises and neighbourhood inhabitants continually produce new codes and signs that can be accessed and legitimated by the youth culture. From there the signs flow into the production of goods and services, with the help of "coolness-hunters" or the activities of local creative and innovative microenterprises.

Creative and innovative microenterprises tend to cluster in particular neighbourhoods and even in particular buildings - either old warehouse factories or empty office spaces. For formal and informal co-operation and networking, these buildings are optimal. Microenterprises, as code predecessors, are well networked with one another and know whith what and where they can satisfy their needs. Most of them are well-embedded in their surroundings. Inexpensive overhead, in particular rent for housing and workspaces, is necessary to ensure a microenterprise´s success. Although many of these creative and innovative microenterprises turn up in the high glamour brochures of Zurich's tourist office, or in the design of business reports of large banks, or as national artists with international recognition, their profits remain below average.

The presence of artists and creative enterprises also raises the attractiveness of their neighbourhoods, thereby increasing investments in housing and in local retail and business enterprises. Gentrification has begun. Rents for flats and rooms increase, and as a consequence poorer inhabitants, shop-keepers, and small entrepreneurs are pushed out. Newcomers and visitors that want to enjoy the new leisure facilities breathe a new and different life into the neighbourhoods. Creative and innovative microenterprises experience increasing economic pressure as gentrification progresses. Temporary users of abandoned industrial areas ran under the constant threat of demolition. Through these processes, clusters of creative innovative microenterprises that were alive and kicking dissolve, and social capital is destroyed along with them. As a result, Zurich´s attractive urban setting is also compromised, because the disappearance of innovative microenterprises means that the creative output that helped to create an attractive city in the first place also vanishes. The only enterprises that manage to survive such economic fluctuations are those based on co-operatively organized housing, a form of housing that can resist real-estate speculation.

Conclusion

The transformation of Zurich´s economy and the urban revolt of the 1980s initiated a basic change in the cultural and public life of the city. Free theatre companies, designers, vibrant parties, trendy bars, concerts, and festivals became an integral part of Zurich´s daily life, and as result, Zurich became a captivating and "cool" place to live and work. Worldwide processes of culturalization of the economy and commodification of culture have supported this development.

The fight for free spaces fostered a culture of entrepreneurship. Many creative and innovative microenterprises started in the 1990s. They took advantage of the opportunity to occupy abandoned industrial areas, flourished in central city neighbourhoods, and created and distributed subculture signs and codes. These creative forces in many ways nourished Zurich´s urban setting. The signs created by the creative and innovative microenterprises that were taken up in fashion and design, represented a new urban culture that is widely accepted throughout urban society today. Furthermore, there is still a market for their activities and products. Yet, most of these microenterprises can only afford minimal wages which is characteristic (if not typical) of flexibilized production systems.

The mixing of subculture with the globalized economy has reached a high intensity and is earmarked by creative and innovative microenterprises. Interestingly enough, these enterprises receive little, if any support. Perhaps a policy that protected low rent spaces from speculation would be one way to sustain Zurich's creative potential, as gentrification and the demolition of warehouses put creative and innovative microenterprises under pressure. Many niche products, which exist under the specific requirements of informal networking and low fixed-costs, cannot survive rising rents for work and living spaces. As clusters of creativity dissolve, so does their social capital and know-how, from which transnational and other enterprises profit.

Endnotes

[1] 360,000 inhabitants in the city, 1 million in the whole region.

[2] *Die Wochenzeitung* 13.4.2000

[3] *Neue Zürcher Zeitung* 17.1.2002

References

Beaverstock, J.V., R.G. Smith and P.J. Taylor (1999), "A Roster of World Cities", in: *Cities*, 16(6), 445-458.

Bundesamt für Statistik, *Pressecommuniqué* 13, Soziale Sicherheit, Neuenburg März 2001.

Hall, Peter (2000), "Creative Cities and Economic Development", in: *Urban Studies*, Vol. 4, 639-649

Helbrecht, Ilse (2001), "Postmetropolis: Die Stadt als Sphynx", in: *Geographica Helvetica* 3/2001, 214-222

Klaus, Philipp (1999), "Subculture and Production of Culture in the Logic of Global Urban Development - in the Case of Zurich", in: INURA Zurich (eds.), *Possible Urban Worlds. Urban Strategies at the End of the 20th Century*. Basel, Boston, Berlin: Birkhäuser-Verlag.

Klaus, Ph (1996), "Leisure in Abandoned Industrial Areas: Between Marketing Concept and Self-Help Project", in: *FUTURES*, Vol. 28, no 2, Oxford, March 1996, 189-198

Klein, Naomi (2001), *No Logo! Der Kampf der Global Players um Marktmacht. Ein Spiel mit vielen Verlierern*. München: Riemann-Verlag.

Krätke, Stefan (2002), *Medienstadt: urbane Cluster und globale Zentren der Kulturproduktion*. Opladen: Leske und Budrich.

Lash, Scott, John Urry (1994), *Economies of Signs and Space*. New Delhi: SAGE Publications, Ondon, Thousand Oaks.

Le Galès, Patrick (1999), "Is Political Economy Still Relevant to Study the Culturalization of Cities?", in: *European Urban and Regional Studies*, Vol. E(4), 295-302

McRobbie, Angela (2001), "Arbeitsplatz auf der Kulturbaustelle. Die Kultur als Wegbereiterin der New Economy", in: *Die WochenZeitung* Nr. 46. 15.11.01

Schmid, Christian (1999), "The Dialectics of Urbanisation in Zurich: Global City Formation and Urban Social Movements", in: INURA (eds.), *Possible Urban Worlds. Urban Strategies at the End of the 20th Century*. Basel, Boston, Berlin: Birkhäuser-Verlag.

Scott, Allen (1996), "The craft, fashion, and cultural-products industries of Los Angeles: competitive dynamics and policy dilemmas in a multisectoral image-producing complex", in: *Annals of the Association of American Geographers* Vol. 86 (1996) Nr. 2. 306-323.

Sennett, Richard (1998), *Der flexible Mensch. Die Kultur des neuen Kapitalismus*. Berlin: Berlin-Verlag.

Taylor, Peter J. and D.R.F. Walker (2000), "World Cities: A First Multivariate Analysis of their Service Complexes", in: *Urban Studies*. Vol. 38.

Wolff, Richard (1999), "A Star is Born - Rote Fabrik Cultural Centre", in: INURA Zurich (eds.), *Possible Urban Worlds. Urban Strategies at the End of the 20th Century*. Basel, Boston, Berlin: Birkhäuser-Verlag .

Zukin, Sharon (1995), *The cultures of cities*, Cambridge (MA): Blackwell.

TEXT....................Andreas Wirz
TRANSLATION....................Maik Lindemann
PHOTOS ....Andreas Wirz, Reinhard Zimmermann and Sabina Altermatt

KraftWerk1 More than Just Nice Living

In the boom quarter of Zürich West [1], surrounded by faceless office buildings, a colourful and vivid oasis has been created. The housing development KraftWerk1, whose name was chosen in reference to the former industrial area [2] of this neighbourhood, is located next to a colossal aluminium-cased office building. Three shiny orange five-story houses were built around a nine-story and 150m long dark brick apartment building. However, what is particular is not the building's appearance, but its interior. 350 people live there in different groupings. Because of its wide range of apartment sizes (between 2 and 14 rooms) the housing complex offers space for all kinds of living arrangements. There is, for example, one household with 12 people: two couples, one of them with a child, a single mother with one child, and five other adults, either single or not living with their partner. Another household is home to eight adults (among them three couples) and one child. The child lives there only half the week; a boyfriend of one of the residents also lives in the building in his own apartment, and a girl-friend of another inhabitant is in a shared living situation in another housing project. There are also single-person households. One mother, for example, lives alone, and has a grown up daughter who shares an apartment with her boyfriend. There are other living arrangements as well: small families, singles, etc.

3.5 Zimmer Wohnung
KraftWerk1

KraftWerk 1
PROJEKT FÜR DAS SULZER-ESCHER WYSS ARE
Kraftwerk
c/o P
Hohlstrasse 8
8004 Züri

One of the three five-story buildings stands along a highly frequented street and provides space only for offices and businesses. About 100 people are employed there. On the ground floor, there is a hairdresser, a flower shop (which also sells fruits and vegetables), and a restaurant, which also serves as a meeting-point for the residents of KraftWerkl and the surrounding neighbourhood. The remaining floors are rented to other firms, such as a fund-raising organization, social services, book editors, and photographers. There are also three shared office spaces for graphic design, architecture, planning, communication, and internet design.[3]

Industrial Areas for Alternative Living-Design

How did such a lively project develop in a neighbourhood, which was known only as an ideal location for back-offices of banks, telecommunication firms, or for a soccer stadium?

In 1993, with the clearing of the Wohlgroth premises next to the main station, the squat movement came to an end. One reason for this development was that the real estate market slackened, as the economic recession led to a decline in the demand for office space. For the first time in Switzerland, there were banners on office-buildings with the words “Offices to rent”. Not surprisingly, many landlords did not know what to do with the empty industrial areas.

As an answer to this, in 1993 a book entitled, “KraftWerk1 - Ideas for the Sulzer Escher Wyss-Areal” was published and became well known in the left wing scene [4]. The central idea was to use the empty industrial areas as a chance to realize alternative living forms that fostered social and environmental awareness, equality, and justice. These ideas attracted individuals from rural communes built in the 1970s, who had also believed in these concepts. New, however, were the size and location - 700 people would be housed in an urban space. KraftWerk1 was not understood simply as an opportunity to build a pleasant community. It also represented a systematic approach towards a better world at the local level. The “1” in the KraftWerk1 emphasized its confidence, and that more projects should follow.

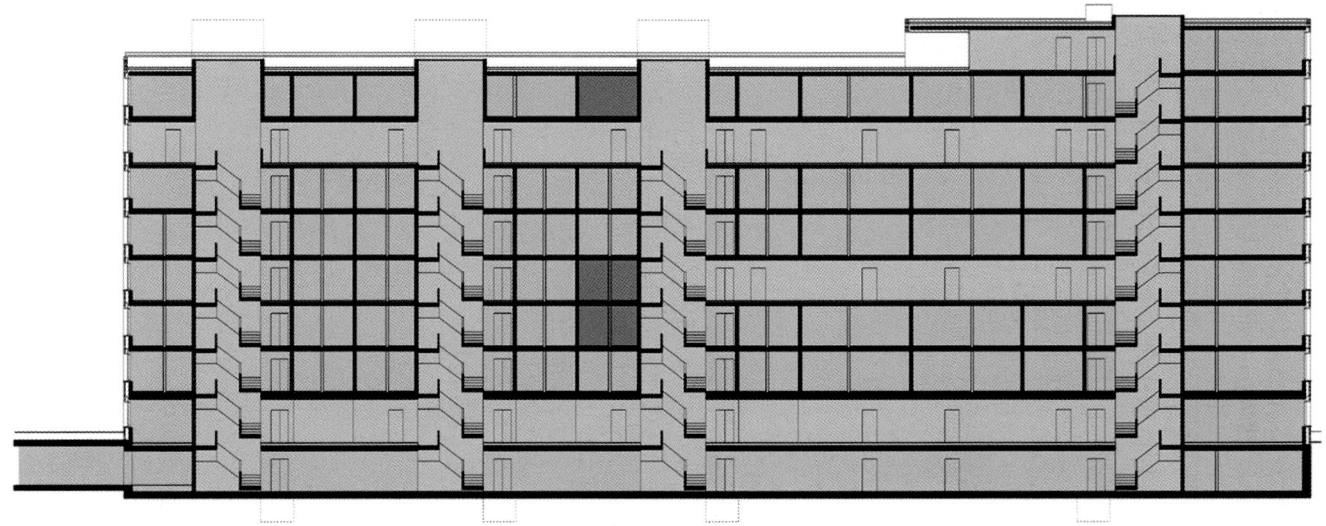

"main house: longitudinal section"

Dream and Count - a Long and Stony Path

Interest in the project grew quickly and the Association of KraftWerk1 was founded. Different working groups were formed to discuss public relations, architecture, ecology and the environment, living styles, and co-operation. To put the project on its feet, two series of events were organised, called "KraftWerk Summer" (*KraftWerkSommer*). In 1994, the first took place in the Schoeller premises [5], together with an extensive cultural program. In 1995, the second one was organized in the "Shedhalle" of the Rote Fabrik,[6] in the form of a "Sofa University" ("*Sofa-Universität*"), during which the focus was on specific project topics. Discussions circled around social infrastructures, optimal uses of consumer goods and services, environmental sunstainable means of food supply and distribution, integration of flexible working conditions, building economic networks among residents, and at the end, as a summary and as a declaration of minimal consensus, the Charter (*Charta*).[7] The discussions took place in a 1:1 model of a possible large-size apartment, which itself was part of the accompanying exhibition.[8] These events resulted in the creation of many pragmatic ideas to be carried out in the planned project. They also showed clearly that the dreaming phase was over, and that calculating had begun.[9] As a first important step, the housing co-operative KraftWerk1 was founded, thus instituting KraftWerk1 into a legal framework. For this, the century-old model of co-op housing was chosen.[10]

The next steps were to find an appropriate site, to create a financing concept, and to hold many meetings in which all interested parties could be kept informed of the progress being made. In this professional phase, there were only a few opportunities for participation, and since much of the work was necessarily shifted to members of the co-op´s board of directors, it was very important, in this phase, to keep all developments transparent and all parties informed. To sustain communication and the co-operative decision-making process, general assemblies were held. Here progress in development could be reported and important decisions could be ratified.

In mid-1998, two pieces of land of the same size were presented to the general meeting of the housing co-operative. Both were located in Zürich West on former industrial sites and both were suitable for the realisation of the project.[11] However, KraftWerk1 still had financial difficulties that created obstacles for the development of the project, as potential inhabitants were reluctant to invest before they could judge the project. This financial problem could only be solved with help from outside. As it was, developer Allreal agreed to finance the project in advance. This led to the decision to build the project on the Hardturm West site.

In December of 1998 the planning application was submitted, and in the summer of 1999 the construction of four buildings began. At the same time, the housing co-op began renting out units. The buildings themselves were designed to respond to flexible and ever-changing living styles. As a result, no two units were built alike. This variety continues to make the project adaptable to changing trends in lifestyles.

From Utopia to Reality

In summer 2001 a new phase began. Inhabitants moved in. The theoretical models were now confronted with reality. From this moment on, inhabitants could engage themselves and give further impetus to the project. Through general meetings and member committees, possible models of organisation were established. Actions could then be delegated and carried through by the members.

KraftWerk1, however, is not a new invention. New was the goal of integrating all spheres of living into a concept of social, ecological and economical sustainability. In KraftWerk1 this resulted in many different projects. There are, for example, two cooking-clubs ("*Circolo*" and "*Circolino*"), with 50 and 20 participants respectively. They both operate the same way: every week a meal is prepared, and the participants rotate the cooking. For the members of Circolo, this means that each participant has to cook once a year for 50 people, and for the rest of the year he/she can enjoy the meals cooked by someone else. The one who cooks also pays - this avoids difficult accounting. There is also the *Pantoffelbar*, a bar operated by volunteers that serves as a meeting-place. It is a self-service venue, where money is paid into the cash box. The Child Commission stands for a child-friendly outdoor environment, and organises afternoon events for children. Government funds provide a kindergarten and a day-care center. A Landscaping Committee organizes care-taking of the plants, the infrastructure around the building, and the common use of the roof terrace. To preserve a clean environment three car-sharing automobiles are available in the underground garage.[12] The use of a car is generally limited to necessary trips. Further environmental action is pursued by the Ecology Committee. At regularly scheduled "Eco-bars" ("*Ökobars*"), critical environmental issues are discussed. The group also seeks ways to reduce the project's impact on the environment - for example by seeking ways to reduce the demand on water or electric energy. All of the projects at KraftWerk1 are funded by special "infrastructure funds" that are maintained by all inhabitants. The contributions are in relation to personal incomes.

KraftWerk1: an Instrument Towards Change in Society?

Many of the initial ideas have been realized. Some have also failed. The aim of having a wide social mixture, for example, was not and could not be fully reached, even though, every resident of KraftWerk1 with an income is required to pay a “solidarity contribution” (*Solidaritätsbeitrag*) [13], which gives KraftWerk1 the possibility of offering a 20% rent reduction to 10% of the tenants. This reduction, however, is still not enough for people who must or want to live with extremely low incomes. In addition, despite the fact that the dwellings were built at a cost that was 20% below average, they remained too expensive for low income individuals/families. The average rent, including monthly utilities, amounts to approximately 600 SFr per person. Older and subsidized houses cost half as much in Zürich.

KraftWerk1 aimed to create employment alternatives that would not be dependent on wider economic business cycles. Today, KraftWerk1 offers in-house employment to individuals to look after daily maintenance and administration. Four individuals are employed approximately 15 hours per week - a volume of employment that would be created by any conventional housing development of this size. In addition, some people at KraftWerk1 practice an alternative, non-monetary economic system (LETS). However, many of the residents earn a steady income and therefore do not find the barter system useful. In fact, one may ask if the barter system inhibits voluntary neighbourly relations.

Another aim of KraftWerk1 was to improve relations between city and countryside. There was the idea, for example, to exchange work for food, whereby people from the city would work on the farms in exchange for produce. Another idea was to spend vacation time on farms as an opportunity for education and communication. These ideas have not yet become a reality.

KraftWerk1 cannot be seen as a microcosm for the renewal of society, which is what, at least in part, the original founders had hoped. KraftWerk1 is not a squatted house, which sees itself as part of a political struggle. In fact, and on the contrary, KraftWerk1 is strongly occupied with itself. The board of directors manages the property, and the inhabitants partecipate in committees that deal with various aspects of the project. Nevertheless, KraftWerk1 is a community where members can enjoy a better life through social exchanges in a shared common infrastructure, a community that is ready and willing to redistribute its wealth to those with less money.

shared office space for graphic design

KraftWerk1 Strengthens the Neighbourhood

At present, political engagement is limited to the neighbourhood. The construction of a new stadium that will house three games of the European Soccer Championship, to be held in 2008 in Switzerland and Austria, is planned in KraftWerk1´s immediate vicinity. Since the City of Zurich did not want to be financially involved, the development of the project was given to a private investor [14], who, as *quasi* compensation, was also allowed to build other profitable projects in the stadium-building, such as a shopping centre. Residents of the neighbourhood are now afraid that the already highly congested neighbourhood will become even more so as these projects generate more traffic. Therefore, residents are lobbying for more housing, which creates less traffic than service and shopping uses. Because KraftWerk1 attracts politically motivated and politically active people, the inhabitants of KraftWerk1 are very actively involved in their neighbourhood. They play an important role, too, in this specific conflict by using the media and initiating a political movement - something that the longer standing residents of the neighbourhood (outside of KraftWerk1) may not easily have been able to do. In a neighbourhood which is infrastructurally underdeveloped and already burdened by excess traffic, a project like KraftWerk1 can make a significant contribution towards the improvement of the area because it can identify with the other inhabitants and share with them the same concerns regarding neighbourhood development. By working together, both residents of KraftWerk1 and residents from outside can profit from improvements in their neighbourhood.

flat with 11.5 rooms: living room

KraftWerk1 was and remains one possible way among many others. It is definitely not a place that will change society as a whole, but it has proven to be a model for neighbourhood renewal and sustainable development. For this reason, we can work confidently towards KraftWerk2, and continue working towards KraftWerkX. At the same time, however, we should not forget to think beyond the boundaries of neighbourhood, and not ignore the world around us.

The project is documented on the internet at http://www.kraftwerk1.ch.

Endnotes

[1] In this chapter, see also Christian Schmid.

[2] In Zürich West, the company Sulzer Escher Wyss had produced 16,000 turbines for power plants all over the world between 1844 and 1994. (trans. note: Kraftwerk means powerplant.)

[3] The INURA common office and the INURA Zurich Institute are also part of one office at KraftWerk1

[4] P.M., Blum, Hofer 1993: KraftWerk1: Projekt für das Sulzer Escher Wyss-Areal. Paranoia City Verlag, Zürich.

[5] Schoeller was an industry that specialised in dyeing yarns. After giving up business in 1988, the premises on the Limmat in Zürich West were used for various interim uses like theatre projects and small businesses. In 1997, the former factory buildings were torn down and the 340-unit housing project Limmat West was built. The first phase began in 1999 and the second in 2002.

[6] The Rote Fabrik was formerly a silk weaving factory. As of 1972, this land has belonged to the public. In 1980, it was turned into a culture centre, first partly illegal, and then provisional. After a plebiscite in 1987, the cultural activities received public subsidies. See also R. Wolff, "A Star is born - Rote Fabrik Cultural Centre". In: INURA: Possible Urban Worlds. Birkhäuser, Basel 1998, p. 226-231.

[7] Excerpts of the Charta:
"We can imagine to ...
... create a living space for some hundred people by ourselves
... combine privacy and community living
... accept and be generous to difference in the name of supporting and encouraging diversity
... handle contradictions in a creative way
... build affordable, but ecologically and architecturally sensible houses
... move without cars, but not marginalize those who require them
... combine a multifaceted and intensive urban lifestyle while at the same time having respect for those who are disadvantaged
... develop new forms of collective solidarity in times of a shrinking labour market and social insecurity
... keep our uniqueness, but remain open to the wider neighbourhood and the city.

[8] Illustrations: see also INURA-Zurich (1999), *Possible Urban Worlds: Urban Strategies at the End of the 20th Century.* Birkhäuser; p. 52-59.

[9] "Dream and Count" was a book that has not been published by Andreas Hofer and Andreas Wirz. It was intended to summarize the results of the KraftWerk1 Summers of 1994 and 1995. The publication was deferred several times because all time and energy had been put towards the search for a piece of land. Later, publication was replaced by the intention of publishing a book after the realisation of the project - a book that would evaluate the entire process. This book is still in progress.

[10] Housing co-operatives have a long tradition in Zürich. They were originally associated with the working class movement. Today, 19% of all housing in Zürich belongs to housing co-operatives (35,800 flats).

[11] The potential risks and benefits of both the Sulzer Escher Wyss site and the Hardturm West site were evaluated.

[12] A contract was made with a Car-sharing co-operative Mobility - a company that has 1700 cars all over Switzerland - that gave the members of KraftWerk1 special conditions (http://www.mobility.ch).

[13] As a newly founded co-operative, KraftWerk1 also depended on capital input from the tenants. Today one must buy a share of SFr 15,000 per 35m2 unit, for which one receives interest. To avoid the exclusion of individuals without capital, the amount of capital required can be reduced. For this purpose, internal funds were established. These funds for share payments today amount to SFr 750,000. As with the solidarity contribution, an external commission determines their distribution.

[14] Credit Suisse, which has already funded similar stadiums in Basel and Genf, is responsible for the development of the stadium. The City of Zürich participates by providing real estate valued at approximately SFr 37 millions.

restaurant "Brasserie Bernoulli" — hair dresser — "laundrette"

TEXT........Richard Wolff
TRANSLATION........Richard Wolff, Chris Lüthi, Geraint Ellis and Michael Edwards

The Rise and Fall of Great Railway Station Redevelopments The Case of Eurogate / HB Südwest

Eurogate was Switzerland's largest-ever real estate project. For more than 30 years, it was the focus of Zurich's development process. It symbolised the city's ambition to become a truly international metropolis and was bitterly opposed. This chapter will analyze the political struggle, which involved a generation of politicians, architects, investors, bankers and local activists. Special emphasis will be put on the final stage of this 'high-noon'-like story, which surprised everybody, even those involved. What really happened? What were the expectations of the various agents? What does this controversy mean for Zurich's further development? Are there general conclusions to be drawn for the analysis of global city competition?

Railway Lands for City Expansion

Throughout much of Europe, inner cities continue to be contested terrains of urban development. Whereas part of the demand for strategic city centre locations can be diverted to the edges and suburbs, there remains great pressure on the city cores. This is reflected in high rent levels and soaring land prices, which decline only in relatively short and sporadic economic downturns. The continuing high demand has led to a number of different approaches for a more intense use of inner city space, one of them being the redevelopment of railway lands.

Developers and city planners often look at railway lands as some of the last development sites in the inner city. They offer a number of advantages and inspire imagination. They are centrally located with excellent public transport access. On these sites the interests of both the real estate industry and politicians meet those of railway companies, which in many countries are under pressure to make better use of their land assets. In short, railway station redevelopments often appear to be an attractive option for inner city expansion.

In various European cities, similar plans have been designed to cash in on these 'underused' sites. In almost every case the proposed railway station developments have aroused fierce controversies about their social, environmental and economic impact on the city and the neighbourhood. Some projects have been realised, like Euralille in Lille, the Utrecht Centrum Project, Gare du Midi in Brussels, Stockholm City West, or Montparnasse in Paris (Bertolini / Spit 1998). Others, like King's Cross in London, have been heavily contested and are still not built. The reasons for success or failure depend on a variety of factors, from the global economic sphere to very local and personal relations. The analysis of Zurich's Eurogate scheme, formerly known as HB-Südwest or Main Station Southwest, will illuminate the driving forces as well as the obstacles that influence the development path of this kind of mega-project.

The 1960s: Dreams of Growth without Limits, the 'Grand Scheme'

The 1960s were a time of unprecedented economic prosperity for Switzerland and Zurich in particular. After the Second World War, a largely intact industrial base, an efficient service sector, and a stable political system gave Switzerland a substantial lead over most competitors. Although Zurich became one of the world's most important financial centres, its political and economic leaders had even higher ambitions for their 'little big city' [1]. In the words of the president of Zurich's most influential business lobby group, the City Vereinigung, it was an issue of Zurich becoming "either a provincial town or a European metropolis" and he added: "The historic mission of my generation is to deliver the infrastructure for the next century" (Blanc / Ganz 1986). With a series of large-scale urban projects, the city was to be launched into a new era.

Decisions taken by the Swiss government fully supported this 'grand scheme'. Zurich became the site for Switzerland's main international airport and the centre of the national motorway system, which provided the city with a dense network of innercity highways. Both of these infrastrucural prerequisites for metropolitan growth were heavily subsidized by federal tax money. On the regional and local level, the 'grand scheme' was complemented by plans for a metropolitan underground railway, which was to connect the airport, city centre and future central business district extensions. To celebrate its coming of age as an international metropolis, Zurich planned to host the Winter Olympics of 1976. It was hoped that this world event would also serve as catalyst for the rapid transformation of the city.

In order to translate this massive infrastructural boost into economic growth, office space had to be increased drastically. The expansion of the central business district was crucial, but was blocked by an already tightly built-up city centre as well as by strict building regulations. Long before deindustrialization would open up new brownfield areas at the urban fringe, viable construction sites were practically non-existent. The only available space was above waterways and railway lands. Therefore, it was proposed that the Sihl River and the railway tracks be decked over with a combined motorway and linear city office development. The centrepiece of this masterplan was the redevelopment of the main railway station. This grand idea, launched in 1965, was to; a) provide Zurich with a new and modern railway station; b) solve the problem of connecting the inner city motorways; c) produce an ample supply of additional office space. HB-Südwest was to become the flagship project of metropolitan Zurich.

6 Models of HB Südwest / Eurogate from 1969 to 2000

b c

a

a) Model of HB-Südwest project by Ziegler. First prize in first competion of 1969/70. Total demolition of old main station and new high-rise buidlings.
Source: SBB: Bahnhofzytig HB Südwest, 1985
b) Model of HB-Südwest project by Baenziger-Bersin-Schilling. First prize in third competition 1980. The old station remains untouched. No more high-rise buidings.
Source: Rudolf Schilling: 'Ideen für Zürich', 1982
c) Model of 'inflated' HB-Südwest project proposed for the second referendum in 1988.
Source: RBAG Doku 16.11.1994
d) Model of 'improved' HB-Südwest project recommended by 'board of advisors' in 1990
Source: RBAG, Photo by Monika Bischof
e) Model of 'revised' Eurogate project submitted for planning permission in 1996.
Source: RBAG Doku 1996
f) Model of the 'best' Eurogate project, which was almost built after 1999. View from south
Source: RBAG

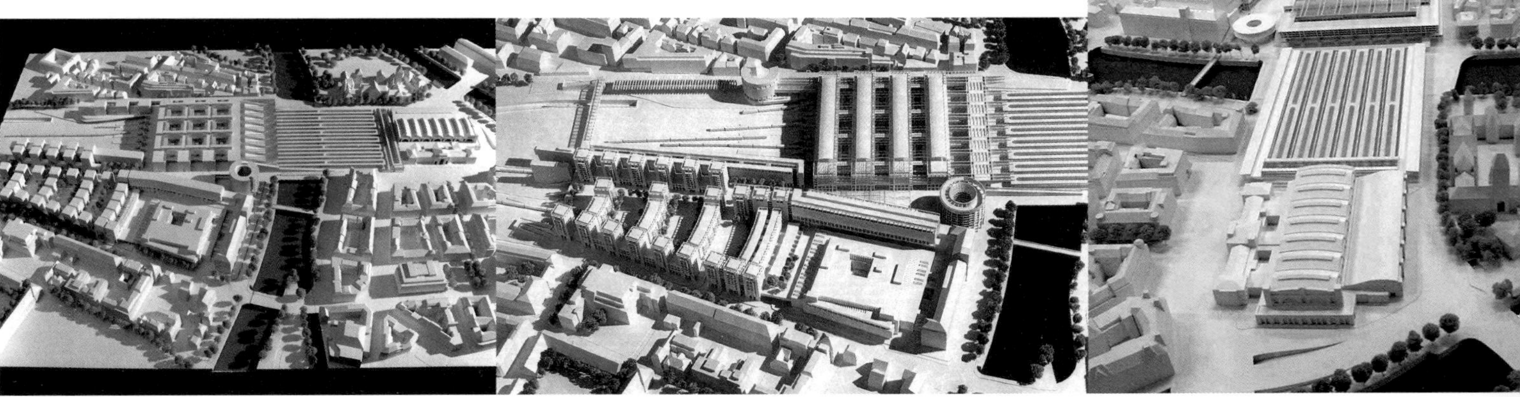

d e f

First Attempt 1969 - 1973: The Radical Project Versus the People

In 1969, an alliance of public and semi-public institutions consisting of Swiss Federal Railways, the Canton of Zurich, the City of Zurich, and the Federal Post launched a competition for a multipurpose main station development. The original idea was to enlarge the station at the cost of private investors who, in turn, would be allowed to develop the land above the rails with huge office blocks. Besides a new station, Swiss Railways hoped to receive a rent of several million francs a year.

The competition was won by the architect Ziegler, who - in a spirit of unclouded optimism - proposed a new station with 400,000 m2 commercial floor space, a 43-floors hotel skyscraper, 40 flats and 4,000 parking lots. The proposal was not well received by the public, which - over the past years - had become increasingly worried about large scale projects. People feared the impact of a 25-year construction site, rising taxes because of cost overruns (beyond the estimated Sfr 1.5 billion), as well as increasing traffic and pollution. Because HB-Südwest would extend the scope of the traditional central business district around Bahnhofstrasse into the inner-city neighbourhoods 'Kreis 4' and 'Kreis 5', it was in these working class areas where the sharpest critique was voiced, warning about detrimental effects like rising rents, gentrification and a general decrease in the quality of life.

These widespread concerns about the proposed urban development became manifest in a referendum in 1969, when the Olympics were rejected by 78% of the voters and, in 1973, when the proposal for a combined underground and metropolitan railway was turned down. Campaigns to stop the completion of the inner-city motorway were yet another expression of this anti-growth attitude of the early 70s (Blanc 1993). This political sea-change, along with the global economic recession which hit Switzerland in 1973 and the fact that the historic main railway station building was listed for preservation in 1972, brought further planning for HB-Südwest to its first halt.

Second Attempt 1978 - 1992: The Improved Project Versus the Government

In 1978 a new architectural competition was launched with guidelines that took into account the changed political-economic situation as well as the now listed old station building. The new project was considerably smaller. Floor space was reduced to 120,000 m2, with 70 flats, and 1,350 parking lots. However, the winning architects, Baenziger-Bersin-Schilling, suggested additional uses, including a new commuter station, a pedestrian passage across the sixteen railway tracks with a shopping mall, a hall for public events, a hotel, a town square and another 310 flats.

While the project was being adapted and revised time and again, the sudden outburst of the 'movement of 1980' [2] brought street rioting and some of the most violent confrontations the city had ever seen. Predominantly young protesters demanded 'the right to the city' (Henri Lefebvre) and the 'fulfilment of the urban promise (Rudolf Luscher), i.e. more freedom and spaces of expression, as well as a fairer share of cultural subsidies. The city as 'space of the everyday' became a focus of this cultural and political movement, adding new strength to the critique against growth-oriented urban development in Zurich.

'Growth above everything? HB-Südwest No'
Advertisement for second referendum in 1988.
(Source: FabrikZeitung 45 / Sept. 1988 special section for 'Città Frontale')

The consortium of developers that was established in 1981, HB City Immobilien AG, mainly banks and large contractors, were confronted with a heavy headwind right from the start. This was enforced to gale strength in 1983, when a citizens' association collected 4,000 signatures for their people's initiative "HB Südwest - So Nicht!" (Main Station Southwest - Not like this!). They demanded that the project be reduced by half, which would have made it economically totally unattractive. Even though this request was clearly rejected in September 1985 by 70% of the voters, the promoters of HB-Südwest did not proceed speedily. Instead, trying to capitalize on the favourable outcome of the vote, and to fulfil Swiss Railways' desires for more space, the project was enlarged again by 50%.
In their somewhat naïve optimism they had not reckoned with the sturdy obstructionism of Ursula Koch, the new head of the City Council's building department. Obtaining planning permission from this outspoken opponent of the project would prove to be a long and difficult matter. By proposing another referendum on a revised area development plan, promoters hoped to sideline opponents of this 'inflated' project and to speed up planning permission. They invested more than a million Swiss francs into a PR campaign that aimed to win public approval for the 'real estate development of the century'. Even though the opposition forces had only very limited resources to fight the 'Folly above the rails' (Snozzi 1987), they lost only by a nose-length. In September 1988, 50.7% voted in favour of the promoter's area development plan.

After this narrow victory, the developer's consortium was looking for wider public acceptance, and therefore installed a so-called 'board of advisors', aimed at helping the architects to reconsider the project in the light of the massive critique that had come from concerned citizens, professionals and politicians. It was mainly the lack of architectural quality and the the sense of overdevelopment that were criticized [3]. Baenziger-Bersin produced new plans with lower buildings and a further reduced floor space. This 'improved' project was rather favourably received by the media, public opinion and the city administration. In the summer of 1990, everything seemed to be in place for a successful progression of HB-Südwest. Instead of asking for planning permission, the promoters could not agree on how to proceed. When they demanded that other architects be included in the planning process, the leading architect, Ralph Baenziger, refused to accept the challenge to his authority and was then dismissed outright in May 1991.

As everybody knew, Baenziger was the key to the project. For almost 20 years, he had been the one who had kept the project going through all the vagaries of changing governments, quareling promoters, uncertain investors, and contested referendums. He was the only one who had been involved with the project since the beginning. Sacking the architect was like cutting the heart out of the project. There was no way of getting around him, and he had made it clear that he would defend his copyright on HB-Südwest all the way through the courts. The promoters had manoeuvred themselves into a dead end. The 1991 collapse of the real estate market and the following economic recession were the final blow for HB-Südwest. At the time there were about 1 million m2 of vacant office space in the Zurich region. In 1992, when the developer's consortium refused to invest more money, it folded, and HB-Südwest was officially buried.

DIENSTLEISTUNGSZENTRUM...

Cross-section of station building above tracks. Artist's impression of HB-Südwest in 1988. (Source: Interessengemeinschaft HB-Südwest: 'Zürcher Geleiseüberbauung HB-Südwest', 1988)

Third Attempt 1996 - 1999: The Revised Project versus the Ecologists

Baenziger refused to accept its death and continued acting behind the scenes, trying to save his lifetime project. The architect-cum-promoter finally succeeded in convincing a newly set-up group of investors to revive the developer's consortium 'HB-Südwest' with the aim of re-launching the old project under the fashionable label 'Eurogate'. The signs of the time seemed favourable. The long recession was coming to an end, and the main objector in the administration, Ursula Koch, had lost her support in local government in the elections of 1994, so a 'revised' project was presented in 1996.

In May 1997, and against Koch's vote, planning permission was granted - for the first time in the history of HB-Südwest / Eurogate. However, as head of the City Council's building department, Koch attached a long list of more than 200 conditions to the planning permission. Some of them had the potential of killing the project. The demands to diminish floor space by 13% and to reduce the number of parking lots from 1250 to 643 undermined the project's profitability. The promoters therefore challenged the most threatening conditions in court. When their appeal was approved in April 1998 at first instance by the Canton of Zurich, both the City of Zurich and the ecological transport association VCS (Verkehrsclub der Schweiz) demanded a legal re-evaluation, spawning a long and tiresome lawsuit. In the meantime, the general prospects for Eurogate had become brighter still when, in the elections of 1998, a worn out Ursula Koch was replaced by Elmar Ledergerber as head of the building department. Although he was a Social-Democrat like Koch, Ledergerber had a 'New-Labour' view on economic policy and was an open supporter of Eurogate. From the promoters' standpoint he was sure to be a reliable partner in upcoming negotiations on unresolved planning matters.

Just like their predecessors, the new group of promoters failed to take advantage of a favourable situation. Instead, they grew increasingly tired of endless legal quarrels, which were nibbling away at their - expected - profits, at a time when a booming stock market was offering easy money. Thus, in 1999, the investors announced their withdrawal and dealt another 'final blow' for Eurogate. Generations of opponents rejoiced.

Fourth Attempt 1999 - April 30th 2001: The Best Project versus the Market

Too early though, as in November 1999, as a total surprise, three of Switzerland's biggest contractors [4] along with the world's third largest bank, UBS, as lead investor, formed a new consortium. This was the most powerful of all the alliances that had ever attempted to realize the mega-project. When they declared their commitment to pick up the pieces and implement Eurogate, it looked like the fourth attempt would finally be the successful one, especially as the political and economic conditions seemed so advantageous. The prospering economy had led to a severe shortage of office space. Political support for the development of the railway lands was now broader than ever, with opposing voices having practically disappeared. Therefore, in July 2000, the City of Zurich granted planning permission for a 1.5 billion Sfr project with 250,000 m2 for 5,000 jobs and 500 flats. Despite the pending law suit regarding the number of parking lots, the local administration conceded 891 parking lots against the officially still valid number of 643. As could be expected, VCS immediately filed a complaint against this unlawful decision.

Meanwhile, time was quickly running out. Swiss Railways, as landowners, had set a deadline for April 30th, 2001 to sign the contract with the developers. Major infrastructural upgradings of Zurich's main station and a new subterranean station that would have to be coordinated with Eurogate could not be further postponed. Despite this tight schedule, promoters were in no hurry and even suspended negotiations with VCS to resolve the car parking issue unilaterally. Instead they seemed to trust the growing political pressure that was exerted on VCS by local government and the media. Behind the scenes there were also some dubious attempts of arm twisting. Rumours about large sums of money being offered in return for a withdrawal of the complaint were never confirmed, but it is a fact that VCS representatives were approached by government representatives, developers and the architect asking them to renounce their resistance. On April 6, 2001, the cantonal administrative court reaffirmed the position of VCS and the validity of 643 parking lots.

After this verdict, everybody expected concessions from the developers or a gentlemen's agreement with VCS, but time elapsed with no shift in positions. Without any further negotiations with VCS, UBS Bank had invited Swiss Railways executives to sign the contract on the very last day of the deadline. Only on this day did they seem to remember the unresolved parking issue. At 9.21 in the morning, a few hours before the scheduled meeting with Swiss Railways, UBS sent a fax to the local VCS representatives demanding their unconditional surrender on the parking-lot front by 10.00 a.m. Unsurprisingly, VCS did not give in. After years of dedicating time and energy to resistance there was no reason to relinquish their position unilaterally. As a next step, UBS turned to the VCS national head office in Berne asking at least for some concessions.

Because they were waiting for a reply from VCS, the bankers arrived half an hour late to the arranged 2 p.m. meeting with Swiss Railway officials. The bankers' request to postpone the signing of the contract for another few days was not well received by the already annoyed Railways representatives, who demanded that the contract be signed that very day. At 15.15 they left the meeting, only 15 minutes before VCS faxed a statement which would have given UBS representatives the opportunity to go ahead. In this statement VCS agreed to compromise on minor issues, in order not to be branded as a total denier. They did not, however, give up on their main point regarding the number of parking lots. This compromise was intended to serve as a face-saving tactic for both sides.

Swiss Railways refused even to consider another meeting. For them, the time window was definitely closed. They argued that their other infrastructural projects in Zurich's main station permitted no more delays. What followed was a bizarre soap opera of mutual recrimination. UBS first made VCS responsible for the 'failure of the century' and then accused Swiss Railways for lacking flexibility, before denouncing their greediness. The Railways explained their rigidity on deadlines with technical and organizational requirements. What they did not say was that their enthusiasm for HB-Südwest / Eurogate had already slowly been eroded over the years. With every new project the developers proposed they had seen their share of the profits melt away. The thought of no revenue in exchange for unforeseeable problems of coordinating Eurogate with the necessary improvement of the tracks and the construction of the new subterranean station was becoming a nightmare. One may, therefore, assume that a heavy burden was taken off the shoulders of Swiss Railways executives when they were given a chance to walk out of the meeting. UBS, on the other hand, eventually admitted that their doubts about the profitability of Eurogate contributed to their somewhat reluctant behaviour.

All in all, it looks as though VCS' obstruction came in handy for both UBS and Swiss Railways. One could even be led to believe that UBS purposely provoked VCS in order to find an 'elegant' way out of an impossible situation. Had they not promised to do everything to get Eurogate going? Had they not postponed their promised declaration to finance the project several times? And why did Swiss Railways not show more flexiblity? It is simply unimaginable, that one signature by VCS, 15 minutes, and a few hundred parking lots should have decided the fate of Eurogate and a 1.5 billion Sfr. investment after 30 years of planning.
HB-Südwest / Eurogate died another death, possibly the last one. Swiss Railways have gone ahead with re-aligning the tracks in the station area and for at least another ten years there will be no technical opportunity for building above railway lands in Zurich's main station. This does not mean that there will be no further attempts to take advantage of this exclusive location. However, theory and practice of urban development have changed over the last 30 years and render a different framework for any type of future development on this site. If there will ever be a fifth attempt, it will surely be approached and conducted in a very different manner. The lessons learnt in three decades of fruitless planning, wasted energies and political shambles will hopefully guide future generations along a more prudent and thoughtful path.

Conclusion - Considering the Multiple Errors, Traps and Shortcomings of 32 Years of Wasteful Planning

There are different ways to explain the failure of the HB-Südwest / Eurogate megaproject(s). First of all, the reason that HB-Südwest / Eurogate became such a heavily contested public affair was the sheer scale of proposed development and its location in the middle of a densely built-up city centre. The arguments for and against Eurogate were equally convincing. Supporters praised its positive impact on the economy, the supply of much needed office space in a prime location in the city centre and ten minutes from an international airport, its excellent accessibility by public transport and hence its ecological quality, and its role as a flagship in global city competition. Opponents denounced the damage the building across the rails would have on the fragile urban landscape, its adverse ecological impact, and its devastating effect on adjacent working class areas. For both political camps HB-Südwest / Eurogate became a symbolic issue of urban development, where proxy wars were fought out.

Over the years and decades, the composition of the camps changed. The crucial role in this game of alliances was played by the City of Zurich. After its initial support, until the early 70s, the 'limits to growth' argument prevailed and the City of Zurich turned from a reluctant supporter to a rather overt opponent. For many years, it was Ursula Koch's unambiguous rejection, supported by an important section of the public, that slowed the planning process. Only after the neo-liberal shift of 1994 did the City change its position, ultimately becoming a fervent supporter. Unaffected by the City's stance, a broad and ever-changing coalition of opponents kept up the struggle. Neighbourhood initiatives, critical planners and architects, leftist and green parties, and the ecological transport association VCS took turns in orchestrating popular resistance. Considering their very limited resources, the impact of this coalition was enormous.

This disproportionate influence of green, leftist, and grassroot politics is partly due to the Swiss regulatory framework. On the one hand there are quite elaborate participatory rights in the planning process. Two referendums, even though both of them lost, slowed down the planning process and caused considerable (and decisive) delays. Much momentum on the developer's side was lost, capital lay idle, plans grew old, the economic and political situation changed. Under direct democracy, where almost every major issue has to pass a referendum, public opinion can become a powerful regulator of exaggerated ambitions.

On the other hand, the regulatory framework contains relatively strong environmental legislation. The clean-air act (Luftreinhalteverordnung) was instrumental in controlling the development process. This rather strict law gave VCS, as a nation-wide environmental organization, the legal opportunity to challenge the number of parking lots. Whereas developers were fighting for more parking space in order to attract more customers to the shopping mall integrated into HB-Südwest / Eurogate, VCS argued that more parking would cause more traffic in an already highly polluted area. Consequently what looked like a side issue suddenly became crucial.

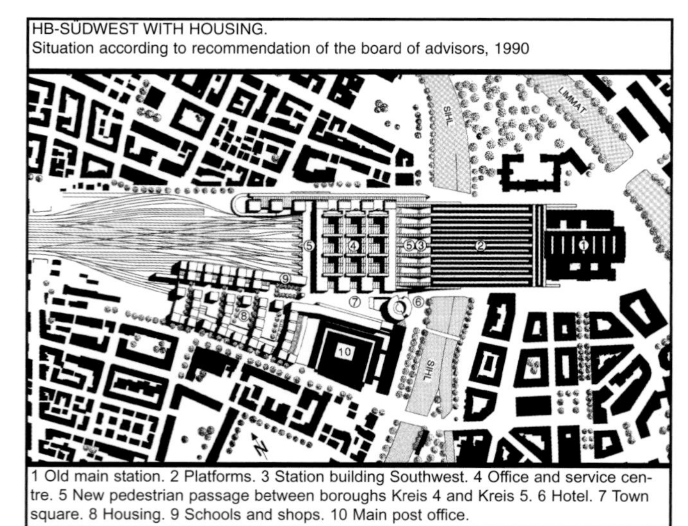

Plan of 'improved' HB-Südwest project recommended by 'board of advisors' in 1990 (Source: RBAG)

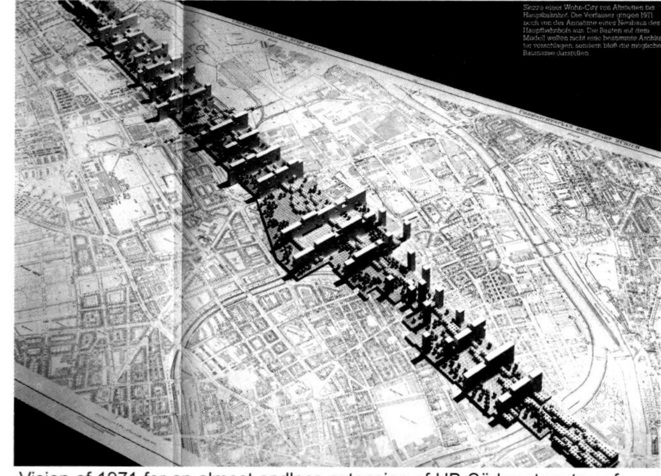

Vision of 1971 for an almost endless extension of HB-Südwest on top of railway tracks to the north. (Source: Rudolf Schilling 'Ideen für Zürich', 1982)

These political and legal struggles clearly show that without a very broad consensus, projects of this size and scope cannot easily progress. Still, there were several windows of opportunity, when the HB-Südwest or Eurogate project could have been realized. To understand why this did not happen, we have to look at the economy. Every time there was a chance to proceed, the economic situation was unfavourable. In 1973, in 1992, and in 2001 the state of the economy was too fragile, the global situation was uncertain, the banks as principal investors saw themselves in trouble some times. Again, the size of the project and the required investments were too large to say 'yes' lightheartedly to a long-term commitment. Perhaps one of the major problems of the project was that it could not be phased. For operational reasons, the decking of the tracks had to be done all at once and did not allow for piecemeal development. Or, as Stuart Lipton, one of the world's most experienced and respected real estate developers, once said: "HB-Südwest is too large for a city like Zurich. The market can't take it" [5].

Finally, one can also put the blame on personal imcompetence on the part of the developers. They were never able to convince a solid majority of the public about the quality and the benefits of their project. They did not conquer the minds and hearts of the people. And they couldn't even find a spokesperson who represented their cause with conviction and charisma. Right from the beginning, HB-Südwest / Eurogate failed to overcome its image of having a purely technocratic and profit-led approach. In an open democracy it is difficult to prevail just with arguments of this kind. This stigma was confirmed when architect Ralph Baenziger, the only one who had given his heartblood for the project, was sacked. Without a powerful and committed captain on the bridge, a project of this dimension cannot be navigated through the stormy weathers of economic cycles and democratic decision taking processes. At all the crucial moments, investors (the banks in particular) lacked the determination and courage needed to get involved in a huge, difficult, long-term project. The deplorable part played by UBS in the dramatic final showdown of 2001 is a perfect illustration of this dilemma.

32 years later, this type of mega-development over the rails has has become obsolete. Industrial decline has opened up new development opportunities. Huge brownfield sites have become available at the fringes of the inner city, where it is easier and cheaper to build than on top of a busy main station. Areas like Zurich West or Zurich North have drawn attention and investments away from the inner city. It is also in these areas that a new and more flexible planning paradigm has proved successful [6]. Eurogate has become a dinosaur in a world that has changed.

References

Bertolini, Luca and Tejo Spit (1998), *Cities on Rails - The Redevelopment of Railway Station Areas*. London
Blanc, Jean-Daniel and Martin Ganz (1986) 'Die City Macher', p. 86f. In: Ginsburg, T., Hitz, H., Schmid, C., Wolff R., (Eds.), *Zürich ohne Grenzen*. Zürich
Blanc, Jean-Daniel (1993), *Die Stadt ein Verkehrshindernis?* Zürich
Snozzi, Luigi (1987), *Das Unding über den Gleisen*. Zurich

Endnotes

[1] Quote Zurich Tourist Board.

[2] See the articles in this book by Christian Schmid and Philipp Klaus.

[3] For a good summary of the critique, see Bruno Odermatt: 'Hauptbahnhof Zürich Projekt Südwest'. In: *Schweizer Ingenieur und Architekt* Nr. 29, 19. Juli 1990, p. 820f.

[4] Karl Steiner Immobilien AG, Göhner Merkur AG, and Bührle Immobilien AG.

[5] Stuart Lipton of Rosehaugh & Stanhope, one of London's major developers with projects like Broadgate / Liverpool Street Station, in a personal communication.

[6] See article by Andreas Hofer in this book.

A B
FIRST·DAY
JANE AND WILSON
ISLINGTON AND ELMHURST
KEEP CLEAR
HIER WIRD GEBAUT.
254 Bitte Schalter
730 Bitte Schalter
267 Bitte Schalter
SINES
CENTR
TAX
PLACE
LEMMENS
NIGHT SHOP
NIGHT SHOP
TUNISIA
GSM 0.35€
TOGO
0.30
LEBANON
BENIN
TRAM
POET
POET
FUME
GROS
WO IST BOB?
HAVE A BREAK
R
IN
PAYAN
NO
FUME
#kaos
BEET AND RUN AWAY art
6de
entrée EST
EST
Tour des Lois
En cas d'intempéries, il est recommandé
RUN
YOU ARE HERE
YOU ARE LOST.
AR
Schuh- & Schlüsseldienst

VERNISSAGE
20 Uhr 24.10.
NOT OPEN
PHONE
X
Nous
on di koi
KARIM EXPORT
ACHAT - VENTE
L'HABIT MODE
HYPE
E.H.S.
Ladend
IMPORT
EXPOR
T
DEMOLITION AUTO
TOUTES PIECES DE RECHANGE
CITROEN
DOWNTOWN
Healthy Home
SALES OFFICE
SOLMAR
PROGRESS PARK
Centre
DR. S. STARKMAN
FAMILY DENTISTRY
INSURANCE
13
quartier ouvert
quartier ouvert
INVENTATI!
154
BALI
-
AFRICA
RENT LARGE
DOUBLE ROOM
300€
BERLIN

Afterword

berlin bruxelles/brussel firenze london toronto zürich

TEXT....Fred Robinson
PHOTOS ....Raffaele Paloscia

The Spirit of INURA

Years ago – back in 1991 – I found myself holed up in a hostel halfway up a mountain in Switzerland. I wasn't at all sure what I was doing there, but I had been persuaded to join a group of people trying to create a new organisation. It was a disparate group – of academics, planners and activists – all committed, in various ways, to changing the world. We had a lot in common, even though we were from different countries and were engaged in different struggles. Unlike most left-wing political groups, our differences didn't set us apart but seemed to be a strength, generating creativity.

Somehow, at the end, we did create something: a new organisation called INURA. It sounded good – the International Network for Urban Research and Action – and it's turned out to be good. It's even better than we hoped for when we hammered out the INURA principles late into the night, fuelled by beer, halfway up that Swiss mountain.

That first meeting, at Salecina, was convened by a small group of Swiss activists (yes, I know, some of us were also surprised to discover that there are Swiss activists). Without their vision, INURA would never have been established and we have a lot to thank them for. Their idea was to create an international network of academics and activists, thinkers and doers, who could exchange ideas and support each other. That has, undoubtedly, been achieved. But INURA has grown and developed to become even more than just a unique network organisation.

INURA is an international network of fellow-travellers, people opposed to global capitalism, exploitation, sexism, racism, consumerism, and keen to bring about change. But, in addition to all that, it is a network of friends. I think that is very important. It may sound trite but, for me at least, the friendliness of INURA is its greatest strength and most remarkable achievement. People engaged in struggle can often feel isolated, not least because they stand outside the dominant culture. Consequently, they need friends – people who share the same concerns and also care about them. At the annual INURA conferences it is obvious that people care and share. How different that is from most academic conferences where competition and petty rivalries are rife. It's rather different, too, from many political movements where debate is angry, divisive and destructive.

When I was at that first meeting in that memorable snowy Swiss wilderness, one of the many new friends I met was Raffaele Paloscia. Curiously, at that hostel we all had to sign the register and give our date of birth, and Raffaele and I discovered we were born on the same day in the same year. Since then, we've called each other 'twin' but it's hard to see how: he, the bearded, dark southern Italian; me, the blond, fair skinned Anglo-Saxon. Stemming from that connection, he has invited me to say something of the spirit of INURA, at the end of a book inspired by INURA and written by its members. He liked the symmetry: he writes at the start of the book, I write at the end. That's typical of INURA, I think. It indicates a playfulness and sense of humour that isn't exactly common in academic circles or in political organisations.
I suppose I was also asked to write this piece because I am a veteran of INURA, having been privileged to be at the first meeting and at almost all of the subsequent conferences. As I think back, many memories come to mind, memories which, in one way or another, convey something of the spirit of the organisation.

For most 'INURANS' the annual conference is the most important connection with the organisation and the people in it. These conferences comprise some formal presentations, good debate, lots of laughter and real engagement with place. Each conference is organised by members from various cities and regions. Somehow, at the end of each conference, brave souls volunteer to organise the next conference in their own country. Joining INURA is a good way of getting to see the world – particularly for me, as someone who generally has to be cajoled to leave home and venture into the unknown.

The engagement with place is a vital element. In such places as Rostock, Florence, Toronto, Amsterdam, Zurich, Brussels, Caen, Berlin and my home, North East England, we have had the opportunity to meet with local people and see projects and activities for ourselves. The local conference organisers put considerable effort into enabling us all to have an insight into the life of the place. We get to see aspects of the place that tourists don't see. I particularly remember the asylum seekers' centre in Brussels and the food bank in Toronto. Often, conventional conferences are placeless jamborees; INURA recognises the spirit of place and seeks not only to explore but also lend support to local progressive movements.

These conferences have also developed the tradition of having a 'retreat'. The second half of the conference is held in somewhere usually 'away from it all' – often somewhere in beautiful countryside (ah, Tuscany was fantastic). There, discussions can be more intimate, wide-ranging, often chaotic, and participants have the opportunity to share their thoughts and fears – with friends. At the retreat we recognise that we have much in common and that everyone has a valid point of view, based on their own particular experience. The academics and the activists debate together, producing a creative mix of theory and practice, bringing together the general and the particular.

For many, the annual conference is the main, perhaps only, engagement with INURA. But for many others, there is regular, frequent contact with the network. Some are involved in shared INURA projects – this book is such a project. Some are heavily involved with others in the network, working together and exchanging ideas. The growth of the Internet has really helped to make so much of that more possible; it's great for networking organisations. And, of course, we mustn't forget our Swiss friends, Richard and Philipp, who work throughout the year to maintain the website, deal with enquiries and generally, behind the scenes, keep things going.

I realise that, in talking about the spirit of INURA, I haven't really said much about the actual interests and concerns of the members. What do we care about – what do we talk about at our conferences? Well, the contents of this book provide a good guide to INURA interests – housing, planning, economic development, globalisation and so on; broadly, the consequences of capitalism, the workings of the state, and the possibilities of resistance. What INURA is about is also conveyed by the principles we drew up at the start. Indeed, what INURA is about may be well understood by the fact that the first task when it was founded was to draw up a statement of principles. If there is one overarching theme it is liberation, collective and personal liberation from the structures and forces of oppression.

INURA is still growing and new members add to the diversity and vitality of the network. But it is still run on a shoestring, with very little income and a do-it-yourself-for-everyone-else philosophy. There may come a time when we will have big sponsored projects and I think that would be valuable, making the network stronger and more productive. There may come a time when we will have a sponsor, an individual or agency, enabling INURA to support members who cannot afford to come to the conferences. That would be great – and we would love to hear from anyone out there who might consider doing that! For now, though, INURA remains an organisation supported only by its members; and, however it may develop in the future, INURA's membership is its strength.

So, dear reader, if you're not already a member of INURA, please do give it a try. Check out the website (www.inura.org), talk to existing members, come to the annual conference. You will be warmly welcomed and I think that you will find, as I have done, that you learn a lot and you'll enjoy the comradeship. Joy in struggle!

An Alternative Urban World is Possible

A DECLARATION FOR URBAN RESEARCH AND ACTION

berlin bruxelles/brussel firenze london toronto zürich

January 2003

Generated, discussed, and agreed upon at the INURA annual meeting in Clinchamps sur Orne, France, June 22, 2002

An urban world

Cities are home to more than half of the world's population. Urbanization rates in the global South continue to rise as rural in-migration reaches new heights due to displacement, droughts, and shifts in global markets. While urbanization in the global North (or West) has slowed or even receded in terms of population growth, the metropolitan centres of industrial countries are still sprawling across their regional hinterlands towered over by eve denser central business districts and edge cities.

A global city

The current period of urbanization is global. It occurs everywhere on earth and, as a material process, is a tangible representation of globalization. Urbanization now means linking urban worlds across a variety of scales from the sub-local to the global. Globalization occurs at all city sizes but also leads to the formation of distinct new spaces of accumulation of money, commodities and power.

Disempower global players

Among these new spaces are global cities, international trade zones and flexible production complexes. In the uneven distribution of the effects of globalization in various parts of the world and at different scales, the colonialist and imperialist legacy continues to determine the relationships between Northern and Southern cities, and what the North does has severe impacts on the South.

Migrant cities

Make

In-migration from the South to the North is occurring as people search for better conditions of life and as millions escape from wars, economic and environmental crisis and social or political repression. However immigrants too often find exploitation, racism, repression, and exclusion. The urban world, both in the North and in the South, is more and more characterized by social polarization, spatial segregation and legal disintegration (sans papiers). Basic social needs are not met for a growing part of the population. Wealth and poverty continue to be geographically differentiated as expressed in segmented housing, public and social spaces, health services, education, access to basic resources such as land, water, and food).

Unsustainable urban-natural relations

profits

The globalization of urbanization has created unprecedented pressures on urban natural environments, the health of humans and the sustainability of human-natural relations. Pollution levels, energy consumption, waste generation continue to rise in the North, as cities still deal with the legacies of the industrial era such as contaminated soils, degraded watersheds and bioregions. In the South, the basic metabolic processes such as urban hydrosocial cycles and regional airsheds are corrupted beyond imagination and perhaps beyond repair. Everywhere in the urban world, albeit to different degrees and in different ways, there have been grave violations of environmental justice.

Neoliberalization: The market rules

unsustainable

The globalization of our cities has coincided with a pervasive neoliberalization of governments, markets, and civil societies at all scales. This has meant that governance, service delivery, and planning have been marketized, privatized, and de-regulated. Cities are viewed as private corporations locked in a global competition with few rules and little protection for local and regional interests and popular demands. Simultaneously, citizens are being recast as clients, and urban politics comes under the spell of the abstract rhetoric of economics and fiscal prudence rather than the concrete goals of social justice and community well-being.

Attacks on democracy

No borders for people

In the period of neo-liberalization, democratic constitutions – already in the past more often than not smokescreens for and facilitators of class rule in capitalist societies – and political processes of self-regulation are either instrumentalized or entirely abandoned in favour of so-called efficiency, flexibility, and lean administration. In the countries of the West, a power shift has occurred from accountable forms of representative democracy and welfare state institutions to private modes of governance, shareholder democracy and open oppression. In the process, citizens, workers, and residents have lost control over the globalized mechanisms that govern their lives. In transitional and developing countries, neoliberalization has meant shifting all attempts to create viable and powerful social and political institutions to check the unfettered powers of global markets. Local governments have often become the ones doing the dirty work of globalization and acting as the block busters in fights over contracting out and privatizing of public services, one of the main mantras of the neoliberal consensus.

Autonomy and social justice in everyday life

Community vulnerability

Economic globalization has increased the vulnerability of local communities to the rules and whims of world markets, transnational corporations and free market trade agreements. As a consequence, life in cities both in the North and in the South has become less secure, more expensive and increasingly unhealthy. Marginalization, homelessness and unemployment has led to widespread despair. Simultaneously, the communities of the wealthy have prospered, as they have barricaded themselves in gated housing complexes protected by private police forces and serviced solely by the market place. Cities have come to be expected to subsidize global corporations in doing their business whereas social services have been defunded and local states have increasingly moved to concentrate on expanding their police forces, penitentiary systems and other forms of social control.

Racism on the rise

Globalizing cities have become very diverse cities. Yet, as racism ethnic violence and intolerance have become natural ingredients of the neoliberal global order, forms of social organization based on solidarity among communities of urban residents and workers have come under attack both ideologically and physically. Whereas cities have often been the laboratories of progressive social experiment, democratization, autonomy, collective organization and urban liberation, they have now come to be associated more frequently with dystopic forms of hate-filled politics and more or less organized populist or even fascist violence.

The Alternative: INURA's urban imagination

Liberate

The neo-liberal project itself cannot be unified and leaves cracks for us to sow our seeds of resistance. Not all cities experience the same degree of commodification of social reproduction and collective consumption, militarization of public space, and deterioration of general living conditions. Many cities in some nations continue to operate on the assumption of the viability of welfare state policies and more collective forms of solutions to mounting social and environmental problems. An important role has been played by the current urban mobilizations in many places from Porto Alegre to Quebec City, and from Seattle to Genoa. The meeting in Porto Alegre and the mobilizations against capitalist globalization have shown the growing presence of movements and action groups located in different parts of the world that join in the fight against neoliberalism and war. They are combining resistance with living and creative alternatives that are under construction and place themselves in the perspective of a new world freed from exploitation, discrimination, dispossession, and violence. These mass events, and other ongoing initiatives at many scales, create potentially new horizons for urban social change beyond both the Fordist past and the neoliberal present. This change of direction goes along with redefined political communities that defy both the traditional the welfare state (where it existed) and neoliberal, asocial individualization. We may witness and advocate the emergence of a new model of urbanity that far exceeds the mere structures of state and corporate economy and remakes the way we live our life in cities and the fundamental assumptions we make about this life.

the urban

INURA's urban imagination is fundamentally opposed to and in struggle with the neo-liberal urban project the contours of which we have described above. Based on the hopeful experiences in the shadows of the globalization and neoliberalization of our cities, we are proposing enthusiastically the construction of a new global urban world based on the solidarity and cooperation of human collectives in justice, democracy, and harmony with non-human nature. We emphatically defend radical and redistributive notions of social and environmental justice, equality of opportunity and rights to diversity. We understand these substantive rights to be enmeshed with the liberation of decision making processes, particularly enhancing the participation of all relevant parties in decision making and modes of collective (self) organization that avoid hierarchies and discrimination.

imagination

INURA sees it as its mandate to support the liberation of urban everyday life from the false demands and constrictions of neoliberal globalization. This, in other words, is fulfilling the promise of the “right to the city”.

nive
sal
NTE .

List of Contributors

Ahmed Allahwala is a political science graduate of the Free University in Berlin and is now a Ph.D. candidate at the Department of Political Science at York University in Toronto, Canada. His research interests are urban theory and politics, state restructuring and questions of citizenship and identity. His research focuses mainly on Germany and Canada.

Ayar Ata was born in 1957 in Saqqiz, eastern Kurdistan. He came to England as a refugee in 1989 and has been working both on a voluntary and paid basis with various refugee groups in London. Ayar studied at SOAS, the University of London and Middlesex University between 1993 - 2000. He now works as co-ordinator of the Hammersmith and Fulham Refugee Forum.

Giovanni Allegretti, architect, teaches 'Urban Management' at the Department of Town Planning of the University of Florence, Italy. He was awarded scholarships that allowed him to study in Tokyo, Copenhagen and Newcastle Upon Tyne, after which his Ph.D. research on the Porto Alegre Participatory Budget and changes in the informal town reclaiming strategies was carried out in Brazil. He is currently working on a study of participatory urban planning and managing practices in Europe. He is a member of INURA and the 'Démocratiser Radicalement la Démocratie' international networks.

Ingo Bader is a geographer and community activist. His work focuses on urban and economic geography and environmental justice. He studied at the Ruhr University in Bochum and the Free University in Berlin, and he is currently writing a book on the interaction between subculture and the global music industry in Berlin's inner city

Adrian Blackwell is an artist and urban designer who teaches urban design and architecture at the University of Toronto. He recently was a visiting professor at Chongqing University in China. His sculpture and photographic projects focus on the problems of social separation within urban space.

Susannah Bunce lives in Toronto and is an urban planner and activist. She is also a Ph.D. student in the Faculty of Environmental Studies, York University, and a member of Planning Action.

Constance Carr holds a Master's degree from the Faculty of Environmental Studies, York University, Toronto. She is now writing her doctoral dissertation at the Humboldt University in Berlin. Her research interests include urban social movements, local urban political economics, and the role of (dis)place and identity in urban spatial planning.

Axel Claes, An artist who is currently working with Ruimte Morguen (Antwerp), has performed recently with the Karin Vyncke Compagnie and is a founding member of PTTL, a Brussels-based bi-lingual collective of artists and unemployed people sharing a camera/edit-suit and a Japanese printing machine.

Bob Colenutt works for the London Borough of Haringey as a regeneration manager. He has particular responsibility for neighbourhood renewal programmes, and for community participation in neighbourhood management. He lives in London and was previously involved in campaigns over the redevelopment of the South Bank and London Docklands.

Manuela Conti, architect and photographer, is a founding member of the ogi:noknauss video collective. She has experience in graphic design, digital editing, and as a videoreporter in community projects, activism and alternative events.

Gabriele Corsani is Associate Professor at the Department of Urban and Regional Planning of the University of Florence, where he teaches the History of City Planning. He is a member of the editorial staff of History of City Planning – Tuscany. He is also on the teaching staff of the Doctorate of Landscaping Department and the Postgraduate School of Parks and Landscaping Architecture. He has published writings on the urban history of Florence and of smaller Tuscan towns, and on city planning in Italy, England and the United States.

Stefan De Corte has long been active as a member of BRAL (Brusselse Raad voor het Leefmilieu), teaches Geography at the Geografisch Instituut of the VUB (Vrije Universiteit Brussel) and is part of the research unit COSMOPOLIS (City, Culture & Society) of the same university sdecorte@vub.ac.be

Walter De Lannoy is professor of Geography at the VUB (Vrije Universiteit Brussel)

Michael Edwards has taught planning at the Bartlett School of Architecture and Planning (University College London) for 30 years and was a founding member of INURA. His work is mainly on planning and development in London, where an essentially Marxist approach is ever more to the fore.
m.edwards@ucl.ac.uk;
www.bartlett.ucl.ac.uk/planning

Volker Eick works as a political scientist at the John F. Kennedy Institute, Department of Political Science, Free University of Berlin. He is currently working on a 3 year-research project entitled "From Welfare to Work? The Transformation of Local Social and Employment Policies and the Role of Non-Profits: A Comparison of Berlin and Los Angeles", funded by the German Research Council. In his research work he focuses on local social and security policies, new governance models, workfare programs and (community) policing.

Kanishka Goonewardena was trained as an architect in Sri Lanka and an urban planner in the US, and now teaches urban design and critical theory at The University of Toronto. He writes on urbanism, globalism and nationalism, while working on two book manuscripts: The Urban Sensorium and The Future of Planning at the End of History.

Christine Goyens worked until recently at the Secrétariat Régional au Développement Urbain (SRDU) and is a long-time resident and activist in the European Neighbourhood (Quartier Léopold) in Brussels.

Andreas Hofer studied at the architectural department of the Swiss Federal Institute of Technology in Zurich. He works as a partner in the planning office 'archipel'. His main interests are the conversion of former industrial land, sustainable city development and public and co-operative housing. He teaches at various universities and publishes regularly on issues regarding architecture and planning. He was a co-founder of the cooperative KraftWerk1 and is a member of the board of the Association Housing Cooperatives in the Zurich region.

Roger Keil teaches urban and environmental politics at the Faculty of Environmental Studies, York University in Toronto. His book on Urban Environmental Policy Making (with Gene Desfor) will be published in 2004 by the University of Arizona Press. The Global Cities Reader (with Neil Brenner) is forthcoming with Routledge.

Stefan Kipfer is an assistant professor in the Faculty of Environmental Studies, York University, Toronto. His interests are urban social theory and urban politics and he has been involved in a number of leftwing oriented urban projects in Toronto.

Ute Lehrer is professor in the Department of Geography, Brock University, Canada, and was a founding member of INURA. She has published widely on the production of space and globalization, on the contested terrains of public versus private space, as well as on urban design and architecture.

Marvi Maggio was a founding member of INURA. She has been an activist in social movements from the seventies. She obtained a Ph.D. in Physical and Urban Planning and has carried out many research projects in Italy, Great Britain, the Netherlands and Canada (Ontario). Her interests cover urban planning and governance of urban change, the conflict between use values and exchange values, landed property and real estate markets, participation of residents in decision-making processes, social rights and accessibility, urban/social movements.

Alberto Magnaghi is Professor of Planning at the University of Florence's Department of Town Planning, where he leads the Laboratory of Ecological Design of Settlements (LAPEI); he is also Head of the Department of Urban, Regional and Environmental Planning of the University of Florence in Empoli. Founder of the "Italian territorialist school", he acts as national coordinator for a number of research projects promoted by the University and Research Ministry and the Council for National Research, as well as for experimental workshops and projects on self-sustainable local development and local identity representation.

Ogi:no Knauss is an independent research group dealing with language, media and human environment's trasformation.
www.oginoknauss.org

Giancarlo Paba is Professor of Town Planning at the Faculty of Architecture and Lecturer at the post-Graduate School of Urban, Regional and Environmental Planning of the University of Florence (Italy). He has conducted numerous research activities in Italy and abroad in the fields of town planning, urban analysis and community planning. He has also acted as advisor for various public organisations and scientific institutions and published numerous books and articles.

Raffaele Paloscia is Professor in Territorial Analysis at the Department of Urban and Regional Planning of the University of Florence. He was a founding member of INURA and is co-ordinator of INURA, Florence. He was also a founding member of the "Laboratorio per la Democrazia" (Laboratory for Democracy) in Florence. He co-ordinates the international activities of the LAPEI (Laboratory of Ecological Design of Settlements). His current main field of research and work concerns projects for development co-operation, self-sustainability and participatory planning in Africa and Latin America.

Michael Parkes has worked for 18 years as a self-employed community planner, providing independent technical assistance to community / disadvantaged / tenants groups, etc involved in regeneration projects / partnerships in inner London. For the last 13 years he has been the Planning Worker to the Kings Cross Railway Lands Group and more recently the Independent Master Planner to the Community Forum / DET at Elephant and Castle. He is also currently working for a Rom organisation on a housing / neighbourhood renewal project in Botosani, Rumania.

Anna Lisa Pecoriello has recently completed her Ph.D. in Urban, Territorial and Environmental planning at the University of Florence. Her main field of research is community planning and the relationship between children and the city. As member of the European association 'Atelier ambulant d'architecture' she carried on experiments in "self-building" as a form of animation of communities and places.

Camilla Perrone has been a practicing architect since 1999 and since 2002 holds a Ph.D. in Urban, Landscape and Environmental Design at the University of Florence, with a thesis on governance and planning in the multicultural (and multiethnic) city. She is currently a visiting fellow at the Faculty of Environmental Studies, York University of Toronto (Canada), with a research project on urban and multicultural planning. She is a member of the Laboratory of Ecological Design of Settlements (LAPEI) Dept., Faculty of Architecture, University of Florence, and participates in national research projects on self-sustainable local development and participatory planning.

Barbara Rahder is the Graduate Program Director and the Planning Programs Coordinator in the Faculty of Environmental Studies at York University in Toronto. Her research focuses on participatory planning with marginalized communities to promote equity and access to community services. Her art work includes line drawings, watercolours, and clay sculptures. Many of her drawings have appeared on the cover and in the pages of "Women & Environments" Magazine.

Fred Robinson is at St Chad's College, University of Durham. His main research interests are the evaluation of regeneration policy and also critical studies of structures of governance in North East England. He is active in a number of local voluntary sector agencies which provide social support and promote social inclusion.

Leonie Sandercock is Professor in Urban Planning and Social Policy at The University of British Columbia. Her research interests include cultural diversity and integration; participatory planning, fear and the city. Her best-known recent writings on urban themes are *Cities for Sale* (1995); *Making the Invisible Visible: A Multicultural History of Planning* (1998); *Towards Cosmopolis: Planning for Multicultural Cities (1998*), *Cosmopolis 2: Mongrel Cities of the 21st Century (*2003). She loves the irrepressible chaos and contradictions of cities, but worries about their 'sustainability', in the broadest sense.

Christian Schmid studied geography and has been involved in a number of action groups in Zurich. He was one of the founding members of INURA and has carried out research projects on urban development in Zurich, Frankfurt, Paris, and Geneva. His Ph.D. thesis is on Henri Lefebvre's theory of the production of space. Today, he is a lecturer in the Faculty of Architecture, Swiss Federal Institute of Technology (ETH), Zurich.

Myriam Stoffen is a member of the coordinating team of the Zinneke Parade, Brussels and part of the research unit COSMOPOLIS (City, Culture & Society) at the VUB (Vrije Universiteit Brussel). She is active in the Parcours citoyen (a citizens' network).

Louanne Tranchell. Born in Glasgow, lives in Hammersmith, West London UK. She has worked as a theatre designer and now is working as a planning and information officer. She is a member of numerous associations, including the Hammersmith Community Trust, the Development Trust Association, Social Enterprise London and the London Rivers Association. She is a former local councillor for the London Borough of Hammersmith & Fulham. Her main concerns are urban studies, equalities and local regeneration.

Lorenzo Tripodi is a Ph.D. candidate in Urban, Territorial and Environmental Design at the University of Florence, and member of ogi:noknauss, a video collective researching on visual language and interaction in public space. His main interests are in urban cultures, conflicts for space, and knowledge exchange in informal and non-competitive contexts.
loreso@oginoknauss.org

Joyce Wade Brought up in St Johns, Grenada, she has lived in London since 1969, when she came to join her parents and to study 'Hair & Beauty' at the Morris School of Hairdressing, Piccadilly. She is involved in costume and textiles for the Notting Hill Carnival, with the masquerade bands 'Stardust' and 'Dragon's Mas Band'. Since 1999 Joyce has been the centre manager of the Emerald Centre, a local community centre where tutors run courses and residents hold autonomous social and family events.

Daniel Weiss was born in 1967 and lives in Zurich. He has studied history and the history of art and since 1994 has worked in the archive of the Institute of History and Theory of Architecture, Swiss Federal Institute of Technology (ETH). He is an activist in various leftist groups and social movements in Zurich.

Tristan Wibault is an artist who is involved with the Universal Embassy in Brussels.

Karen Wirsig is a reporter on urban issues in Toronto and has been active in feminist, anti-racist and green campaigns among labour-community coalitions that aim to challenge the marginalization of large groups of people in the city.

Andreas Wirz lives in Zürich and runs an architecture office at KraftWerk1. He is a member of the board of directors of the housing co-operative KraftWerk1 and has been involved in the development of the project since 1994. wirz@archipel.ch

Richard Wolff is an urban researcher, campaigner and activist. He grew up in Switzerland and Venezuela, studied anthropology and geography, traveled the seven seas and has worked with the Ssenter for Applied Urbanism SAU, Rote Fabrik Cultural Centre, the Swiss Federal Institute of Technology ETH, and the INURA Zurich Institute Ltd. He was an activist in the urban and cultural movement of 1980 and continues his involvement with community groups and social movements. He lives in a cooperative house in Zurich with his partner Talila and has three boys, Jonathan, Noah and Nicolas.

Clive Wren was born in Oxford, UK and trained in architecture at Kingston College. He lives on a narrow-boat on the Thames. His expertise is in waterside sites, spatial management and masterplans and he has extensive experience in UK planning applications and public inquiries into local schemes. He worked for seven years for British Waterways and now has own practice. Clive is grateful to his aunt, who took him for walks and ice creams as a boy and who introduced him to places with a good balance of social function with natural elements. Living on a boat, he has always felt 'on holiday - already packed'.

Douglas Young teaches Urban Studies at York University in Toronto, where he is also a PhD candidate in Environmental Studies. He is an architect and a member of the Toronto-based group, Planning Action.

4080

Anne & Jerome Fisher
FINE ARTS LIBRARY
University of Pennsylvania
Please return this book as soon as you have finished with it. It must be returned by the latest date stamped below.